Challenge of the Big Trees

Sequoia and Kings Canyon National Parks preserve many natural and cultural resources, but they owe much of their fame to the presence of the world's largest trees–the giant sequoias (*Sequoiadendron giganteum*). This 1936 view of the California Tree only hints at the size of the biggest trees. Photograph by George A. Grant, of the National Park Service, October 18, 1936.

Challenge of the Big Trees

The History of Sequoia and Kings Canyon National Parks

A Revised Edition by
William C. Tweed and
Lary M. Dilsaver

with a new foreword by
Jonathan B. Jarvis, Director,
National Park Service

GEORGE F. THOMPSON PUBLISHING
in association with the
Sequoia Parks Foundation and
American Land Publishing Project

Sequoia and Kings Canyon National Parks protect the scenic heart of the High Sierra, a wonderland of high peaks and stunning glacial gorges. This photograph of LeConte Canyon and the Middle Fork of the Kings River by Richard Frear, of the National Park Service, taken in the 1970s, captures the essence this spectacular region.

CONTENTS

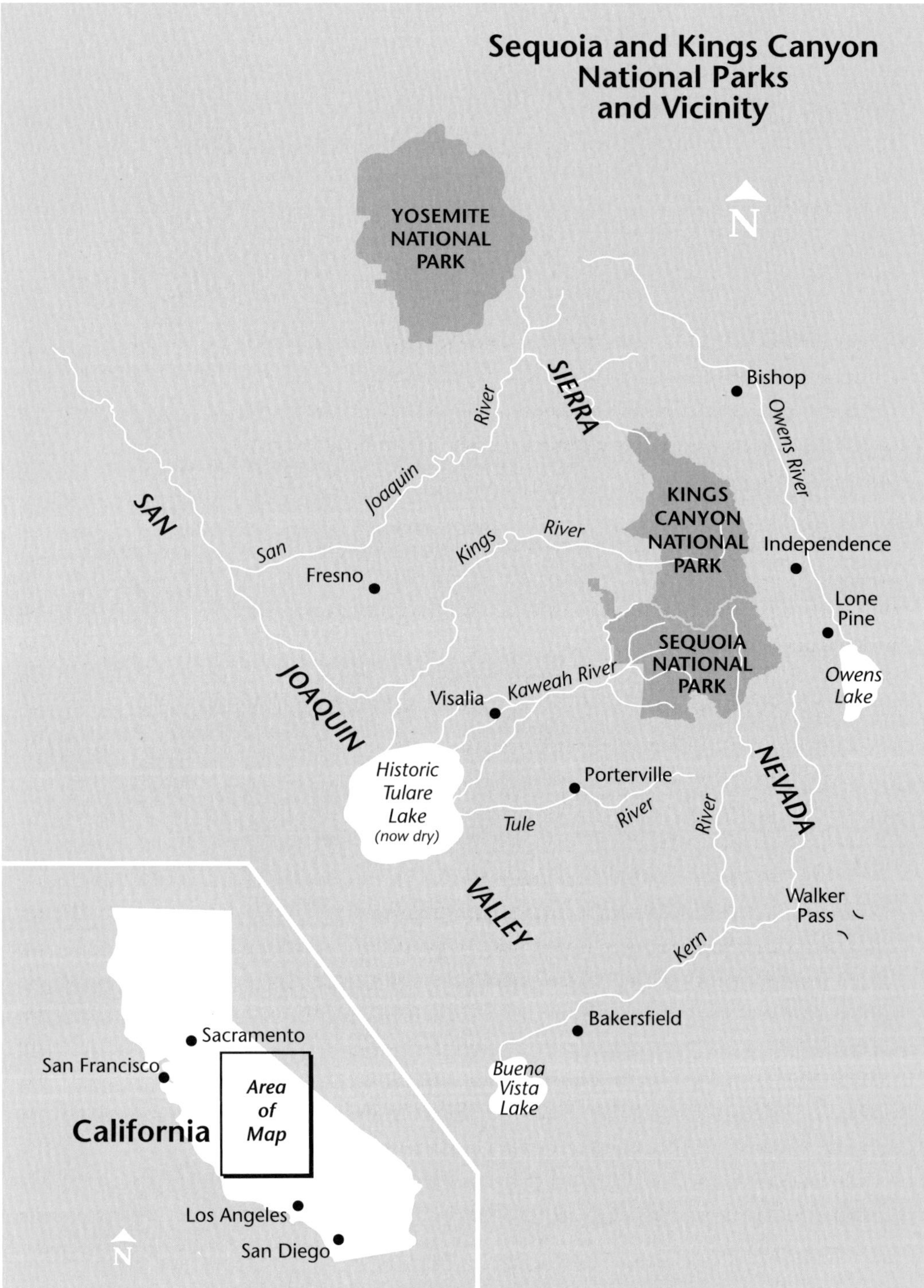
Sequoia and Kings Canyon National Parks and Vicinity
YOSEMITE NATIONAL PARK
N
SIERRA
NEVADA
SAN
JOAQUIN
VALLEY
San Joaquin River
Bishop
Owens River
KINGS CANYON NATIONAL PARK
Kings River
Independence
Fresno
Lone Pine
SEQUOIA NATIONAL PARK
Owens Lake
Kaweah River
Visalia
Historic Tulare Lake (now dry)
Porterville
Tule River
Kern River
Walker Pass
Bakersfield
Buena Vista Lake
Sacramento
San Francisco
California
Area of Map
Los Angeles
San Diego
N

LIST OF MAPS

Note: All maps were rendered by Eureka Cartography, of Berkeley, California, except as noted.

LIST OF PHOTOGRAPHS

Note: All photographs appear courtesy of the Sequoia National Park Photo Archives, Ash Mountain, California, except as noted. Also, "n.d." means "no date" or "date unknown."

From its founding in 1916, the National Park Service sought to market the national parks and monuments under its management by finding ways to make them interesting to visitors. The giant sequoia that became the Auto Log fell in 1917 and was promptly outfitted with a ramp that allowed visitors to drive their automobiles onto the surface of the fallen monarch. Photographer and date unknown.

FOREWORD TO THE REVISED EDITION (2016)

by Jonathan B. Jarvis,
Director, National Park Service

THIS REVISED EDITION of *Challenge of the Big Trees* comes at an important time. As it is published, we celebrate the 125th anniversary of Sequoia and Kings Canyon National Parks. In addition, we look forward to the celebration of the 2016 centennial of the creation of the National Park Service, the federal agency that has overseen the parks for a full century.

The first edition of this book came out in 1990 to mark the centennial of the designation of the two parks. It told the story of how the parks grew to protect the heart of the southern Sierra Nevada of California and how the parks' managers wrestled with the myriad of challenges inherent in the protection of wild ecosystems in our industrialized world. This new edition extends that story into the twenty-first century, a period that has seen both major accomplishments within the parks and the arrival of new challenges to our precious natural resources.

Much has come into better focus since 1990. The decades-long effort to restore the Giant Forest to a more natural condition was finally completed, and the parks continued to wrestle with ongoing illegal cultivation of marijuana on the parks' lands. At the same time, however, new and even larger issues arose—questions like global climate change and the role of nature-based outdoor recreation in a world dominated by computers, video games, and television. These are likely to be among the key questions the parks will face as this century progresses.

The authors of this book, William C. Tweed and Lary M. Dilsaver, bring to this volume seven decades of experience in the field of national park history. Dr. Tweed pursued a career in history, park planning, and education with the National Park Service, mostly at Sequoia and Kings Canyon National Parks. Dr. Dilsaver taught geography for three decades at the University of South Alabama, a position that allowed him to research national park history in several important park units. Together, they make a strong team—one that understands the complexities and nuances of the stories associated with these and other national parks and monuments.

In his foreword to the 1990 edition of this book, William Penn Mott, Jr., who served as Director of the National Park Service from 1985 until 1989, emphasized how national park history reflects the efforts of those who care about these special places. Looking back over his long association with the parks, he wrote:

> [*Challenge of the Big Trees*] is a story of how the dedication and sustained effort of a small group of interested citizens awakened the consciousness of the American people and their government. As a result, the Sierra's giant sequoias and wonderful high country were saved from selfish destruction. In my lifetime of park work, I have witnessed many similar stories; people do make a difference.

As I look back over my nearly forty years of national park experiences, I can reflect both on our accomplishments of the past and our challenges into the future. We need periodic reminders, like this fine book, of how far we have come, most often the result of dedicated citizens and professionals. We also need inspiration and optimism that we will succeed in caring for these special places. Within these pages I invite you to wander but, more importantly, to spend time with the Big Trees, for they have seen many challenges, and yet they still stand.

FOREWORD TO THE CENTENNIAL EDITION (1990)

by William Penn Mott, Jr.,
Director of the National Park Service, 1985–1989

MORE THAN HALF A CENTURY AGO in 1933, I accepted a position with the National Park Service in the agency's Region IV office in San Francisco. This was at the height of the Great Depression, and I was very glad to be able to put my newly acquired master's degree in landscape architecture to work. Soon, I was at work in the woods designing and overseeing construction of the Generals Highway, the roadway the National Park Service and the Bureau of Public Roads were constructing to connect Sequoia and General Grant National Parks. A few years later, I returned to the Sequoia/Kings Canyon region to explore the Kings Canyon backcountry on horseback to see if the area met the Park Service's criteria for inclusion within the national park system. For these reasons, *Challenge of the Big Trees* is for me a very personal and exciting opportunity to renew old memories.

Now, as Sequoia National Park celebrates its centennial and Kings Canyon National Park achieves its golden anniversary, I am struck by how much the Sierra has changed since I first went to work in the region. The highway I helped to design now allows nearly a million visitors a year to see the beauties of the southern Sierra, and the Kings Canyon region I studied is now the heart of one of America's greatest wildernesses.

Challenge of the Big Trees tells of the changes I have seen and more. It is a story of how the dedication and sustained effort of a small group of interested citizens awakened the consciousness of the American people and their government. As a result, the Sierra's giant sequoias and wonderful high country were saved from selfish destruction. In my lifetime of park work, I have witnessed many similar stories; people do make a difference.

The story of Sequoia and Kings Canyon National Parks is also a fascinating bit of history. The authors detail not only how the parks came to exist, but also how the parks were repeatedly threatened with over-development and how they were fortunate enough to ward off those threats. Again, the critical efforts of a few key persons made all the difference. All too often national park histories tend to end with the creation of the parks. *Challenge of the Big Trees* avoids this weakness and explores in substantial detail the critical actions that made the two parks what they are today.

As we face the environmental challenges of the future, it is wise to review the challenges of the past and the lessons they provide. Much can be learned from reading this book; I commend it to you.

The physical extent of the High Sierra, as captured by Richard Frear, of the National Park Service, in the 1970s, gives Sequoia and Kings Canyon National Parks much of their character. A backpacker can wander for weeks on the twin parks' 700-plus miles of wilderness trails. The photograph shows the Sphinx and Kaweah Basin, looking southwest from Kern Point.

INTRODUCTION

THE FIRST EDITION OF THIS BOOK came out in 1990 in celebration of the centennial of the establishment of Sequoia and General Grant (later, in 1940, Kings Canyon) National Parks.[1] The mood at the time was celebratory, but the story we told sought to be something more. It was our goal to capture the full and often complicated saga of a century of national park management in the southern Sierra Nevada. Now, several decades later, the story has become even more complex. Within the parks, much has happened that was far from inevitable when first we wrote. And, even more importantly, our perceptions of the broader world and the "national park idea" have evolved.

This revised edition of *Challenge of the Big Trees* seeks to address several needs. As a history, it now provides a narrative about events in the parks through the first fifteen years of the twenty-first century. This allows the book to resolve important stories left unfinished in the original edition, including the many-decades-long effort to restore the Giant Forest. At the same time, the book addresses a powerful suite of issues that had not yet come into focus during the late 1980s, things such as the evolving state of Central California, the shrinking capacity of the federal government, and global climate change.

We know, of course, that, by updating this work, we still cannot complete it. The story of Sequoia and Kings Canyon continues, even as we share this new edition. It is our hope, however, that the stories and ideas we have captured here will strengthen the ability of the parks' managers and users alike to understand the chapters still to come. The story, undoubtedly, has a long way yet to run.

National parks are more than land, more than just protected resources, more than policy or law, more than their histories, more than the people who use and love them. Our national parks are places where the people of the United States have undertaken a great and still-evolving experiment. Can a modern society preserve "unimpaired" not just isolated natural features but entire natural ecosystems, while at the same time intensively use them for recreation? Further, should these idealistic goals be pursued through gentle, hands-off protection or through intense and persistent management? Is it possible to define at what point human use begins to conflict significantly with effective preservation of resources? Should the natural ecosystems in national parks be allowed to evolve unimpeded towards some uncertain but natural future—or should they be stabilized or frozen to perpetuate the features or systems that attracted public attention to the park in the first place?

A century and a half after the initiation of this grand American experiment began at California's Mariposa Grove and Yosemite Valley in 1864, none of these questions have really been answered. Perhaps in the definitive sense they never will be. Each national park and monument has contributed in its own way to the ongoing debate about what parks really are and how they should be managed. The national park system and the agency that operates it have received increasing attention from scholars in recent years, yet few of these studies have focused in depth on the history of individual parks. It is a premise of this book that our understanding of the national park system can be significantly improved by detailed appraisals at the individual park level. There are two reasons for this: First, because the origins of many system-wide policies can be found in episodes and conflicts within individual parks, and, second, because the addition of park-level detail refines the picture we have of the entire parks system and the political forces that spawned it. In this light, the histories of the oldest national parks are, perhaps, the most significant. Created well before the national park idea was clearly codified in 1916 and long before the dawn of ecological biology, these parks have been the scenic battlegrounds where the critical and defining issues that still haunt the parks were first articulated and considered.

Several early national parks, notably Yosemite and Yellowstone, have received prolonged and serious attention from historians and other students of the national park idea. Other parks have not been so fortunate, although their stories are every bit as important. Two of these occupy and protect the spectacular southern climax of California's Sierra Nevada. Here on the rugged flanks of the highest mountains in the forty-eight contiguous states grow the largest living things of our planet—the incomparable giant sequoias (*Sequoiadendron giganteum*). And surrounding them is a land of enormous scenic and biological fascination, a land that has captured the imagination and spirit of uncountable numbers of people from around the world.

Today, the two national parks of the southern Sierra Nevada are known as Sequoia and Kings Canyon. In 1890, when the U.S. Congress first set them aside as the second and fourth parks of the national park system, they were known as Sequoia and General Grant National Parks. Twelve decades have now passed since that event. During that time, much more than is realized, Sequoia, General Grant, and later Kings Canyon repeatedly played critical roles in the evolution of modern national park philosophy and management. Within these parks, precedents were set that still bear fruit throughout the American park system. This book is the story of these two parks.

If the critical question about national parks is, "How has humanity perceived and modified the land according to its evolving values?," then the state of the land itself becomes the primary historical record. Thus, in this book we describe through time the changing state of the lands and ecosystems that are now Sequoia and Kings Canyon National Parks. From the mid-nineteenth century on, how have individual people and the societies they lived in acted upon the southern Sierra? What did they assume? What did they value? What impact did they have on the land and the ecosystems—and how did this affect subsequent perceptions of resources and values? Our geographical focus is on the lands now within the two national parks we seek to understand. But just as the modern national parks cannot stand divorced and separated from the surrounding world, neither can our study of them ignore adjoining lands. We thus place the two parks in a larger historical and geographical perspective. Out of necessity, we observe and document the fate of the mountain lands that now surround the parks and look at the lands to the west, for their fates also are inseparable from Sequoia and Kings Canyon.

Both parks are situated mostly in three definable regions or watersheds. The western half of Sequoia, west of the rugged alpine ridge known as the Great Western Divide, is drained by the five forks of the Kaweah River. East of the Great Western Divide, the other half of Sequoia National Park is the headwaters of the North Fork of the Kern River. The main portion of Kings Canyon National Park is drained by the Middle and South Forks of the Kings River, which join a few miles west of the park's boundary, while the Grant Grove Section of Kings Canyon Park occupies the forested divide between the Kings and Kaweah Rivers and provides water to both river systems. Small portions of northern Kings Canyon and southern Sequoia are drained, respectively, by the San Joaquin and Tule Rivers. These lands, together with the downstream canyons and valley delta regions of the Kings and Kaweah Rivers, are the focus of our landscape study.

Several themes appear so regularly that they must be introduced before we can begin. One, already stated, is that this is a history of the land and our relationship to it. Another, basic to understanding the Sequoia and Kings Canyon National Parks during the twenty-first century, is that contrasting land-management goals have worked inexorably to make the parks an increasingly isolated biological island. Yet another theme is that, although the parks are places where national policies were executed, they also were the birthplaces of policy, where management philosophy and procedures were created and refined—and not just for the two parks themselves but for the national park system as a whole.

We bring to this project the outlooks and field experiences of two intellectual disciplines: William C. Tweed is an historian and Lary M. Dilsaver a geographer. We believe that only an interdisciplinary combination of these two perspectives can adequately explain the complex reality of Sequoia and Kings Canyon National Parks.[2] Ultimately, the natural and human worlds cannot be separated.

In closing, we wish to establish one additional point: Despite the cooperation of the National Park Service in the preparation of this history, the opinions and interpretations (and errors, if any) presented here are solely those of the two authors and in no way represent the National Park Service or any other organization.

Challenge of the Big Trees

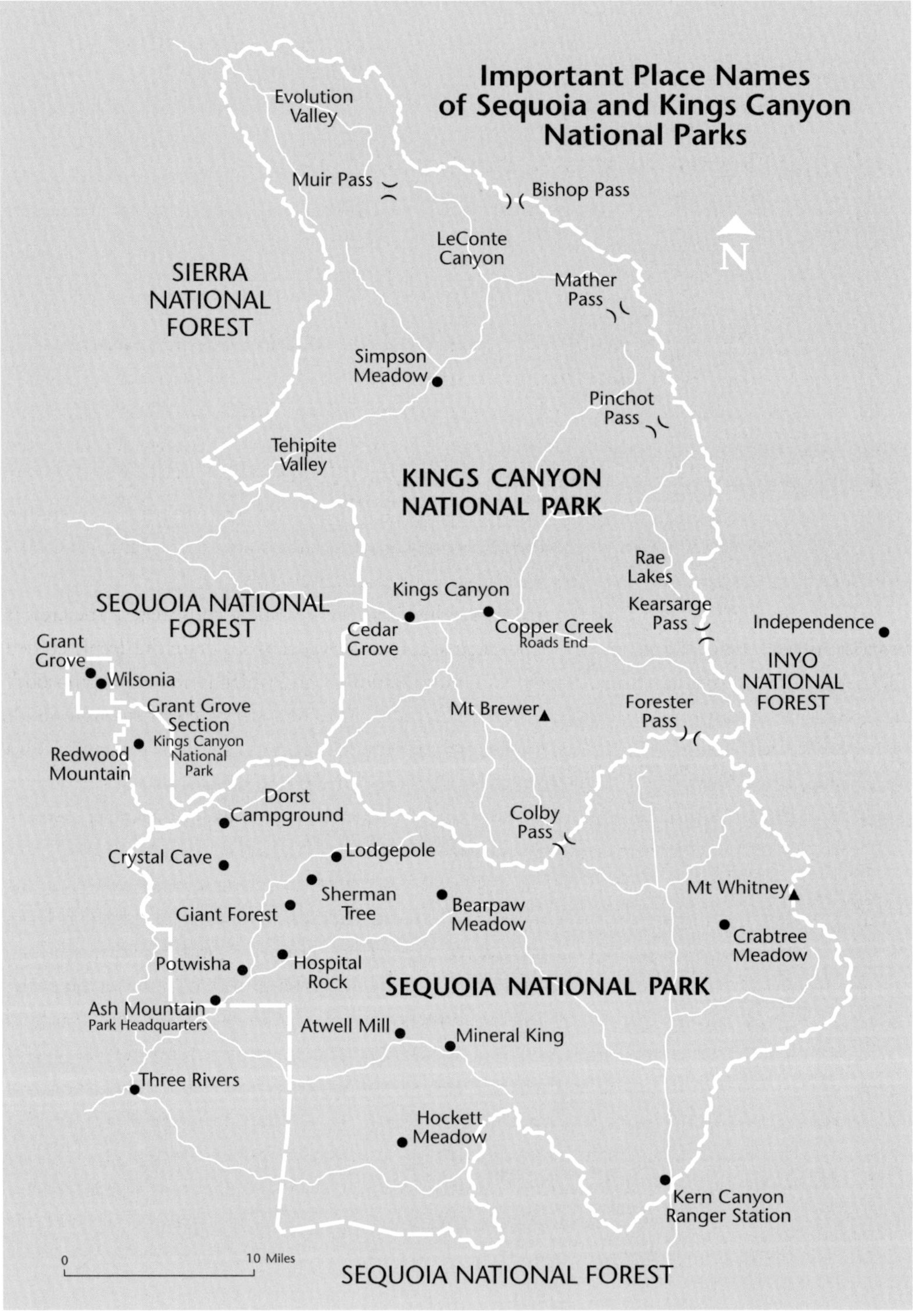
Important Place Names of Sequoia and Kings Canyon National Parks
Evolution Valley
Muir Pass
Bishop Pass
N
LeConte Canyon
SIERRA NATIONAL FOREST
Mather Pass
Simpson Meadow
Pinchot Pass
Tehipite Valley
KINGS CANYON NATIONAL PARK
Rae Lakes
Kings Canyon
SEQUOIA NATIONAL FOREST
Kearsarge Pass
Independence
Cedar Grove
Copper Creek
Roads End
Grant Grove
Wilsonia
INYO NATIONAL FOREST
Grant Grove Section
Kings Canyon National Park
Mt Brewer
Forester Pass
Redwood Mountain
Dorst Campground
Colby Pass
Crystal Cave
Lodgepole
Sherman Tree
Mt Whitney
Giant Forest
Bearpaw Meadow
Crabtree Meadow
Potwisha
Hospital Rock
SEQUOIA NATIONAL PARK
Ash Mountain
Park Headquarters
Atwell Mill
Mineral King
Three Rivers
Hockett Meadow
Kern Canyon Ranger Station
0
10 Miles
SEQUOIA NATIONAL FOREST

CHAPTER ONE

The Natural World of the Southern Sierra

THE SIERRA NEVADA DEFINES THE INTERIOR of California in a way that overwhelms all other topographic features. The "great snowy mountain range" takes its name from the description offered by a Spanish explorer in 1776. Missionary Pedro Font first saw the great snowy mountains, "*una gran sierra nevada*," from the low hills that separate San Francisco Bay from the Great Central Valley of California. His vista disclosed the central portion of the range—the area that, in 1848, would become the focus of the California Gold Rush. Altogether, the Sierra is nearly 400 miles long, with the northern end of the range often defined as Lake Almanor, near Lassen Peak, and the southern end at Tehachapi Pass. [1]

Over the northern two-thirds of its length, the Sierra has a striking consistency. The crest is consistently far east of the center of the mountains, and long river canyons drain the deeply eroded but relatively gentle western slope. North of Yosemite National Park, which is near the north–south midpoint of the range, only a small part of the Sierra is above timberline. From Yosemite south, however, the range is higher and more rugged. Starting at Mt. Dana, just south of Yosemite's Tioga Pass, and continuing south for more than 100 air-miles, the Sierra Crest consists of continuous high, sharp peaks, each successively more rugged. The ultimate summits of the Sierra rise near the southern end of this high, barren land, in the headwaters of the Kings and Kern Rivers.

Despite the increasing heights of the ridges, the Sierra Nevada retains its westerly trending drainage pattern as far south as the Kings River canyons. The two major forks of the Kings River are born on summit peaks very near the eastern edge of the mountains and flow through long deep canyons down the west side of the mountains to the San Joaquin Valley. In the region of the Kaweah and Kern Rivers, however, the shape and texture of the Sierra change radically. South of the Kings River, the Sierra Nevada has a double crest. The main crest—the home of the highest peaks in the range—remains far to the east, but a second, parallel crest also appears: the Great Western Divide. West of this divide, the five forks of the Kaweah River drop steeply into the San Joaquin Valley. East of the Great Western Divide but still west of the Sierra Crest is the fifteen-mile-wide canyon complex of the Kern River, draining not west, like every other Sierra river, but instead south for many miles and only finally, almost reluctantly, west into the extreme southern end of the San Joaquin Valley.

These two factors—the presence of the highest peaks in the Sierra and the well-spaced double crest with extensive uplands between—make the southern Sierra very different from the remainder of the range. Nowhere else is the Sierra so high. Nowhere else are the canyons so rugged and deep. And nowhere else does the Sierra rise so steeply from the west. The peaks of the Great Western Divide are much closer to the floor of the Great Central Valley than any other alpine area in the range. The headwaters of the Middle Fork of the Kaweah River, on summits more than 12,000 feet high, are less than thirty air-miles from the nearly-sea-level valley floor. In the Yosemite and Tahoe regions, the distance is much greater.

GEOLOGICAL BACKGROUND

Why the structure of the Sierra varies so distinctly at its southern end is not entirely obvious. A study of the surface rocks alone certainly does not disclose a clear answer. In most of the southern Sierra, the bedrock is granitic: hard, crystalline rock that cooled slowly from a molten state while still deep within Earth's mantle. Revealed by erosion. these rocks usually appear as speckled ("salt and pepper"), massive, light-colored granites, which when closely inspected consist entirely of small, hard crystals. Other types of rock sometimes appear with the granites. Most often these are brown or reddish with visible layering, and usually the layers are severely deformed. These layered rocks are older than the granites and are more common in the foothills than the high country. Occasionally in the south and more frequently to the north, a third type of rock appears: surface volcanics in the form of weathered lava flows and cinder cones.

After a century of study, the origins of these three rock types can now be explained. At the end of the Paleozoic geological era, about 225,000,000 years ago, the region that would become today's Sierra Nevada was near the western oceanic margin of North America. According to plate tectonic theory, two large, moving plates collided along this continent–ocean edge. One plate, of relatively heavy rock, formed the floor of a large oceanic basin; the other, lighter plate formed the North American continent. The two plates were being slowly forced against each other with the result that the heavier, oceanic plate dove beneath the lighter, continental plate. Geologists describe this process as subduction. Minerals trapped in the intense heat and pressure of the resulting collision zone eventually melted and began moving upward through Earth's crust.

As the large masses of molten minerals slowly moved upward, the molten rocks began to deform the oceanic sediments above them. Some sediments hardened and recrystallized; others probably were completely melted and became part of the magma pool. Eventually, some portions of the magma reached the surface and vented as volcanoes, forming an island chain similar to modern Japan. From these eruptions, extensive beds of marine and terrestrial volcanic sediments accumulated, each subject to deformation by the next eruption. Some of these eruptions were extremely violent, so entire mountains exploded and disappeared, leaving behind empty craters, or calderas, which filled with sediments from yet other eruptions. Much of the magma did not reach the surface, however, and began slowly to cool beneath Earth's surface. This process continued for tens of millions of years until ultimately an enormous mass of cooled igneous material was embedded beneath the coastal edge of the continental plate. Eventually, the zone of magma intrusion and deformation shifted to the east, apparently because the angle of collision between the two tectonic plates shifted.

By roughly 80,000,000 years ago, both major rock types that now form the southern Sierra had been formed and positioned. On the surface, weathering away, could be found an extensive, severely distorted mass of volcanic and marine sediments. Beneath these older rocks but sometimes nearly surrounding them were even larger amounts of now-cooled magma. Today, geologists call the distorted sediments "metamorphic" (changed) rocks, while the cooled magmas are grouped together as "igneous" (fire-caused) rocks. The cooled, igneous magmas of the Sierra are what we now see on the surface and call granites.

The mechanism that caused the Sierra to rise to its current height is less well understood than the forces that created the range's rock types. It is known, however, that, about 25,000,000 years ago, the tectonic plate collision ended that had been going on for so long along the western edge of North America. In its place, new forces exerted themselves. Instead of collision, the dominant mode became continental stretching and uplift. The brittle continental plate began to fracture, and volcanic material again came to the surface through these cracks. The northern Sierra was ultimately buried beneath these flows, and even the southern portion of the range saw scattered eruptions. Then, for reasons that are still debated, the gigantic block of cooled magma began to rise up out of the continental plate. One contemporary explanation for this phenomenon is that the relatively light granites had been "frozen" into the continental plate at the time of their formation, and they had thus long been held in place, as a block of ice might hold a cork embedded within it as long as the ice was solid and intact. When tectonic stretching "broke the ice," so to speak, the granite was freed and began to float upward.

In recent geological time, the granite block we call the Sierra has been rising rapidly. The uplift has occurred more strongly on the eastern edge of the block, explaining the strongly asymmetrical shape of the range. Nowhere is the power of this process more apparent than in the Owens Valley along the eastern edge of the Sierra in the Kings and Kern Rivers regions. Here, the visible displacement along the fault is more than two vertical miles. And the uplift almost certainly is not over. Every several hundred years, the Sierra jumps further into the sky in a violent earthquake that shakes most of California. The last one occurred in 1872, when the vertical difference between the summit of Mt. Whitney and the floor of Owens Valley immediately to the east increased by more than twelve feet.

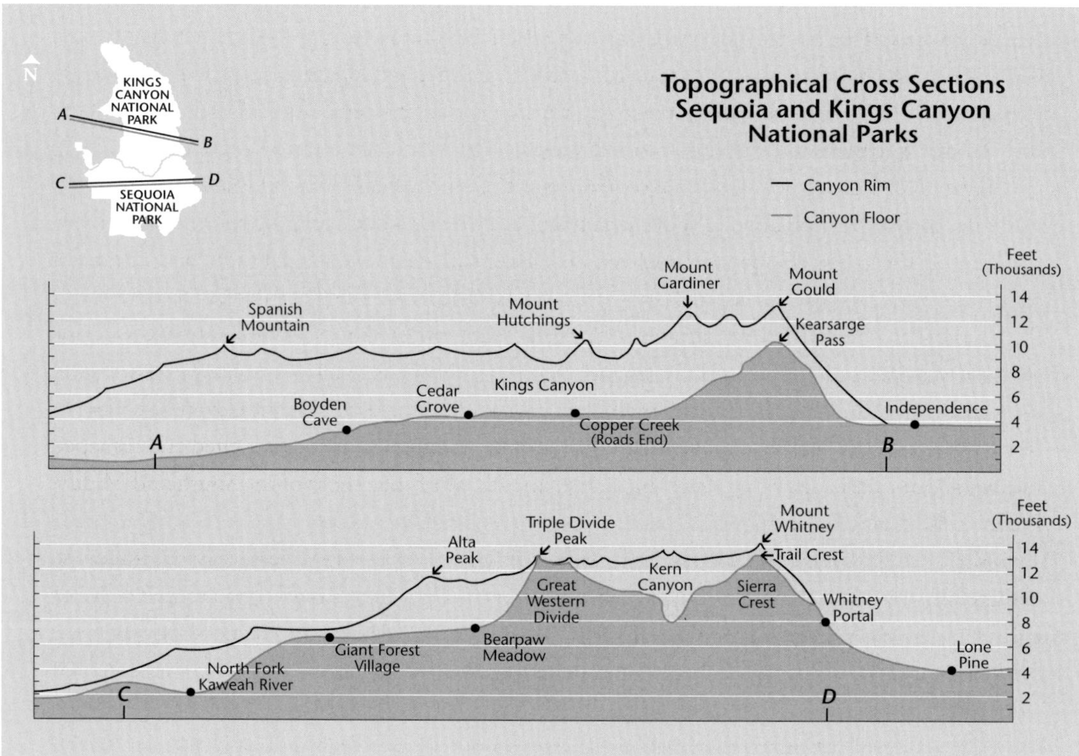

Topographical Cross Sections
Sequoia and Kings Canyon
National Parks
N
KINGS CANYON NATIONAL PARK
SEQUOIA NATIONAL PARK
A
B
C
D
Canyon Rim
Canyon Floor
Feet (Thousands)
14
12
10
8
6
4
2
Spanish Mountain
Mount Hutchings
Mount Gardiner
Mount Gould
Kearsarge Pass
Kings Canyon
Boyden Cave
Cedar Grove
Copper Creek (Roads End)
Independence
Alta Peak
Triple Divide Peak
Mount Whitney
Trail Crest
Great Western Divide
Kern Canyon
Sierra Crest
Whitney Portal
Giant Forest Village
Bearpaw Meadow
North Fork Kaweah River
Lone Pine

THE ICE AGE

At the same time that the Sierra Nevada was rising toward its modern height, Earth's atmosphere was cooling. Sometime between two and three million years ago, a deep and extensive ice cap began to accumulate over the range. During the Pleistocene epoch, ice accumulated in the High Sierra to depths of more than 2,000 feet in some of the highest alpine basins; then it began to flow slowly downhill, scouring and reshaping the landscape. Several times the ice melted, only to return again after a few tens of thousands of years. As recently as 20,000 years ago, the Sierra was once again icebound, and the last major glaciers melted away barely 12,000 years ago.

Glacial erosion fundamentally reshaped much of the surface of the Sierra. In the southern portions of the range, glaciers formed in most basins above 9,000 feet. From these locations, the ice flowed downhill through existing river canyons, reaching down to an altitude of 6,000 feet in the Kern and Kaweah watersheds, and below 4,000 feet in the two major canyons of the Kings River. In the high mountains, where they were born, the glaciers quarried and removed enormous amounts of rock, leaving behind narrow, cliff-rimmed ridges and barren open basins dotted with bedrock-lined lakes. In the middle and lower canyons, the ice widened and reshaped like a giant bulldozer, carving out U-shaped mountain valleys like those of the South and Middle Forks of the Kings River. [2]

Since the last large glaciers melted about 12,000 years ago, the Sierra has continued to change. Plant pollen trapped in muds in meadows and lakes suggests that, 7,000 to 10,000 years ago, the Sierra was considerably drier than it is now. On the western slope, extensive acreages of sagebrush and Jeffrey pine grew in a landscape reminiscent of modern Mono County on the east side of the Sierra. This same research suggests that, in more recent times, a more water-loving forest eventually replaced that open, dry forest. From about the fourteenth through the eighteenth centuries, the Sierra even experienced a "Little Ice Age" that saw the formation of new glaciers on the higher peaks. Since about 1800, the climate has again warmed, and, with the effects of the Industrial Revolution now being realized, additional warming seems inevitable.

A LAND OF BIOLOGICAL VARIETY

Nineteenth-century explorers of the Sierra Nevada found a finely tuned biological world, responding to the changing conditions of the post–Ice Age period. As the ice melted, plant and animal populations shifted in response to the warming climate. During the Ice Age, numerous northern cold-tolerant plants and animals colonized California. As the weather warmed, these organisms found their ranges increasingly restricted. At the same time, the shift towards warmer, drier weather increased habitat for many plants and animals of meso-American origin. In recent millennia, northern plants have been confined mostly to the upper altitude portions of the southern Sierra; at lower altitudes, more drought-tolerant species of southern origins now dominate.

Regardless of where they live, nearly all the organisms that survive today in the Sierra have had to accommodate to several inescapable truths. Exact climate data for the southern Sierra is largely limited to the past seventy-five years, but, even so, it is complete enough to give some idea of the patterns that have prevailed during the past 10,000 years. Temperature variation, for example, is a predictable function of altitude: Every thousand feet increase in altitude results in a drop in temperature of three to five degrees Fahrenheit. The implications of this fact on a mountain range with 14,000 feet of altitude variation are easily appreciated. On an average day, the summits of the highest peaks will be forty to sixty degrees colder than the western base of the mountains. Variation in precipitation is nearly as predictable. During the past fifty years, average annual values for the region have varied from about ten inches of precipitation in Visalia and Fresno to a probable sixty inches annually at the 9,000-foot level, an increase of 600 percent. Another critical factor in any understanding of the Sierra's climate in recent times is the Mediterranean cycle of precipitation. Under this pattern, which seems to have applied to the Sierra since the end of the Ice Age, precipitation comes mostly during the winter months, at a time when many plants are unable to use the moisture due to cold and lack of sunlight. A necessary corollary is summer drought, another inescapable fact of life (or death) for most Sierra Nevada life-forms.

In an endless cycle of experimentation and adaptation, the Sierra's plants and the animals have found ways to survive and even prosper in the face of these challenges. Up to about 5,000 feet in altitude, mild, sometimes rainy winters and intense summer drought have formed a distinctive world. In this zone, vegetation is typically oak-dominated broadleaf forest or dense brush, a plant community called chaparral. Above 5,000 feet, not only does precipitation increase to an average of about thirty-five to forty inches, but also a critical winter temperature threshold is reached. Around 5,000 feet, winter storms usually produce more snow than rain. At 7,000 feet, average annual snowfall during the twentieth century exceeded 250 inches. At 9,000 feet, the total was probably thirty percent greater.

Plants life reflects these changes in temperature and precipitation. Between 5,000 and 9,000 feet, the southern Sierra Nevada is clothed with an extensive conifer "snow forest." Nearly a dozen species of tall, narrow, evergreen trees grow together in this zone. The annual pressure of heavy snowfall makes the pines, firs, and cedars similar in superficial appearance, but each is uniquely adapted to fill a slightly different ecological niche. Many of these species grow quite large, with six-feet-thick, 200-foot-tall trees common. Here also grow the giant sequoias, with the largest

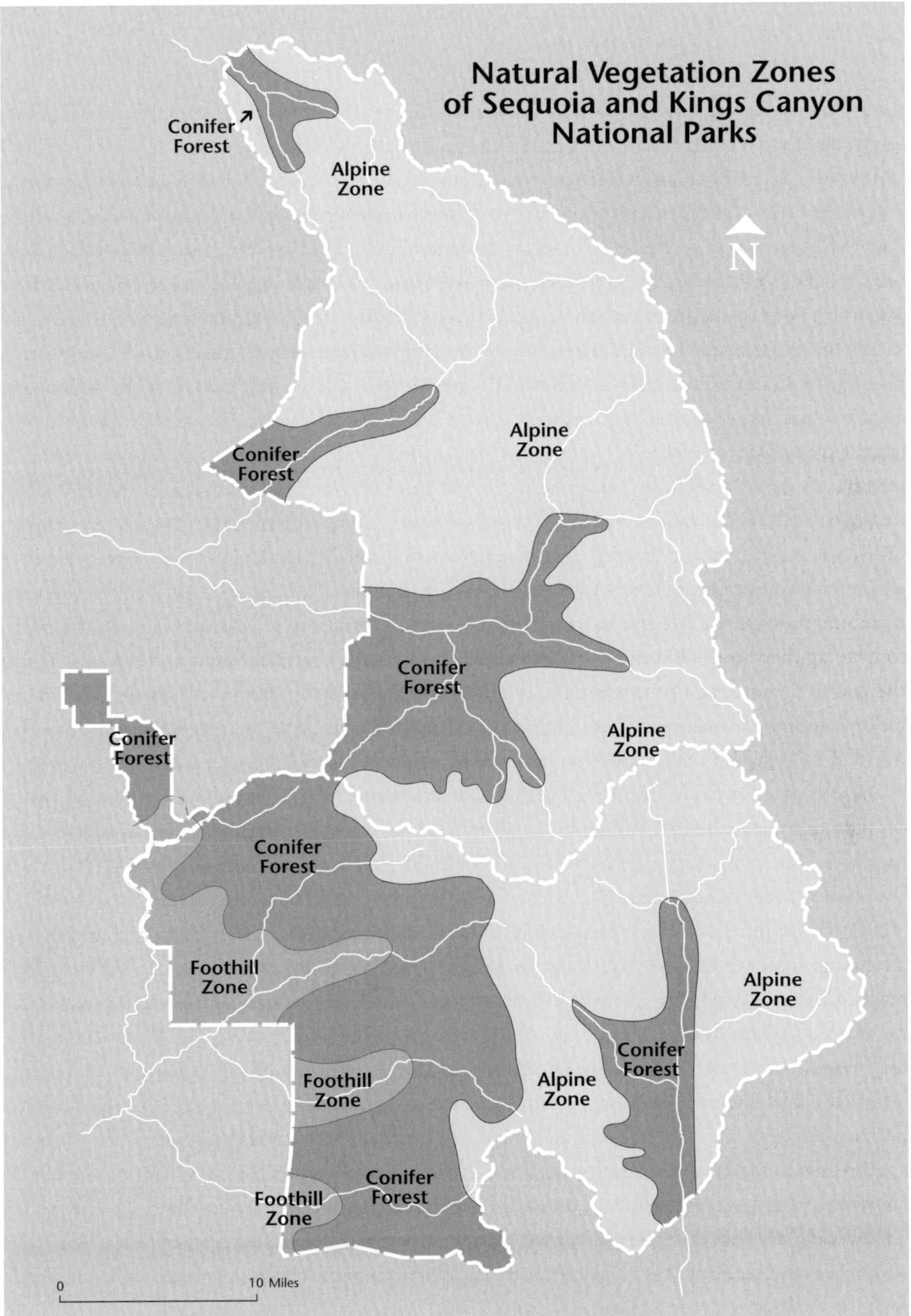
Natural Vegetation Zones of Sequoia and Kings Canyon National Parks
N
Conifer Forest
Alpine Zone
Conifer Forest
Alpine Zone
Conifer Forest
Conifer Forest
Alpine Zone
Conifer Forest
Foothill Zone
Alpine Zone
Conifer Forest
Foothill Zone
Alpine Zone
Foothill Zone
Conifer Forest
0
10 Miles

specimens exceeding 300 feet in height and thirty feet in basal diameter! Scattered through the forest, where soils are too wet for trees, are lush wetlands or meadows.

Above 9,000 feet, a third natural world appears. Here, winters are long and cold, spring snowmelt is slow, and summers are cool and short. Life is difficult here for many reasons, and the vegetation shows it. Tree growth tends to be patchy and sparse, and above 11,000 feet there usually is no forest, only rock and small, ground-hugging alpine perennials. This is tundra, a land of constrained biological productivity and of limited ability to recover when damaged.

At the foot of the mountains, on the floor of the Great Central Valley to the west, was a fourth world, one now largely superseded by modern human activity. Much of the valley floor was dry, seasonal grassland that blended seamlessly into the spare oak savannas of the lowest foothills. But here and there, mostly along rivers, better watered freshwater marsh and deciduous forest areas could be found. The richest of these were within the lush deltas of the Kings and Kaweah Rivers. Both streams supported extensive riparian mazes that began as soon as the rivers exited the mountains. Ultimately, both streams, together with the smaller Tule River and even part of the Kern terminated in a giant freshwater basin known as Tulare Lake. With a thousand square miles of wetlands, Tulare Lake was an enormously productive biological engine, supporting millions of birds and fish.[3]

BEFORE WE CAME

At the end of the sixteenth century, before a single European had entered the great valley that is the true heart of California, before anyone but Native Americans had seen the mountains we call the Sierra Nevada, the world that now contains Sequoia and Kings Canyon National Parks was an unseamed, unitary whole.

From the human point of view—and humans were already very much a part of the landscape—the heart of the region was the great tule swamp later known as Tulare Lake. The lake itself, if seen from the air, was a giant oval of concentric rings. The innermost ring, miles across, was open water, too deep for tules or other reeds but green with other kinds of floating life made possible by the warm water of summer. Closer to the lakeshore were miles of the thick tules that would ultimately share their Spanish name with the lake itself. Six to ten feet tall, grey-green and tubular, the reed-like plants were a world unto themselves, endless and regular.

On the eastern side of the lake, the marshlands fringed into the oak forest. If still on wing, an observer would look down into a confusing forest of dark, drooping, rounded oaks and slightly higher and drier islands of grass. Scattered along meandering streams, bright green marshes added another hue. The forest belt of the Kaweah River delta averaged perhaps fifteen miles in width.

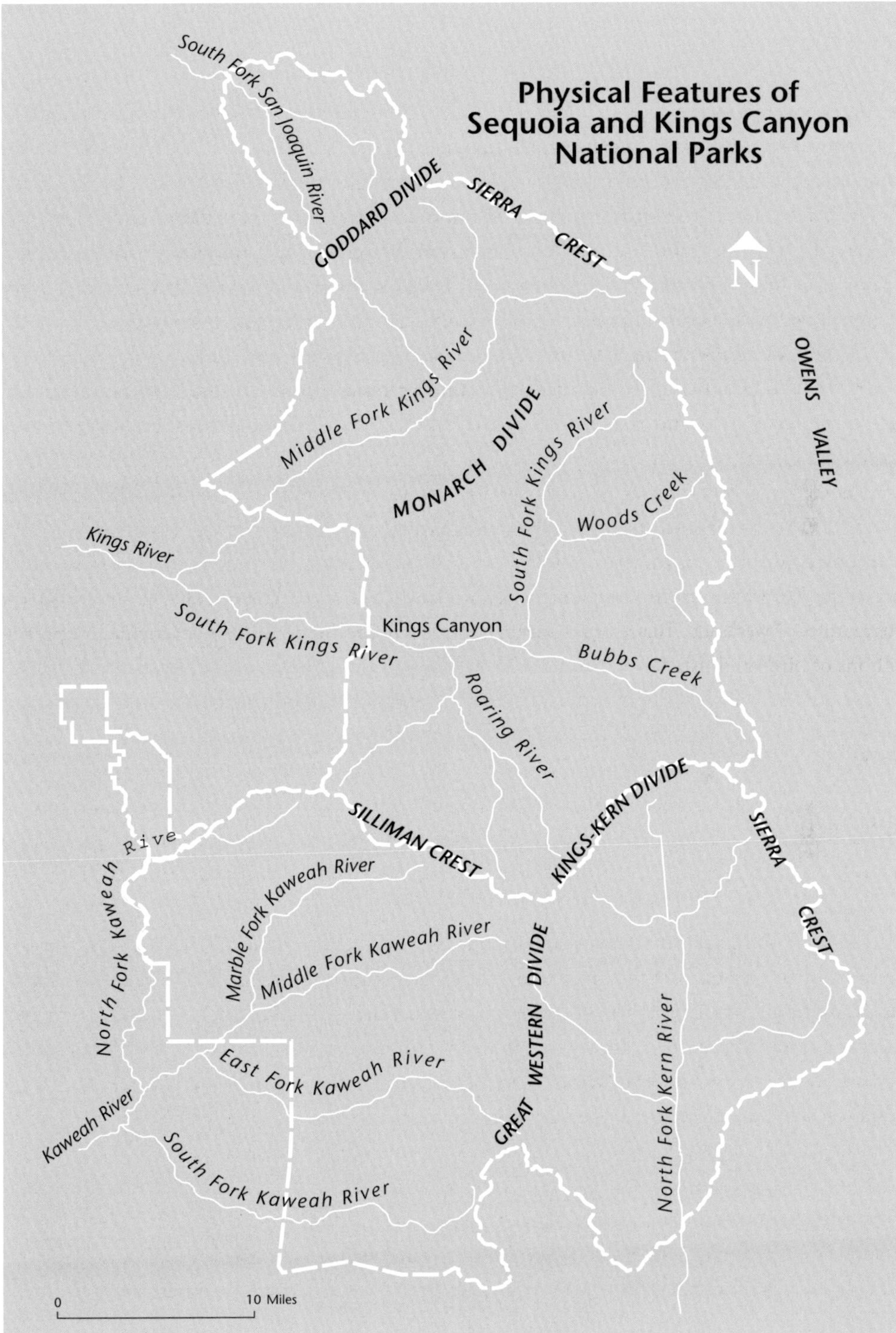

Physical Features of Sequoia and Kings Canyon National Parks
N
South Fork San Joaquin River
GODDARD DIVIDE
SIERRA
CREST
OWENS
VALLEY
Middle Fork Kings River
MONARCH DIVIDE
South Fork Kings River
Woods Creek
Kings River
South Fork Kings River
Kings Canyon
Bubbs Creek
Roaring River
SILLIMAN CREST
KINGS-KERN DIVIDE
SIERRA
CREST
Rive
North Fork Kaweah
Marble Fork Kaweah River
Middle Fork Kaweah River
GREAT WESTERN DIVIDE
North Fork Kern River
East Fork Kaweah River
Kaweah River
South Fork Kaweah River
0
10 Miles

To the north and south, brown, open grassland stretched toward seeming infinity; herds of pronghorn and tule elk lived in the brown openness. To the east, distantly visible above the oak forest, rose a miles-high blue and grey mountain wall: the Sierra Nevada.

No clear color line separated the foot of the Sierra from the valley floor. The first foothills did arise abruptly from the surrounding prairie, but they shared the same colors and textures as the lowlands they bordered. A little higher up, particularly on slightly less arid northern slopes, the first of the dryland oaks appeared—well-spaced, compact trees making no pretense to being a forest. Above, on the looming mountain face, darker and denser forests began to come into view. These were the forests that gave the mountain its dark blue cast from the distant lake on clear days. First, there were oak forests of increasing density; then steep, thick mountainsides of intertwined brush; and, higher yet, the great conifer forests.

The forests of tall, densely packed, angular trees rose steadily, rank upon row, up the steep flanks of the Sierra—broken only occasionally by a small, wet meadow or a gleaming, gray-granite dome or ledge. Above this forest belt, visible from 100 miles away, the granite asserted itself at last as the dominant and crowning feature of the range—clean and spare, angular and symmetrical: bare rock in summer; shining ice in winter and spring. And above the rock, on hot summer afternoons, would grow towering, blue-white thunderstorms, rising another four or six miles into the sky.

All this was visible to any creature that chose to look. And looking at this land already, and changing it in many ways, were thousands of people. It is time to remember them.

CHAPTER TWO

The Native Americans and the Land

When significant numbers of Europeans first entered the interior of California during the mid-nineteenth century, they were immediately impressed with the land they found. Everywhere they looked they sensed potential. They found people, too, sometimes lots of them, but the Europeans were not nearly so impressed with them. In a way, the separation of the two was odd, for the land and the people were inextricably bound together.

Just when people first came to live in the southern Sierra is not entirely clear. Archaeologists are now confident that human beings have lived in California for at least 13,000 years, and some evidence suggests much earlier occupation. In the Great Central Valley, sites 3,000 to 4,000 years old have been excavated, and it now seems apparent that humans have occupied Central California, including portions of the Sierra, for at least 6,000 or 7,000 years and quite likely much longer.[1]

In the Sequoia/Kings Canyon region, the record is much more vague, with much of the area archaeologically unexplored even today. Most of the limited archaeological work within the parks' areas, moreover, occurred many decades ago. For our purposes, the most useful excavation took place at several locations along the main stem of the Kaweah River. Three sites were explored in the late 1950s during construction of Terminus Dam on the Middle Fork of the Kaweah River below Sequoia National Park. At Hospital Rock, six miles upstream from the parks' boundary on the same river, additional work was done in 1960. During the same year, limited excavation took place in Kings Canyon less than a mile from Cedar Grove.[2]

Taken alone, these excavations provide only very limited information. None demonstrate occupation of great antiquity, although deposits of cultural material at Hospital Rock were up to six feet deep. Remaining physical evidence suggests the basic directions of subsistence and culture but little more. Only when the excavations are placed in the broader context of regional anthropological research does the haze of the past begin to recede.

NATIVE AMERICANS OF THE SOUTHERN SIERRA

At the beginning of the nineteenth century, two distinct groups of people occupied the southern Sierra Nevada. In the higher mountains and also down into the western foothills lived hunters and gatherers known as the Monache or Western Mono. West of the Monache, in the lowest foothills and also across the expanses of the Great Central Valley, was a second group, the Yokuts. Both language and history separated the two tribes. The Yokuts spoke a Penutian language, which related them to many of the other tribes of interior California, while the Monache language makes it clear that their ancestors were relatives of the Shoshone or Paiutes who still occupy the Great Basin region to the east of the Sierra.

The Monache apparently were fairly recent arrivals on the western side of the Sierra. Their language still strongly resembled that of the Owens Valley Paiute. Certainly, if the two groups had been separated for a long time, their two languages would have begun to diverge. The Owens Valley Paiute, or Eastern Mono, were a well-established desert culture relying for their survival upon a variety of resources. Their main villages occupied sites near streams in the dry desert valleys east of the Sierra, where they lived largely on a diet of gathered seeds, fish, and game. Nuts from the pinyon pines that grew extensively in the desert mountains east of the Owens Valley and also on the eastern slope of the Sierra were an important food staple. Rich in fats and calories, the nuts are one of the few foods of the early Native Americans of California still to be consumed in any volume today.[3]

The pursuit of pine nuts and game as well as the summer climate of the desert valleys where they made their homes sent the Eastern Mono seasonally to higher elevations. The Sierra Nevada, with its pinyon-forested eastern foothills and herds of deer and bighorn sheep, certainly attracted these people. The Eastern Mono had other reasons to ascend into the High Sierra and, perhaps, even cross the range, for west of the high peaks were other peoples with goods to trade. A surprising amount of Native American commerce seems to have occurred across the high ridges of the southern Sierra. From the east, the Owens Valley Paiute brought salt, pine nuts, mineral paints, obsidian, and many other critical items not obtainable west of the mountains. Traded eastward across the mountain were other unique commodities, including fresh water and saltwater shells, acorns, manzanita berries, and bear skins. This trade benefited both groups and increased their contact with each other. Modern archaeological work confirms the pattern. Most west-side arrow points, for example, were fashioned of obsidian that came from the east, while desert camps, when excavated today, almost always include fragments of jewelry made from seashells.

Eventually, for reasons that can only be surmised, some Eastern Mono began to winter west of the Sierra Crest. In some ways, the change was not a big one, for the Mono pattern of life had long been to winter in the lowlands and range higher during the warm summer months. Perhaps they were invited west; perhaps the western slope enticed them with its wetter but less severe winter climate; perhaps a portion of the tribe found itself cut off from the desert by an early winter and sought refuge. We will probably never know. The exact date of this change is not completely clear, but it appears to have been about 500 or 600 years ago. Interestingly, the apparent division of the Mono into western and eastern bands came at about the same time as the onset of the Little Ice Age, with its increased snowfall and resumption of glaciation in the southern Sierra.

Whatever their initial reasons for developing winter settlements west of the Sierra Crest, the Monache successfully adapted to the available resources of their new home. Their pattern of establishing permanent villages at relatively low altitudes and then ranging much higher during the summer months fit easily to the west slope. The intense cold and heavy snow found above 5,000 feet on the west slope required that the permanent villages of the Western Mono be located in the foothill region. Village sites in the Central Valley were already occupied by the much more numerous Yokuts, a group perhaps ten times the size of the Mono and far too large to displace from their main residences; thus, the Western Mono established, over time, a line of winter village sites in the middle foothills of the western slope. Several of these village sites, including Hospital Rock and Potwisha along the Middle Fork of the Kaweah River, are now within Sequoia National Park. Other Western Mono groups located permanent villages on foothill lands along the North Fork of the Kaweah and in the lower Kings River watershed.[4]

The Western Mono did not displace the Yokuts from their main homelands along the lower stretches of the Kaweah and Kings Rivers and around Tulare Lake, but they probably did displace them from the foothill areas they previously had occupied. Certainly, as we have noted, these areas had witnessed human activity before the arrival of the Monache. The oldest and deepest archaeological sites on the western slope generally show a significant cultural change around the thirteenth or fourteenth centuries CE. Many aspects of physical culture altered, and the brownware pottery of the desert Paiutes began to show up where none previously had been seen.

THE WESTERN MONO

As the Monache brought new technology to the western slope, they also were forced to adapt to different natural resources. In this shift, they inevitably looked to many of the techniques already developed by the long-time residents of the less-arid environment of the western foothills. Many new plants were present, and many familiar ones missing. The staple nuts of the pinyon pine occurred only in a few isolated areas, but several varieties of oak provided often-enormous annual crops of nutritious acorns. The technology was different, however, for, unlike pine nuts, the acorns had to be treated to make them edible. Acorn meal ultimately became the single most important food staple for the Monache. Similar shifts in hunting habits were required.

For several centuries, the Western Mono effectively adapted to life on the western slope of the Sierra Nevada. By the time Europeans arrived on the scene, the Monache had divided into

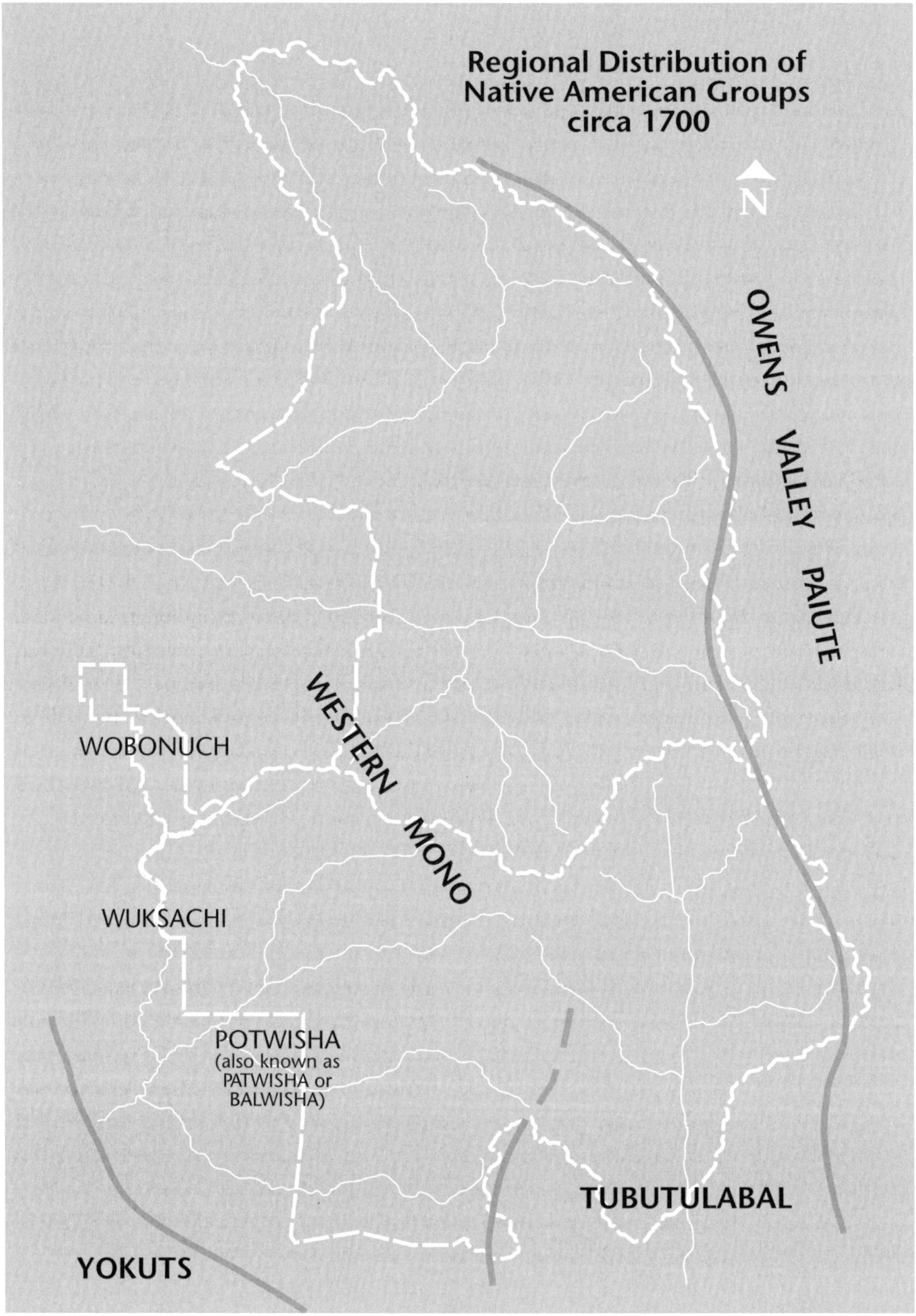
Regional Distribution of
Native American Groups
circa 1700
N
OWENS VALLEY PAIUTE
WESTERN MONO
WOBONUCH
WUKSACHI
POTWISHA
(also known as
PATWISHA or
BALWISHA)
TUBUTULABAL
YOKUTS

approximately half a dozen bands, united by language but by no apparent political structure. Three of these bands were north and west of present Sequoia and Kings Canyon National Parks and are not a part of our story; the other three lived in and near areas that are now part of the two parks. The Wobonuch lived in the foothill country west of Grant Grove that drains mostly north into the Kings River. South of the divide between the Kings and Kaweah Rivers, occupying valleys in the upper foothills near the head of the North Fork of the Kaweah, resided the Wuksachi. Occupying the remainder of the Kaweah watershed were the Potwisha (also variously spelled Patwisha or Balwisha). To the west of the Monache, on the floor of the Great Central Valley itself, Yokut bands dominated, as they also did in the Tule River watershed immediately to the south of the Kaweah. In the Kern River country, well south of what is now national park, the Tubatulabal, another Paiute-Shoshonean group, made their permanent home. [5]

The Potwisha are the best known and remembered of the Monache bands in the parks' region. Apparently, they ranged throughout the watersheds of the Marble, Middle, East, and South Forks of the Kaweah. The western boundary of their world, which they shared with the Yokuts, was approximately where Terminus Reservoir is today. The Potwisha exploited their native range in a thoroughly omnivorous fashion. No plants were cultivated for food, although some plant manipulation, including use of fire, may have been helped increase yields. Actually, there was little in either the plant or animal kingdoms that was not occasionally consumed. Acorns were the staple of their diet. Several species were consumed, but preference went particularly to those of the black oak (*Quercus kellogii*) of the upper foothills. Acorn crops varied annually in abundance and quality, and the various Monache bands learned to store the nuts in specially designed granaries. Because they contain tannic acid, acorns required water leaching before they could be consumed. This usually was accomplished through a process that began with grinding them into flour and then continued through a hot-water treatment to the resulting flour. The de-acidified flour was then used to make gruels and cakes. Many other plants were used seasonally, including pine nuts, yucca, and manzanita berries.

Hunting provided another critical food source, and the native peoples pursued many different creatures. Larger mammals were brought down with the bow and arrow, but the Monache also made extensive use of snares to catch game. Bows commonly were made of California laurel, although more elaborate ones of western juniper reinforced with deer sinew also were fabricated. Obsidian for arrow points came through trade from the Owens Valley area. The addition of certain substances to arrowheads resulted in poisoned points, which were not uncommon. Sun-dried deer liver, sometimes fortified with rattlesnake venom, was the most common toxin. Deer provided the most useful targets, being relatively plentiful and having many useful parts, but various other animals also were taken. Throughout the year, deer might be taken by arrow or trap, bears ambushed as they came out of winter dens, migratory fish forced into weir-like woven traps, and small rodents smoked out of their tunnels. Generally, the environment provided abundant food.[6]

Befitting the usually gentle climate, housing and clothing were simple. Small, dome-like thatched shelters or conical houses of cedar bark provided shelter. Villages normally had sweathouses, which were sometimes so popular that groups had to alternate using them. During warm weather, clothing was limited to a few small garments worn below the waist, and moccasins were used only for longer journeys. The largest known Potwisha village apparently occupied the narrow river terrace along the Middle Fork of the Kaweah now known as Hospital Rock. Located at an altitude of 2,700 feet, the site offered a nearly perfect combination of the elements important to Western Mono life. Several types of oak forest, including black oak, grew nearby. The same variety of plant communities provided excellent habitat for game. Immediately below the camp flowed the Middle Fork of the Kaweah River, with excellent fishing. Camp water came from a spring and stream that flowed across the village site. Nature had even provided extra shelter in the form of a talus boulder nearly sixty feet long with a natural cave beneath it.[7]

From their Hospital Rock camp, the Potwisha pursued their seasonal search for food. Individually and in family bands, they wandered widely across the landscape, following traditional foot-trail routes they shared with other mountain creatures. During summer and fall, the Monache often moved into the higher mountains. Here, just as many others have since, they escaped the summer heat of the lower canyons, while they harvested acorns and late-summer berries, hunted, and traded with desert Indians who had come into the high country from the east. Throughout the parks' region, evidence of summer mountain camps can still be seen. Bedrock mortars—conical holes worn into the rock by the repeated grinding of acorns, pine nuts, and other seeds—are the most common sign of these camps. At major village sites in the foothills, more than 100 mortar holes can sometimes be found. Smaller sites are scattered throughout the mid-altitude forests, where modern visitors often discover them. The Wobonuch and Wuksachi apparently moved up in summer to areas that include modern Dorst Campground, Grant Grove, and the floor of the Kings Canyon. Bedrock mortars at these sites provide irrefutable evidence. The Potwisha also moved up; their mortar sites are still visible at the Giant Forest and Mineral King, among other places.

We can only estimate the total number of Monache to inhabit the parks region. During the early twentieth century, pioneer anthropologist A. L. Kroeber, of the University of California in Berkeley, calculated that the Western Mono could not have totaled more than 2,000 individuals in the early nineteenth century, with the Eastern Mono of the Owens Valley region numbering perhaps twice that many. Thus, Kroeber concluded, the total world of the Mono peoples probably did not exceed 6,000 persons. The Yokuts, having the rich biological resources of the Central

Valley's wetlands to draw upon, were much more numerous. Kroeber estimated 15,000 to 20,000, and some recent estimates are much higher.[8] All this leads to the final question of this chapter: How did these people perceive, react to, and affect the lands that are the subject of this book?

NATIVE AMERICAN IMPACTS ON THE LAND

Modern Americans tend to assume that the Native Americans who first inhabited this continent lived in almost perfect harmony with the environment. There is some truth to this assertion and a great deal of dangerous misinformation. A fundamental beginning for understanding the relationship between pre-contact Native Americans and the natural environment is to understand that they would never have asked the question. Before the arrival of Europeans in California, the people who lived here saw themselves as inseparable from the natural world of plants and animals. The Western Mono lived in a unified world of predator and prey, of spirits and totemic clan groups. Their mythology related them to their fellow creatures and to the landscape. But this does not mean they had no impact upon their world, for they certainly did.

One of the more difficult historical question modern wilderness managers face in the Sierra is defining how pre-industrial human beings affected the ecosystems we now seek to preserve. Were early human actions so insignificant they really are of no modern consequence? Or were they critical to the development and maintenance of the landscape we now call "natural" and that we so deeply appreciate? The final detailed answers to these problems are still deeply hidden, but a preliminary picture is emerging, and that picture suggests that Native Americans were a major factor in development of the California landscape.[9]

Many Native American impacts on the landscape were localized. Hale Tharp, apparently the first white man to visit the Monache village at Hospital Rock, reported that, in 1858, he found several hundred Indians living at the site, that the camp was occupied all year, and that campfires were never allowed to go out.[10] Perhaps not all the people Tharp met that day actually lived at Hospital Rock, but even a complex of several villages with this many people would have had significant local impacts. To support several hundred people through hunting and gathering involves a great deal of resource manipulation, and keeping camp fires burning 365 days a year would definitely affect local vegetation. Without doubt, a camp like Hospital Rock, which, according to archaeologists, had been occupied for at least 500 years prior to Tharp's arrival, inevitably changed the appearance and biological functioning of the surrounding landscapes. Quantifying this change, unfortunately, is as yet impossible. We simply do not know enough about exactly what the Indians were taking from the environment, how they were taking it, or even exactly what the environment was at the time.

Native American impacts were not always local, however, and at least one of their cultural habits affected the entire landscape. Throughout North America, anthropological research makes it clear that Native Americans frequently used wildland fire to modify vegetation. Fires were kindled for various reasons, including improvement of forage for game animals, encouragement of valuable plants, herding game, and improvement in visibility. From all we can tell, the Western Mono, Yokuts, Tubatulabal, and Eastern Mono all set fires at various times for various purposes. Understanding the impacts of these fires is difficult. Fires change both the density and composition of vegetation, and frequent fires, from any cause, can profoundly change ecosystems. We know that Native Americans frequently lit fires.[11] We do not know, however, how many fires burned or what percentage of those fires were kindled by Native Americans rather than by natural causes. Thus, we cannot, as did the early European pioneers, separate the land from its Native American inhabitants.

During the mid-nineteenth century, when Europeans first studied the resources and landscapes of the southern Sierra Nevada, they profoundly misperceived what they saw. Because they refused to take seriously the technologically simple people they found living there, they completely missed how significantly the Native Americans had changed the landscape and its natural systems. Because the early Europeans missed these crucial relationships, they convinced themselves that they were looking at a virgin, primeval landscape, the work of God. The rapid disappearance of the Indians during the 1860s, which we detail in the next chapter, only served to reinforce this perception. Ultimately, this mistaken idea of a primeval landscape would be taken up not only by pioneers, but also by politicians and conservationists and would, in time, become a subtly flawed foundation block in the formation of Sequoia and Kings Canyon National Parks.[12]

CHAPTER THREE

Exploration and Exploitation (1850–1885)

DURING THE MIDDLE DECADES of the nineteenth century, the Native Americans who had lived relatively undisturbed in the southern Sierra for countless generations found themselves suddenly and permanently displaced as the dominant mountain culture. The agents of change, of course, were people and cultures of European descent. California is a long way from Europe, yet, within fifty years of the first voyage of Christopher Columbus across the Atlantic Ocean, Portuguese sailor Juan Rodriguez Cabrillo made crude maps of the cold, foggy coast of Alta (Upper) California. Cabrillo found little to excite the Spanish colonial mentality, and more than two centuries passed before Spain finally thought Upper California worthy of organized exploration and settlement. In 1769, responding to perceived international threats in the North Pacific from Russia and England, the staid, already centuries-old Spanish colonial administration of the Americas began to establish a tenuous string of European outposts along the Alta California coast.

Anchored by the small military posts (*presidios*) at San Diego, Santa Barbara, Monterey, and San Francisco, the chain of Spanish settlements was secured by Christian missionary settlements sponsored by the colonial government, operated by the Franciscan Order, and populated largely by unenthusiastic Native Americans from the coastal tribes. None of the twenty-one missions the Spaniards ultimately established were more than a few dozen miles from the coast, yet the impacts of these settlements on California and its residents were widespread and significant. Even the southern Sierra was not immune.

In a way, it is deceptive to call these Spanish settlements "European," for the number of pure-blooded Europeans in Spanish California was never very large. Most of the mission residents were California Indians, and most of the "Spanish" immigrants were actually of *mestizo* (mixed Indian–European) blood. Only a tiny handful of civil and ecclesiastical colonial appointees were truly European, born on the eastern shores of the Atlantic. But if the new people who came to Alta California were more truly "American" than European, the material culture they brought was not only European, but specifically Mediterranean. The connection was highly fortuitous, for many of the plants and animals the Spaniards brought to California were actually better suited to life in the new California settlements than they had been in Mexico and the Caribbean Islands. The Spaniards brought to their settlements many crops that are still California staples, including oranges, olives, peaches, corn, and wheat. They also brought with them European grazing animals, including cattle, sheep, goats, burros, and horses. The crops the Spaniards introduced to California were limited by water and climate largely to the places where they were put, but the grazing animals imported by the Spaniards and the weedy plants that inadvertently came with them would ultimately change the face of much of California, including the southern Sierra.

Initially, the Spaniards were content to explore the lands near the coast, but, within a few years, they had begun to penetrate inland California. During the 1770s, several expeditions sought understanding of the lands to the east. It soon became apparent that beyond the coastal mountains was a large, often swampy inland plain, and that east of that was a high, rugged mountain range, or "sierra," as the Spaniards called serrated ridges. In 1776, Franciscan missionaries Francisco Garces and Pedro Font, both members of the first overland colonizing party to come to California, explored the northern and southern extremities of the San Joaquin Valley. To Font fell the accidental honor of naming the high eastern mountains. In his journal, he described, as he looked eastward across the marshlands near the confluence of the Sacramento and San Joaquin Rivers, "*una gran sierra Nevada*" ("a great snow-covered mountain range"), which ran from north to south. Font's intentions were merely descriptive, but the mountains east of the San Joaquin have henceforth been known as the Sierra Nevada, the "snowy mountains."

Time passed slowly in Spanish California, and a new century began before much more was officially known about the eastern mountains. During two expeditions in 1806, Spanish Navy Ensign Gabriel Moraga mapped and named a number of features along the eastern edge of the San Joaquin Valley, including the San Joaquin, Merced, and Kings Rivers. In the Spanish fashion, each feature received an ecclesiastical name appropriate to the day of discovery. Because Moraga camped on the banks of the Kings River on January 6, the twelfth day of Christmas, he named the stream *el rio de los santos reyes* ("the river of the holy kings"), after the three magi of the Christmas story.[1]

Moraga was not the only Spanish Californian to enter the interior during the early years of the nineteenth century. Increasingly, Spanish activity along the coast affected inland areas. The coastal missions had led to a severe and spreading disruption of California Indian life. Refugees from the coastal tribes often sought escape among the tribes of the interior, and they brought with them both a hatred for the Spaniards and an appreciation for the tastiness of European grazing animals. Eventually, horse and cattle theft became a way of life for many interior Indians, a development that required a Spanish response. As the early decades of the nineteenth century passed, this situation worsened, with the ultimate victims being the valley Indians themselves. Their cultures diluted by refugees from other tribes, their security reduced by raiding parties of soldiers and mission Indians from the settlements, and their numbers threatened by the introduction of European diseases, the Native Americans of interior California found their world crumbling. Least affected were the Indians of the Sierra, but as their valley neighbors suffered, so was their protecting buffer zone slowly eroded.

ARRIVAL OF THE ANGLO-AMERICANS

Not until 1827 did the Sierra first succumb to a crossing by people of European descent and, then, it was not the Spaniards who finally accomplished the feat but a new breed of naturalized Euro-Americans emanating from the upstart republic of the United States of America. These men were motivated not by the larger goals of empire or salvation, as the Spaniards had been, but by ambition for personal advantage and simple curiosity. During the 1820s, the rapid harvesting of the beaver of the Rocky Mountains had sent adventuresome fur trappers farther and farther afield in search of un-trapped beaver. It was only a matter of time before the trappers of the Rockies found their way into the Mexican settlements of Upper California. (Mexico had separated from Spain in 1821 and took California with it.)

Contact between the two cultures had already been made in New Mexico. Nevertheless, authorities in California were not pleased when trapper Jedediah Smith succeeded in crossing the Great Basin and finding his way to Mission San Gabriel in late 1826. Mexican Governor Echeandia ordered Smith out of California, but, during the winter and spring of 1827, Smith instead wandered north through the San Joaquin Valley, trapping the numerous beaver of the valley's rivers and noting the lay of the country. His first attempt to cross the Sierra took him up the Kings River, where extremely rugged terrain and the earliness of the season stopped him cold. Finally, in May, on his second try, Smith succeeded in crossing the mountains in the vicinity of the Stanislaus River, east of modern Stockton. In 1828, Smith returned to trap in the San Joaquin, and, in 1829–1830, employees of the Hudson's Bay Company trapped the same areas. As knowledge of California spread, the number of trappers increased.[2]

In 1832–1833, a party that included Ewing Young and J. J. Warner trapped the Kings River "some distance into the mountains." During 1833 and 1834, a party led by Joseph Walker crossed the Sierra from east to west in the Yosemite country and then proceeded south along the western foothills of the Sierra. Finally, taking the advice of local Indians, the party departed eastward through the Kern River route still known as Walker Pass. Once across the Sierra a second time, Walker turned north and explored the Owens Valley, taking a hard look at the severe eastern face of the Sierra. Finally, he connected with his route of the previous year and turned east.[3]

It did not take long to exhaust the beaver populations of Central California. Unlike the Rockies, the Sierra had beaver only at the lowest altitudes. California beaver depended mostly upon cottonwood trees for their sustenance, and since significant cottonwood groves were limited to foothill and valley riverbanks, the fur trappers had little cause to explore the high country. But, in late 1844, Second Lieutenant John C. Frémont, of the U.S. Topographical Engineers, while illegally exploring the fringes of Mexican California for the U.S. Army on the eve of the Mexican War, made a serious attempt to cross the high country of the southern Sierra. It was late December, and Frémont's goal was to rendezvous with the remainder of his party on the eastern side of the mountains. He left Sutter's Fort (modern Sacramento) on December 14 and ascended the Kings River, following the north bank. As the canyon narrowed, Frémont climbed higher and followed the ridges to the northeast. Finally, having ascended all the way to timberline, he found himself not on the crest of the Sierra but somewhere on the divide between the North Fork of the Kings River and the South Fork of the San Joaquin River. To the east rose masses of 12,000-foot peaks. That night a snowstorm began, and by morning the explorer abandoned all further thought of crossing the Sierra. Only with difficulty did Frémont and his party succeed in regaining the floor of the San Joaquin Valley. Had they been another day or two's travel into the mountains, they might not have escaped at all.[4]

Smith, Walker, and Frémont established basic truths about the southern Sierra. Along the western slope, deep canyons made travel very difficult. To the east, the high snow-peaks of the crest stood as a barrier visible for 100 miles. Between was a difficult land of dense forests, high ridges, and nearly impassible gorges. If one wanted to get to the other side of the southern Sierra, it was best to go around.

CAUCASIAN SETTLERS COME TO THE SOUTHERN SIERRA

At the end of the Mexican War on February 2, 1848, all of California officially became a part of the United States. Almost simultaneously, the discovery of gold in the central Sierra foothills east of Sutter's Fort began a new chapter in the history of California. During 1849 and 1850, several hundred thousand argonauts descended upon California from all over the world. Initially, the gold seekers focused upon the areas where gold had initially been discovered, well to the north of the future area of Sequoia and Kings Canyon National Parks, but the arrival of so large a group inevitably came to affect the remainder of the California landscape as well.

On the scene in the Tulare Lake basin at the moment of transition was Lieutenant George H. Derby, another representative of the U.S. Army's Topographical Engineers. During 1850, Derby, assigned to search for the best location for a military post to control the Indians of the basin, visited not only Tulare Lake, but also the lowland deltas of the Kings and Kaweah Rivers. He noted the by-now well-known topography of the valley region as well as the great changes ongoing in the Indian world.[5] Even as Lieutenant Derby made his reconnaissance of the Tulare Basin, Caucasian settlement was beginning in the oak forests of the nearby Kaweah River delta. The Indians, long embittered by their experiences with Spaniards and Mexicans, killed those first settlers, but, a few months later, another settlement called Visalia popped up nearby. Within two years, Visalia was a county seat, and, with emigrants spilling out of the northern gold country looking for settlement and business opportunities, life would never be the same again for the Native Americans of the Tulare Lake basin and its tributary mountain rivers. From Visalia, the first permanent Euro-American settlement in the region, settlers began to disperse in search of opportunities. Before the decade ended, they had invaded the mountain canyons to the east.

The story of Hale Tharp, the first Anglo to settle in the Kaweah River canyons, reflects a typical experience among those who came to California during the early 1850s. Born in Michigan, Tharp was twenty-three in 1851, when he was hired by an Illinois widow with four young sons to take her family to California. Driving a prairie schooner with two teams of oxen, Tharp succeeded in delivering the Swanson family to Placerville. There, noting that good women were in short supply, he made Mrs. Swanson henceforth Mrs. Tharp. He worked in the mines for several years, with fair success, but the work did not agree with him. Eventually, like many a disenchanted miner, Tharp sought another way to make a living.

The rapid growth of the mining and trading cities of the gold region created a substantial demand for foodstuffs, and good opportunities existed for an ambitious young man. Tharp settled upon cattle raising as a likely means of livelihood. He wandered south, away from the heavily populated region, in search of open land that would support cattle. Sometime during 1856, Tharp followed the Kaweah River into the foothills east of Visalia. In the broad, open valley where the Kaweah leaves the Sierra, Tharp found what he was seeking. Grass covered the hills and surrounding highlands, while the Kaweah River provided a reliable and ample water supply. Years later, Tharp recounted his positive impressions of the new land:

> There was abundance of game and other animals in this country when I first came here. Deer were practically everywhere, with lots of bear along the rivers; occasionally a grizzly bear, too. Lions, wolves and foxes were very plentiful. There were a great many ground squirrels, cottontail and jackrabbits; quail were seen in coveys of thousands. I never saw elk or antelope in the Three Rivers country. There were plenty of fish in the rivers below the rapids, lake trout and suckers; once in a while a speckled trout could be caught.[6]

Tharp also noted the substantial Native American population, which, to its later dismay, welcomed him graciously:

> I first located my ranch where I now live in the summer of 1856. There were about 2,000 Indians then living along the Kaweah Rivers above where Lemon Cove now stands. Their camps extended up along the rivers on the South Fork to the Cahoon Ranch, the North Fork to Kaweah, the East Fork to Kane's Flat, and the Middle Fork to Hospital Rock in

> Sequoia National Park. The Indian chief was named "Chappo" and he was a fine man. The Indians told me that I was the first white man that had ever come to their country. But few of them had ever seen a white man prior to my arrival. The Indians all liked me because I was good to them. I shot many deer for them to eat as they had no firearms and knew nothing about firearms. I liked the Indians, too, for they were honest and kind to each other. I never knew of a theft or murder amongst them.[7]

It is possible that Tharp was not the first Caucasian to enter the Kaweah Canyons. Nearly thirty years had passed since fur trappers first entered the region, and someone must have penetrated the lower canyons of the Kaweah during those curious times. No recorded attempt, however, had been made to penetrate the higher mountains. Because there were no beaver above the low foothills, all the early entries into the high country were attempts to cross the Sierra, and nowhere else in the southern Sierra did the mountains appear more formidable than at the headwaters of the Kaweah. From clearings in the oak forest of the Kaweah delta, peaks as high as 13,000 feet were clearly visible. In comparison, from the floor of the San Joaquin, even the Kings River country, which concealed one of the deeper canyons on the continent, looked more feasible as a possible trans-Sierra route.

Two years later in 1858, with his brother-in-law, John Swanson, Tharp returned to the Kaweah and began to develop a ranch. That first year he built a log cabin and a barn. He also explored the mountain country to the east:

> I made my first trip to the Hospital Rock camp during the summer of 1858. Chief Chappo and I had become the very best of friends and he asked me to come up and stay with him overnight. He sent down two young Indian men to pilot me in, as there were no trails in the country, just Indian footpaths. I went on horseback and it took me about 8 hours to work my way in, the distance being about 18 miles from my Three Rivers ranch. When I arrived at the Camp, Chappo and his men extended me a cordial welcome and gave me the best his camp afforded. He called out every individual in the camp and with much dignity and long ceremony introduced me to all. There were over 600 Indians then living at the camp. My arrival excited the curiosity of most of the Indians, as I was the first white person that had ever visited their camp, and only a few of their leaders had ever seen a white person before. As for myself, I did not attract half so much attention as did my horse and saddle, my weapons, and the clothing that I wore. These were all new to most of the Indians . . .[8]

Having caught a glimpse of the high country, Tharp's curiosity increased, and he made arrangements to explore further to the east:

> Accompanied by two Indians, I made my first trip into the Giant Forest during the summer of 1858. We went in by the way of the Middle Fork and Moro Rock and camped for a few days at Log Meadow, after which we came out by the same route that we went in. I do not remember the dates that we were there, but I carved with my knife on the big hollow redwood log my name and the date on the same day that we got there.[9]

Tharp was now convinced that the Kaweah country offered what he was seeking, and he moved to strengthen his situation. He relocated his wife and children from Placerville to Farmersville, near Visalia, explored the mountains as far north as Kings Canyon and as far south as Mineral King and, in 1861, began grazing his horses at Log Meadow during the summer months.[10] All this was necessary because, increasingly, Tharp had company. In 1859, Hopkins and Martha Work became Tharp's first Caucasian neighbors, and, during the next few years, William Swanson, Joseph Palmer, and Alfred Everton began a parade of settlers that, in some ways, has yet to end. And the Kaweah region was not unique in the attention it was receiving. As early as 1858, a party led by J. H. Johnson, of Tulare County, succeeded in crossing the Sierra via what is now known as Kearsarge Pass, a route that took them through the Kings Canyon.[11]

The immediate human losers in this influx of Euro-Americans were the native peoples. Nearly half a century later, Tharp recalled their fate:

> By the spring of 1862 quite a number of whites had settled in the Three Rivers section, and the Indians were gradually forced out. Then, too, the Indians had contracted contagious diseases from the whites, such as measles, scarlet fever and smallpox and they died off by the hundreds. I helped to bury 27 in one day up on the Sam Kelly place. About this time Chief Chappo and some of his men came to see me, and asked me to try and stop the whites from coming into their country. When I said that was impossible, they all sat down and cried. They told me that their people loved this country, did not want to leave it, and knew not where to go. A few days later Chappo came to me with tears in his eyes and told me that they had decided not to fight the whites, but would leave the country. From that time on, they moved out little by little and from time to time until all were gone. I think by the summer of 1865 the Indians had left the district. Their Hospital Rock camp was the last vacated, and they left it as clean as a ribbon.[12]

EXPLOITATION BEGINS

The effective replacement of the Native American population of the southern Sierra with a population of Caucasian settlers had a profound effect upon the land. Both cultures looked to the land for sustenance but in very different ways. Through many centuries, the Indians, with their hunting-and-gathering economy and their use of fire, had established a relatively stable relationship with the ecosystems of the Sierra. Human impacts on the natural systems were real and significant, but an approximate equilibrium had been established that later residents of the region misperceived as purely natural. All this disappeared in a decade with the arrival of a new culture and new ways of life.

The new culture that washed over the Sierra in the twenty years following Tharp's arrival held values far removed from those of the Native Americans. These new people valued not nuts, berries, and game but pasturelands, timber, and minerals. The new people saw nature not as a part of the same psychological world as that of humanity but as something provided by God for their consumption and use. The new people did not seek stability and equilibrium; instead, they had a strong predisposition towards change, even if it involved total consumption of the places and resources at their disposal. Not surprisingly, the change in cultures that took place in the southern Sierra during the second half of the nineteenth century modified the Sierra much more profoundly than had the previous several centuries of Native American habitation.

During the 1850s through the 1870s, the southern Sierra was closely searched for resources of value. First came the cattlemen and sheepmen. With the rapid growth of the mining industry and the development of California's first real cities during the 1850s, grazing activity expanded into the interior valleys of the new state. Tharp's arrival in the Kaweah Canyons was a part of this process. In those early days when transportation was still very primitive, the highest value for many remote areas was to use the lands for grazing. Once the grass had been consumed, the animals could walk to market, however far that might be. During the early 1860s, after a rapid buildup of interior grazing activity, two successive events, the great Central Valley flood of 1862 and the severe drought of 1863–1864, shook the grazing industry to its foundations. The drought especially, with its near total failure of winter-pasture grasses, sent stockmen desperately searching for previously unused rangelands. What resulted was the first utilization of the Sierra for large-scale livestock feeding. During the drought years, hungry cattle from the lowlands swarmed over the Sierra foothills and forests, while the high country suddenly found itself assaulted by huge herds of domestic sheep. Tharp and his Three Rivers neighbors had claimed their mountain ranges none too soon. By the summer of 1864, as many as 4,000 cattle were in the Giant Forest area.[13]

Within a few years, much of the herbaceous vegetation of the Sierra was either destroyed or replaced. In the foothill's grasslands, annual Eurasian grasses replaced the grazing-sensitive native perennial species. In the high country, entire basins were so thoroughly denuded that parties traveling on horseback lamented the almost total lack of feed for their animals. Particularly hard hit was the alpine, northern portion of the Kern River watershed. The change was apparent to all who knew the country. Geologist Clarence King, who had first visited the "green and lovely" Kern Plateau in 1864, reported, in 1873, that the same country had become "a gray sea of rolling granite ridges no longer velveted with meadows and upland grasses."[14]

The search for resources was not limited to grass, however, for timber and mineral deposits also had potential value. Accessibility was the key to much of this resource-prospecting activity, and accessibility was exactly what the southern Sierra did not naturally offer. The logical result was the beginning of a trail system. The initial trail-building impetus in the southern Sierra was not so much to get into the mountains as to cross them. The Native Americans had regularly crossed the mountains on trading and even social journeys, and they had worked out the best routes long before the arrival of the Europeans. Indian paths were of limited use to the new wave of mountain travelers, however, because the Native Americans had not used beasts of burden. Since they traveled only on foot and seldom with heavy loads, their trails were usually little more than light foot paths. Euro-American pioneers, however, wanted to travel on horseback with freight loaded on mules, a practice that required better trails.

As noted, trans-Sierra travel began as early as the late 1850s but only with terrible hardship. Soon, however, the development of mining communities in the Owens Valley and Coso Mountains immediately east of the southern Sierra led to attempts to improve transportation across the mountains. Anyone looking at the western side of the Sierra from the San Joaquin Valley could tell that the high peaks of the Sierra, which stretched north almost indefinitely, ended immediately south of the Kaweah watershed. It was for this natural target that the early trails headed. The first route, used by the summer of 1860, was known as the Dennison Trail. It ascended the western slope of the Sierra along the Tule River, south of the Kaweah country, crossed into the Little Kern drainage, and eventually came out on the east side at Olancha. Little is known about the Dennison, because it was soon supplanted by the better known Jordan and Hockett Trails.[15]

John Jordan petitioned Tulare County for permission to build a toll trail across the mountains in November 1861. He was at work on his trail when he drowned while attempting to cross the Kern River in June 1862. Others completed his trail, which was largely an improvement of the Dennison route, and used it for many years. That December, Tulare County chartered yet another trail across the mountains, this time in response to a petition from John B. Hockett. His trail ran farther north than either the Dennison or Jordan routes, and it passed through portions of what later became Sequoia National Park. The Hockett Trail began near Tharp's Ranch on the Kaweah River, ascended the South Fork of the Kaweah to the area now known as Hockett Plateau, then crossed into the Little Kern; it briefly combined with the Jordan Trail only to diverge to the north again, pass over Coyote Pass, and then descend to the main branch of the Kern River in the vicinity

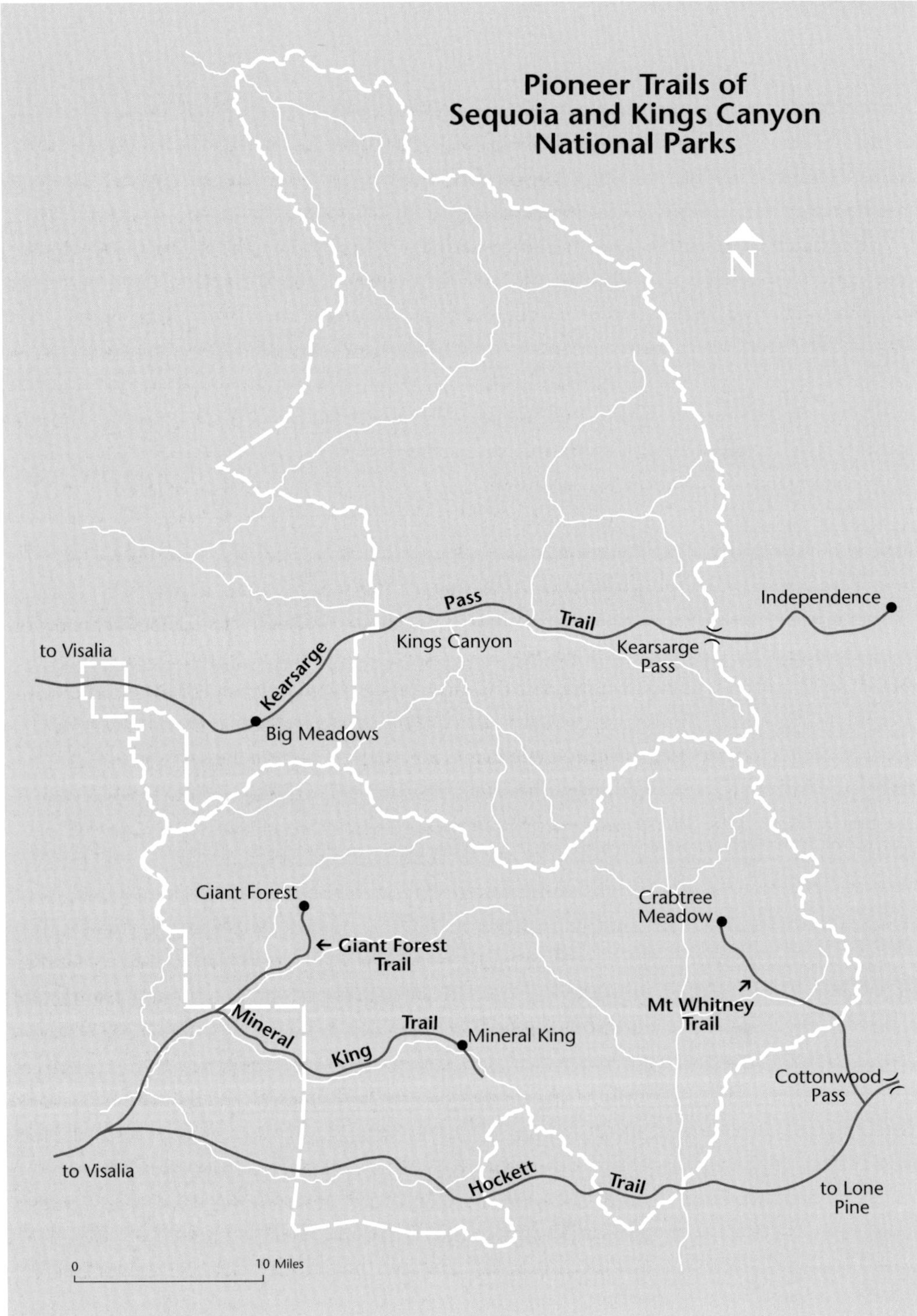
Pioneer Trails of
Sequoia and Kings Canyon
National Parks
N
Independence
Pass
Trail
Kings Canyon
Kearsarge
Pass
to Visalia
Kearsarge
Big Meadows
Giant Forest
← Giant Forest
Trail
Crabtree
Meadow
Mt Whitney
Trail
Mineral
Trail
King
Mineral King
Cottonwood
Pass
to Visalia
Hockett
Trail
to Lone
Pine
0
10 Miles

of Kern Lake. East of the Kern, the route climbed Golden Trout Creek (then "Whitney Creek") to Big Whitney Meadows, crossed the Sierra at Cottonwood Pass, just south of the southernmost major peaks, and then descended steeply to Owens Lake and the desert.[16]

In 1865, traders pushed a wagon road over Walker Pass, providing business headed from Visalia to the Inyo mines a longer but much easier route. The trails farther north remained, however, and they opened up the southern flank of the High Sierra to sheepmen, hunters, mineral prospectors, and anyone else interested in looking at the country.

THE GOVERNMENT SURVEYS

In all this activity, there remained a gap. Trails and even a wagon road now took travelers around the southern end of the Sierra. Sheepmen and cattlemen, each jealously guarding their own discoveries, poked through much of the range, seeking forage; mineral prospectors, too, combed the ridges seeking their fortunes. No one, however, had yet attempted to explore and map the heart of the southern Sierra for public purposes. Into this gap stepped the California Geological Survey. Created by the state legislature in 1860 "to make an accurate and complete Geological Survey of the State, and to furnish maps and diagrams thereof, with a full and scientific description of the rocks, fossils, soils, and minerals, and of its botanical and zoological productions, together with specimens of the same," the survey was California's first formal public attempt to inventory its resources. In charge was Josiah Dwight Whitney, forty-one years old and a graduate of Yale University. Under his supervision were several brilliant selections, including especially William Brewer, thirty-two at the time of his appointment and also a graduate of the Yale Scientific School. To Brewer fell responsibility for supervising the actual field activities of the survey.[17]

Although the survey began work late in 1860, it was not until 1864 that it turned its attentions to the southern Sierra Nevada. During that wartime summer, while the fate of the nation was being decided on eastern battlefields, Brewer and his men focused on the largest remaining blank spot on the map of California: the high mountain country south of the San Joaquin River watershed. From the drought-ravaged San Joaquin Valley, Brewer led his small party up into the mountains along the divide between the Kings and Kaweah Rivers. In early June, they camped just west of modern Grant Grove near a recently established logging enterprise called Thomas's Mill that was beginning the assault on the timber resources of the Sierra. After re-provisioning and making a visit to the Big Trees now called Grant Grove, the survey party struck out to the southwest, following the ridges into the higher mountains. As they climbed high enough to begin to get a sense of the country, they noted many high peaks to the east and south. Their plan, based on the false assumption that the southern Sierra was structured much like the Yosemite country, was to follow the Kings-Kaweah Divide to the crest of the Sierra. Soon, the ridge they were following rose up to form a sharp granite peak. After a difficult scramble, they attained the summit.

It was June 28, 1864, when Brewer climbed and named Mt. Silliman after one of his Yale professors. From the summit, now measured at 11,188 feet, Brewer got his first real impression of the complexity of the southern Sierra. To the east and north, forming the headwaters of the Kings River, Brewer could see an endless jumble of canyons and barren, serrated ridges. To the southeast, much closer, rose other peaks, equally high. To Brewer's surprise, a number of the visible summits were obviously as high as anything in the Yosemite country. The party named the highest-visible summit in the Kings River area "Mt. Brewer," and, since their original geographical strategy for exploring the country had proven flawed, they now struck out for this peak, which they hoped to ascend.

Several days of rough travel took the survey down off the Silliman Crest, across the Sugarloaf Valley and Roaring River (which they called the South Fork of the Kings River), and up the canyon at the western base of Mt. Brewer. On July 2, Brewer and Charles Hoffman struggled up the steep, talus-guarded peak and, after several dead ends, finally found their way to the summit, which they correctly estimated to be more than 13,000 feet high. The view stunned Brewer:

> Such a landscape! A hundred peaks in sight over thirteen thousand feet—many very sharp—deep canyons, cliffs in every direction almost rival Yosemite, sharp ridges inaccessible to man, on which human foot has never trod—all combined to produce a view of sublimity of which is rarely equaled, one which few are privileged to behold.[18]

When they returned exhausted that evening to their camp in the sparse, rocky forest below, Brewer and Hoffman shared the important things they had seen. Mt. Brewer was not the highest peak in the region—at least eight or nine were visibly higher—and the barren alpine region they had glimpsed was totally unlike anything they had seen elsewhere in the Sierra or expected to find here. From the summit of Mt. Brewer, they also had finally glimpsed the true climax of the southern Sierra. The highest peaks in the range, they now realized, lay to the southeast along a second ridge, hidden behind the peaks that formed the headwaters of the Kaweah River. That night at camp, Brewer called the newly discovered mountains the "Snow Group." Other had seen these mountains from the Owens Valley, and they were visible also from points along the Hockett Trail, but until Brewer and Hoffman's discovery, no one had seen them from the west and recognized their true significance.

The "Snow Group," possibly the highest mountains in the then United States, captivated survey volunteer Clarence King. Initially, Brewer resisted King's pleas to be allowed to make a closer reconnaissance. Supplies were short, and the intervening country looked impossibly difficult.

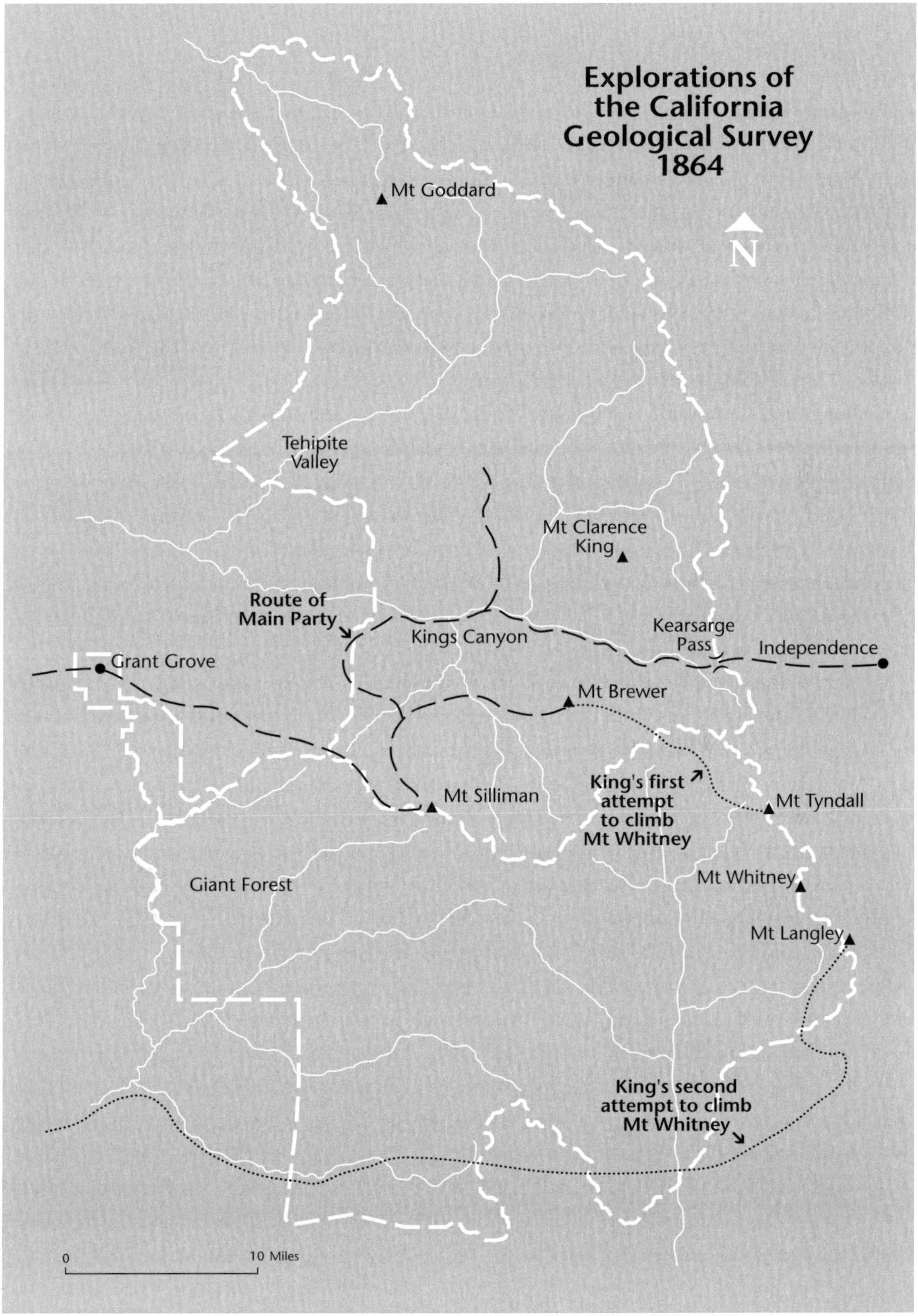

Explorations of the California Geological Survey 1864
N
Mt Goddard
Tehipite Valley
Mt Clarence King
Route of Main Party
Kings Canyon
Kearsarge Pass
Independence
Grant Grove
Mt Brewer
King's first attempt to climb Mt Whitney
Mt Silliman
Mt Tyndall
Giant Forest
Mt Whitney
Mt Langley
King's second attempt to climb Mt Whitney
0
10 Miles

King was persistent, however, and Brewer, truthfully, every bit as fascinated. On July 4, with Brewer's blessing and crude knapsacks filled with six days' provisions, King and Dick Cotter set out to explore the highest mountains in the then United States.

From the shoulder of Mt. Brewer, they attempted to follow the Brewer Ridge (now called the Great Western Divide) south to the Kings-Kern Divide. Finding this impossible, they dropped down into the headwaters country of East Creek and then climbed onto the Kings-Kern Divide. On the second day, they got over the divide, using lariats to lower themselves down the cliffs, and then headed out across the alpine landscape that gives birth to the Kern River. The "Snow Group" was now immediately before them, and they made for what had appeared to be the highest peak. Reaching the summit after considerable difficulty (which was exaggerated rather shamelessly in King's later writings), they found themselves again frustrated. From the summit, yet higher mountains were visible immediately to the south. In his notes, King referred to one of those higher peaks as Mt. Grant. When on Mt. Brewer, they had named this new summit they had just scaled "Mt. Whitney" after their chief. Several days later, however, when they finally made their way back to Brewer's camp, it was decided that the highest peak should be Mt. Whitney, and so the lower mountain became Mt. Tyndall. Also named at the same time were Mt. Williamson, Table Mountain, and Milestone Mountain.

From their reunited camp at the foot of Mt. Brewer, the surveyors moved on. They dropped into the Kings Canyon, and from there they attempted to cross the Monarch Divide to gain access to the Middle Fork of the Kings River but found the route too difficult. Noting and naming Mt. Goddard and the Palisades, still the preeminent landmarks of the upper Kings River, they returned to the floor of the Kings Canyon and then made their way east over the Sierra Crest via Kearsarge Pass and dropped into the Owens Valley. Later in the summer, they explored the headwaters of the San Joaquin, located Mt. Goddard from the north, and then tied that country in with the already known peaks in Yosemite.

In one summer, the California Geological Survey permanently changed the map of California. It confirmed the presence, already locally suspected, of the highest mountains in the then United States, located and named the major landmarks, and, unlike nearly everyone else who had been into the high country, made its discoveries public. From the surveyors' efforts came the first useful maps of the southern Sierra and a number of popular and broadly read books. Even today, King's *Mountaineering in the Sierra Nevada* (1872) and Brewer's *Up and Down California in 1860–1864* (1930) remain in print. Yet, in another way, they added very little to what had already been discovered by Jedediah Smith, Joseph Walker, and John C. Frémont: That the heart of the southern Sierra was a rugged, hostile place, best avoided unless one could find something of value within its forbidding granite recesses.[19]

Clarence King's fascination with Mt. Whitney did not end. He unsuccessfully attempted to climb Whitney from the southeast later in 1864 and returned in 1871, when, in a climb obscured by clouds, he made a successful attempt on what he thought was Whitney but actually was later proven to be what is now Mt. Langley. After that confusion was publicized in 1873, King returned again and finally made it to the top of the real Mt. Whitney, only to discover that others had preceded him that summer.[20]

THE PROSPECTORS

Increasingly, other people entered the mountains. After the drought of 1864, domestic sheep, often attended by Basque shepherds, became an annual summer feature in all but the most remote parts of the range. Lower on the western slope, most of the meadows had long since been appropriated for summer grazing by cattle ranchers. The Brewer party met a group of prospectors in the Kings Canyon in 1864, and, in 1869, Frank Dusy made his first trip to Tehipite Valley on the Middle Fork of the Kings Rivers. By 1877, sheep were grazing in the Middle Fork Canyon, having been brought over the crest of the Sierra from Owens Valley.[21] We have already mentioned that Hale Tharp visited both the Kings Canyon and Mineral King in 1861. In 1864, Harry O'Farrell, a meat hunter working north from the Hockett Trail, entered Mineral King from a more southerly angle. All of these people were seeking a way to make a living or even a fortune in the mountains. Not until 1873, however, did anyone discover a resource of sufficient value to attract real attention.

Repeatedly, prospectors had been frustrated by the apparent lack of minerals in the southern Sierra. Some "color" in the streams had attracted attention to the Kern River area well to the south near Walker Pass and to a small gold-mining district on the White River in extreme southern Tulare County. Neither area had produced much, however. Most of the southern Sierra, it seemed, consisted of barren, gray granite. In those limited areas where the bedrock was not granitic, prospectors continued to hope that something valuable might be discovered. As the population of the valley and foothill towns continued to grow, the level of resource pursuit intensified. Harry O'Farrell, for example, continued to return to the Mineral King area after his first visit in 1864, and, in 1872, he located a likely looking mineral prospect high on the reddish metamorphic slopes of Empire Mountain. During the summer of 1873, O'Farrell found two other prospecting parties in the Mineral King area, one from Three Rivers and the other from the southern Tulare County community of Porterville. In late July, it was the Porterville group, led by James Crabtree, which finally found something.

Crabtree's story reflects the similarity of experiences that tied together the generation that came to California seeking gold. Like Hale Tharp, Crabtree was born in the Midwest and came

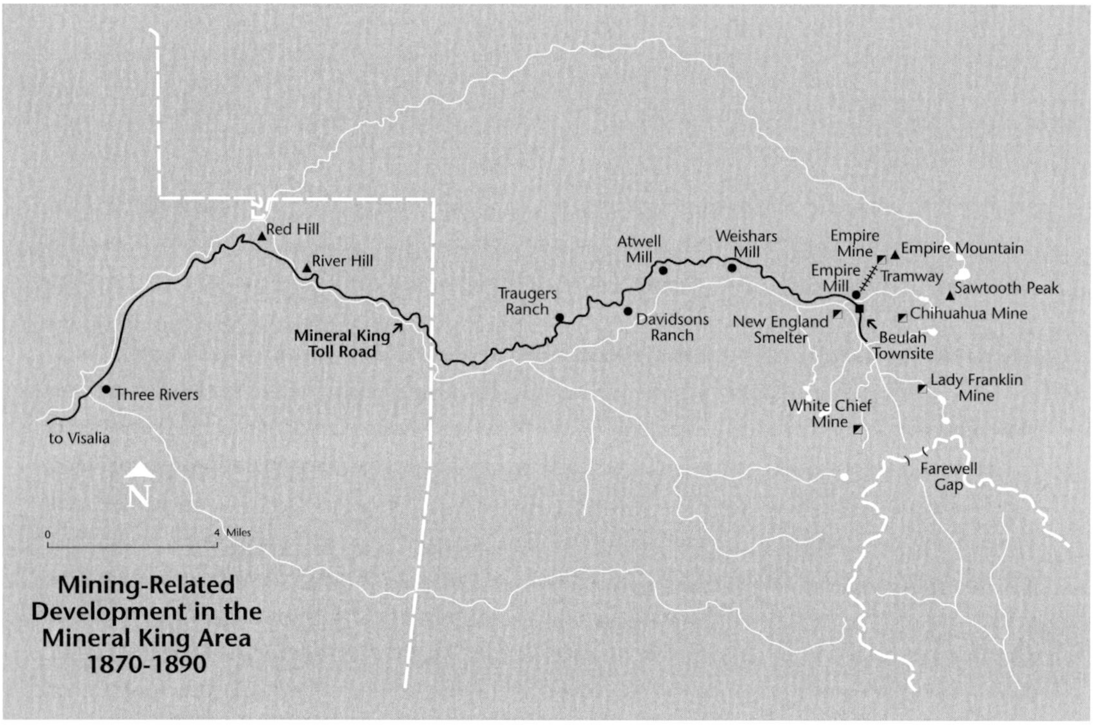
Red Hill
River Hill
Mineral King
Toll Road
Three Rivers
to Visalia
N
0
4 Miles
Traugers
Ranch
Davidsons
Ranch
Atwell
Mill
Weishars
Mill
Empire
Mine
Empire Mountain
Empire
Mill
Tramway
Sawtooth Peak
New England
Smelter
Chihuahua Mine
Beulah
Townsite
Lady Franklin
Mine
White Chief
Mine
Farewell
Gap
Mining-Related
Development in the
Mineral King Area
1870-1890

west as a young man. He was twenty-three when he arrived in California in 1852. When opportunities in the northern mines dwindled, he wandered south to farm 160 acres of land in the southern part of Tulare County. Not far away was the White River mining district. Regularly, when the seasons allowed him to be away from his farm, he prospected in the local Sierra.[22] On July 26, 1873, Crabtree located the White Chief lode in the Mineral King area at the head of the East Fork of the Kaweah River. According to Crabtree, he had been guided to the site by an Indian, who came to him in a dream—hence the name. There may have been an Indian in his dreams, but it seems no accident that Crabtree stumbled into Mineral King Valley. The area was just a short distance north of the Hockett and Jordan Trails and was already known for its odd rock formations. Once he was sure he was on to something, Crabtree did what many other prospectors have tried. He went home quietly and recruited some friends to join him in getting rich. The enlarged Porterville group unobtrusively returned to the mountains in early September, laid out their claims, organized a mining district, and elected themselves to the key positions. A few days later, the word was out in Visalia and Porterville, and the rush was on.

Fall weather arrived in the mountains before Crabtree's discovery became public knowledge, but, with fortune beckoning, mineral seekers wasted no time worrying about an early storm. Before winter snows finally buried the area in November, ninety-three hopeful prospectors filed a total of sixty-five claims. Of these, at least seventy-five were residents of Tulare County, and among them at least forty were local farmers.[23] The winter passed quickly, and eager prospectors pushed their way up the East Fork well before the snows melted in the spring of 1874. During the summer of 1874, the subalpine valley the miners optimistically called "Mineral King" swarmed with humanity. Cabins and houses were erected from lumber cut nearby, and, by the end of the season, 166 additional mining claims had been filed; the value of claims sold during the year was recorded at more than $36,500. Although more than 200 mining claims had now been filed in the district, no real mines had been developed. Development of mines required that the many small claims be consolidated into workable units and that adequate capital be raised to construct a road to the district and a mill to treat the ores. At the end of 1874, none of these necessary events had yet occurred, but, in 1875, the New England Tunnel and Smelting Company arrived with the goal to carry out the consolidation and development work required to make Mineral King a real mining district.

During the second full summer of excitement at Mineral King, the New England Company energized the district with hope, and consolidation began. A number of prospectors traded their claims for stock in the new company. The company carried out exploration work on its holdings, especially the White Chief Mine, and talk continued about building a road and an ore-processing mill. One hundred and forty additional claims were recorded during 1875, and optimism remained high. But soon another reality asserted itself: During the centennial summer of 1876, the New England Company ran out of money. It had never succeeded in collecting the full sales price for its shares, and much of its stock had simply been traded for mining claims within the district. But development demanded hard cash, and, during 1876, the company assessed its stockholders three times. Each time, if the assessment was not paid, the stock was repossessed and resold by the company. The local prospectors who had traded their claims for stock soon found themselves being forced out, unless they had additional cash to invest. By the end of the year, the New England Tunnel and Smelting Company had been locally renamed the "New England Thieving and Swindling Company."

The new year, 1877, brought little to improve the situation. Still short of funds and now under new ownership as a result of the assessments, the company constructed a simple smelter to treat ores from the White Chief Mine. Arguments over milling technique soon disclosed that the company was still unable to produce silver bullion from its ores. After a desperate special stockholders' meeting in early September, the New England Tunnel and Smelter Company filed for bankruptcy. Court-appointed management, under the control of the creditors, attempted to continue operations, but, on February 18, 1878, a powerful avalanche destroyed the company's main facilities at the White Chief Mine. The thirty-by-sixty-foot bunkhouse, already straining under twenty feet of snow, was shattered. Miraculously, no one was killed, but operations were suspended until spring, and, when spring came, the New England Company was dead. During the summer of 1878, only ten new claims were filed in the district.[24]

In 1878, after five years of mining activity in Mineral King, little of a permanent nature had actually been accomplished. Several hundred mining claims had been filed, but most were nothing more than insignificant scratches on the mountainsides. A few had received some minimal development, but none had produced enough ore to be termed fairly a real mine. A number of simple cabins had been scattered about the valley, but the lack of a wagon road kept development minimal. Only accessible by a long, rough mule trail, and apparently without a successful mine, Mineral King certainly had failed to live up to its name. The mining history of Mineral King should have ended with a whimper at this point, and the fact that it did not is testimony to the energy, wealth, and poor judgment of one individual: Thomas Fowler. In mid-September 1878, Fowler purchased the Empire Mine from a group that included Harry O'Farrell. Almost overnight, Fowler's purchase rekindled interest in the dying mining district. Local residents responded vigorously to Fowler's involvement, because he was a well-known and well-to-do local politician. In 1878, he was described as one of the largest cattlemen and landowners in California. So, if Mineral King were good enough for Tom Fowler, there must be something to it after all! In the last four months of 1878, ninety-two new mining claims were filed versus ten in the first eight months. Mineral King had come back to life.

During the next twelve months, Fowler poured most of his personal fortune into the Empire Mine. Tunnel work began, high above the timberline on Empire Mountain, and continued throughout the winter. In March 1879, with Fowler's support, a toll road company was organized. By August 15, after an incredible burst of road building, wagons entered the Mineral King Valley for the first time. Soon, construction began on a fifteen-stamp ore processing mill and a mile-long bucket tramway connecting the mine with the mill in the valley below. By September 27, all the materials for the mill and tram were on the site, and, two months later, both facilities were operable. Fowler had built more in one summer in Mineral King than everyone else together had done in the previous five years.

In December, Fowler closed the mill for the winter but attempted to continue work at the mine. The risk involved was not fully apparent until a huge avalanche destroyed much of the Empire works in the late evening of April 16. Again, no lives were lost, but the main bunkhouse and several other buildings were destroyed. A little snow was not going to close the Empire, however, and activity resumed at the mine as soon as the winter snowpack melted. On July 23, 1880, the mill resumed operations, and *The Visalia Times* headlined "TOM'S BONANZA—MILLIONS IN SIGHT." But millions were not in sight, and it soon became apparent, despite denials, that the Empire Mill was not producing silver. Fowler was silent about the mine's problems, but the obstacle was getting the silver out of the ore. The Empire announced next that it would build a small smelter to treat ore prior to stamping, but that did not solve the problem either. Before the summer ended, Fowler found himself in money trouble; to keep the mine operating long enough to find a way to produce bullion, he turned it over to a court-appointed trustee. The following summer, Fowler resumed direct control of the mine and attempted to reopen the facility, but very little actually happened. The same scenario occurred in 1882. Fowler was broke, and the Empire Mine was not the bonanza that would save him. In 1884, depressed and worn out, he slipped while stepping off a train and injured himself. Within a day, he was dead.

In hindsight, it seems that Fowler, a successful rancher and politician but not a miner, did almost everything wrong at Mineral King. He bought an unproven mine and invested everything he had in it. The stamp mill he constructed was designed to process gold and free-state silver, substances not found in the Empire ores. At best, Fowler was terribly careless in his Mineral King investments and developments; at worst, he may have been swindled by the mine's previous owners and the manufacturers of the stamp mill. Either way, he proved that Mineral King was not a significant mineral district, a verdict that has been repeatedly challenged but never overturned in the years since.

THE RICHEST RESOURCE: LUMBERING

Minerals and grazing were not the only resources to be found in the mountains. Everywhere above 5,000 feet, extensive conifer forests clothed the southern Sierra, and, with the valley below completely lacking usable softwoods, a natural market existed for lumber. The principal problem was transportation. Trees were available in the mountains almost for the asking, but getting them to market was a difficult proposition. The most accessible timber lands in the future parks' region were on the lower portions of the divide between the Kings and Kaweah Rivers. Here, extensive forests of ponderosa pine grew on rolling terrain. A crude mill may have been operating near the present town of Miramonte, west of Grant Grove, as early as 1856.[25] In 1864, as we have noted, the California Geological Survey found Thomas's Mill operating at Mill Flat Meadow, a site immediately west of Grant Grove that is today flooded by Sequoia Lake. By the late 1860s, the Hubbs and Wetherbee Mill was operating in the mountains above Porterville, where again it was possible to get a wagon with only reasonable difficulty. In the Kaweah drainage where the mountains rose more steeply, not until completion of the Mineral King wagon road did serious logging attempts began. Although several small mills had served the mines before the road opened in 1879, not only was there renewed interest in mining, but also a rush to appropriate timber lands suddenly made valuable by the construction of the Mineral King road.

Initially, the impact of these early sawmills on the landscape was quite limited: a natural result of the size of the trees involved and the existing low level of technology. But soon, with rapidly improving steam equipment, the pace of destruction accelerated. In 1874, Hyde's Mill, operating on Redwood Mountain near the western boundary of modern Kings Canyon National Park, managed to cut 2,000,000 board feet, much of it sequoia. Still, the cutover zones that surrounded the noisy mills were no more than localized blemishes on the almost endless forest that grew along the western slope of the southern Sierra. The pace of cutting was still held back by the cost of hauling lumber down from the mountains by wagon. It was often cheaper for valley residents to buy lumber shipped by railroad from farther north. Valley residents, however, because they hated the railroad with its near monopoly on transportation, took pride in their local mills and encouraged the development of additional mountain enterprises. The U.S. Congress also worked to enhance the western lumber industry. The Timber and Stone Act of 1878 allowed any citizen to purchase 160 acres of timber-covered land from the government for $2.50 per acre, and many locals took advantage of its generous provisions.

A VOICE AGAINST RESOURCE EXPLOITATION

Not everyone who came to the Sierra during the 1870s came solely to seek a fortune. The mountains were still big and wild enough to offer both solitude and adventure. Eccentrics and hermits of all sorts sought quiet niches. Many left no record whatsoever; others left their names on the creeks or canyons where they made their homes. One of these men, however, initially by his own admission nothing more than a tramp, eventually reshaped the entire culture's perceptions of nature.

John Muir, born a Scot and reared in Wisconsin, first came to California and the Sierra in 1868. He soon discovered the beauty of Yosemite and, with the help of a series of part-time jobs, made that area his home. Muir's curiosity regarding the Sierra was boundless, and, after several years of exploring the Yosemite country and studying its forests and glacial tracks, he began to feel the need to expand his geographical knowledge of the range. What lay to the south, he wondered? Finally, in September 1873, Muir got a chance to find out. In the company of several Yosemite friends, he set out to explore the southern Sierra. In early October, they entered the Kings River watershed from the north, followed the North Fork of the Kings down to the main river, crossed the river in its enormous lower gorge, and then climbed to Thomas's Mill on the south side of the canyon near Grant Grove.

On October 9, Muir got his first look at the Kings Canyon. Fascinated by the obvious similarities to Yosemite Valley, whose glacial origins he was still working out, Muir found the glacial gorge of the South Fork of the Kings River a true southern rival of his home canyon. Worried by the lateness of the season, Muir's party moved on toward Kearsarge Pass and the Owens Valley. In the upper canyons, Muir strayed to climb what he thought was Mt. Tyndall (actually, he was on the Kings-Kern Divide), spending a cold night bivouacked beneath the high peaks. When he returned to camp the next day, his friends were gone, having already given him up for lost. Muir soon caught up and accompanied them to Independence.

Mt. Whitney had caught Muir's attention. At Independence, he left his party and, using the Hockett Trail for access, attempted to climb the highest mountain from the south. He made the same mistake Clarence King had made two years previously and found himself not on Whitney but on Mt. Langley. Muir recognized the error and attempted to follow the ridge north to his destination, only to find himself trapped by nightfall at 13,000 feet in his shirtsleeves. Muir survived the bitter cold October night only by forcing himself to dance until dawn to keep himself warm. He returned exhausted to Lone Pine, only to sally forth again a few days later, this time directly from the floor of the Owens Valley. On October 21, he reached the top, the first to ascend the peak from the east. On the summit, he found the records of the previous parties who had climbed the peak that summer, including Clarence King, who had been there five weeks earlier. [26]

Not even giant sequoias live forever. Each Big Tree eventually crashes to the ground, creating a roar that echoes through the forest like thunder. Without the park ranger in this photograph, taken after this tree near the Congress Trail fell in 1964, it would be difficult to grasp the overall size of the log. Photographer and date unknown.

During July 1875, Muir, again with a party of friends, returned to the Kings Canyon and Mt. Whitney. At Grant Grove, he found a party busy at work felling a Big Tree to send to the Philadelphia Centennial Exposition planned for the following summer. Already belying his self-proclaimed status as a casual tramp, Muir sent accounts of this trip to *The San Francisco Daily Evening Bulletin*, which counted Muir as one of its field correspondents. His essays on the Kings Canyon and Mt. Whitney were both published by the newspaper in August.

Late that same summer, Muir again traveled south from Yosemite, this time alone except for a reluctant mule named Brownie. On this trip, Muir eschewed the high ridges and focused on the middle-altitude forest belt and its resident sequoia trees. For several years, his curiosity about the range and distribution of the sequoias had been intensifying, and the purpose of this journey was to seek out as many of the groves as possible. Starting south from the Mariposa Grove in the Yosemite country, Muir first searched the San Joaquin River watershed for sequoias, wondering as he did why so few Big Trees grew in that region. From the San Joaquin, he crossed again into the region of the North Fork of the Kings River. He had traveled through this area before, but this time he climbed farther east and caught his first glimpse of the Middle Fork Canyon and Tehipite Valley. After crossing the main Kings River somewhere below the confluence of the Middle and South Forks, he climbed 4,000 feet up the southern wall of the canyon and entered the northern end of the Tulare County sequoia belt.

For the next several weeks, he wandered through the places we now know as Converse Basin, Grant Grove, Redwood Canyon, Muir Grove, the Giant Forest, Atwell's Grove, and Garfield Grove. Here, Muir found what he had always suspected must exist: an almost continuous forest of giant sequoia, with countless Big Trees scattered amongst the pines and firs. As he wandered, Muir studied the growth patterns and reproduction habits of the forest giants. He also noted several sawmills busily whittling away at the forest landscape. In the Giant Forest, which he named during this trip, he met either Hale Tharp or Tharp's hired man James Wolverton and stayed for several nights in the hollow log, where Tharp made his main camp. In the groves along the East Fork of the Kaweah River, Muir productively passed several days watching a forest fire creep through the sequoias. Eventually, Muir and his mule left the Kaweah drainage and continued their studies of the sequoia in the Tule River and Deer Creek watersheds. In the Tule country, in particular, he found considerable logging activity underway. Finally, with winter imminent, he reached what he believed must be the southern end of the sequoias.[27]

Muir now knew more than anyone else about the natural history of the sequoias. The following August, the American Association for the Advancement of Science published his conclusions, in which he outlined, for the first time, an accurate description of the tree's range, discussed its reproductive habits, and proposed a theory that accounted for the geographical gaps between the groves. Muir's essay ended on a somber note: The grand trees were being destroyed at a fearsome rate, and if they did not soon receive some sort of protection, the oldest specimens would eventually all be felled.[28]

Muir made one more trip to the south during the 1870s, when he finally visited the nearly inaccessible Tehipite Valley. Again, the season was late. Muir and a newly acquired hiking companion followed the well-known trail to the Kings Canyon and then ascended the Monarch Divide, crossing its summit during a nighttime snowstorm. Dawn found them on the rim of the Middle Fork Canyon. They dropped into the canyon near Simpson Meadow and traveled downstream, through Tehipite Valley, to the confluence of the Middle and South Forks. The entire journey was rushed, and the two were short on food. By the time they returned to the Grant Grove area, Muir's companion had lost nearly twenty pounds![29]

At the time, Muir's trips to the Sequoia/Kings Canyon region were of limited importance. From his newspaper accounts came some larger appreciation of the features of the area, and his writings about the sequoias added to the understanding of the Big Trees. The primary significance of Muir's visits, however, would not become apparent for a number of years. Muir perceived in the Sierra several points that largely escaped his contemporaries. He saw first that the resources of the Sierra, extensive as they seemed, were finite and that a few decades of human activity could severely impair them. He saw also that the mountains had values above and beyond those that produced immediate monetary gain. To his contemporaries, especially in the 1870s, Muir was a peculiar eccentric, a man who did not understand the "realities" of his time. Muir's genius, of course, was that, unlike his contemporaries, he perceived that the pioneer era of unrestrained resource consumption could not go on indefinitely.

After his 1877 trip to Tehipite, Muir did not return to the southern Sierra for more than a decade. During those years, he married, started a family, and operated a successful fruit-growing venture in the hill country east of San Francisco Bay. He did not forget the Sierra, however, and, when he returned, the ideas he originally put forth during the 1870s would spread far beyond his original hopes.

THE BEGINNINGS OF RECREATION

During the late 1870s and early 1880s, John Muir was not totally alone in his appreciation of the beauty of the mountains. Even some of the cattlemen, miners, and lumbermen whose activities so upset Muir were not unappreciative of the scenery. Many residents of the Mineral King mining area seemed to treasure the summer climate nearly as much as they did the possibility of striking it rich; in fact, after the Empire Mine failed, Mineral King became a summer resort. The same thing happened in the sequoia logging areas in the Tule River country, where a resort community called Mountain Home developed. Even Mt. Whitney was not immune. In the summer of 1878, a party of nearly thirty residents of the Porterville area, including four women, crossed the mountains and ascended Mt. Whitney. The women apparently were the first of their sex to ascend the peak. In 1881, another party from Tulare County, this one consisting of three friends named William Wallace, Frederick Wales, and J. W. A. Wright, crossed the mountains on the Hockett Trail, climbed Mt. Whitney, descended into the upper Kern Canyon, and even made the first ascent of Mt. Kaweah from the Chagoopa Plateau.[30]

These three found themselves with a surprising amount of company when they arrived at the western base of Mt. Whitney in late August 1881. In place, accompanied by a rather elaborate scientific party, was Professor Samuel Pierpoint Langley, Director of the Allegheny Observatory near Pittsburgh, Pennsylvania. On the advice of Clarence King, Langley had selected Mt. Whitney and vicinity as the site for an attempt to determine the amount and quality of the heat being sent to Earth by the sun. Using the Hockett Trail from Lone Pine and the faint track that had been in use for some time that led north from Tunnel Meadow to the western base of Mt. Whitney, Langley set up his base camp at 12,000 feet, the highest point to which he could easily get stock. There, he erected a "bolometer," a device that measured the radiant heat of the sun by correlating the radiation-induced charge in electrical resistance of blackened metal foil with the amount of radiation absorbed. Hauling sufficient wood to the site to construct the low, 400-foot-long trestle the device required was a considerable challenge.[31] Langley was not satisfied to take measurements only at the base of the mountain, and eventually he tried to establish a camp on the summit. It was already September, and high winds and biting nighttime cold made readings on the summit difficult. Portions of the Langley party nonetheless spent several nights on the summit, and, on at least one night, they were joined by Wallace, Wright, and Wales.

The results of Langley's scientific efforts were inconclusive, but from of his group came one of the first attempts at resource protection in the southern Sierra. Attached to the Langley expedition from the U.S. Army was a Captain Otho E. Michaelis, temporarily assigned to the Signal Corps, and from his involvement apparently resulted the creation, in September 1883, of the Mt. Whitney Military Reservation. The reservation withdrew from sale much of the Sierra Crest in the upper Kern region, including Mounts Williamson, Whitney, and Langley. In 1883, the Weather Bureau was still attached to the Army Signal Corps, and the reservation supposedly was created for additional scientific work under these auspices. Little came of the designation, however; and the reservation was abolished after the turn of the century and most of its lands were added to the Sierra Forest Reserve.[32]

INCREASING ACTIVITY IN THE LUMBER INDUSTRY

By the mid-1880s, the pioneer era in the southern Sierra was coming to an end. A generation of mountaineers had crawled over the range, seeking resources and opportunities. From their efforts had come the development of significant livestock-grazing enterprises, a realization that the southern Sierra probably did not harbor any great mineral treasures, and a growing lumber industry. This growing world of sawmills resulted both from improving technology for handling large trees and from a steadily growing market for lumber in the San Joaquin Valley. The Timber and Stone Act of 1878 had been designed to encourage private ownership of timberlands, and, together with the ongoing land survey efforts of the government in the early 1880s, a timberland rush of sorts developed.

Theoretically, the entire Sierra Nevada had been for sale by the federal government since California became a part of the United States in 1850. Practically, this was not the case, because the land had not been surveyed. Most early timber operations simply took trees from public land. The survey's first priority, of course, went to the valley lands below, but, during the early 1880s, the Jeffersonian grid system of surveying by township and range (officially, the Northwest Ordinance of 1789) was extended across much of the southern Sierra. As the six-mile-square townships were surveyed, lands within them became available for private purchase at the General Land Office in Visalia. A few pioneers had already claimed homesteads in the mountains, and in areas such as Mineral King mining claims had been established. Still, the majority of the land remained unassigned. Several federal laws made the most valuable portions available to the public. The Swamp and Overflow Act transferred "swamp" lands to the state to be sold to raise money for reclamation purposes. Another act decreed that section 36 in each township should be transferred to the state to raise money for schools. The Timber and Stone Act, as mentioned, made land endowed with timber or building stone available inexpensively.

Using these laws, various groups interested in the Sierra pursued the lands appropriate to their needs. The cattle industry found in the Swamp and Overflow Act a way to take permanent title to the mountain meadows they already controlled. Lumbermen used both the school section provision and the Timber and Stone Act to assume control of forested areas. Only the sheepmen trusted to the continued openness of the public domain, a trust that, ultimately, would leave them without a land base in the Sierra.

Though the Timber and Stone Act was designed to give individuals ownership of 160-acre timber tracts, in reality it often served to put large blocks of forest land into corporate ownership. When a new tract opened for entry, a lumber company would recruit a number of individuals, have each make his perfectly legal purchase, and then buy the lands from them. All this could be arranged so that the person who actually "bought" the land from the government received nothing more than a little pocket cash and a pleasant trip to the mountains. During the mid-1880s, this strategy was applied to lands in the Kings, Kaweah, and Tule watersheds.

Some of the same men were involved in logging enterprises along the Kings and Tule Rivers—specifically Smith Comstock and a partnership consisting of Hiram Smith and Austin Moore. Comstock, in 1883, had begun cutting sequoias near Grant Grove at what is now known as Big Stump. During the middle years of the same decade, Smith and Moore, operating as the Kings River Lumber Company, acquired almost 30,000 acres of timberlands in the same vicinity. In the middle of this sea of private lands, the government retained title only to the four square miles of land containing the Grant Grove itself; these had been withdrawn unilaterally from sale in 1880 by Theodore Wagner, U.S. Surveyor General for California, to prevent their sale and destruction. On the North Fork of the Tule River, Comstock, Smith, and Moore operated as partners in the Tule River Lumber Company. Eventually, several different generations of ownership cut over most of these lands and returned them to the government. Immediately north of Grant Grove, in Converse Basin, Smith and Moore destroyed the largest of all the giant sequoia groves between 1892 and 1908. Ironically, despite the large scale of logging, transportation costs remained so high that no profit was ever made.[33]

In the Kaweah country, transportation also remained a critical problem. Because the terrain was so rugged, only one road—to Mineral King—entered the Kaweah forests, and that road was so steep it was not used much for lumber hauling. Nevertheless, the Kaweah area was also surveyed and opened to purchase. Here, the story takes an odd turn, for the parties that responded were not the usual corporate interests but rather a loose association of frustrated labor-union socialists from the San Francisco Bay area.

The Kaweah Colony, as this group called itself, grew out of a San Francisco organization known as the "Cooperative Land Purchase and Colonization Association." Organized primarily by Burnette Haskell, a lawyer and self-appointed leader in the local labor movement, the association had as its goal the development of a worker's cooperative based on the philosophies of German socialist Laurence Gronlund. Late in the summer of 1885, association member Charles Keller found himself seated on a train immediately behind P. Y. Baker, the land surveyor who had been directing work in the Giant Forest area. As he listened to Baker tell about the forests of the Kaweah country, Keller concluded that, here, was an opportunity of which his association might be able to make something.

Keller presented the scheme to the group, and a scouting party visited the area in September 1885. They liked what they saw, and, in the following month, forty members of the association filed Timber and Stone Act claims in the Giant Forest area. Altogether, they claimed ten square miles of forest. In Visalia, after they filed their claims at the land office, a seemingly small problem developed. George Stewart, editor of the newspaper in which legal notice of their claims had to

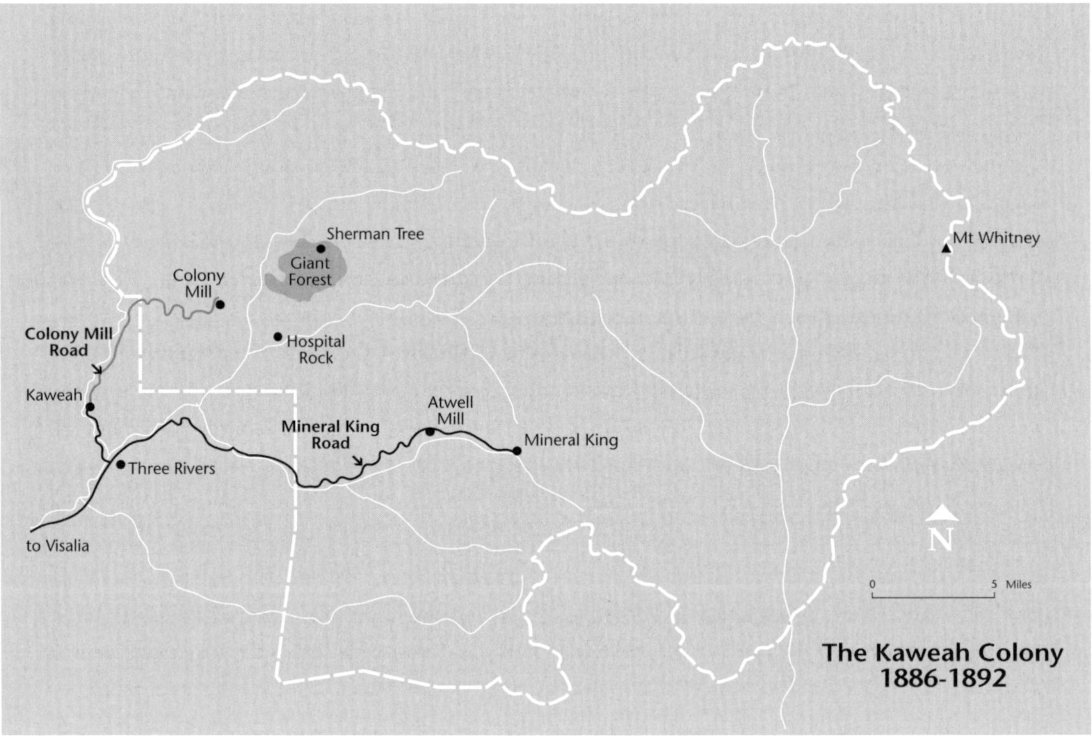

Sherman Tree
Giant Forest
Colony Mill
Colony Mill Road
Hospital Rock
Kaweah
Atwell Mill
Mineral King Road
Mineral King
Three Rivers
to Visalia
Mt Whitney
N
0
5 Miles
The Kaweah Colony 1886-1892

be printed, noted that nearly all of the claimants gave the same San Francisco address. Suspecting that yet another timber swindle was in the making, Stewart requested a government investigation. In response, the local land office suspended the claims until their validity could be studied.

The problems generated by Stewart surprised the colonists but did not discourage them. They knew they were not part of anything illegal and proceeded to implement their scheme. In the spring of 1886, Haskell and the first contingent of colonists arrived. They established themselves along the North Fork above Three Rivers at a settlement they called "Kaweah" and went to work. The major obstacle to their success was that the timber they had claimed, including the Giant Forest with its immense sequoias, was far from any usable transportation route. Only Hale Tharp's cattle trails entered the area, and there was no way lumber would ever travel over them. Briefly, they considered building a railroad, and they talked to the Southern Pacific Railroad Company about possible junction points. But when it became apparent that such a project was beyond their means, they settled upon building a wagon road. For the next several years, they labored to construct a road across the rugged terrain west of the Giant Forest. By the late 1880s, they had built twenty miles of road and were poised to begin logging just a few miles west of the grove.[34] The fate of their plan and its connection to the campaign to create Sequoia National Park are explored in the next chapter.

THE IMPACTS OF EXPLOITATION

As the 1880s ended, so did the first generation of use of the Sierra Nevada by Euro-Americans. With only a few exceptions, the generation that replaced the Native Americans sought opportunities to use the resources they found. At first, the number of people involved was tiny, and the resources of the Sierra seemed limitless. How could so few ever affect so large and richly endowed a place? Yet, after three decades, the pioneers had influenced the mountains and valley far more than most of them realized. They had destroyed the lifestyle and culture of the Native Americans and thus ended the impacts of their activities, including their forms of hunting and of burning vegetation. On the floor of the Central Valley, the spread of farming had disrupted native vegetation and wildlife and had begun destruction of the riparian oak forests. So much water was being diverted for irrigation that, before the century ended, Tulare Lake would go dry for the first time. In the foothills, three decades of heavy grazing, with periodic droughts, had led to the destruction of the perennial native grasses and their replacement with less-nutritious Eurasian annuals. Heavy grazing also had badly damaged many middle-altitude meadows and the high country. Much of the High Sierra had been so ravaged by the grazing of domestic sheep that the land had been almost completely denuded. Along the lower edge of the forest belt, three decades of logging had begun to create significant gaps in the once-continuous forest, and much bigger lumber enterprises seemed imminent. Only a tiny fraction of the total forest had yet been affected, but they were in limited areas with good access to the valley. The damage was locally appalling, especially around Grant Grove and on the North Fork of the Tule River.

In short, everywhere one looked there was resource consumption and environmental change. In barely thirty years, the pioneers, with their widely shared ethic of unlimited resource use, had changed the mountains forever. Against these trends had been raised only a few voices, and, until the mid-1880s, those voices had been easily ignored by a culture that saw itself as building a new civilization. Inevitably, as population and resource use continued to grow, the free, largely individualistic consumption patterns began to run into limits. The world of the pioneer was becoming increasingly complicated, and the perception of unlimited resources had begun to unravel.

CHAPTER FOUR

Parks and Forests: Protection Begins (1885–1916)

By the mid-1880s, local groups had begun to compete for access to key natural resources. Increasingly, the actions of loggers and stockmen in the mountains conflicted with the activities of farmers and city residents in the valley. From these controversies would emerge a new set of rules governing the use of the Sierra and new controlling groups. Significantly, resolution of these issues would fall to the federal government, which would itself undergo revolutionary changes in its land-management policies during the period.

As the agricultural communities of the southern San Joaquin Valley grew during the 1870s and 1880s, their attitudes toward the mountains began to diverge from those of the men who were actually living in and exploiting the highlands to the east. Initially, the grazing, mining, and lumbering enterprises in the mountains had served to increase economic activity in towns such as Porterville and Visalia. Eventually, valley towns developed stronger economic bases, founded largely on the spread of irrigation farming, and residents of the valley began to discover reasons to oppose limitless resource consumption in "their" mountains. Opposition centered on two issues: the impacts of grazing and lumbering on stream runoff and the effects of these same activities on mountain recreation and scenery.

From the beginning, both concerns were inextricably linked. In the days before reservoirs were constructed on the rivers of the Sierra, farming by irrigation depended completely on natural stream flow. As logging, sheep grazing, and wide-ranging fires often set by sheepmen changed the nature of the Sierra's vegetation, so, too, were seasonal stream flow patterns changed. Generally, to the valley settlers of the time, it seemed like the consumption of mountain resources resulted in less water flowing from the mountains, especially during the dry season.[1] Changes in seasonal stream flows made little difference to mountain loggers and sheepmen, but they could be critical downstream, where survival of a field crop in August could make or break a farmer. Significantly, too, as the number of valley residents traveling to the mountains for pleasure increased, so did their concern over the state of the mountains. The intense heat of July and August in the San Joaquin Valley sent many families to the high country seeking relief. There, all too often they discovered their favorite camping areas logged or their favorite meadow areas denuded so thoroughly by sheep that parties could find no feed for their stock.

GEORGE STEWART CAMPAIGNS TO PROTECT THE MOUNTAINS

Sometimes, all it takes to turn a concern into a political movement is a single individual with vision and drive. Fortunately for the ecosystems of the southern Sierra, one such individual appeared in Tulare County during the late 1870s. George W. Stewart came from a new generation of Westerners. Born in Placerville, California, in the waning years of the gold rush, Stewart saw the California landscape in ways far removed from the perspectives of his father's generation. In 1872, only fifteen years old, Stewart moved to Tulare County, where he soon found the vocation that would occupy much of his life—journalism. It was in 1876 when Stewart began writing for *The Visalia Delta,* one of two newspapers in the growing town. Two years later, Stewart assumed the position of city editor for the paper.[2] In that same year, Stewart, only twenty-one years old, first addressed the destruction in the mountains east of Visalia. In an editorial, he called for a state law to prohibit the cutting of giant sequoias.[3] Nothing concrete came from the suggestion, but Stewart had chosen sides in a battle that was just beginning. As a native Californian, he had convinced himself that the Big Trees deserved a better fate than being converted into fence posts and shingles.

During the early 1880s, Stewart was not entirely alone in his interest in protecting the mountain country. The U.S. Surveyor General for California had "temporarily" withdrawn from sale four sections of land surrounding the General Grant Tree in 1880, an action supported by the valley residents of Tulare County. And the Mt. Whitney Military Reservation had been created in 1883, after the meeting of the Langley expedition and the Wallace-Wales-Wright groups in 1881. Upon their return, the Wallace party also began actively to advocate a Sierra Nevada alpine national park that would focus, as had their journey, on the Mt. Whitney region. In this proposal, they received considerable support from several members of Langley's scientific group.[4]

Stewart championed a similar idea. General John F. Miller, seeking support for his 1880 candidacy for the U.S. Senate, had come to Visalia to talk with the *Delta's* editors. During Miller's visit, Stewart filled his ear with local concerns about the mountains. After his election to the Senate by the California Legislature, Miller introduced Senate Bill 463, "a bill to provide for setting apart a certain tract of land in the State of California as a public park." Miller's proposal, which did not receive serious attention from his colleagues, sought to protect an extensive tract of land, including most of what are now Sequoia and Kings Canyon National Parks. Its significance lay not in its fate, for it was premature in many ways, but in its expression of what Stewart and his friends had in mind nearly a decade before any Sierra Nevada national park came into being. Within a few short years, Stewart had moved from trying to protect certain species of trees through state law to attempting to protect the entire southern Sierra through federal action.

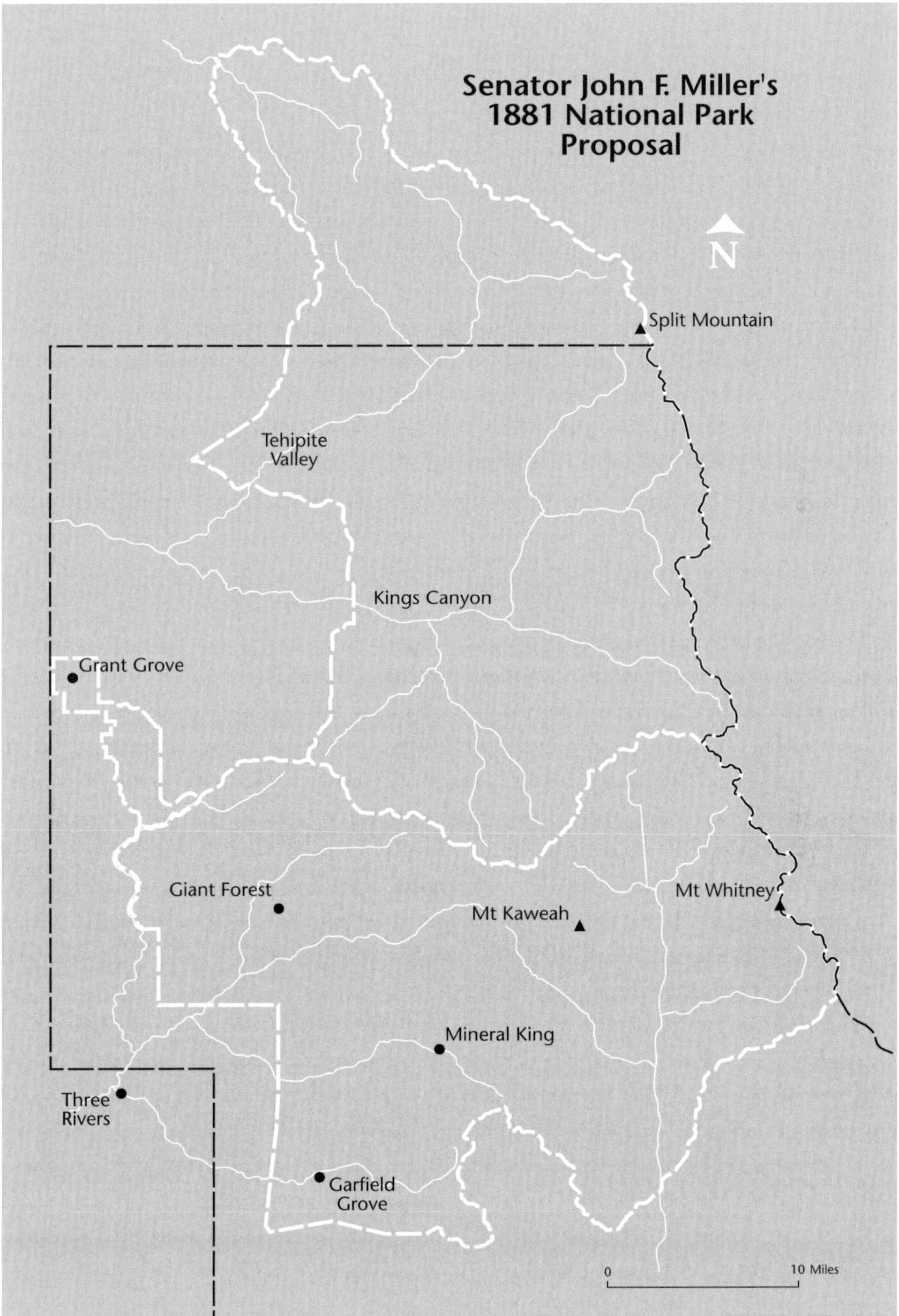
Senator John F. Miller's
1881 National Park
Proposal
N
Split Mountain
Tehipite
Valley
Kings Canyon
Grant Grove
Giant Forest
Mt Kaweah
Mt Whitney
Mineral King
Three
Rivers
Garfield
Grove
0
10 Miles

In their proposals for a federally established public park in Tulare County's mountains, Stewart and William Wallace drew upon several existing western precedents. In 1864, recognizing that it was in the public interest to preserve the Yosemite Valley and the nearby Mariposa Grove of the Big Trees, the U.S. Congress withdrew the two tracts from the public domain and transferred them to the State of California to be managed for the public good. After an idealistic start, however, California's administration of the Yosemite reservations eventually proved subject to political intrusions of all sorts. The state granted numerous concessions, and its administration of the reservations could only be described as haphazard. In 1872, a similar situation arose in the northern Rocky Mountains, with a proposal to preserve in public ownership the thermal areas near the head of the Yellowstone River. This time, however, there was no state government to put in charge of the lands. Hence, Congress had no choice but to create a "national" park. Again, like Yosemite, the early administration of Yellowstone was replete with difficulties, many of which negatively affected the landscape and its natural residents. Nevertheless, as a national park, Yellowstone represented an alternative to the Yosemite model, and, after 1886 when the frustrated Department of the Interior turned protection of Yellowstone over to the U.S. Army, the model began to look increasingly attractive.

It was into this milieu that the Kaweah colonists stumbled in late 1885, when they filed their Timber and Stone Act claims on lands in the Giant Forest area. Suspicions about the colonists being fraudulent "dummy entrymen" led the *Delta* to request that the General Land Office (GLO) look closely at the situation. As a result, GLO Inspector G. C. Wharton reviewed the status of claims in eighteen townships in the southern Sierra. In many of these, he saw evidence of possible fraud, and he recommended that nine full townships, including all the colony's claims, be withdrawn from the market until the situation could be clarified. GLO Commissioner W. A. J. Sparks, a self-appointed critic of the Timber and Stone Act, suspended all eighteen townships. In 1887, Sparks was forced out of office, but his replacement, S. N. Stockslager, continued the withdrawals Sparks had initiated.[5]

When Republican Benjamin Harrison defeated incumbent President Grover Cleveland in the presidential election of November 1888, a more traditional attitude returned to the Department of the Interior. John Noble, the new Secretary of the Interior, made it clear that he disagreed with the policies of his predecessors and that he would work to return as much withdrawn land as possible to the market. In response, Stewart and the *Delta* initiated a campaign for permanent withdrawal of the townships in question. Stewart's plan called for the federal government to retain title to these tracts, a policy he hoped would protect Tulare County's forests and the interests of valley farmers. The effort began in earnest in January 1889, when California, taking advantage of the section 36 school statute, claimed a portion of the Grant Grove. Since the claim fell within the four sections that had been "temporarily" withdrawn from sale in 1880, the GLO rejected it. In April, sensing that the national political change might be to their advantage, several private parties also filed claims in the area. On April 25, Stewart editorialized that the land was already "regarded as a public park" and that it needed to be designated permanently as such. Stewart also organized a flurry of letters to GLO officials, reminding them of the importance of the four sections to local residents. The GLO responded that, at best, the withdrawal was only temporary and that it was up to Congress to provide permanent protection for the area.[6]

During the summer and fall of 1889, Stewart pursued his goal of protecting large portions of the local mountains. Using the *Delta,* he kept the issue before the public and worked to create a consensus. Several local farmers' organizations offered public support, and, in October, a meeting with interested individuals from adjacent Kern and Fresno Counties went well. Park backers developed a petition and collected signatures. During the winter, however, the petition disappeared. Supposedly, it had been forwarded to Washington, D.C., but even the governor of California could not discover its whereabouts. By June, Stewart was a little discouraged. Speaking of the sequoias he so loved, he wrote:

> Nearly all have already passed into private ownership. Certain tracts, like the Giant Forest, that were once on the market and filed on by applicants in good faith, should be restored to the market. This would be nothing more than justice under the circumstances; but every acre of unsurveyed timber lands in the Sierra Nevada should be reserved immediately and for all time.[7]

THE CAMPAIGN TO CREATE SEQUOIA NATIONAL PARK

The General Land Office confirmed all of Stewart's worst fears when, on May 23, 1890, the agency canceled the suspension on township 17, range 30, and opened the area once again to land purchase. Eager land claimants immediately filed on portions of the thirty-six-square-mile township, which contained most of the timber adjacent to the Mineral King road, including several large sequoia groves.[8] Soon, rumors circulated that township 18, range 30, would also be put back on the market. This tract, in the timber belt of the South Fork of the Kaweah River, contained several large sequoia groves, including the spectacular Garfield Grove on the northern side of Dennison Mountain. Stewart responded with a change in his strategy. For the time being, he would defer his goal of large-scale protection for the entire southern Sierra and concentrate instead on protection of township 18, range 30. Stewart believed that this township represented the best chance to preserve a large tract of sequoia land in permanent federal ownership. Title to all the other major groves, including the Giant Forest, he believed, was impaired in one way or another.

With the nearly full-time help of Frank Walker, another interested Tulare County man, Stewart initiated a campaign to protect the critical township. In early July, a shower of editorials appeared in the *Delta*, and letters were sent to Interior Secretary Noble. During the next few weeks, Stewart's proposal evolved slightly, when he discovered that a bribery dispute between a surveyor and a squatter stockman had resulted in the extensive Hockett Meadows not being declared Swamp and Overflow land. Since the meadows formed the heart of the township immediately east of the one Stewart was fighting to preserve, he added the second township to his scheme, thinking it would make an excellent summering area for mountain visitors. When it was discovered that four sections in the township to the north also contained sequoias and had not yet been claimed, Stewart also added those sections as well.

Having initiated the publicity effort, Stewart now turned to the political arena. On July 28, General William Vandever, representative of California's Sixth Congressional District, introduced H.R. 11570, which was based closely on Stewart's proposals. Interestingly, Vandever had that year already introduced a bill to create a Yosemite National Park, a result of efforts by John Muir and other Bay Area individuals. With a southern Sierra park bill now in place, Stewart and Frank Walker next worked to broaden support and undertook a media campaign that involved sending materials to newspapers and magazines across the nation. They managed to get a supportive editorial in *The New York Tribune* and gained the ear of Robert Underwood Johnson, editor of *Century Magazine*. By August 5, they even had the public support of California Governor S. W. Waterman.

With the end of the congressional session not far off, it was important that the bill move quickly. On August 23, Lewis E. Payson, of Illinois, Chairman of the House Committee on Public Lands, received permission to bring the bill before the House of Representatives. With his support and no organized opposition, the bill passed the House on a voice vote and was referred to the Senate Committee on Public Lands.[9] As September began, support continued to build. The California Academy of Sciences entered the effort early in the month, led by Gustavus Eisen. Other support came from *The San Francisco Chronicle*, *The San Francisco Examiner*, *The San Francisco Bulletin*, *The Oakland Tribune*, *The Sacramento Bee*, and *The Fresno Expositor*. In Tulare County, papers in Porterville and Traver opposed the bill, while the *Delta's* chief rival in Visalia, *The Tulare County Times*, remained silent. Organized local opposition was limited mostly to the mountain-grazing interests, a relatively small group. The general feeling of the valley people that it was time to control grazing, logging, and fires in the mountains, along with the limited nature of Stewart's goals, prevented the bill from becoming controversial.

On September 8, U.S. Senator Preston Plumb, of Kansas, Chairman of the Senate Committee on Public Lands, received unanimous consent for the immediate consideration of H.R. 11570.

Following his favorable report and without debate or amendment, the Senate passed the bill. A bit more than two weeks later, on September 25, 1890, President Benjamin Harrison signed it into law. Jubilant, the *Delta* editorialized that "the first step in a great work" had been accomplished.[10] His immediate goal of protecting one township of sequoias achieved, Stewart could now return to the larger effort of ending sales of timberland in the entire southern Sierra Nevada.

Stewart, Walker, and a number of other Tulare County citizens had succeeded in permanently withdrawing from sale some seventy-six square miles of Sierra Nevada forest containing one large and truly first-class sequoia grove and another half-dozen smaller groves. In the eastern part of the new reservation along the Hockett Trail, they also had taken away from the grazing interests a series of extensive mountain meadows that would henceforth be available for recreational purposes. The bill did not specifically designate the area a "national park," but it did state that the lands in question were to be "set apart as a public park, or pleasure ground, for the benefit and enjoyment of the people . . ." The act assigned responsibility for protecting the new park to the Secretary of the Interior, together with the authority to make and publish necessary rules. Included in the bill were instructions that required the secretary to "provide for the preservation from injury of all timber, mineral deposits, natural curiosities or wonders within said park, and their retention in their natural state." The "wanton destruction" of fish and game was to be prevented, and leases of up to ten years were allowed for the "accommodation of visitors."[11] America had gained its second national park.

In retrospect, with only Yellowstone as a possible model and with the concept of a true national park only beginning to appear even there, Vandever's bill was an effective and innovative charter. And, through the efforts of George Stewart and Frank Walker, it had been created after a campaign lasting barely four months.

EXPANSION OF SEQUOIA AND THE CREATION OF GENERAL GRANT

Stewart made no secret of his intention to protect more of Tulare County's mountain lands. But the next move in this direction, which occurred within a week of the signing of the act he had worked to create, came as a total surprise to almost everyone in Tulare County, including Stewart. On October 1, 1890, President Harrison signed another national park bill that had been introduced by Vandever. This one had been introduced in the House on March 18 as H.R. 8350, a bill to create a Yosemite National Park to surround the existing state reservations that protected Yosemite Valley and the Mariposa Grove of Big Trees. The bill, supported by a group of northern Californians almost totally separate from Stewart's group, had moved slowly, and not until September 30 did it come before the entire House. As was the case with the Sequoia bill,

Representative Payson, of the House Committee on Public Lands, represented the bill on the floor. Payson's recommendation, however, was not that the House pass H. R 8350 but that the House instead agree to a substitute bill, H.R. 12187, also sponsored by Vandever.

The substitute differed radically from Vandever's original bill. It still contained provisions for a Yosemite National Park, but it called for a reservation five times larger than that called for in original bill. Vandever's original Yosemite bill had proposed a relatively small federal reservation surrounding the state park; the new bill called for an extensive federal park very similar to that proposed the previous year by John Muir. The substitute bill also contained an entirely new section, which would add five townships of thirty-six square miles each to Sequoia National Park as well as permanently preserve the four sections of land surrounding the Grant Grove that had first been temporarily withdrawn from sale nearly a decade earlier.[12] Within the five townships proposed for addition to Sequoia were all the Timber and Stone Act claims of the Kaweah colonists.

As historian Douglas Strong later noted, there is little evidence that the congressmen who passed H.R. 12187 understood what they were doing.[13] The Yosemite portions of the bill were relatively clear, but section three, which affected Tulare County, was a model of evasion. The lands in question were to be "reserved and withdrawn from settlement, occupancy, or sale under the laws of the United States, and . . . set apart as reserved forest lands . . .," subject to the same management provisions as were included within the Yosemite Park section of the bill. Nowhere was there any mention of H.R. 11570 (passed a week earlier), Sequoia National Park, or even Tulare County.

Despite some grumbling from the floor over the substitution, Payson read the bill and got it through the House that day with no recorded debate. The following day, the penultimate of the session, Senator Plumb, of Kansas, brought H.R. 12187 to the floor of the Senate. After the bill was read, Senator George Edmunds, of Vermont, complained that it could not be understood and should be printed. Then, someone spoke quietly to Edmunds, and he withdrew his objections. The bill passed the Senate without further debate and was signed by President Harrison the following day, on October 1, 1890.

To this day, the origins of and motivations behind H.R. 12187 have never been adequately explained. No one ever admitted to drafting the substitute bill. Congressional archives contain nothing, not even the original draft of the substitute bill. So the question remains: Who was behind the political intrigue that increased Yosemite's acreage by 500 percent over what Vandever had proposed the previous March, nearly tripled the acreage of the newly created Sequoia National Park, and created a third entirely new national park—soon to be named after General Ulysses S. Grant.

Two historians, Holway R. Jones and Oscar Berland, tackled this question in the 1960s. Berland focused on Sequoia's enlargement. First, he followed Stewart's trail, when, late in his life, Stewart undertook a prolonged and unsuccessful attempt to answer the question himself. Eventually,

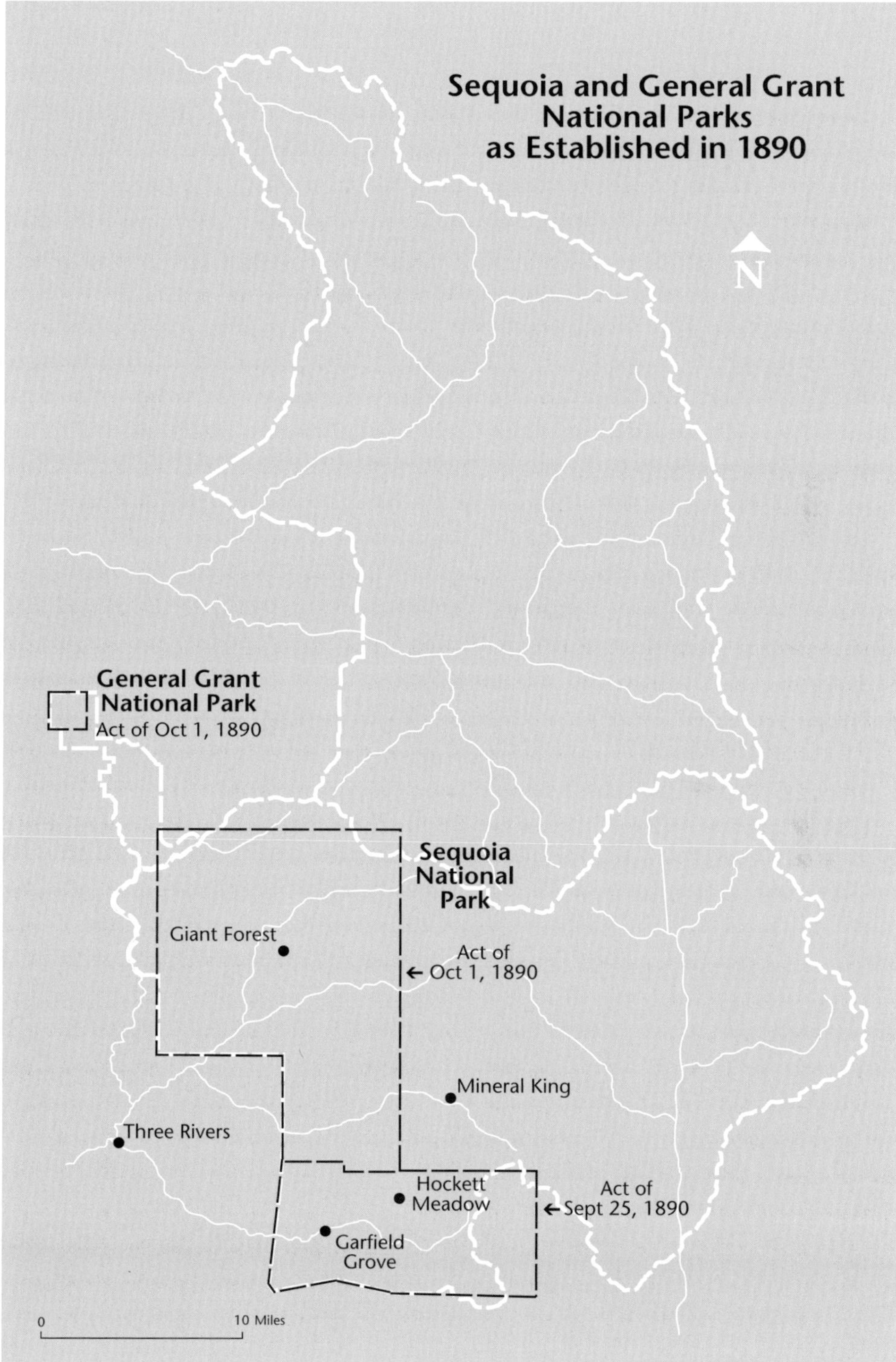
Sequoia and General Grant National Parks as Established in 1890
N
General Grant National Park
Act of Oct 1, 1890
Sequoia National Park
Giant Forest
Act of Oct 1, 1890
Mineral King
Three Rivers
Hockett Meadow
Act of Sept 25, 1890
Garfield Grove
0
10 Miles

Berland pieced together a circumstantial case focusing on the organization that, in 1890, was arguably the most influential and powerful in California—the Southern Pacific Railroad Company (SPRR). Berland found only one hard piece of evidence connecting the enlargement with the railroad, a map drafted by the company showing the revised boundaries of Sequoia Park and the presence of the new General Grant reservation and dated "San Francisco, October 10, 1890." At this date, no one else in California yet knew of the enlargement. Stewart and his friends in Tulare County did not realize what had happened until October 21. Beyond the map, Berland looked for likely connections and found Daniel K. Zumwalt, a Tulare County lawyer who had regularly represented the railroad in its Tulare County affairs. Zumwalt also knew the mountains; during the summer of 1889, he had made a trip to Kings Canyon in the company, among others, of the same William B. Wallace who had first proposed a Mt. Whitney national reserve back in 1881. Moreover, Zumwalt was in Washington, D.C., during early September, as a personal guest of Vandever.[14]

Berland's research proved that the SPRR (apparently alone at the time) was fully aware of what H.R. 12187 implied and that it had an agent on the ground who knew the situation. But what was the railroad's motive? Here, only speculation remains. Certainly, the railroad would profit from development of tourist enterprises along its lines, and, in fact, the railroad sent a photographic party to the new Sequoia National Park during the park's first month of existence. Probably more important, however, according to Berland's speculations, was the railroad's deep involvement in the California lumber industry. On its lands in Northern California, the SPRR controlled enormous amounts of saw timber, and it made a substantial profit transporting wood products to Central and Southern California. The SPRR also owned major tracts of agricultural land in Tulare County and, thus, would benefit from the same watershed protection efforts that the county's independent landowners had supported. Finally, it was rumored that the railroad was involved financially in the Smith and Moore lumbering enterprises active in sequoia groves immediately north and south of the new park. Perhaps, Berland implied, the ultimate goal of the SPRR was to destroy the Kaweah Colony and its competitive lumbering potential. Holway Jones, studying the Yosemite aspects of H.R. 12187, found the same trail of confusion and deceit. He was unable to provide more than suggestions as to who was actually behind the substitute bill.[15] But one more hint does exist, according to Berland. In 1913, Zumwalt, by then an old man, took credit for helping create General Grant National Park; he never said anything, however, about his relationship with the remainder of the same bill.[16]

The full story of how Sequoia National Park came to include the Giant Forest, how General Grant National Park came into existence, and how Yosemite National Park blossomed to include much of the central Sierra may never be known. What is obvious is that, through the use of a cooperative congressman who undertook to sponsor several local causes and then through the very careful and quiet substitution of carefully thought-out alternative legislation, some unknown agents created or enlarged three national parks for reasons that can only be surmised. Probably, the agent was the SPRR, representing its own interests and possibly also those of some of its individual local representatives; presumably the motivation was nothing less than corporate greed—an irony seldom appreciated by modern students of the national parks of the Sierra Nevada.

THE END OF THE KAWEAH COLONY

The acts of September 25 and October 1, 1890, provided little specific instruction for administering the new reservations. It was left to the Secretary of the Interior to develop the procedures and regulations required to execute the acts' rather general goals. In late October, Secretary Noble responded. On October 21, the same day that Stewart and his friends learned of the enlargement of Sequoia, the Department of the Interior issued a list of eight regulations governing the new reservation. The first named the reserved tract "Sequoia National Park." Additional provisions prohibited hunting, fishing, and the possession or use of alcohol, while another section designated that the park would be under the immediate control of a government officer entitled "Superintendent of Sequoia National Park."[17] The rules and regulations were printed on cloth and forwarded immediately to local agents of the GLO, with the instruction that they be posted in and near the park. On the same day that the regulations were issued, Secretary Noble addressed the War Department, enclosing copies of the acts creating the three new national parks in the Sierra Nevada and requesting that military authorities in California investigate whether the parks would require military protection during the coming winter. By December 3, Secretary Noble had his answer from the Secretary of War:

> From the best information I can obtain, the best protection these park reservations can have during the winter consists of the heavy snows which cover them. . . . I therefore recommend that action be deferred until spring, when small parties of mounted men might be sent there to warn off, and, if necessary eject, timber cutters and sheepmen with their herds . . .[18]

In all his initial actions regarding Sequoia and General Grant National Parks, Secretary Noble followed rather closely the precedents set in the nation's only previous national park—Yellowstone, established in 1872. Troops had been detailed to Yellowstone in 1886, after an unsuccessful attempt at civilian law enforcement, and the rules and regulations for the California parks strongly resembled those issued for Yellowstone. Even the name "Sequoia National Park" imitated the earlier "Yellowstone National Park."

The immediate problem faced by the Department of the Interior in Sequoia National Park was what to do about the Kaweah Colony and its land-title claims. During the summer of 1890, prior to passage of either act, the colonists' road had finally reached the edge of the conifer timber. There, they erected a small, portable, steam-powered sawmill at a place they called Colony Mill. By late summer, at the same time that Stewart's campaign to protect the Garfield/Hockett country reached its climax, the colonists were beginning to cut pine and fir trees and mill them into lumber. No sequoias had yet come under the axe, as several miles of rugged canyon country still separated the colonists from the Giant Forest.

Despite the confidence shown by continued road-building activity and the initiation of logging at Colony Mill, the question of the colony's title to its five-year-old land claims in the Giant Forest remained unsettled. The temporary withdrawals that had been placed on the lands the colonists had claimed in 1885 remained in effect. In June 1890, the GLO had initiated a new investigation of the situation. Assigned to this task at the request of Congressman Vandever was temporary special land agent Andrew Cauldwell. The land agent's first report, filed in mid-July, represented the colony favorably and recommended that it be given an opportunity to take title to the Giant Forest. The following month, again at Vandever's request, Cauldwell undertook a general survey of the state of the Big Trees under the control of the federal land offices in Stockton and Visalia. His report, dated September 18, 1890, documented a radical and mysterious change of heart regarding the colonists. Suddenly, he saw them as illegal squatters on government land, operating an illegal sawmill. When he visited Colony Mill in August, Cauldwell warned the colonists that they were operating outside the law.[19]

Representative Vandever, still driven by an agenda we may never fully understand, continued his involvement. Twice, once late in October and again in early November, he wrote the GLO of his concerns about the actions of the colonists in the new park. In late November, apparently at Vandever's urging, Cauldwell returned to the scene. In a stormy meeting, colonist J. J. Martin told Cauldwell that the colony would continue cutting timber until the government stopped them with force. Cauldwell reported the confrontation, and on November 30, U.S. Marshal Myron Tarble, backed by two deputies, arrested four of the colony's directors: J. J. Martin, Burnette Haskell, H. T. Taylor, and William Christie. The four were taken to federal court in Los Angeles on December 1, 1890, where they entered pleas of "not guilty" and posted bail. Interestingly, Cauldwell reported all this at some length in a letter to Congressman Vandever, which survives in the National Archives. In the letter, Cauldwell called the colonists "rascals" and offered to resign, perhaps implying that he had now completed his work for Vandever now that the colony's key officials had been prosecuted.[20]

The fate of the Kaweah Colony rested upon the shoulders of Interior Secretary Noble, to whom fell the decision as to whether to honor the colonists' properly filed land claims. The question was whether the claims would be treated as public lands and, therefore, a part of the new park or whether the claims would be recognized as valid, with the result that the tracts would be private lands and, thus, subject to the clause in the legislation that specifically recognized the continued privacy of previously alienated lands within the new reservation.

On April 6, Noble announced his decision: Since the land claims in question had never formally been transferred to the claimants and since Congress had made no provision for the colonists, it was the duty of the GLO to reject the claims and manage the lands in question as a part of Sequoia National Park. Seven weeks later, the GLO itself responded with a contrary opinion from the assistant attorney general, citing a number of rulings, which suggested that land claimants who had followed all procedures were entitled to their lands and noting the *ex post facto* nature of the suspensions of land sales that were the heart of the issue.[21] Nothing came of the internal disagreement, and when the colonists had their day in court in mid-April, they were found guilty of timber trespass and fined several hundred dollars each. In Tulare County, where the colonists had been popular, the court's decision was not well received. George Stewart, speaking for a probable majority of his neighbors, found the whole spectacle disturbing. If the enlargement of the park had been carried out properly, he complained, none of this would have happened.[22]

THE FIRST SUMMER

While the Secretary of the Interior, the GLO, and federal court system debated the future of the Kaweah Colony, the U.S. Army prepared to assume responsibility for the physical protection of the new national parks of the Sierra Nevada. On May 14, 1891, the fifty-eight men of Troop K, Fourth Cavalry, under the command of Captain Joseph H. Dorst, rode out of the Presidio of San Francisco, crossed the San Francisco Bay by ferry to Oakland, and boarded a Southern Pacific train for Tulare County. On the evening of the sixteenth, the troops, traveling with sixty horses and twenty mules, arrived at the western boundary of Sequoia National Park, above Three Rivers. There, they came face to face with a myriad of problems.

Dorst brought to his new assignment nearly twenty years of military experience. An 1873 graduate of West Point, he had spent fourteen years in the field during the Indian Wars, mostly in the Southwest. During the last years of the 1880s, he returned to West Point as a cavalry instructor. Assigned in 1890 to the Fourth Cavalry in San Francisco, Dorst now faced a new and distinctive challenge: protection of America's second and fourth national parks.

Dorst's first problem was to locate the boundaries of the new national parks on the ground and then to develop plans for policing the tracts. The winter had been relatively wet, and much of Sequoia National Park remained snow-covered when Dorst and his troops arrived. He soon discovered that two roads entered Sequoia: the 1879 wagon road to Mineral King and the recently built Colony Mill Road ending at the temporary sawmill several miles west of the Giant Forest. While the Colony Road led to nothing but the now-closed mill, the Mineral King road, despite difficult grades, led to an area that had become a summer resort. Since most people entering the new park would do so via the Mineral King road, Dorst focused his initial interest on this area, even though the new park did not include Mineral King Valley itself. From a temporary camp at Red Hill, just above Three Rivers, Dorst sent troops to assist Tulare County in repairing winter damage to the roadway. On June 7, he entered Mineral King Valley, although the melting snowpack prevented establishment of a permanent camp there until June 29.

Once the snow melted, Dorst turned to exploring the rugged reaches of the two new reservations. Almost before he could start, however, he ran into the problem that would dominate his summer—the Kaweah Colony's attempt to cut sequoias at Atwell's Mill. Arrested and convicted for their efforts to cut trees at Colony Mill, the determined remnants of the colony regrouped after the trial in Los Angeles. On May 1, barely two weeks after the end of the trial, they signed a one-year lease allowing them to log on the 160-acre Atwell Tract along the Mineral King Road.[23] Logging had begun among the sequoias at Atwell's Mill during the last days of the Mineral King silver rush, but the mill never produced much, owing to its remote location. Now, under the leadership of Irwin Barnard who negotiated the lease for the remaining colonists, another attempt was to be made to make Atwell's Mill profitable. At risk was the existence of the colony itself, for, since the loss of their Giant Forest lands, the whole enterprise had fallen into doubt. In the way stood Captain Dorst and the U.S. Army, reluctant agents of the new and still vague national park idea.

On the scene again was Congressman Vandever's man, GLO Special Agent Andrew Cauldwell. Cauldwell learned of the colony's lease of Atwell's about June 1, while he was looking into the organization of the new Yosemite National Park. On June 12, Cauldwell talked with Dorst at his Mineral King camp. Cauldwell told Dorst that, under the rules and regulations that the Secretary of the Interior had decreed for the park the previous fall, the felling of standing timber, even on patented land, should not be allowed. According to Cauldwell, this was the rule that the army was enforcing in Yosemite. Cauldwell had already requested clarification on this issue from the secretary, when he first reported the potential conflict. Two weeks later, the commissioner of the GLO told the secretary's office that, as private land, Atwell's Tract was not subject to the rules promulgated for Sequoia National Park. The problem, however, was that Secretary Noble, like most other officials in hot and humid Washington, D.C., had left the city for a prolonged summer vacation.

Hence, the commissioner's recommendation did not receive immediate attention. The secretary's office did warn Cauldwell, however, to take no action at Atwell's until the secretary returned.

Though the Secretary of the Interior was on vacation, the Kaweah colonists were not. After Dorst found several trees freshly cut at Atwell's Mill on June 18, he sought the foreman, a Mr. Purdy, and told him that, until he received answers to the questions he had sent to Washington, Purdy was not to cut any trees in Sequoia National Park, even on patented land. Purdy strongly objected to both the order and to the fact that it was coming from a military officer. Dorst explained that the order was based on a cautious reading of the secretary's rules for the new park and that he was serving as acting superintendent of Sequoia National Park, a civilian office, not as an agent of the War Department. Purdy politely thanked him for the explanation and told him he did not intend to comply. Alone and unarmed, Dorst left the scene, heading for Visalia, where he hoped to find Cauldwell and make some sense of the escalating situation.[24]

The following day, June 19, at Dorst's request, Lieutenant J. E. Nolan visited Atwell's Mill. Nolan found Purdy, and Purdy denied being told by Dorst not to log; for spite, he added that if he had been told such a thing, he would not obey. Nolan renewed Dorst's order not to cut trees. The next day, Nolan returned to the mill, where Irwin Barnard presented him with a written statement strongly protesting the illegality of Dorst's order. The colony would sue, if necessary, to carry out its legal rights, he threatened. Meanwhile, Dorst proceeded to Visalia, where he failed to locate Cauldwell but did find the secretary's telegram of June 16, warning Cauldwell to take no action until he received further instructions.[25]

On the stage back to Three Rivers from Visalia, Dorst met Barnard, and he told the colonist of the secretary's telegram, which seemed not to threaten the colonists' interests. For the next week, believing that the situation was resolved, Dorst turned his attention to other matters. Then, in early July, he received a long-delayed response to his initial request for clarification on this issue. This letter, from Acting Secretary of the Interior George Chandler, instructed Dorst to prevent destruction of the "great trees" in the park. Confused, he telegrammed Washington: Which instruction from the Department of the Interior was he to follow? Should he take no action, or should be protect the trees aggressively? On July 9, the acting secretary telegrammed an answer: "You will not permit the cutting of any timber within the park until further orders."[26]

Dorst's military sense of duty expressed itself clearly in the letter he had hand-delivered to Irwin Barnard as soon as he received the July 9 telegram:

> In reply to a question of mine addressed to the Secretary of the Interior, concerning the cutting of timber at Atwell's Mill, I have received a telegram of which the enclosed is a copy. You will see that I am directed not to permit the cutting of timber within the park until

> further orders. I have the honor to request therefore that you will cause the cutting of timber to be discontinued on the tract of land in the vicinity of Atwell's Mill, which you have leased or claim to control, for I am informed that all that land lies with the limits of the park.

On July 15, Dorst visited the mill to see if his instructions had been carried out. Barnard was present and told Dorst he would cease only under threat of direct force or court injunction. The situation was getting completely out of hand.

Nearly half the summer had now passed, and the controversy over the colony's activities at Atwell's Mill had thus far prevented Dorst from undertaking any serious work in the remainder of the two new parks. Because the mountain terrain was so poorly known, Dorst's commanding general had authorized him to hire a civilian guide to help explore the new reservations but for no more than four weeks. During the lull before Chandler's telegram arrived, Dorst had hired a guide. Now, with the Atwell's situation heating up again, one of the four weeks of the guide's time had already been wasted. Determined to see the rest of the two parks, Dorst prepared to leave Mineral King for the Giant Forest area on July 18, only to have the colonists purposefully fell a tree in front of one of his soldiers on the 17th. Apparently, the angry socialists had gone so far as to cut a young sequoia nearly through and then wait to fell it until a soldier came by. Dorst sent a corporal and several troops to the mill, while he stubbornly took most of his troops north over Timber Gap toward the Giant Forest. The scouting party sent to the mill reported that no trees had been cut, and Dorst continued his exploration of Paradise Ridge. By the morning of the 21st, his party had worked its way down to Red Hill, on the lower Mineral King Road. There, news arrived that the colonists had cut more trees, and Dorst ordered Lieutenant Nolan and a dozen troops to proceed up the road to Atwell's Mill to investigate. Just before Nolan left for Atwell's, Dorst received a telegram from Cauldwell that told him to "carry out the orders of the Secretary."

Early in the evening of the 21st, after a blistering-hot eighteen-mile ride, Nolan and his troops arrived at Atwell's Mill. Under strict orders to avoid violence, Nolan met briefly with Barnard, who told him that the colonists would cease logging only if physically forced. Worried, Nolan took his troops to camp a half-mile away for the night. The next morning, Nolan's troops returned to Atwell's to be met by thirty colonists armed with axes and supported by a deputy sheriff, who threatened to arrest the troops if they interfered with the colonists' logging activities. Sensing that the situation had reached a dangerous point, Nolan again withdrew and took his men back down the long, hot ride to Red Hill, where he reported to Dorst. Frustrated that his exploration time was being lost, Dorst nevertheless ordered his entire command back up the Mineral King Road that same afternoon. Late in the afternoon, as they climbed the steep, dusty road, they met Barnard coming down, heading for Visalia to swear out warrants for the arrest of Nolan and Dorst. After an inconclusive conversation, Barnard continued down the road. By midnight, the troops were bivouacked at Nolan's camp near the mill. At dawn, they moved past the mill, seeking a better campsite for the large party, and, as they passed, the colonists dropped a tree they had readied for the occasion. Dorst, bone tired and sick with a fever, ignored the provocation and moved on up the road.

The following morning, July 24, 1891, Dorst felt no better but realized he must act. On Dorst's orders, Nolan returned to the mill, where he found angry colonists chopping away at the trees. Several times he approached individuals, ordered them to cease cutting, and then laid his hand on the logger. In each case, the colonists ignored the symbolic application of force. Again, Nolan withdrew. Later the same day, however, foreman Purdy entered Dorst's camp and told him that all logging had been voluntarily stopped, because his men were so excited that nothing could be accomplished anyway. Dorst, sensing an opportunity, ordered Nolan and all the troops who had been directly involved at the mill to prepare to leave the next morning for the northern portion of the park with the civilian guide. At least, he hoped, that would make it difficult for the county sheriff to arrest them.

Lieutenant Nolan, with nineteen troops and a civilian guide, left Mineral King on the morning of July 25. That same day Dorst received a telegram from Cauldwell enclosing a message from Washington:

> It appears that Atwell's Mill is on private land. If this is correct, instruct Captain Dorst to defer action on all patented land until I can communicate with Secretary, now absent on his vacation, and obtain his directions. [signed] George Chandler, Acting Secretary

Dorst forwarded a copy of the telegram to Barnard, together with the message that he would cease his interference with the colony's activities at Atwell's Mill.

With the unfortunate incident at Atwell's Mill stabilized, Dorst was finally able to turn his attention to the two national parks under his control. Between July 25 and August 9, Lieutenant Nolan's patrol made the first official visits of the U.S. Army to the northern part of Sequoia and to General Grant National Park. After his 207-mile journey, Nolan noted that the Giant Forest was the most interesting part of the new parks yet the least visited, owing to remoteness. Within the grove, Nolan wrote, were more than forty simple cabins built by the colonists in their attempt to claim the land. At the confluence of the Marble and Middle Forks, Nolan recorded the presence of squatter Jim Wolverton's cabin and gardens. A few miles downstream, just inside the park, another squatter named Bonivie also had settled.[27]

While Nolan explored the north, Dorst sent out several additional detachments of troops from his Mineral King camp. Between July 18 and August 31, Sergeant Patrick Daugherty and his men rode 970 miles, patrolling the area around their camp at Zimmerman's (Hockett) Meadow.[28] Another detachment camped at Colony Mill to look after the Giant Forest and Grant Grove country.

Early in August, Andrew Cauldwell returned to the park to inspect Dorst's efforts. On August 10, the two men visited Colony Mill, where they met Colony Director Horace Taylor and told him to remove the mill's equipment but not the cut lumber, since that was the property of the government. Cauldwell also visited Atwell's Mill, where he reported that the colonists had resumed cutting sequoias, although, because of their inexperience, they were losing much of the wood to breakage. Cauldwell thought they were operating at a loss. One hundred persons, he reported, had left the colony in the past year. [29]

The troops remained in the vicinity of the parks until the winter rains began on November 16. In his annual report, Dorst recommended that Sequoia Park be extended to the east to protect the Mt. Whitney area, which was so heavily grazed that tourist parties could not visit it, that the boundaries of the two parks be surveyed, and that legal penalties be provided to support the parks' rules and regulations.[30] Andrew Cauldwell resigned his position as special agent on September 17. In a cover letter attached to Cauldwell's resignation by the new local congressman, W. W. Bowers, Bowers complimented Cauldwell's work and summarized the feelings they apparently shared about the ill-fated enterprise: "Suffice it to say at this time—that this Colony Scheme is the most . . . bald-face piece of villainy I ever knew of—and I intend to fully to ventilate it."[31] Attached in the files to Cauldwell's resignation was an additional note remarking that Cauldwell's only recent project had been the Kaweah problem and that it was now resolved.[32] Helping to resolve the "Kaweah problem" was the fact that the colony was dying. Cauldwell's suspicion that its logging activity at Atwell's Mill was unprofitable proved to be true, and the colonists never succeeded in making a significant dent in the forests at Atwell's Mill. By May 1892, when the time came for the colony to renew its annual lease on the tract, the organization no longer formally existed.

Today, it is difficult to survey the story of the colony and its demise without mixed feelings. Undoubtedly, the logging of the Giant Forest would have been a tragic mistake; certainly, we are fortunate that it survived intact as the center of a national park. Yet, in many ways, the colonists—a hard-working and dedicated group—were treated unfairly. Their claims to the Giant Forest appear to have been legally filed, and, by the precedents of the time, the lands they claimed should have been transferred to them. The road they built, which for many years served as the main route into Sequoia National Park, was taken from them without compensation. And, certainly, their treatment at the hands of the army during the summer of 1891 was unjustified by any legal doctrine. Why did Andrew Cauldwell change his mind so completely about their efforts, and what was his real role in their destruction? Why did Congressman Vandever involve himself so deeply in the affair? What was the hidden role of the Southern Pacific in the destruction of the colony? More than a century later, these questions are still unanswerable and likely to remain so.

THE SIERRA FOREST RESERVE

With the lands of Sequoia and General Grant National Parks permanently withdrawn from sale and under the summer protection of the U.S. Army, George Stewart and his supporters resumed their efforts to protect the remainder of the southern Sierra. Owing to a move by Interior Secretary Noble, a new tactic for forest preservation was now available. On March 3, 1891, President Harrison signed a bill that contained, among other things, a provision that allowed the President to create forest reserves for conservation purposes. The clause had been added to the bill at the suggestion of Secretary Noble, during a late-night conference session as Congress prepared to adjourn. When the House and Senate endorsed the conference bill, primarily an act to repeal the old timber-culture laws, few members of Congress apparently noted the clause about the reservation. Noble's addition gave the President the right to decree the permanent withdrawal of selected public lands from sale, so they might be preserved in public ownership, a radical change in federal land policy.[33] President Harrison quickly exercised his new authority, when he created the first forest reserve in Wyoming less than a month after he signed the act.

Meanwhile, Stewart was enjoying broader political help than he had received during the 1890 campaign. His new allies included Robert Underwood Johnson, editor of *Century Magazine,* and John Muir. Muir's particular focus was the Kings Canyon. As early as April 1890, when the effort to create Yosemite National Park was just beginning, Muir had promised Johnson that he would write an article for the popular magazine to publicize the canyon and its beauty. Muir hoped that fall to visit the gorge, which he had last seen in 1877, but a family illness prevented the journey. The following spring, Muir returned to the project. On May 18, 1891, Muir mailed Johnson a map, showing his proposal for an enlarged Sequoia National Park, which included not only the Kings Canyon and the Sierra Crest peaks immediately to the east, but also Mt. Whitney and all the sequoia groves from the Kings River south through the Tule River country.[34]

On May 28, Muir finally departed for his trip to the Kings Canyon, taking with him artist Charles Robinson. On May 31, they arrived in the glacial gorge, where they spent a wet, cold week, while Muir renewed his impressions of the place for his article and Robinson sketched illustrations for the article. Muir spent much of the summer trying to provide Johnson with a concise Kings Canyon article of 8,000 words. Published in the November 1891 issue of *Century*

Magazine as "A Rival of the Yosemite," the article described the region's features in detail, included Muir's map of his proposed additions to Sequoia National Park, and recommended congressional action to preserve the region.[35]

Johnson maintained excellent connections with government officials, and, within a few weeks of publication of Muir's article on Kings Canyon, Interior Secretary Noble himself promised Johnson that he would discuss the matter with President Harrison. Actually, responding to local interest, the GLO had already initiated a study of the forest reserve's potential in the Sierra Nevada. In October 1891, the GLO assigned Special Agent B. E Allen to the project. Allen began work immediately and continued his field efforts during the summer of 1892. As 1893 began and the end of Harrison's term approached, Allen received orders to speed up the preparation of his proposal, so that the lame-duck President could sign the decree before his successor entered the White House. Allen completed work on the draft proclamation on February 10, and Harrison signed it four days later. The day before the Sierra Forest Reserve was formally proclaimed, Secretary Noble wrote Johnson, telling him that the new reservation would contain more than 4,000,000 acres and protect all the areas Muir had mentioned in the *Century* article.[36]

Harrison's proclamation of February 14, 1893, permanently withdrew almost the entire central and southern Sierra Nevada from sale to private parties. The move was generally supported in the San Joaquin Valley, with only sheep and mining interests openly opposed. Again, as had been the case three years earlier, the farmers of the San Joaquin, pursuing protection of their water supply, together with a small number of individuals who prized the natural beauty of the area, had turned to the federal government. Creation of the Sierra Forest Reserve brought a final end to the region's pioneer era. Although a number of years would pass before the newly reserved lands were brought under effective management, cessation of the sale of federal timberlands in the Sierra marked a profound change of direction in regional land management.

At the time, most people perceived little difference between the creation in 1890 of the three national parks in the Sierra and the proclamation of the Sierra Forest Reserve in 1893. Special Agent Allen, in his final report, referred to the proposed forest reserve as a "great national park."[37] In many ways, this perception made considerable sense. After all, the law of October 1, 1890, that set aside more than seventy percent of Sequoia Park simply decreed that the lands "be set apart as reserved forest lands." There were significant differences that Allen underestimated, however. The most critical of these was that while the two 1890 acts specifically instructed the Secretary of the Interior to protect the natural features of the new parks, the 1893 presidential proclamation only required cessation of land sales. As a result, the relatively small portion of the Sierra designated as "national park" continued to receive military protection, while the immensely larger Sierra Forest Reserve found itself under the very weak control of a tiny handful of civilian GLO field agents.

Under this regime, for the remainder of the decade, the forest reserve continued to suffer abuse from loggers, miners, and stockmen.

A QUIET DECADE

Despite the presence of military troops, even the national parks of the southern Sierra Nevada received only minimal management. As the summers passed, a military routine developed for protecting Sequoia and General Grant. Late each spring, cavalry troops arrived in the parks, usually from the Presidio of San Francisco. After setting up a headquarters camp somewhere in the Mineral King area, most often at Weishar's Mill (modern Silver City), the acting superintendent sent detachments to outlying areas, usually including General Grant National Park. This work involved patrolling to keep sheep and cattle out of the parks, to suppress fires, and to prevent hunting. Aside from expulsion from the parks, no penalties stood behind the secretary's rules and regulations, a problem that severely limited the troops' effectiveness. In time, ways were found to make the best of the poor situation, including an informal procedure for expelling trespassing sheep on one boundary and the offending shepherds at another location.

Several factors hindered the effectiveness of the military administration. None of the military officers who served as acting superintendent of the two parks during the 1890s served more than two consecutive summers, a policy that worked against long-term planning. Congress appropriated no funds for developing the parks, and the War Department invested only the minimum necessary to support its troops. Of visitors, only a trickle was to be found, owing primarily to a lack of access. Nevertheless, the early military men took seriously their charge of protecting the parks, and, within the limits of their situation, they largely succeeded in their task. The routine crumbled, however, during the summer of 1898, the year of the Spanish-American War. Before troops finally arrived in September of that year, more than 200,000 sheep ravaged Sequoia National Park, and a fire of some size burned in the Giant Forest.[38]

It fell to Second Lieutenant Henry B. Clark, acting superintendent of the two parks during the summer of 1899, to summarize the successes, failures, and visions of that first decade. His report is worth quoting at length:

> The Sequoia Park, although 252 square miles in extent, is crossed by but one wagon road—that one of about 11 miles in length, and called the Mineral King Road. This so-called county road through a National Park is unsatisfactory, and presents many complications and opportunities for dispute with trespassers and stockmen. The county of Tulare spends but very little for its repair, while the General Government contributes nothing, though

both are alike interested in the improvement of this single thoroughfare. The roadway is cut in the hillside, and the grade as now established is wretched.

Previous reports have referred to the Old Colony Mill road, but neglect and want of use for the past nine years have rendered this road impassable to wagons, and unless someone is interested in its repair very shortly this important thoroughfare will return to its primitive condition of a steep mountain side thickly covered with brush. This road was constructed to within 2 miles of the redwoods, though a 9-mile trail is now the only thoroughfare open to the tourist from the end of the Colony Mill road grade. Wagons cannot approach nearer than 20 miles from the forest.

Resort must be had to the mountain trail for all travel through the Sequoia Park. Of these trails there are many, some made by hunters, some by cattlemen, and others by the troops in attempting to eject these trespassers. All are poorly marked, and many were obliterated by the invading sheep last season. No attempt was made to follow anything like an even grade in their construction, and their condition is not inviting to the average tourist.

It is to be presumed that the Sequoia and General Grant National Parks were established for two purposes: First to preserve the redwood trees and, second, to protect the watershed of the rivers which drain this region of the Sierras. The mere detailing of troops, which will faithfully execute their military orders, is sufficient to accomplish both these ends. But, what is a park—a national park? Is it a playground for the people, a resort for the tourist, a mecca for travelers, a summer house where inhabitants of crowded cities can repair and fill their lungs with the pure air of mountain and forest—where poet, artist, clerk, and artisan, without discrimination, can stand on lofty peak and breathe the inspiration of scenes of grandeur? If this makes a park, then the Sequoia National Park is a failure—a failure not because it wants in snow-clad peak, in noble game, in frightful precipice, deep gorge, or ragged canyon, but because the people find its beauties and its wonders inaccessible.

It is time that a systematic development of Sequoia National Park be inaugurated. Money has been spent generously on Yellowstone, Yosemite, and Chickamauga, but not a dollar on Sequoia or General Grant National Park. I would, therefore, earnestly recommend that reasonable appropriation be made at once.[39]

PARK DEVELOPMENT BEGINS

Many Tulare County businessmen shared Lieutenant Clark's concerns. If the parks could be developed for tourism, many Visalia residents believed the incoming visitors would begin to make a significant contribution to the economy of the region. Finally, several Visalians took the matter into their own hands. During the same summer that Lieutenant Clark superintended the two parks, a party of thirteen visited Mineral King, Kern Canyon, Mt. Whitney, and the Giant Forest. The group, organized by Ben Maddox, editor of Visalia's *Tulare County Times* and founder of the new Visalia Board of Trade, also included local Congressman J. C. Needham and representatives of the Southern Pacific Railroad and Santa Fe Railway. The effort paid off. The Sundry Civil Appropriations Act of June 6, 1900, included $10,000 for the protection and improvement of Sequoia National Park.[40] The new fiscal year began July 1, and, on July 16, rehabilitation work of the Colony Mill Road began. Six weeks later, with the road open for wagons to Colony Mill for the first time since the early 1890s, work began on extending the road toward Giant Forest. On September 15, Acting Superintendent Frank West, a captain in the Ninth Cavalry, reported that a route had been surveyed all the way to Moro Rock and Crescent Meadow. The same act that gave Sequoia road money also appropriated $2,500 to build an eight-mile-long fence around General Grant National Park. That work began September 8. Encouraged by the appropriation, Captain West recommended an additional $21,000 of improvements that he thought productive. He also recommended that two civilian forest rangers be employed to protect the parks during the off-season.[41]

West's suggestion regarding civilian rangers had some precedent. During the troublesome year of 1898, Sequoia Park had received useful help from GLO/Forest Reserve Ranger Ernest Britten.[42] In December 1899, after a good deal of lobbying for the new position, Ranger Britten resigned from the Sierra Forest Reserve and assumed the position of Forest Ranger for Sequoia and General Grant National Parks. Late in January 1900, Britten reported that he was in Three Rivers and on duty. He had been delayed, he recounted, because he had to build a house so he could live in the vicinity.[43] Britten looked after the parks until West's troops arrived, and West was impressed enough with Britten's work that he kept him on duty throughout the summer of 1900 and recommended, at the end of the summer, that Britten be retained permanently to protect the parks in the winter and to assist the army during the summer.[44]

West had several good reasons to believe that the parks needed all-year protection. The rehabilitation of the Colony Mill Road meant that, for the first time, the government actually had made improvements in the parks that would require care during the rainy season. Also, appropriations had allowed trail building to start. If the army was only going to be in the parks during the summer, which seemed logical to West and his military successors, someone else needed to watch over the parks for the other eight months of the year. Sequoia and General Grant National Parks had their first real ranger.

During the next several years, the Department of the Interior authorized and supported development of a small but permanent civilian ranger corps. In the fall of 1901, Captain L. C.

Andrews, the acting superintendent of the two parks, issued winter instructions for the two rangers remaining on duty. They were to protect the Colony Mill Road from damage by winter rains, work on three new trails, maintain control of the parks' tools and equipment, put up trail signs, and in their spare time clear brush from existing trails. Captain Andrews ended the document by expressing some frustrations with the general condition of the parks:

> The rangers will habitually work together, especially on trail and road work. It is desired that main trails be straightened and widened and made trails, instead of rambling cow paths as at present, and that attention will be paid to brushing out overhead and on the sides, as well as making a good trail bed. It is assumed that my successor will be able to ride main trails next season without being brushed from the saddle, or traveling 5 miles unnecessarily in order to go 2 miles.[45]

The impetus to develop the two parks came from business interests in Tulare County, and those same interests soon found ways to exploit the improving situation. The packers for the 1899 Visalia Board of Trade party that took Congressman Needham to Mt. Whitney were a Three Rivers partnership known as Broder and Hopping. John Broder and Ralph Hopping both operated ranches in the lower Kaweah River canyons, and, like most small ranchers of the time, they looked beyond their ranches for cash income. During the summer of 1898, operating out of Hopping's ranch at Redstone Park on the North Fork of the Kaweah, the two ranchers organized a packing business for tourists. At Redstone Park they established a simple tent hotel to serve as a way station for their pack-train tours to the Big Trees. They also initiated a stage line between Visalia and Redstone. Considering the problems of Sequoia National Park that summer, it is not surprising they were involved in the Visalia Board of Trade's lobbying effort of the following year. And it is equally unsurprising that, in the same year that the army rehabilitated the Colony Mill Road and committed itself to construction of a wagon road into the Giant Forest, Broder and Hopping opened a tent hotel in the Giant Forest. They called the new resort "Camp Sierra," and Hopping and his wife operated it, while Broder continued to look after their facility at Redstone Park. Broder also started a stage line up the road to Colony Mill once that route had been restored.[46] During 1901, Ranger Britten received an application from another local enterprise, Ellis and Sons, to operate a stage from Visalia to General Grant Grove, using the Stephens Grade, which had been extended into General Grant National Park several years earlier. Britten recommended that General Grant, too, be opened for commercial activity.[47]

The progress that began during the summer of 1900 with the first annual appropriations for the development of Sequoia and General Grant National Parks accelerated during the remainder

Following instructions provided by Captain Charles Young (later a colonel), the U.S. Army began an effort in 1903 to protect some of the most famous individual trees in the twin parks. Fences were erected around both the General Grant (shown here) and General Sherman Trees to keep visitors a few yards away from the trees. On March 25, 2013, President Barack Obama designated the Charles Young Buffalo Soldiers National Monument to commemorate the leader of the African-American military whose duties included protection of Sequoia National Park as acting superintendent. Photographer and date unknown.

of the first decade of the new century. For a number of years, annual appropriations held firm at $10,000 for Sequoia and $2,500 for General Grant. While these sums were not large, they had considerable purchasing power in a world where a full day's labor could be purchased for several dollars. In Sequoia, work continued on the Giant Forest extension of the Colony Mill Road. By the end of 1901, the road had been extended to the Marble Fork Crossing and a wagon bridge constructed across the river. In 1903, the army completed the road to Round Meadow and Moro Rock. On August 15, 1903, Acting Superintendent Charles Young celebrated completion of the project with a picnic beneath the Big Trees. During that same summer, Young, at that time the only African American holding a regular commission in the U.S. Army, fenced the General Grant Tree and General Sherman Tree and obtained options to purchase most private lands within the two parks at reasonable prices. Unfortunately, Congress appropriated no funds for the purchases, and the options expired.[48]

Once the Giant Forest Road was in place, a network of well-graded trails was extended across Sequoia National Park. Included in these early trails were the Alta Trail, connecting the Giant Forest with Alta Meadow; the Sevenmile Hill Trail, leading from near Alta Meadow to Redwood Meadow and the Mineral King country; and the Black Oak Trail, which opened the northwestern portions of Sequoia National Park. By 1907, the summer community at the Giant Forest had grown large enough to warrant the opening of a post office and the stringing of a single-wire telephone line connecting the Giant Forest with Three Rivers. During these productive years, protection of Sequoia National Park continued largely in the hands of the U.S. Army during the summer, although the Department of the Interior maintained three rangers on full-time duty. At General Grant, once the surrounding fence was complete, protection fell mostly to Ranger L. L. Davis, who lived in the park throughout the year.

As the two parks passed through their second decade of existence, the nature of the protection they required shifted. After the turn of the century, trespass grazing by large herds of unregulated cattle or sheep largely ceased to be a problem, but, with the opening of the parks to stage transportation and rental accommodations, people problems began to occur, including illegal hunting and camp sanitation. Fire suppression also rose in importance, a result again of the rising use of the parks. During the summer of 1907, some 1,100 persons visited General Grant National Park, while another 900 entered Sequoia.[49] Although their numbers were still small, the impact of these visitors was locally substantial. Many came to the parks to escape the summer heat of the San Joaquin Valley, and families commonly camped in the forest for two months or more. As a result, camp sanitation eventually required construction of formal latrines. Meadows near camping areas such as the Giant Forest's Round Meadow took a heavy beating from grazing draft and saddle animals, and here, too, the government had to intervene with rules.

THE SIERRA CLUB AND THE HIGH COUNTRY

The increase in visitor interest in the southern Sierra did not limit itself solely to the developed areas within the two parks. As early as 1892, John Muir brought together in San Francisco a number of his friends and other appreciators of the mountains to form the Sierra Club in order to "explore, enjoy, and render accessible the mountain regions of the Pacific Coast; to publish authentic information concerning them; [and] to enlist the support and cooperation of the people and the Government in preserving the forests and other natural features of the Sierra Nevada."[50] Initially, the new club was small, but its members, many of them associated either with the University of California in Berkeley or Stanford University, brought to the organization a deep appreciation for the beauty of the mountains. And many of the club's early members were no strangers to the southern portions of the Sierra. For example, in the summer of 1890 Joseph N. Le Conte, while still a student at Cal, undertook a trip sixty-seven days long, covering some 652 miles to Kings Canyon, Mt. Whitney, and Yosemite.[51] During his long life, Le Conte would make more than eighty backcountry trips in the Sierra and play a major role in opening the Kings Canyon backcountry to recreational use.

Until the 1890s, despite the pioneer mapping of the California Geological Survey and several decades of use by shepherds, the high country remained largely unknown as a recreational resource. Three individuals, all associated with the early Sierra Club, changed this pattern. One was Le Conte; the others were Bolton Coit Brown, an art instructor at Stanford University, and Theodore Solomons, a young man from San Francisco who had been smitten by the mountains during a teen-aged stint on a relative's farm near Fresno. During a decade of summer adventures, these three men led the recreational exploration and mapping of the southern Sierra. Because nearly all previous explorations in the mountains had focused on getting across them, it fell to these three to figure out how to travel north and south within the high country. From their efforts came a wonderful series of articles in the *Sierra Club Bulletin* and, ultimately, the first locally accurate maps of the range. And it was Solomons who put the routes together and came up with the idea that would eventually become the John Muir Trail, a route running the length of the High Sierra and closely paralleling the crest.[52]

Inevitably, as Le Conte, Brown, and Solomons shared their adventures in print, others followed in their footsteps. After the turn of the century, the Sierra Club initiated a program of elaborate annual outings, many of them in the southern Sierra. The club's first "outing," in 1901, occurred at Tuolumne Meadows in Yosemite. The following year, the club traveled to the Kings Canyon, where a permanent camp was set up near the mouth of Copper Creek. Setting a model for similar outing camps that the club would operate for the next several decades, the 1902 camp

The Sierra Club, originally a mountaineering club based in the San Francisco Bay Area of California, began its program of annual outings into the High Sierra in 1901. In subsequent years, many of these month-long trips included the Sequoia and Kings Canyon region. Participants in these trips often became determined advocates for the protection of the Southern Sierra. Photographer and date unknown.

at Copper Creek had 200 residents who required 25,000 pounds of baggage, all transported by mules. More than fifty members of the club made the ascent of Mt. Brewer, where, less than forty years previously, Brewer and King had struggled desperately to attain the summit.[53] Recreation had come to the High Sierra.

HYDROELECTRIC DEVELOPMENT ON THE KAWEAH RIVER

West of Sequoia Park, the canyon country above Three Rivers also began to change. Half a century had now passed since Hale Tharp and a few others became the first non-Native Americans to reside in the area, and new potential uses for the land and its resources were coming into focus. Of these, the most radical departure from the traditional world of small-scale ranching and farming came from the Mt. Whitney Power Company, which began constructing hydroelectric plants on the Kaweah River in 1898. During that year, using sequoia lumber cut at Atwell's Mill, the power company built its first flume and powerhouse, using water from the East Fork of the Kaweah. In June 1899, the turbines began humming at the pioneer Kaweah Number One Plant located at the new town of Hammond, two miles west of the Sequoia Park's boundary on the Middle Fork of the Kaweah. Construction soon began on a second plant, which diverted water from the Middle Fork barely 100 yards downstream from the park's boundary. And, in 1902, three years before work concluded on the Number Two Plant, the company applied for permission to begin planning a third water diversion, flume, and power plant, this time within Sequoia National Park.[54]

In 1902, the Middle Fork Canyon was still an inaccessible and little-visited corner of Sequoia National Park. Since the death of James Wolverton in 1893 and the eviction of squatter Bonivie, the area had been uninhabited for the first time in thousands of years. A poor horse trail still ran up the canyon to the Giant Forest via Hospital Rock, but, with completion of the wagon road to the Giant Forest via Colony Mill, the route seemed even less important than before. The canyons and river flats proposed for development by the power company were too low to support sequoias, and the local agricultural interests offered a critical advocacy, strongly supporting the development proposal, since the power generated would be used to run pumps for irrigation. Faced with a significant proposal to use rather than preserve a part of the park and sensing no significant opposition, the Department of the Interior granted permission to the company to construct hydroelectric improvements.

By May 1913, when the Mt. Whitney Power Company started operations at its Kaweah Number Three Plant, Sequoia National Park had felt twentieth-century industrial technology for the first time. Developments included low-diversion dams on both the Marble and Middle Forks of the Kaweah, nearly five miles of concrete canal, and a concrete power house that straddled the park's boundary. Additional plans called for construction of another power plant in the park, to be called Kaweah Number Five, together with additional flumes and a 100-foot-tall dam on Wolverton Creek east of the Giant Forest.[55] This dam, constructed on private land sold earlier under the provisions of the Swamp and Overflow Act, was thought necessary to provide adequate late-summer flow for the generation of power.

Between 1905 and 1915, the Mt. Whitney Power Company permanently changed the face of Sequoia National Park. Not only did the company dam two of the park's rivers, scar the Middle Fork Canyon with several miles of flumes, and clear-cut nearly a hundred acres of forest at the Wolverton Reservoir site, but it also constructed roads. To facilitate construction of the Kaweah Number Three Flume and the eventually aborted Number Five Plant, the company built a wagon road up the Middle Fork Canyon as far as Hospital Rock. Seeking access to its Wolverton Creek project, the company constructed another wagon road along the northern edge of the Giant Forest, passing the base of the General Sherman Tree. Both roads opened new portions of the park to vehicular tourism.

In hindsight, it is, perhaps, too easy to fault the Department of the Interior for allowing the Mt. Whitney Company's projects to mar the natural face of the park. If proposed two decades later, the projects would have been rejected as inappropriate, but, during the first decade of the new century, the national park idea was simply not mature enough to prevent construction of a locally popular dam. It is worth remembering that, in 1914, Congress itself gave away the incomparable Hetch Hetchy Valley in Yosemite National Park for construction of a reservoir by the City of San Francisco. In the end, further damage to Sequoia was prevented not by the government but by the faulty engineering of the company itself. Had it not unsuccessfully sought bedrock at the Wolverton dam site in a nearly bottomless deposit of loose glacial debris and, as a result, abandoned its reservoir plans, the company might well have gone on to build the Kaweah Number Five project.

THE FOREST RESERVE AND THE NEW FOREST SERVICE

The advent of the twentieth century, with its new land-use pressures, was felt not only in Sequoia and General Grant National Parks, but also on the surrounding Sierra Forest Reserve. Creation of the forest reserves had left most of the southern Sierra open to nearly any use that did not involve outright sale of the land to private parties. The GLO did not ignore the reserve altogether, however, and it assigned to the giant area several forest rangers supervised by the GLO's office in Fresno. But the sheer scale of the terrain involved, together with the GLO's very limited human resources, determined that attention could go to only a few selected issues.

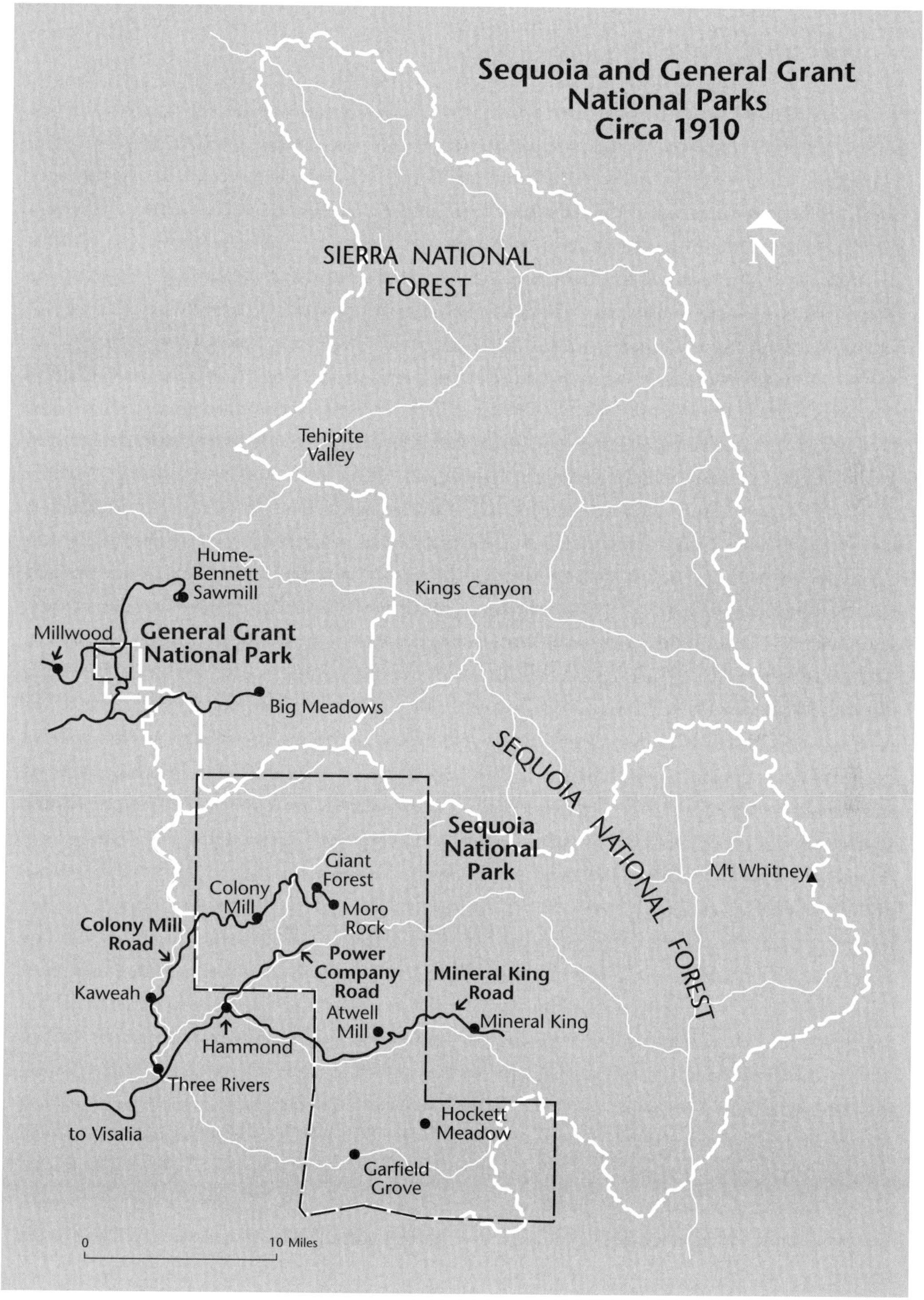

Sequoia and General Grant
National Parks
Circa 1910
N
SIERRA NATIONAL
FOREST
Tehipite
Valley
Hume-
Bennett
Sawmill
Kings Canyon
Millwood
General Grant
National Park
Big Meadows
SEQUOIA NATIONAL FOREST
Sequoia
National
Park
Giant
Forest
Colony
Mill
Moro
Rock
Mt Whitney
Colony Mill
Road
Power
Company
Road
Mineral King
Road
Kaweah
Atwell
Mill
Mineral King
Hammond
Three Rivers
to Visalia
Hockett
Meadow
Garfield
Grove
0
10 Miles

An example of one of those issues was the GLO's attempt to prevent the patenting of the Empire Mill site in Mineral King Valley. Under federal mining laws, which remained in effect on the forest reserves, individuals could claim land where they found mineral deposits and they could also claim other nearby tracts of public land for use as mill sites, where the ores from their mine could be processed. In 1904, the Empire Mine was more than two decades dead, and Arthur Crowley, who had helped to build the mining road into the area in 1879, was using some of the lands in question for a small resort. No ores were being processed at the Empire millsite, but a store, hotel, barn, meat shop, post office, and cabins were all in use. Forest Reserve Supervisor Harrison White contested Crowley's application for a permit for continued occupancy, and the controversy eventually went to court. Ultimately, Crowley received not only a use permit but also a patent, which gave him fee-simple title to the land. Protecting government lands in the forest reserve was not an easy proposition.[56]

Actually, by the time Arthur Crowley received title to his land in Mineral King Valley, a major change had been made in management of the reserves. On February 1, 1905, at the behest of President Theodore Roosevelt, responsibility for managing all the nation's forest reserves had been transferred from the U.S. Department of the Interior to the U.S. Department of Agriculture (USDA); there, they were placed under the control of what had previously been called the Bureau of Forestry but would henceforth be known as the U.S. Forest Service (USFS). The effort to transfer the forest reserves from Interior to Agriculture originated with Gifford Pinchot, the first American to be trained in Europe as a forester and the head of Agriculture's forestry program. Starting about 1902, Pinchot, a close friend and advisor of President Roosevelt, began a campaign to transfer the growing system of forest reserves to his bureau. Pinchot sought support for this move primarily by advertising that his proposed agency would be able to carry on a more vigorous and energetic management program than had been effected by Interior's Division of Forestry.

But the Department of the Interior had been trying. In California, the biggest continuing problem in the forest reserves was unregulated grazing. In 1900, Interior had issued a first set of "Rules and Regulations Governing the Forest Reserves," which had prohibited the pasturage of sheep on reserves in California and a number of other states. The regulation proved impossible to enforce, however, and, in June 1903, the superintendent of the Sierra Forest Reserve estimated no less than 34,000 sheep on the reserve. The Sierra Club blamed this inability to enforce the law, at least in part, on Interior's "venal forest rangers," who were all too often tied to local user groups. In this situation, it might be better, the club thought, to transfer responsibility to a new organization.[57]

The law that passed on February 1, 1905, not only transferred the forest reserves to the USDA, but also set up a funding system for their management by allowing the USFS to retain fees collected from either resource sales or land use. On the same day that President Roosevelt signed the bill, the Secretary of Agriculture signed a carefully drafted policy memo to "Chief Forester" Gifford Pinchot, outlining the directions the new agency should pursue. Drafted by Pinchot, this policy statement charted a clear course based on turn-of-the-century Progressive thought. One sentence summarized it admirably: "All the resources of the forests are for use, under such restrictions only as will insure . . . permanence . . ."[58]

Creation of the USFS, with its clear and guiding multi-use philosophy, unencumbered funding, and progressive leadership, did bring new energy to the forest reserves of California, including the Sierra Forest Reserve. During the next few years, the agency fought a number of critical battles, and if it lost a few, such as its effort to prevent Arthur Crowley from gaining title to his "mill site" in Mineral King Valley, it won most of the big ones. In California, the biggest battle was over sheep grazing in the Sierra. Years later, William Greeley, who, in 1906, became Supervisor of the southern half of the Sierra Forest Reserve, remembered how the battle was finally won:

> "No Trespass" signs in English and Spanish were put up every half mile. In the spring secret lookouts were posted at points commanding the wooly line of march. They were enthusiastic volunteers for this duty from young cow punchers. Soon dust clouds carried the news that sheep were moving up Walker Pass, and headquarters had daily reports on the location of the lead flock. This district ranger ostentatiously left his station with his pack string, for a long trip over the high country.
>
> We waited for days while the sheep grazed along but never across the boundary. Then suddenly they moved in. We held back until the flocks had made a day's drive and a night[']s bedding within the … forest. Then the deputy supervisor rode up with three or four deputized marshals and a Basque interpreter. There were nine thousand sheep in trespass under care of a dozen herders and camp tenders. Through the bedlam of South European expostulations, the deputy made the boss herder pick three men to take care of the sheep. He arrested the others and marshaled them before the United States Commissioner at Bakersfield.
>
> Suspicions of long standing were confirmed when top flight attorneys from San Francisco magically appeared as counsel for the sheepherders. They represented some of the largest land companies in the state. They challenged the power of the Secretary of Agriculture and all his minions to control grazing on public lands of the United States. However, the commissioner bound the Basques over to the Federal court and unwonted peace descended upon the south Sierra ranges. Many months later the Supreme Court received the case of United States vs. Grimaud, Cazaous, and Inda and settled for all time the authority of the Secretary to regulate grazing on national forests.[59]

During the next few years, the remaining shadows of the old Interior Department's forestry organization were swept away. An act approved on March 4, 1907, renamed the forest reserves "national forests," and, on July 2, 1908, President Theodore Roosevelt, through Executive Orders 902 and 904, reorganized the administration of the southern Sierra. The divide between the Middle and South Forks of the Kings River became the boundary between the Sierra and Sequoia National Forests. By 1910, the two national forests were in control of their lands and resources. Tightly organized and adequately funded, the USFS brought grazing under permit and even succeeded in regulating existing resort villages in places such as Mineral King. By 1910, if one wanted to do something on the national forests, one had to ask permission, get a permit, and pay a fee.

WALTER FRY AND CIVILIAN PARKS' ADMINISTRATION

While the USFS perfected the purposes and goals of the Sierra and Sequoia National Forests, Sequoia and General Grant National Parks continued along a separate path, still guided by the legislation of 1890. Troops continued to arrive each summer through 1913 to guard the parks and supplement the small corps of permanent park rangers. During that last summer of military supervision, 3,823 persons entered Sequoia National Park. Of these, forty-one percent went up the Giant Forest Road, while another twenty-two percent entered via the Mineral King Road. Statistics show the state of transportation to the parks: fifty percent of all the parks' visitors entered on horse-drawn wagons, twenty-four percent on horseback, ten percent on foot, and six percent in an automobile, the parks having been opened to motor vehicles for the first time that year. During the same summer, General Grant National Park received 2,756 visitors.[60]

The army's departure after the 1913 season came as no surprise. Ever since the appointment of permanent civilian rangers, military officers assigned to the parks had recommended initiation of a completely civilian administration. By the spring of 1914, with the Mexican Revolution demanding military attention along the international boarder and the condition of the two parks fully regularized, it made sense to make the change. As the first full superintendent of Sequoia and General Grant National Parks (all the military officers had served only as "acting" superintendents), the Secretary of the Interior appointed Walter Fry, a ranger and long-time resident of Three Rivers who had been associated with the parks in one capacity or another since 1901.

Born in Illinois in 1859, Fry first heard of the Tulare County's sequoias while a youth of ten in Kansas. The stories he heard about the faraway place fascinated him, and, in 1887, after a series of setbacks, he resolved to come west and try his luck in the land of the Big Trees. Fry brought his family to Tulare County in March of that year, and, for much of the next decade, he worked in

Following the model established at Yellowstone National Park in 1886, U.S. Cavalry troops came to Sequoia and General Grant National Parks in the summer of 1891. They would return each summer through 1913, providing critical oversight to the parks in the years before the establishment of the National Park Service in 1916. Photographer and date unknown.

and around the city of Tulare, ten miles south of Visalia. His first exposure to the sequoias came during these years, when he worked for a month as a tree feller for the Smith Comstock Sawmill at Big Stump. When Fry discovered through tree-ring counting that one large tree he had helped destroy was at least 3,266 years old, he quit logging forever. Soon after this adventure, Fry met Hale Tharp in Visalia and learned of the Giant Forest. His first visit to this finest of sequoia groves changed his life. Fry's name was a prominent third on the 1890 petition from Tulare supporting the creation of national parks in Tulare County's mountains. In 1895, he relocated his family to a ranch three miles east of Three Rivers, close to the boundary of Sequoia National Park. In 1901, Fry obtained work on the army's Giant Forest road crew, and, during the next few years, he moved into the ranger ranks and finally to the position of chief ranger. When the army left, he was the logical person to take charge of the two parks. In his first summer as superintendent, Fry supervised a staff of three permanent and eight seasonal rangers in Sequoia and one full-time ranger at General Grant.

Like all other national park superintendents at that time, Fry reported directly to the Secretary of the Interior, a procedure that was growing more cumbersome as the number of national parks continued to grow.[61] A result of this casual organization was a large degree of inconsistent policy within the national park system, a situation that appeared increasingly unsatisfactory in contrast to the efficiency of the USFS. The creation of separate systems for national parks and national forests had occurred accidentally, mainly because Pinchot's Forest Service, with its utilitarian philosophies, found itself responsible for the forests but not the parks. Pinchot and his organization would have liked to merge the two systems, and USFS officials actually inspected Sequoia and General Grant National Parks at one point with that thought in mind. That this did not occur is the result of efforts by a group of men who were troubled by the management direction of the user-oriented USFS. Californians who knew the Sierra and its national parks played a critical role in this effort, including Interior Secretary Franklin Lane, a graduate of the University of California in Berkeley; Stephen T. Mather, another Cal grad who was a later member of the same fraternity there as Lane; and Mather's assistant, yet another Cal grad named Horace M. Albright.

THE SIERRA'S PARKS AND CREATION OF THE NATIONAL PARK SERVICE

The saga of the creation of the National Park Service (NPS) and Stephen T. Mather's influential role in establishing and directing it has been told many times, so it is not necessary to detail that story here. Sequoia did play a part in the campaign to create the NPS, however, and that part is worthy of brief summary, for it sheds light on the condition of the park itself. In the summer of 1915, hoping both to advance the ongoing campaign for a national park bureau and to give wider exposure to the beauties and potential of Sequoia National Park, Stephen T. Mather brought to Sequoia a party of twenty-five carefully chosen men. Among them were the head of the House Committee on Appropriations, the vice-president of the Southern Pacific Railroad, the president of the American Museum of Natural History in New York City, Chief of the U.S. Geological Survey, and the editor of *National Geographic Magazine*. For twelve days, at Mather's expense, the party traveled by pack train from the Giant Forest to Mt. Whitney and finally to Lone Pine. Along the way, they saw what Sequoia needed and what it could become. All came away convinced of the value of national parks, in general, and Sequoia, in particular. At the end of a second, similar high-country trip the following summer, Mather learned happily that President Woodrow Wilson had signed the National Park Service Act on August 25, 1916.[62]

That act, which created the NPS, had been drafted by Mather and his advisors such as Horace Albright to codify the national park concept in a way that separated the parks from the national forests. The new legislation made the difference clear:

> The Service thus established shall promote and regulate the use of the Federal areas known as national parks, monuments, and reservations hereinafter specified by such means and measures as conform to the fundamental purpose of said parks, monuments, and reservations, which purpose is to conserve the scenery and the natural and historic objects and the wild life therein and to provide for enjoyment of the same in such manner and by such means as will leave them unimpaired for the enjoyment of future generations.[63]

Critical to the national park concept that Mather and Albright held was a balance between the seemingly contradictory goals of resource preservation and visitor use. Preservation was the long-term goal they sought, but both felt strongly that visitor use must play an important role in the parks. As a result of this perspective, the creation of the NPS would lead to a period of unprecedented visitor development in Sequoia and General Grant National Parks.

THREE FORMATIVE DECADES

The creation of the National Park Service marked the final step in the federal assumption of control of the Sierra Nevada. When George Stewart and his allies first turned to the national government in 1890, they initiated a course that ultimately took control of the land away from Tulare County altogether. Sequoia and General Grant National Parks and the Sierra Forest Reserve had all been created in response to regional demand for better protection of mountain resources. No one intended initially that the two types of federal reservations would go forward forever in different directions, but ultimately they did. And no one intended that the reservations would cease to respond to local needs, but ultimately that is what happened. Just as surely as the creation of the USFS reduced the locals to permittees on national forest land, so creation of the NPS would move control of the two parks from local residents, subject to direction from Washington, D.C., but still in close touch with the community, to a new and professional bureaucracy. Initially created by the residents of Tulare County largely for their own ends, Sequoia and General Grant National Parks and the Sequoia National Forest were, by the end of 1916, truly national reservations, supported and controlled by the federal government.

During the thirty years between 1886, when the Kaweah Colony began constructing the Colony Mill Road, and 1916, when the NPS assumed responsibility for management of Sequoia and General Grant National Parks, the land-based resources of the southern Sierra underwent significant changes, mostly for the better. During the 1890s, just as local populations, technology, and transportation reached the critical mass necessary to allow the devastation of the region, an effort began to slow and limit that destruction. As a result, in the same decade when locals witnessed the destruction of Converse Basin, the largest natural Big Tree grove, they also saw creation of two national parks to preserve giant sequoias and the withdrawal of all remaining forest lands in the Sierra Nevada from sale.

The political decisions made in 1890 and 1905 about the southern Sierra led ultimately to land-management policies that ended the era of unlimited resource consumption. In Sequoia and General Grant National Parks, the primary goals of this effort were to prevent large-scale grazing and hunting and to control fire. Unregulated grazing in the parks took a decade to stamp out, but it was gone, except from some small inholdings, by the turn of the century. Nevertheless, residual scars marked the slopes and valleys. In the foothills, heavy grazing had destroyed native grasses, which had been replaced by annuals of Eurasian origins. In the high country near timberline, much of the vegetation was gone, leaving behind a landscape far more barren and stark than had existed before the late-nineteenth century. Fires also were not a problem in those early years, for, although it would not be understood for another fifty years, the unlimited burning during the late-nineteenth century had so thinned the Sierra's vegetation that it would be several decades before the fire hazard rose again. Early national park management affected wildlife, too. Although the prohibition against hunting gave many animals protection not found outside the parks, management also felt free to "improve" wildlife situations. Predators were often shot on sight, and trout were introduced into many previously barren streams. Early in the century, a well-intentioned if misguided attempt at wildlife preservation had even witnessed the introduction into Sequoia National Park of some of the last tule elk from the San Joaquin Valley, an attempt that was defeated by the inability of the prairie animals to adapt to life in the mountains.

Because the goals of the Sequoia and Sierra National Forests diverged from those of Sequoia and General Grant National Parks, different protection measures were undertaken in the forests. The USFS, for example, controlled but by no means eliminated grazing. In 1917, in the Great Western Divide country, the USFS administered more than a dozen grazing allotments, including several designed for sheep.[64] According to USFS policy, other consumptive activities, including logging, were appropriate forest uses, but, in reality, resource demand was not yet sufficient to justify much activity in these areas. The USFS suppressed fires aggressively and with increasing efficiency, and hunting and fishing regulation began in cooperation with the State of California.

In 1916, despite their widely divergent management policies, the biological systems of the national parks and national forests of the southern Sierra had not yet diverged significantly. In most places, the only real change along their shared physical boundaries was the transition from no grazing to regulated grazing or the shift from no hunting to low-intensity recreational hunting. In 1916, the parks were better protected than the lands of the surrounding national forests, but both types of lands were far better treated than they had been during the late-nineteenth century. Rational management by outside federal agents had come to the Sierra.

Moro Rock is a towering dome of granite, an igneous rock formed from magma that cooled and solidified beneath the surface. Weathering and erosion exposed it to the surface, and exfoliation began whereby sheets of material peeled off like layers of an onion. At an elevation of 6,725 feet, it provides outstanding views of the Great Western Divide of the Sierra Nevada to the east and, on clear days, more than 100 miles of the San Joaquin Valley and the Coast Ranges to the west. Photographer and date unknown.

CHAPTER FIVE

Selling Sequoia: The Early Park Service Years (1916–1931)

The founding of the National Park Service (NPS), in 1916, brought radical and immediate change to Sequoia and General Grant National Parks as well as the rest of the fledgling national park system. For the first time, this loose aggregate of land withdrawals had a unified and dedicated administration. For the first time, the two parks escaped the threat of a takeover by the U.S. Forest Service (USFS), with that agency's entrenched multiple-use policy in support of forestry, grazing, and other utilitarian activities. And, for the first time, a group of men zealously committed to preservation and the recreational use of parks would administer the parks.

The NPS, however, was young and politically weak, and the system of lands it inherited was insignificant compared to the USFS and its vast tracts. In addition, the NPS faced a complicated problem of blending two nearly incompatible purposes—recreational use and preservation of natural and cultural resources. These challenges demanded leaders who would be extraordinary in their vision, skills, and devotion. Upon their shoulders would fall the very future of the national park system. The decisions they made, the policies they adopted, and the infrastructure they approved would become a permanent legacy for the NPS's future.

From 1916 to 1931, the NPS would find four such leaders at the national level and in the two parks of the southern Sierra Nevada. Given the times, all were men: Stephen T. Mather, the first director of the NPS who ran the agency from 1916 to 1929; Horace M. Albright, his trustworthy assistant who became the second director during the years 1929 to 1933; Walter Fry, the first civilian superintendent of the two Sierra parks; and Colonel John White, the second, longest-tenured, and, ultimately, key park superintendent. During NPS's first decade and a half, these four men would define the parks' goals, establish patterns of "visitor use" and development, and create two administrations, national and local, that would guide the parks through the remainder of their history.

Among their tangible accomplishments at Sequoia and General Grant were elimination of nearly all private land holdings, especially in the Giant Forest; the enormous expansion of Sequoia National Park to near its present boundaries; establishment of a highly successful program in natural history that incorporated the now-familiar and popular campfire talks and ranger-led hikes; installation of a unified, monopolistic, and financially stable concessions company, with vastly improved and expanded infrastructure; and construction of nearly all the significant roads and trails found today in the two parks. Products of their time, these men favored development of parks for visitor use, and their greatest accomplishments lie in that realm. Yet it was also these remarkable leaders who first questioned the wisdom of such practices and who took the first tentative steps away from relentless tourism development and toward control or even elimination of some recreational activities and the construction necessary to promote them.[1]

Stephen Mather combined the rare and fortunate qualities of a preservationist philosophy, extraordinary dedication and ambition, and a considerable personal fortune garnered by mining borax in and around Death Valley. Horace Albright, his young second-in-command, matched that dedication and intelligent ability and added uncommon persuasive skills, particularly in the arena of Washington, D.C., politics. Upon the successful conclusion of the battle to create the NPS, the two men returned to the business of putting the system's house in order. For decades, the parks had suffered from a lack of purpose and a shallow, almost aimless philosophy of management. One of the earliest and most far-reaching accomplishments of Mather and Albright was firm establishment of a management philosophy for the national park system. They performed this through the curious but politically typical technique of personally composing a letter for Interior Secretary Franklin Lane that would, in turn, be sent to them, instructing them on the rules and practices of national park management.

Over the years, historians have argued about who wrote this letter: Mather or Albright? Albright maintained that he wrote the letter, basing it primarily on the ideas of Mather but also incorporating ideas from William Colby, Francis Farquhar, and Joseph LeConte, all of the Sierra Club, Gilbert Grosvenor, of the National Geographic Society, J. H. McFarland, of the American Civic Association, Robert Marshall, of the U.S. Geological Survey, and Robert Sterling Yard, of the National Parks Association. This cast of advisors gave the letter a considerable tilt toward preservation values, very much a minority opinion in those early NPS days. Mather and Lane both approved the document, which then reappeared on the director's desk dated May 13, 1918. It embodied "an outline of the administrative policy to which the new Service will adhere . . ." and has subsequently been called the "creed for the National Park Service."[2]

It was in this roundabout way that Secretary of the Interior Lane recommended three basic management principles to shape future park policy. First, "that the parks were to be preserved unimpaired for future generations," a restatement of the earlier congressional act; second, "that the parks were to be used for the observation, health and pleasure of the people;" and, third, "that the national interest must dictate all decisions affecting public or private enterprise in the parks." Because the statement of preservation preceded that of popular use in the letter, it has provided justification, during the ensuing decades, for administrative changes toward preservation and away from recreational use.

The letter went on to give twenty-three specific directives on various issues ranging from grazing permits to concession activities. The general tenor of the letter reflected the limited knowledge of ecology at the time but made a strong statement toward the preservation of objects and scenery, both still novelties in this recent frontier country. Cutting trees, grazing cattle, and constructing roads and buildings were to be permitted but only if these activities proved absolutely necessary and harmonized with the natural setting. Camping, concession operations, and automobile use were to be encouraged within the limits required for persistence of "natural conditions." Park rangers were to encourage educational use of the parks in every way, while allowing "appropriate" recreation. In addition, Lane's letter addressed issues of expansion of the national park system, maintenance of proper standards within each unit, acquisition of adjacent park-quality lands, and elimination of private inholdings within existing parks.[3]

At Sequoia and General Grant, the directives of Lane's letter were greeted by Superintendent Walter Fry as welcome confirmation of most existing practices and affirmation of ambitious and worthy goals. Since taking over the superintendency in 1914, Fry had established a reputation based on his knowledge of the two parks and his total dedication to their protection. Now, he skillfully implemented the new policies emerging out of Washington, D.C., and helped establish Sequoia and General Grant under the new NPS in those first few critical years. Fry's real love, however, lay not in administration but in the forests and among the wildlife of his park home. During his years in the parks, he had become obsessed with the study of nature, an obsession that would soon pay rich dividends for visitors. His opportunity came in 1920, when he was offered the position of U.S. Magistrate at Sequoia and, two years later, leadership of an incipient natural history program. At age sixty-one, Fry accepted the new challenges and, for the next two decades, helped build the nature-guide service at Sequoia, a program that became a model for other national parks.[4]

Mather, meanwhile, had been searching for a younger generation of men with "the right stuff" to operate the parks and carry out his philosophy. He found such a man for Sequoia and General Grant in Colonel John White, late of the Philippine Constabulary and, arguably, the most important individual in the history of the two parks. John Roberts White was born in England and attended Oxford University before joining the U.S. Army as a lowly private in 1899. Assigned to the U.S. garrison trying to pacify the Philippines, White soon found himself a colonel in the Philippine Constabulary, commanding a small army of Filipino soldiers with distinction during the guerrilla war in that turbulent place. In the process, White contracted malaria and tuberculosis, which forced his retirement. Nevertheless, he rejoined the U.S. Army during World War I and rose again to the rank of colonel while serving in Europe. In 1919, he retired again from the military, and, looking for outdoors work that would maximize his administrative talent as well as restore his health, White stumbled across Albright and Arno Cammerer, who would become the second and third directors of the NPS. Although Albright had nothing available that he thought proper for a colonel, White persisted, until Albright offered him a position as a ranger at the newly established Grand Canyon National Park in Arizona. Within a year, White assumed the superintendency of Sequoia, the second oldest of America's extant national parks.[5]

In White, Mather had a man committed to the principles of nature appreciation, preservation of the parks' resources, and encouragement of visitor use and education—ideas the director himself espoused. With Mather and Albright directing policy from Washington, D.C., White tirelessly operating his benign dictatorship within the two parks, beloved Walter Fry building one of the nation's great natural history and public interpretation programs, and a codified creed of policies and philosophical tenets, Sequoia and General Grant entered a new era of development and popularity and a new level of debate over the two purposes for which they and the youthful agency were founded: use versus preservation.

USE: GAINING PARK TERRITORY FROM WITHIN AND WITHOUT

One of the first problems that Director Mather and his staff tackled in Sequoia and General Grant was acquiring privately held lands within the two parks. From the earliest days of the military administration, superintendents and civilian officials had pleaded with the U.S. Congress to appropriate money for the purchase of these lands, which included many of the finest tracts of meadows in the sequoia belt. Indeed, the options Captain Young had obtained in 1903 on all 3,877 acres held in the parks were for a paltry $73,000 or $19.00 an acre. Not until 1916 did Congress finally appropriate $50,000 to buy just 670 acres in the Giant Forest owned by two Tulare County ranchers. Unfortunately, this appropriation still fell well short of the ranchers' $70,000 asking price. Here, Mather's great personal skill and persuasive ability combined to carry the day. The director appealed to friend Gilbert Grosvenor and his National Geographic Society for the remainder and was rewarded with a well-publicized $20,000 donation in November 1916. Once the purchase of this important tract of the Giant Forest was complete, the first for any national park using a congressional allocation, Mather turned his attention and his own personal fortune to other plots. From 1919 to 1927, the NPS acquired another 2,166 acres, relying heavily on contributions from the National Geographic Society, Tulare County Board of Trade, wealthy industrialists such as George Eastman, and Mather himself, who spent more than $55,000.

In addition to buying and donating lands within the two parks, Mather was instrumental in obtaining title to Redwood, Wet, and Funston meadows outside Sequoia but within the area to be included in a hoped-for park expansion. The Sierra Club and its directors held title to

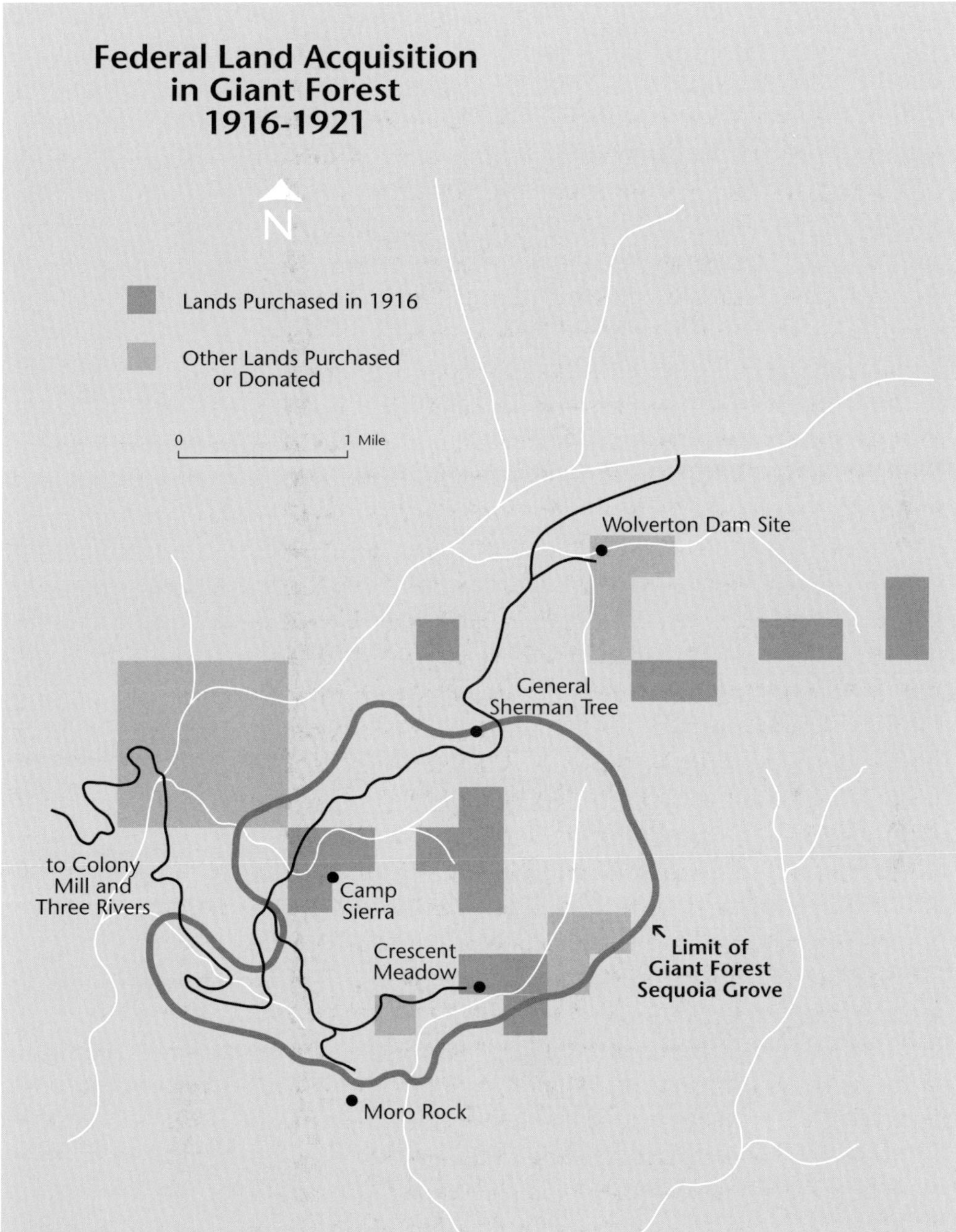

Federal Land Acquisition in Giant Forest 1916-1921
N
Lands Purchased in 1916
Other Lands Purchased or Donated
0
1 Mile
Wolverton Dam Site
General Sherman Tree
to Colony Mill and Three Rivers
Camp Sierra
Crescent Meadow
Limit of Giant Forest Sequoia Grove
Moro Rock

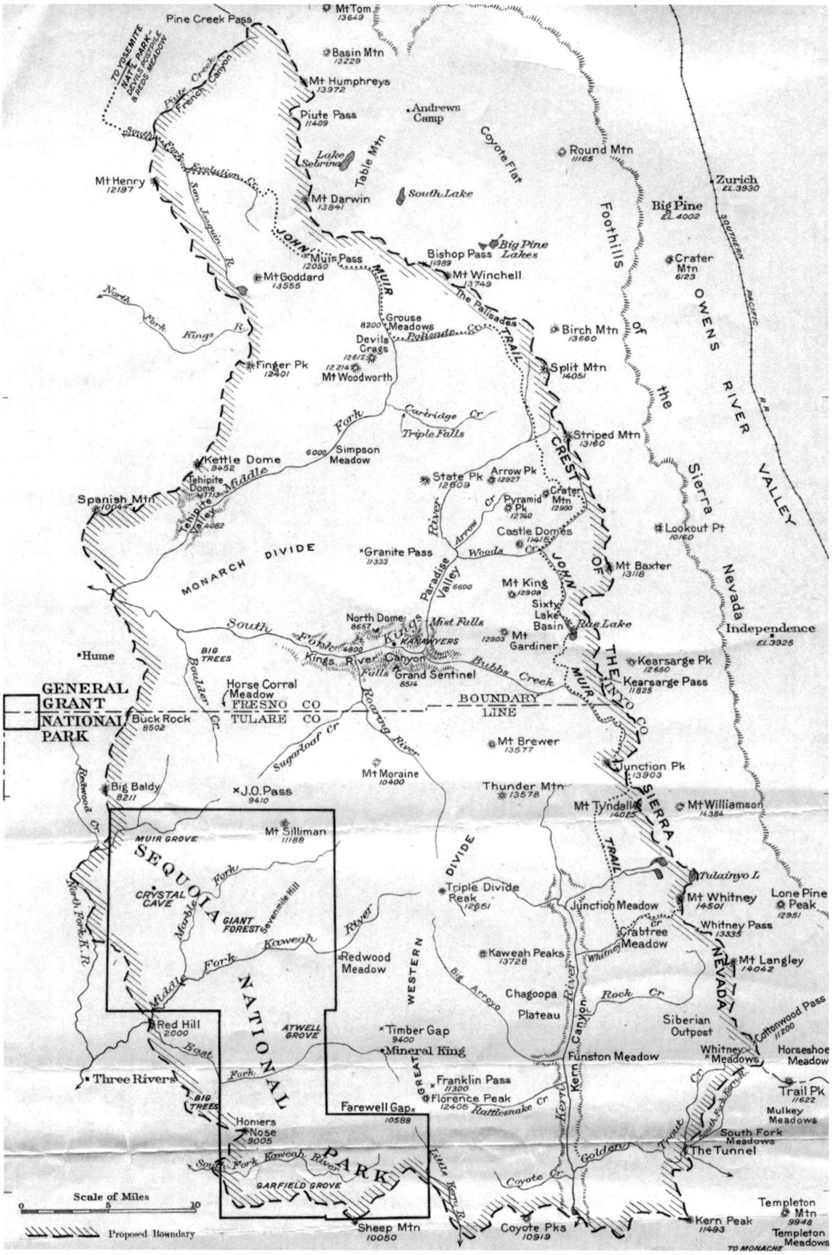

Sequoia National Park was considered one of the "crown jewel" parks when the U.S. Congress established the National Park Service on August 25, 1916. Director Stephen Mather and others soon urged enlargement of the park to encompass the crest of the Sierra Nevada as well as much of the Kings River drainage. This National Park Service map of 1919 shows the two 1890 parks and the proposed boundary for a much larger Roosevelt-Sequoia National Park.

the land until 1926 when Sequoia was enlarged to include the area surrounding these choice meadows and sequoia groves. During this period, the National Geographic Society and the Save-the-Redwoods League provided the beneficial publicity that encouraged landowners to maintain or even depress their prices until Mather, his friends, and the government could gather the funds. During the decade, the Giant Forest was entirely freed of private lands, and many other popular visitor areas also came into the fold. Southern California Edison donated outright its large holding at Wolverton Meadow, which it had absorbed along with the remainder of the Mt. Whitney Power Company's assets. The only piece of highly desirable private land the government failed to get was a 160-acre plot in General Grant that was developed for summer cabins, beginning in 1919. That private enclave still exists today as Wilsonia Village in Grant Grove, near the park's visitor complex.[6]

As Mather and his wealthy associates endeavored to eliminate private holdings from the two parks, a much larger and more important battle swirled around the floors of Congress and the meeting rooms of local businessmen and preservationists. Since the establishment of the parks in 1890, successive superintendents and secretaries of the Department of the Interior, prodded by preservationists, had campaigned for enlargement of Sequoia to include the majestic high country to the east. Indeed, for years it was confidently expected that the new additions would be forthcoming momentarily. But proponents of the park underestimated the variety and numbers of anti-park forces. Local farmers, cattlemen, timber interests, and even advocates of recreation were leery of NPS control and the restrictions that would inevitably be placed on commercial and personal activities. The USFS, on the other hand, imposed few limitations on mining, lumbering, summer cabins, or even reclamation projects. It was the preferred agency among those who stood either to benefit from the tangible resources of the region or to lose upon their withdrawal for preservation. Not incidentally, USFS men lost no opportunity to foster this attitude and cling to their territory against what they perceived as aggressive land grabbing by the new NPS.

The principal problem in the initial proposals by Mather and other park backers was the magnitude of their suggested enlargement. Sequoia National Park contained 252 square miles of woodland, meadows, and chaparral. Under the proposals offered from 1916 to 1919, a new Roosevelt-Sequoia National Park would contain more than five times that much land, encompassing the Kern River drainage south to Coyote and Kern peaks, the South and Middle Forks of the Kings River westward nearly to the General Grant area, and part of the San Joaquin drainage in and around Evolution Valley. (The Roosevelt portion of the name came from attempts to make the enlarged park a memorial to Theodore Roosevelt.) The component of this huge proposed park that presented the greatest controversy was the Kings River drainage, which we review in depth in Chapter Seven. Another area of contention was the Mineral King Valley, where dozens of private cabins formed a popular summer recreation zone for residents of the San Joaquin

Valley. Still another problem arose from the potential commercial timberlands on the western and southern edges of the proposed park. Indeed, lumbermen and the USFS were already casting covetous eyes on the timber resources of the southernmost and rarely visited portion of the existing park.

Mather initiated efforts to enlarge the park immediately upon his appointment as the director of the new NPS, and he engaged in a series of meetings with Chief Foresters Henry Graves and William Greeley aimed at hammering out some sort of compromise. Both Forest Service men drove hard bargains, but, in 1921, it seemed that a solution was imminent. Mather agreed to sacrifice the three southern townships of the existing park, the same area that had first inspired George Stewart to work for creation of the park, as well as the J. O. Pass area of the proposed parkland. Greeley looked forward to receiving these valuable timberlands within the park, in exchange for a huge tract of worthless rockland. Accordingly, local Congressman Henry Barbour, who had earlier opposed any notion of park expansion, introduced the compromise bill to Congress. Unfortunately, proponents of irrigation had not been consulted in these negotiations, and they sent up a crescendo of opposition to withdrawal of the Kings River area. In addition, an assistant curator of the American Museum of Natural History, one Willard Van Name, flooded the media and Congress with letters and bulletins opposing exclusion of any portion of the existing park. Proposed exclusions included the Garfield Grove of giant sequoias, one of the finest and largest groves, as well as Hockett Meadow, an area that was far more popular for visitors during the early years of the park than it is today. Van Name vilified the USFS as greedy and unprincipled and saved enough anger to accuse the NPS of irresponsible dereliction of its duty. The combined outrage of these dissimilar opponents crushed the Barbour Bill and delayed the park's enlargement for nearly five years.

Immediately, Mather, Albright, and White took up the negotiations again. After some years of delicate discussion, it became apparent that the Kings River addition was simply too embroiled in controversy and counterclaims to be acquired. Likewise, the Mineral King Valley drew too much antagonism and presented too much of an administrative headache. Hence, in early 1926, Mather, the Sierra Club, USFS, and most proponents of irrigation agreed to a compromise bill that would expand Sequoia National Park to include the Kern River drainage and readjust the park's northern boundary to follow the divide between the Kaweah and Kings watersheds. On July 3, 1926, President Calvin Coolidge signed the bill, which increased the park's acreage by 140 percent to 604 square miles. The bill also designated twenty-five square miles in the Mineral King area as the "Sequoia National Game Refuge" but left that area under the USFS's control; this was meant to protect the wildlife in the area, which moved freely in and out of the surrounding park. The loss of the Kings River country was a particularly bitter pill for the park men, and Min-

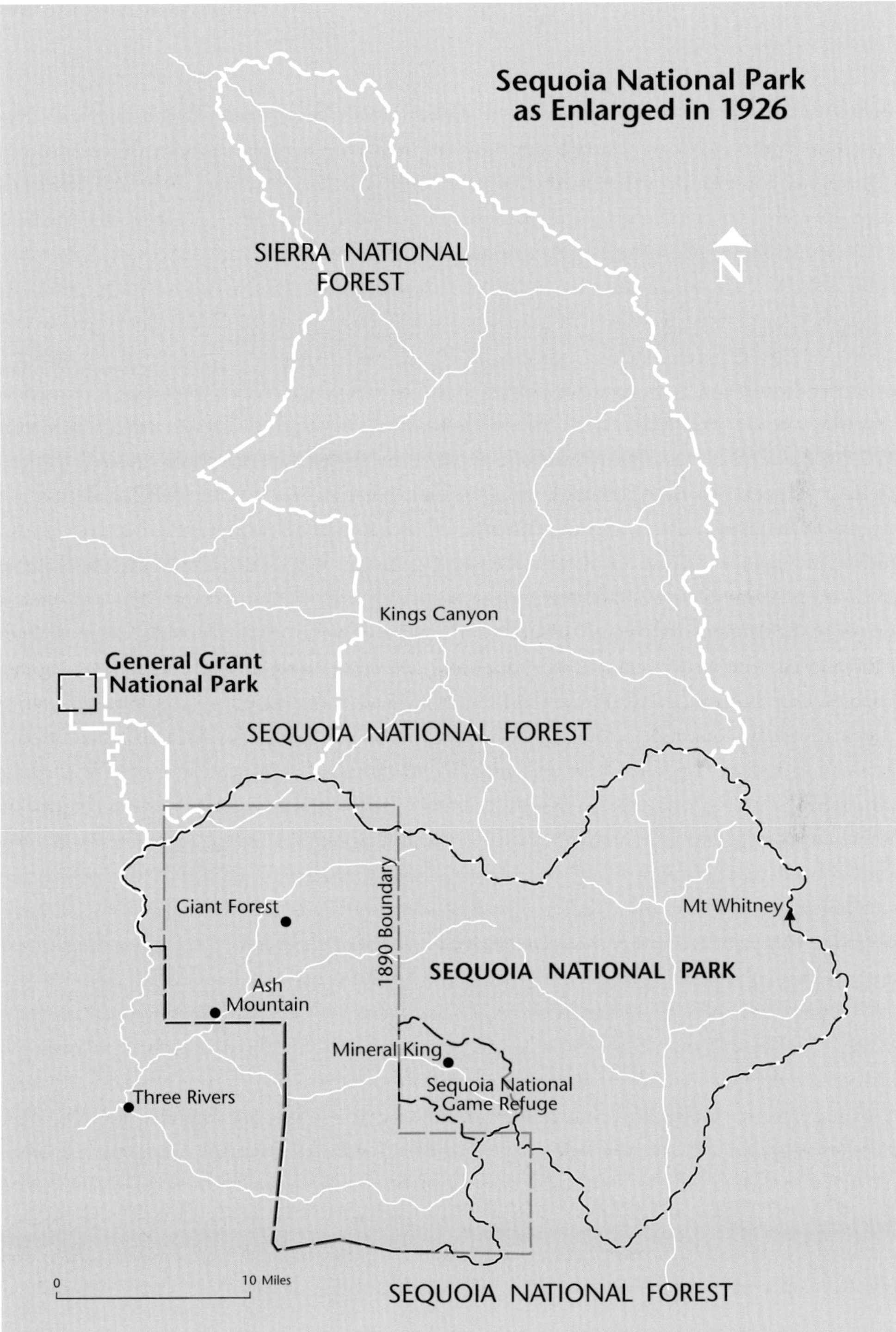
Sequoia National Park
as Enlarged in 1926
N
SIERRA NATIONAL
FOREST
Kings Canyon
General Grant
National Park
SEQUOIA NATIONAL FOREST
1890 Boundary
Giant Forest
Mt Whitney
SEQUOIA NATIONAL PARK
Ash
Mountain
Mineral King
Sequoia National
Game Refuge
Three Rivers
0
10 Miles
SEQUOIA NATIONAL FOREST

eral King remained like a knife of potential development plunged into the southern boundary. Nevertheless, the 1926 act retained the southern townships, for which Van Name had campaigned, and added a vast and magnificent new area to the park. Assistant Superintendent Dan Tobin later wrote gleefully that the addition made Sequoia not only the "biggest tree" national park, but also the "biggest mountain" national park as well.[7]

USE: PUBLICITY AND THE NATURAL HISTORY PROGRAM

For nearly thirty years, Sequoia and General Grant National Parks had offered visitors the chance to see the largest living things on Earth and some of the most spectacular scenery in the world. Yet a combination of insufficient publicity and the towering shadow of their famous neighbor, Yosemite, left the two in relative obscurity. Mather, Albright, and White shared the view that this was an unfortunate, even intolerable state of affairs. One reason for their dismay certainly arose from Mather's realistic appraisal of his agency's future. Without a massive display of public sympathy for each park as well as the system in general, the NPS and some of its parks might not survive. This survival instinct, however, was not the only motive for the pro-tourism attitude of the director and his top assistants. Mather and Albright, both businessmen at heart, saw the parks as good and proper places for public recreation and for the establishment of a tourism infrastructure to foster and profit from that activity. Secretary Lane's policy letter was replete with instructions for operations by concessions and camping privileges. It ordered that "every opportunity should be afforded to the public, wherever possible, to enjoy the national parks in the manner that best satisfies individual tastes."[8] And Colonel White's early annual reports were filled with recommendations for tourism developments and pleas for the money to build them.

One of the best ways to protect the parks was by public use, and the best way to encourage public use was via publicity. Mather encouraged articles in high-profile magazines such as *The Saturday Evening Post* and *National Geographic,* and he and Albright made the convention circuit rounds and filled the radio waves with enthusiastic invitations to visit the national parks. At Sequoia and General Grant, the NPS, in 1916, released a slick, forty-seven-page information booklet that became a model for later guides to the two parks. Of greater significance, *National Geographic* published a lengthy and well-illustrated article on Sequoia, bringing the "Big Trees" to the attention of millions. Meanwhile, Colonel White visited state and local newspaper offices and attended various business and social affairs to publicize his two parks. The Automobile Club of Southern California helped by printing a series of popular maps, brochures, and advertisements, while railroads, towns in the San Joaquin Valley, and the State of California added their efforts to the publicity campaign.[9]

Once visitors began arriving in ever-increasing numbers, the question became one of controlling the amusements and pursuits they sought. To the minds of Mather and White, the proper technique was to offer visitor activities consistent with the high moral and intellectual opportunities available in the sublime setting. White, in particular, was loath to regulate or control visitors, an ironic position considering his later stance on such matters. He much preferred the carrot of education and spiritual enrichment in the parks to the stick of rules and enforced limitations. To educate the public, a program was necessary whereby trained park officials could demonstrate the fascinating natural processes and fragile complexities that nature offered. Museums, nature hikes, occasional lectures, and an entire program to "interpret" the natural world were necessary. Mather initiated the scheme by encouraging Dr. C. M. Goethe to conduct nature walks and campfire talks in Yosemite during the summer of 1920. The reaction was so positive that, before the year was over, Mather had directed that each national park should have a trained naturalist on staff and a similar program in operation.[10]

In Sequoia, funding problems and many other needs delayed implementation of Mather's order another two years. But, in 1922, White turned to the man whose expertise and enthusiasm for investigating and explaining the natural world of Sequoia and General Grant were already almost legendary—Judge Walter Fry. In his new position as U.S. Magistrate, Fry found himself with a good deal of time on his hands. During the summer of 1922, he tried a total of twelve cases in his park's court, most of which took only a few hours to conduct. Hence, he was free to initiate the Sequoia Nature Guide Service. On his first guided walk in late June, Fry took twenty-seven visitors on a wildflower walk and promptly identified sixty-seven different flowers.

In addition to developing programs with direct contact with visitors, Fry also began collecting assorted specimens of the parks' wildlife and vegetation. Initially, the collection was housed in the new administrative center in the Giant Forest, but, within a year, Colonel White was forced to order construction of a two-room tent museum adjacent to the building for Fry's rapidly expanding collection. By 1925, more than 400 floral specimens had been mounted for public viewing and reference. The growth of the museum was so steady that, by 1926, White reported the collection had taken over the entire Giant Forest administration building, which fortunately had been freed by completion of a new administrative building at Ash Mountain. Mrs. White and her friends waged a constant fund-raising effort to support the museum and employ an attendant.

By 1926, Walter Fry's advancing age plus the ever-growing popularity of the nature-guide program compelled the recruitment of three new naturalists with money from the volunteer museum's fund. During that season, more than 1,200 people attended nature walks, and almost 18,000 heard the nightly campfire programs. Fry, meanwhile, continued to publish an extraordinarily

The development of ranger-guided walks to educate visitors "properly" began during the early 1920s and immediately became extremely popular. One of the most desirable walks accessed Moro Rock, where workers replaced an earlier wooden structure with nearly 800 feet of steps carved into the granite in 1931. Landscape architect Merel Sager and engineer Frank Diehl designed the new stairway to blend into the natural scenery. Photographer and date unknown.

popular series of pamphlets called "Nature Notes." The naturalist program had matured to the point where its benefits and popularity now exceeded even the predictions of White and Mather. In his 1926 annual report, Colonel White wrote:

> The expansion of museum, nature walks and campfire lectures is the surest protection against degeneracy into jazzy amusements. If we do not lead the public into amusements and sports which harmonize with the purposes of the park, we must not be surprised if the public and the operators clamor for an atmosphere which may be eventually destructive of the policy of maintaining the parks in absolutely unimpaired form for the use of future generations as well as those of our own time.[11]

White now realized that a more permanent naturalist program was needed in the parks. The importance of the program was fully proven, but volunteer efforts could not continue to meet increasing demand. During the summer of 1927, the concession company hired its own naturalist and specialist on Indians, Herbert Wilson, to supplement the NPS's effort, but even this addition proved insufficient. More than 3,500 visitors attended Wilson's walks alone. It was clearly time to expand the operation and bring it into the park's regular budget.

White now put his considerable political skills to work. Claiming private funds were no longer adequate to operate the nature-guide service, he allowed the effort to lapse in 1928. Only Wilson, of the concession company, continued to provide interpretation for visitors. White's motives for allowing the nature-guide service to expire can only be surmised from the modern perspective. If, by allowing the program to die, he was trying to force the Washington, D.C., office to begin regular support of a naturalist program in Sequoia, he succeeded. The 1929 budget provided funds for employment of a permanent park naturalist. The superintendent hired Frank Been for the new position before the summer season commenced.

Placing a permanent park employee into a full-time, nature-guide position brought new life to the naturalist program. Been's first summer in Sequoia was a busy one. Before the season had ended, he had taken more than 5,000 visitors on guided walks and presented campfire lectures to 66,000. These results so gratified White that he transferred a seasonal ranger from the regular ranger force to Been for the summer. Meanwhile, he continued his lobbying efforts and, in 1931, succeeded in bringing the entire naturalist program into the regular operating budget of the parks. During that year, White hired two seasonal ranger-naturalists, Walter Powell and Walter Van Deest, to replace the borrowed ranger, and he besieged Director Albright for another full-time position. With the opening of a new campfire circle at Lodgepole to supplement the one in the Giant Forest, the naturalist program in Sequoia alone consisted, in 1931, of two nature walks and two campfire programs every day of the season. The program for nature education of visitors had arrived, and the most familiar and positive image that most visitors have of national parks—the friendly and informative ranger at the campfire and on guided walks—was firmly fixed in the public's mind.[12]

It is, of course, difficult to gauge the effect of the nature-guide program except by its popularity. This experiment in public relations—cautiously suggested by Mather, enthusiastically promoted in Sequoia by White, and begun by the sage and grandfatherly Walter Fry—met unhindered success and an almost feverish demand from visitors. As attendance swelled, most tourists came to regard the walks, talks, and museum displays as the most obvious and appropriate functions of national parks. Those visitors, likewise, cannot have failed to adapt to the messages contained in the rangers' words. In the nature-guide program, which now exists as the service-wide Interpretation and Education Division, the NPS molded public attitude about what parks are, what they could and should become, and how their preservation and maintenance is a sacred trust of the present generation for the future.

USE: BUILDING FOR THE PEOPLE

Many accomplishments characterized the first fifteen years of the NPS in Sequoia and General Grant, including an eightfold increase in visitation, establishment of resource-management and interpretation programs, and the enormous popularization of the two parks among the general public. But of all the accomplishments of Mather, Albright, and White, perhaps the most significant and ostensible was the vast development of public infrastructure. From 1916 to 1931, the parks' administrators extensively enlarged and altered both the road and trail systems, built a substantial complex of government facilities for public and employee use, and installed an aggressive and competent concession monopoly to cater to the burgeoning tourist market. In the process, they also developed virtually all the parks' areas and many of the facilities still in use today, and they firmly entrenched a set of procedures and activities as proper and traditional in the minds of both the public and the concessioner. So successful were they that, within a few years, they began to have doubts about their own policies and the effects of those policies on the fragile parks environment.

Roads and Trails

The U.S. Army's completion of the Colony Mill Road to the Giant Forest, in 1903, was a banner event for Sequoia, because it opened the park to the common traveler for the first time. Almost from the day of its completion, however, engineers, park rangers, and visitors commented on the need for a replacement road that would provide a gentler grade and wider, more sweeping turns. With the advent of regular automobile traffic shortly before the founding of the NPS, such suggestions became demands. The Colony Mill Road wound tightly up precipitous slopes at a steady grade of about ten percent, far too narrow and steep for the substantial traffic expected in the upcoming years. A potential solution was provided by the Mt. Whitney Power Company's road along the Middle Fork of the Kaweah River, which extended nearly seven miles up the canyon toward the Giant Forest. As a mechanism for implementing Mather's program of increased visitor use, a new highway into Sequoia National Park became the first and foremost priority, the lifeline by which all else would hang.[13]

During his visit to Sequoia in 1918, Director Mather saw firsthand the limitations of the Colony Mill Road. The bumpy, grinding, dusty trip frustrated the director, who envisioned the tangle that would inevitably result from a summer weekend's traffic. Accordingly, he ordered a survey of an additional road to be undertaken and bids for construction to be accepted by Superintendent Fry. An engineer by the name of Peters completed a preliminary survey from the power company's road terminus at Hospital Rock up over Deer Ridge to the Giant Forest, and a contractor in Fresno agreed to undertake the job. Unfortunately, the funds for construction of a road over this "Peter's Survey" route, estimated at $300,000, remained unavailable for a few years, while Congress contemplated the project's worth.[14]

The delay in construction gave Mather and new Superintendent White an opportunity to review the project and its implications. In the original plans, the new highway would supplement rather than replace the Colony Mill Road. The one-lane power company road would continue as a one-way road into the park, while the old road would furnish a lane for outgoing traffic. Ironically, this concept would reappear repeatedly, as the parks' planners struggled to control traffic and protect the parks' atmosphere. After considerable discussion and consultation, the parks' officials decided to construct a two-lane road up the new route and abandon the old road, due to the high expense of maintaining both.[15]

Meanwhile, a decade-old scheme known as the Park-to-Park Highway steamrolled onto the scene and into the planning. This scheme had been a popular notion among businessmen, publishers, and others who urged the public to "See America First." The idea was to build a network of roads connecting the national parks, upon which Americans and, presumably, Europeans could travel from one spectacular attraction to another. A well-developed road connection from Sequoia to General Grant had been an early and obvious link in this planned scenic chain. By 1920, the idea was being seriously considered as an extension of the road project from Hospital Rock to the Giant Forest. Two years later, the NPS secured the USFS's approval and commitments of funds from the affected counties and state. The "Generals Highway" project was born. Vastly improved

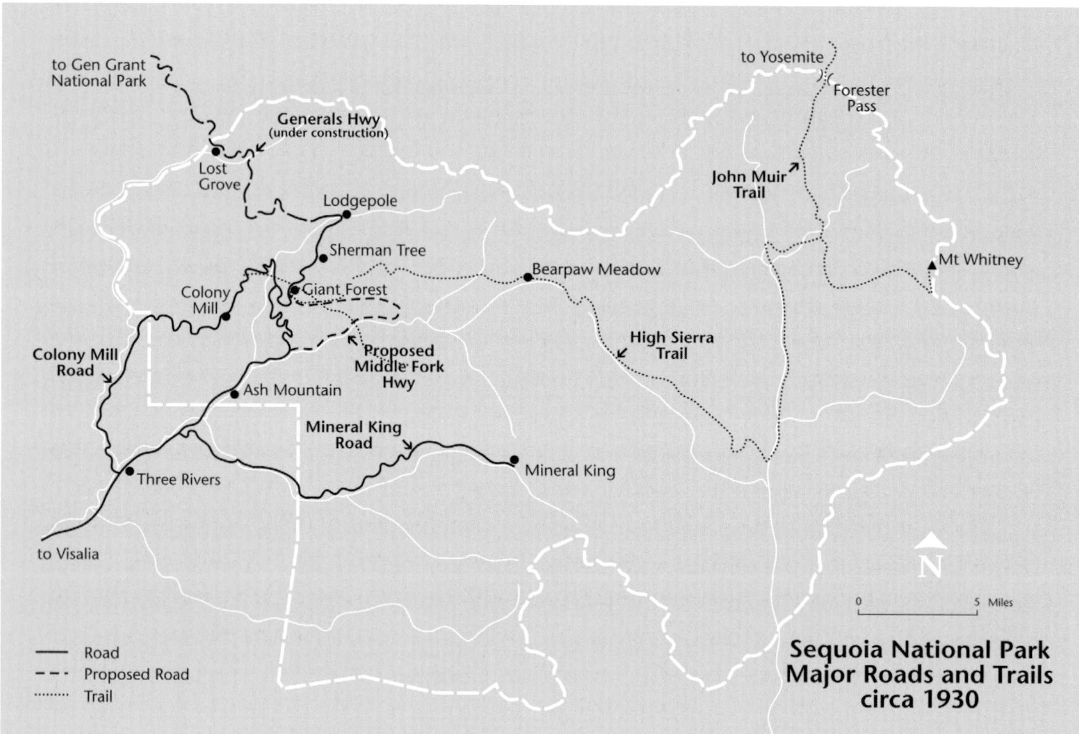

to Gen Grant
National Park
Generals Hwy
(under construction)
Lost
Grove
Lodgepole
Sherman Tree
Giant Forest
Colony
Mill
Colony Mill
Road
Proposed
Middle Fork
Hwy
Ash Mountain
Mineral King
Road
Mineral King
Three Rivers
to Visalia
Bearpaw Meadow
High Sierra
Trail
to Yosemite
Forester
Pass
John Muir
Trail
Mt Whitney
N
0
5 Miles
Road
Proposed Road
Trail
Sequoia National Park
Major Roads and Trails
circa 1930

access roads from Visalia and Fresno to the new parks had recently been promised, and the vision of a comfortable, scenic loop through the spectacular mountain country sparkled in the mind's eyes of the NPS, USFS, and local business representatives. The road would connect the General Sherman Tree with the General Grant Tree and allow visitors to cruise comfortably up to 7,000 feet and through both parks in a day. Work began in 1922, with a total projected cost, including expansion of the existing Mt. Whitney Road and construction of the portion from Hospital Rock to General Grant National Park, of slightly more than $400,000.[16]

In July 1926, the highway opened from Ash Mountain, where a new administrative center had been constructed two years earlier on the bluffs above the Middle Fork of the Kaweah River, to the Giant Forest. The road entered the Giant Forest's plateau from the west near Beetle Rock and proceeded northeasterly toward the General Sherman Tree and the future site of Lodgepole. The new Generals Highway passed through the heart of the old development area in the Giant Forest and necessitated a redesign of the entire area. A few months later, after assumption of the duties and facilities, the new concessioner, Sequoia and General Grant National Parks Company, ceremoniously and literally picked up its stores and dining facilities and moved them from the old site near Round Meadow to a new site on the eastern side of the road across from Beetle Rock. The new location and its facilities became known as Giant Forest Village and would later become the focus of intense efforts by the NPS to remove concession buildings and their respective functions from the Giant Forest.[17]

With completion of the all-important Ash Mountain-to-Giant Forest segment, attention was turned to the slowly progressing connection between the two parks. Blasting and grinding through the rock and cliffs of the seasonally snowbound Forest Service territory came the road builders from General Grant. Northward from the Giant Forest and past the huge General Sherman Tree and the newly developed camping area at Lodgepole came the Sequoia contractors. North of Lodgepole, the builders encountered a series of creeks that demanded expensive bridges—Wolverton, Silliman, Clover, and Suwanee as well as a large one at Lodgepole. The work was slow, and one contractor went bankrupt trying to complete the bridges. Another, the Bechtel Company, devoted some ninety-five men to the project in a desperate attempt to stay on schedule, but, by summer of 1931, they still struggled to finish. Bechtel lost heavily on the job, as did the subcontractors employed for bridge approaches and other related tasks.[18]

The reason for the slowness of work and consequent construction troubles came partly from the quality control exercised by the NPS's landscape architects. The 1920s and 1930s marked the apogee of landscape architecture as a determinant of NPS policy, design schemes, and development. With every decision to build came a studied effort to blend the features into the surrounding environment—to look rustic, scenic, and "appropriate." One of the results of this attitude of preserving scenery was the defeat of a plan to build a large and elaborate hotel, like Yosemite's

Ahwahnee, near Beetle Rock. Instead, the NPS approved a scattering of tiny cabins and tent-tops. Another impact was a set of stringent specifications for the Generals Highway and its bridges. Arches and supports of carefully cut and molded stone pleased the eye and suggested a rustic coordination with the rocky streambeds and towering cliffs nearby. They also called for back-breaking and expensive labor. Bechtel and the other companies suffered from drastic employee turnover that slowed the job even further and exacerbated the cost overrun.[19]

Nevertheless, the job continued. By October 1931, most of the heavy bridge work was concluded, and the contractors faced the easier task of pushing the road ahead to connect the two parks. Four years later, on July 23, 1935, at Stony Creek on USFS land, the Generals Highway was dedicated. It had cost $2,250,000, more than five times the original estimate, yet it provided one of the finest, most scenic highways in mountain America. With its completion, the NPS and the public realized their long-held dreams of a loop road through both parks. Sequoia and General Grant were more firmly bonded together than ever before. The Generals Highway marked the most important piece of road building in the history of the parks, and it continues to be the primary artery of visitor circulation today.[20]

Ironically, even before the construction of Generals Highway began, engineers from the federal Bureau of Public Roads began to consider alternate routes from Hospital Rock to the Giant Forest. Although the new highway would be a vast improvement over the Colony Mill Road, it still required many tight turns and a grade that occasionally exceeded eight percent. From an engineering standpoint, there was another, far superior route available. In 1920, NPS civil engineer George Goodwin proposed that an access road extend far up the canyon of the Middle Fork of the Kaweah River, make one turn back, and proceed along the plateau to enter the Giant Forest from the east. Such a road could avoid hairpin turns and progress at an easy grade to Panther Creek or, perhaps, even as far as Redwood Meadow before executing its 180-degree turn back to the Giant Forest. Goodwin pointed out that this extension well into the roadless backcountry could later be continued over the Great Western Divide and into the Kern River country.[21]

Initially, both Mather and White looked favorably upon this project. Yet there were problems with the route, chief among them the price. This much longer road would cost at least twice as much as the "Peters' Survey" route, and, for that reason, Mather advised Visalia businessmen, in 1921, that the shorter and steeper route would be constructed first and the longer road postponed until more funds became available. For a time, this decision quelled the calls for a "Middle Fork" route, yet it was by no means out of the minds of road engineers and local businessmen who saw any improvement and extension of access as a potential moneymaker. In March 1927, the topic again surfaced among NPS engineers who had had a full season to watch more than 10,400 cars weave up the Generals Highway to the Giant Forest.[22]

In the intervening years, however, Colonel White had studied the proposed new route and found some serious flaws in the proposal and its potential results. After seven summer seasons in the parks, the superintendent had become quite proprietary and had modified his views principally toward those of the landscape architects with whom he worked. He saw three reasons why the Middle Fork Road should not be built. First, it would cost at least $2,000,000, money that was needed on the connection from the Giant Forest to General Grant as well as other roads and projects in the parks. Second, it would necessitate a complete reordering of the road pattern and redistribution of structures on the Giant Forest's plateau and create a good deal of traffic congestion. Third and ultimately most important, the Middle Fork Road would be a visible scar running smack across the vista from the park's major overlook at Moro Rock. As a footnote, White questioned the wisdom of extending a road that far into the backcountry, where hitherto only trails interrupted the sublime wilderness experience available to visitors.[23]

With such extensive and ardent opposition by the superintendent, any project would seem to be doomed immediately. At this time, however, Stephen Mather, in ill health and distracted by other problems and responsibilities, retired and passed the directorship to Horace Albright, his longtime friend and associate. The new director was, if anything, more committed to paving the way, literally and figuratively, for vastly increased visitor use in the national parks. Evidence of his lifetime commitment to the notion of "parks for people" is abundant. He maintained his philosophy long after the NPS had evolved toward preservation and stricter control of visitor use.[24] Albright had regarded the Generals Highway up the "Peters' Survey" route as insufficient and potentially dangerous from the start, and he was no happier with it when, as director, the Middle Fork proposal resurfaced.

Here began the first sparks in what was to become an emotional clash of wills between a strong, passionate, and even dictatorial superintendent and his equally resolute boss. At one point, Albright in disgust referred to the new Generals Highway as a "rathole," an incident and term that deeply offended Colonel White.[25] For years afterward, White brought up the remark when any reference to the road was made and long after serious discussion of the Middle Fork alternative ceased. The conflict, which fortunately never fatally harmed the friendship the two men shared, later spread to a variety of other development issues, particularly in the Giant Forest.[26]

In the case of the Middle Fork Road, the questions of scenic disruption and the rising cost of such a project continued to stall any decision. NPS engineer Frank Kittredge, a future NPS regional director, repeatedly resurrected the notion but could not overcome the twin fears of scenic injury and expense.[27] White, in a letter to Francis Farquhar, of the Sierra Club, dismissed the ideas of engineers: "I have the highest regard for Frank Kittredge, but in dealing with engineers you must not always follow their tangents of thought. They deal so much with tangents on roads that they sometimes think along the same lines."[28]

In the end, White outlasted the opposition and even convinced Albright, after his retirement, to join in opposing the Middle Fork Road. What convinced most NPS administrators was the continued success of the Generals Highway. By 1931, it carried up to 2,000 cars on some summer days. A few years later, the road remained open throughout the winter with no problems. By the mid-1930s, the Generals Highway, including the "Peters' Survey," had proven itself. Agitation for alternative routing faded to a murmur from discontented engineers.[29]

In addition to the Generals Highway, several shorter but important public roads and a network of rough fire roads also commanded the NPS's attention from 1916 to 1931. One of the first to be constructed was a road from Wolverton to what came to be known as Lodgepole. Completed in 1917, the road proved useful later, when the government turned to Lodgepole as an alternate site for both public and concession development.[30] Another important road developed along the old horse trail from Moro Rock to Crescent Meadow. Here, the NPS met some resistance from the Sierra Club, which conducted some of its popular summer camps at Crescent Meadow and opposed opening the area to auto traffic. After construction and oiling of the route was completed during the mid-1920s, the NPS found the road so popular that a tangle of parked cars crowded up to the very base of Moro Rock. For a while, NPS engineers and Colonel White considered a loop road that would bring drivers past Moro Rock, around Crescent Meadow, and back to the Giant Forest via Bear Hill, where another road had been constructed to the garbage incinerator and bear show. After further reflection, White blocked the plans because of the potential damage to the scenery and serenity of protected areas of sequoias.[31]

While the NPS designed, developed, and oiled public roads and access to campgrounds, it also vigorously extended the trail system, especially after the park's expansion in 1926. Where the Sierra Club and other preservationists urged caution or actively opposed road building in the parks, they enthusiastically lobbied for trail development.[32] By 1916, a fairly complete network of trails in the High Sierra already existed, the legacy of years of sheep and cattle grazing as well as hunting and recreational camping. But these trails often consisted of little more than the eroded paths made by past domestic animals. To serve an anticipated boom in backcountry hiking and riding, Sequoia, at least, would need extensive improvement of old trails and construction of new ones. General Grant National Park was simply too small, although a few miles around its principal grove and up to the Paradise overlook needed work.

After the 1926 expansion of Sequoia, the NPS undertook an aggressive trail program, prodded consistently by an eager Sierra Club. In the first full construction season the following year, seventeen men worked on improving or building thirty miles of trail, including the popular Alta Trail from the Giant Forest to Alta Peak and a new trail along the Marble Fork from Lodgepole to Tokopah Falls. The largest job involved reconstruction of nearly sixteen miles of trail at scattered points in Kern Canyon, a part of the recent addition of former USFS land. Toward the end of the season, another eight and one-half miles in the southern part of the park in and around the Garfield Grove were upgraded with fire-prevention funds. In the ensuing several years, park employees accelerated this pace of reconstruction or development of trails both in the Giant Forest, where the routes of heaviest use were lightly oiled, and in the new backcountry.[33]

From 1916 to 1932, however, construction and maintenance of two spectacular and costly "special status" trails commanded the attention and much of the appropriations of Sequoia National Park. One was the premier backcountry trail in California, if not in the entire West—the John Muir Trail. The other was the Sierra Nevada's most elaborate and ambitious trail, a veritable hiker's freeway—the High Sierra Trail. Both projects were the product of high expectations and dreams, both cost years of effort, tens of thousands of dollars, and, in the case of the John Muir Trail, even some lives. And both today form the backbone of the trail system in Sequoia and Kings Canyon.

The California State Legislature officially commissioned the John Muir Trail in 1915, when it appropriated $10,000 toward construction of a high-altitude trail from Yosemite Valley to Mt. Whitney. The route was sanctioned in August of that year after consultations between state engineers, the Sierra Club, U.S. Geological Survey, and USFS, with the latter having actual jurisdiction. Construction began a few weeks later on the 184-mile trail and proceeded sporadically until 1938. In the process, 17.5 miles of the trail were transferred to Sequoia National Park in 1926. The Park Service then undertook extensive repair and rerouting of that segment, which had been among the earliest completed and most heavily damaged by long winters and travelers' pack stock. Although the bulk of the John Muir Trail lay still in Forest Service land, it began and ended in national parks and was most associated with its famous terminus: Mt. Whitney. At Sequoia, the annual maintenance of this trail, which wove through altitudes of 10,000 to 14,495 feet, placed a heavy burden on park-trail appropriations.[34]

The High Sierra Trail was the most colorful of all the backcountry projects, a symbolic step in unifying the original park with its huge backcountry addition; it was also one of Colonel White's pet projects during his first dozen years at the helm. During the 1920s, the superintendent had become convinced that the future of national parks and, indeed, the future of the conservation ethic in America lay in the wilderness, specifically in the public's explorations of it and the education derived from those wilderness experiences. To diffuse stressed and crowded visitors from auto-jammed, urban-like camps of the Giant Forest and show them the wisdom and peace of the natural world, they had to be separated from their cars, cabins, and dingy amusements and propelled into the wilderness. But the average visitor was unprepared for the rough and tumble of the improved sheep trails that lined most of the park's new territory. The solution was a gently sloping, high-quality, and carefully designed trail that would lead visitors through meadows and canyons and over passes between towering peaks from the Giant Forest, one of the park's major attractions, to Mt. Whitney, another big draw. The first hurdle was convincing the Washington, D.C., office of the necessity for such a project and the considerable cost it would entail. This White accomplished by early 1928, when Sequoia received new trail-building funds with provisions for the High Sierra Trail. He secured the temporary assistance of a NPS engineer and began to plan the exact route of his new "tourist" trail.

Initial study convinced White that Crescent Meadow was the logical starting point for the trail. During the first construction season in 1928, ranger Guy Hopping and his crew constructed a mile-and-a-half of gentle pathway along the slopes above the Middle Fork. For the next two years, laborers drove the trail eastward, blasting and hand digging through miles of solid granite on steep slopes, while engineers Guy Edwards and John Diehl studied how to bring the trail over the Great Western Divide. Their options eventually boiled down to crossing either via Tamarack Lake and Lion Lake or via Hamilton Lakes. Either route involved heavy work near the crest of the divide and down the other side. Eventually, Diehl chose the Hamilton Lakes route, which offered the lowest pass at Kaweah Gap but presented one of the most rugged sections of the park's high country. Included in the western approach to Kaweah Gap was an imposing sheer-walled, steeply angled avalanche chute known as Hamilton Gorge. To cope with this barrier, Diehl resolved to construct an elaborate suspension bridge with tons of cable, steel, and concrete brought in twenty-one miles by pack train from Mineral King via Black Rock Pass.

Throughout the summers of 1930, 1931, and 1932, work crews continued the heavy construction, literally carving the trail out of pure stone. By September 1932, the only task left west of the divide was construction of the costly bridge. More than 200 pack animal trips were required to deliver some 41,000 pounds of material. By October 10, the NPS announced that the spectacular bridge was complete and with it the entire trail from Crescent Meadow to and beyond Kaweah Gap. Original plans had called for the trail to continue eastward over Kaweah Peaks and on to the John Muir Trail to connect with Mt. Whitney. The Depression, however, deprived the NPS of funds to finish the job. Instead, the trail connected with existing trails that skirted south of the Kaweah Peaks, through Chagoopa Plateau and back up Kern Canyon, to Junction Meadow and its original planned route. Five years later, red-faced engineers found that the fragile Hamilton Gorge Bridge had plunged into the canyon, a casualty of extremely heavy snowfalls and an avalanche. After rerouting the trail around the gorge, using half-tunnels to make a ledge along the sheer cliff, the High Sierra Trail, as it now exists, was complete. It had taken five summer work seasons and $120,000 to construct the twenty-one miles from Crescent Meadow to Kaweah Gap. Improvement of the trail on the other side cost tens of thousands more. Yet the project initiated a new phase in the use of the Sierra Nevada's backcountry and of Sequoia National Park. The High Sierra Trail was both the first trans-Sierra trail built entirely for recreational purposes and the highest-quality mountain trail in California, if not the entire nation. With its completion, the backcountry's wilderness became easily accessible to the burgeoning number of park visitors and realized Colonel White's dream of bringing wilderness opportunities to the general public.[35]

Campgrounds, Water Lines, and Government Buildings

Important as roads and trails were for making the parks accessible to the public, NPS Director Mather and his men believed that much more was necessary, particularly as guests packed into the Giant Forest and other popular areas. Twenty-six years of previous park use had generated a disorganized array of ramshackle temporary structures, scattered and messy campsites, a profusion of litter and waste, and grossly inadequate water and sewage systems. Mather and Colonel White aimed to correct these problems, and three specific issues had to be addressed. First, the NPS needed to organize and enlarge government-controlled camping. Hitherto, campers had simply thrown up tents or crude cabins wherever they found space. Second, the NPS needed to construct basic infrastructure such as water systems, garbage dumps, and parking lots. Finally, to benefit the touring public, assist the rangers who hosted them, and realize the image Stephen Mather promoted, the park needed scenic overlooks, amphitheaters, museums, visitor centers, and administrative buildings at the Giant Forest, at General Grant, and somewhere in the lower elevations for winter residence. [36]

One of the first tasks was to solve the chaos of miserable camping facilities that beset the Giant Forest. Years later, Colonel White described the grim scene that met his eyes upon his arrival at his new assignment in 1920:

> [I]t was barely possible to see Round Meadow because of the tents which surrounded it. The very choicest places were preempted by public campers and by those who had permits to establish little cabins at Giant Forest. The whole of the Hazelwood, Firwood, Nob Hill and other central camp areas was given over to camping and in every direction there were pit toilets, cess pits, and a criss-cross of water lines under the Big Trees.[37]

During Fry's administration, an effort had been made to improve the situation by installing a sewer system, but this merely encouraged an increased density of campsites, many of them using sequoias as braces for their lean-tos and tents.

The first commercial "village" in the Giant Forest had developed adjacent to Round Meadow when this photograph by Lindley Eddy was taken in 1920. After the Generals Highway opened in 1926, many of these buildings were moved to the new village site one-quarter mile away. At the time, visitors parked and camped wherever they wished among the giant sequoia trees.

White quickly decided that the NPS needed to organize developed campgrounds within the Giant Forest but at the edge of the central belt of sequoias. Here, camping could be restricted to planned sites and excluded from the premier scenic attraction of the park. Thus, from 1921 to 1928, the NPS designed and constructed four campgrounds called Firwood, Highlands, Paradise, and Sunset Rock, with access roads, parking areas, and comfort stations. As rangers moved campers away from Round Meadow, they razed nearly 300 campsites and, by 1932, had restored most of the central area to a semblance of the natural scene. In addition to the four campgrounds in the Giant Forest, the NPS also established a large camp development at Lodgepole five miles from the Giant Forest. By 1928, park officials decided to make Lodgepole the primary camping area for the park, a role it still holds today. Although these steps to clear Round Meadow and the sequoia belt were commendable, later hindsight would find the solution insufficient. Hundreds of campsites still occupied the Giant Forest, albeit in less sensitive sections. And, to the later dismay of park officials, some of the former camping areas were later occupied by the concessioner's cabins and tent-structures.[38]

Even as the NPS worked to relocate and organize the camping chaos at the Giant Forest, it made a startling decision. After surveying the scene in the Giant Forest, particularly the sites occupied by San Joaquin Valley residents for up to two to four months at a time, Mather gave permission, in 1920, for locals to construct "semi-permanent camps." Initially, this meant erection of simple roofs to shelter the campers and their equipment from summer thunderstorms. Within a short time, however, the fifty families who secured permits began to add to their complexes by stringing lines between trees and building walls, sheds, and even rudimentary fences. The reaction of campers was so swift and the implications of "ownership" in a national park so disturbing that the director reversed his decision only a year later. But, as the NPS would come to find out many more times, once something becomes acceptable practice, it is next to impossible to reverse the policy. Colonel White, who dealt daily with local citizens and courted their favor for the bill to expand the park, tried for several years to convince Mather to reestablish the practice, but the director resisted. Meanwhile, each campsite that was not reassumed at the opening of a season was quickly torn down and removed. Thus, in the fall of 1932, only nine sites remained when NPS officials unceremoniously revoked their permits and removed the few remaining structures. The reason for allowing the practice is clear: Local support for a national park was a priority for survival and, in this case, expansion. Still, the policy of allowing semi-permanent camps flew in the face of Secretary Lane's letter, composed from Mather's own ideas, which flatly stated, "you should not permit the leasing of land for summer homes." Colonel White argued that these could scarcely be called homes; nevertheless, even for development-minded officials such as Mather and Albright, the semi-permanent camps constituted an aberration from principles and policies.[39]

As they solved the camping problem in the Giant Forest, park officials also looked for ways to improve the basic infrastructure of the parks' developed areas. Haphazard trash and sewage disposal, inadequate water supply, and confusion created by cars pulled alongside Generals Highway and amidst the trees all begged quick resolution. One of the earliest and most important steps was construction, in 1923, of a new water-supply system for the Giant Forest. Before that date, water came from tiny Sherman Creek near the development area. By 1923, however, Sanitary Engineer H. B. Hommon realized that this supply would always be inadequate, particularly during dry seasons. He proposed that a four-inch redwood pipeline be run from the old Mt. Whitney Power Company's dam site at Wolverton Meadow. The cost was significantly higher, but the potentially disastrous consequences of doing nothing convinced White and his bosses. By the end of the season, the new system brought 350,000 gallons a day of fresh water to the Giant Forest and allowed rapid expansion of both government and concession developments in the grove.[40]

During this same period, the NPS added a new water system at Ash Mountain, sewage systems at General Grant and the Giant Forest, and a new garbage incinerator at Bear Hill, which promised to ease a rapidly mounting problem of garbage and litter. In addition, park officials constructed dozens of new parking areas in campgrounds, at concession facilities, and at scenic attractions such as the General Sherman Tree and Moro Rock. Sequoia, in particular, had become a zone of automobile-using recreationalists, with the number of auto permits rising from 766 in 1918 to nearly 21,000 in 1930. Each of these completed projects enabled the NPS to absorb a greater number of tourists in the parks' popular areas. [41]

Once visitors arrived in the parks, they hungrily combed the developed areas for scenic attractions, visitor contact stations, and various amusements. In response, the NPS concentrated on improving and making available these features. During the 1920s, laborers built amphitheaters, a museum, and several visitor centers. In 1917, an elaborate and somewhat intimidating wooden staircase had been erected to the top of Moro Rock. After fourteen years of exciting climbs, the NPS replaced it with a stone stairway carved into the famous outcrop and added a handrail two years later. A fallen sequoia was graded and converted into an "Auto Log" and quickly became a major attraction. At General Grant, rangers cut dozens of smaller trees to provide a scenic vista of the General Grant Tree, which, as the "Nation's Christmas Tree," had become part of several pageants and rituals. Finally, the NPS built a new winter headquarters building at Ash Mountain and a new maintenance complex at Lodgepole. It was a busy time for the parks' administration, one filled with ambition and optimism and one that met with popular approval every step of the way.[42]

USE: IMPROVING CONCESSIONS

Upon assuming directorship of the new NPS, Stephen Mather faced one of his trickiest duties: designing a comprehensive policy for concessions and implementing it in his new charges. There were two options available—competition and monopoly. Mather chose monopoly as a way to maintain quality and prevent abuse of the parks' scenery and resources. When the director turned to Sequoia and General Grant National Parks, however, he found problems. A variety of operators controlled hotel, dining, transportation, photography, and other services, and each service was small-time and marginally profitable. Mather was reluctant to expel loyal and established businesses, but as long as the situation persisted, development of Sequoia and implementation of his policy would be hindered.[43]

In 1920, the problem of ejecting a loyal business solved itself when Mrs. Kenney decided to abandon her lodging operations, which she had operated with her now-deceased husband since 1914. But, upon studying the situation at Sequoia, Mather found that the difficulty of access to the park severely limited the number of customers. Small-time operations such as those of Kenney or the Sequoia National Park Stage Company could make a small profit scraping by with limited infrastructure or investment, but a larger-scale monopoly, committed to aggressive modernization and expansion, could scarcely hope to survive, let alone make substantial improvements. What Sequoia and, incidentally, General Grant needed was a company willing to hold the concession until the Generals Highway reached the Giant Forest. Mather chose a company with an established concession operation and some capital to spare: the Yosemite National Park Company controlled by Harry Chandler, of Los Angeles and A. B. C. Dohrmann, of San Francisco. The two men formed a subsidiary company called the Kings River Parks Company and commenced operations at the beginning of the 1920 season in the Giant Forest, at General Grant, and outside the parks in Kings Canyon at the old Kanawyer's site.[44]

From the beginning, the Giant Forest became the focus of plans for improvement and the source of most revenue. There, in the first two seasons, the new concessioner built modern cabins, enlarged the dining room, and added bath, laundry, and toilet facilities. The following year, a new lunchroom and more housekeeping cabins brought the capacity at the Giant Forest Lodge up to 234. These improvements, however, were insignificant compared to what General Manager Theophil Fritzen planned. For a projected investment of nearly $2,000,000, Fritzen envisioned a seventy-six-room hotel at Beetle Rock, 125 cabins nearby, and 775 new tent-cabins and cottages at Soldier's Camp about two miles from Giant Forest Lodge. In all, the three developments at the lodge, Soldier's Camp, and Beetle Rock areas would house more than 3,000 people, with additional structures for 800 employees. This was a scale of operation that would make Sequoia National Park one of the greatest tourist attractions in the western United States and easily accomplish the NPS's goal of creating public-recreation grounds in the parks.[45]

Unfortunately for the company, with progress on the Generals Highway maddeningly slow, financial survival became a more immediate concern than any vast expansion. From 1920 to 1924, the Yosemite National Park Company was forced to stake its expensive subsidiary more than $108,000. More alarming was that the amount increased each year until 1924, when a new manager undertook severe and unpopular austerity measures. Efforts at bringing local businessmen into the operation to prop it up until the Generals Highway could be completed failed, due to competing projects in the San Joaquin Valley. In desperation, the company leased its southern operation in Sequoia during 1925 and abandoned it entirely the following year. For five grim years, the company had done Mather and the NPS a favor by consolidating the concession operations in Sequoia and General Grant and by considerably improving the physical plant. By the time the long-awaited Generals Highway finally arrived, however, the Yosemite National Park Company had had enough. It had retired to its popular and lucrative northern park, financially bruised and presumably somewhat wiser.[46]

Determined to install a single, consolidated concession operation at the two southern Sierra parks, Mather turned next to an old friend, Howard Hays. He promised Hays ready cooperation from the government and sure profits when the road reached the Giant Forest. In response, Hays formed a company with the lengthy name of Sequoia and General Grant National Parks Company. Hays had come west shortly after the turn of the century and taken a job with one of the concessions in Yellowstone National Park. During that time, he had become friends with Mather and Albright. After stints as a promoter of tourism for several major railroads and with the National Railroad Administration, where he coordinated projects with Albright, Hays had bought out his old employer at Yellowstone. He had operated that concession until 1924, when health problems forced him to sell.

Mather's desperation and elaborate promises finally convinced Hays, who saw an opportunity to implement plans such as those of former manager Fritzen and to build Sequoia and General Grant into large, famous, and profitable tourist resorts. He signed a twenty-year contract in the spring of 1926 and, three years later, brought in his brother-in-law, George Mauger, to manage the operation. These two men, Hays and Mauger, would operate the parks' major concession for the next forty years. During that time, even as they would vastly expand and update the infrastructure, they would do so amid an atmosphere of steadily growing hostility, as the NPS changed its attitudes toward development and the scale and location of concessions in the Giant

Forest—going to the heart of the promises with which Director Mather had lured Hays back into the national park concession business.[47]

After assuming the concession operations with a secure, long-term contract, Hays surveyed the facilities he had to offer incoming visitors. In Sequoia, the two principal areas were at the Giant Forest, specifically Giant Forest Lodge near Round Meadow, and the Glen Ridge Camp along the eastern side of the new road. Giant Forest Lodge contained a moderate-sized dining room, a lunch counter, ten two-room cabins, thirty tents, an office, and assorted maintenance structures. At Glen Ridge, which was universally described as ugly and dilapidated, there were another thirty-three tents. Near the lodge were a store and the buildings of the smaller concessioners like photographer Lindley Eddy. At General Grant, always a small-time afterthought despite substantial numbers of visitors, a few tiny cabins and tent-tops clustered near a small store and lunch counter. General Grant boasted few attractions compared to its larger southern neighbor. It was popular with residents of Fresno and other San Joaquin Valley towns, but these tourists often made only day visits or camped on their way to Kings Canyon.[48]

Upon completion of the Generals Highway into the Giant Forest, Hays moved quickly to exploit the publicity and overhaul his company's holdings. In his first two seasons, 1926 and 1927, Hays ordered replacement of the thirty tents at the lodge with sixty-eight new shingle and tent-top cabins, nearly tripling the overnight capacity of this popular complex. In addition, he replaced most of the tents at Glen Ridge, while moving them across the road at the request of Colonel White. In late fall 1926, the concessioner moved the lunch counter to the new Giant Forest Village site and commenced construction there of a store and gas station. As part of an agreement, small independent operations such as the post office, photography studio, and barber shop also moved. Across from the village, Hays received permission to develop a new complex of housekeeping cabins near Beetle Rock to be known as Camp Kaweah. By the end of the 1927 season, fifty units were in place along with a washhouse, office, and bathhouse. A dozen more would follow in 1928. Finally, the company built two additions onto the Giant Forest Lodge's dining room and added a large, new hot-water system and bathhouse as well as some warehouses and sheds. In the first two seasons alone, the visitor capacity, or so-called "pillow count," of the Giant Forest rose more than 100 percent and occupied vastly improved accommodations.

Elsewhere in the parks, the Sequoia and General Grant National Parks Company exercised considerable caution. At General Grant, the miserable tents were replaced with four duplex cabins made of redwood. At Hospital Rock, Hays opened the Buck Eye Store to cater to campers and hikers in the foothills' areas. To his dismay, Hays had assumed the transportation concession as well, and it proved to be a burden for some years to come. When he took over managerial duties,

George Mauger expressed considerable interest in the backcountry, and, for some years, the major concession company operated a pack station catering to those who would ride into the park's recently acquired wilderness zone.[49]

By 1930, the company boasted an imposing complex in the Giant Forest area. At Giant Forest Lodge, eighty-five new redwood and bungalow (tent-top) cabins could house more than 250 guests and employees. Two offices, a writing room, several bathhouses, a dining room, and a variety of subsidiary structures together crowded nearby. At the new Glen Ridge Housekeeping Camp, twenty-six tents and a few employee cabins remained. At Camp Kaweah, sixty-three cabins and tents lined the western side of the Generals Highway across from a new Giant Forest Village. In addition, Hays and Mauger had received permission to open a new "auto-camp" at Pinewood, where another thirty cabins had just been completed or were under construction.[50]

There was every indication that this tremendous buildup at the Giant Forest would continue until the area reached a capacity rivaling that planned by Theophil Fritzen and the old Kings River Parks Company. Two events, however, combined to halt the company's progress. One was the shocking crash of the stock market in 1929 and the ensuing Great Depression. No one could be sure how long the Depression would go, and, in that climate, Hays decided on a cautious program. The company had made a profit each year, but those annual profits rarely exceeded $10,000.[51] There was money to be made in the concession business, but it certainly was not a high-profit venture. With so little financial cushion and with the very future of tourism in doubt, caution was an intelligent man's choice. The second event was, perhaps, even more shocking. In early 1931, Hays proposed a small addition to the Giant Forest Lodge. Colonel White refused on the grounds that the company should not be in the sequoia grove in the first place. For the first time, someone had actually rejected a move to bring more tourists to the park's major attraction. At first, Hays was nonplussed, but then he was angry.

UNIMPAIRED BY WHAT MEASURE? RESOURCES MANAGEMENT, 1916–1931

The tremendous popularity of the natural-history program, the meteoric rise in the number of visitors, and the huge infusion of infrastructure spotlighted the government's efforts at natural-resource management. Unfortunately, these advances were not matched by similar improvement in the preservation of the parks' vegetation and wildlife. During the first fifteen years of the NPS, resources were manipulated (or sometimes preserved) for aesthetic and emotional rather than scientific reasons. In addition, surrounding landowners again resumed grazing their cattle and horses in Sequoia. From a modern perspective, the decade of the 1920s represents a period of immature and almost destructive policy in resource preservation. Yet, during this period, questions about resource practices first arose, questions that would later evolve into serious doubts and major shifts of policy and administrative technique.

Management of vegetation during those years consisted of fire suppression and, beginning in 1917, efforts to control native insects. Total suppression of fires became institutionalized by the establishment of regular, annual fire-prevention appropriations in 1928. Although regeneration of sequoias had ceased in all the developed areas as well as in most other groves in the two parks, White and his staff took few active steps to replace the missing seedlings or address the issue through commissioned research.[52] One exception was an important study conducted by Emilio Meinecke, an eminent forest pathologist, at the request of Director Mather.[53] In his 1926 report, Meinecke principally directed his attention to the negative effects of human trampling and construction on the sequoias; he recommended an active but scientifically controlled program of reforestation not only of sequoias, but of all the species eliminated by development. A few years later, White opened a nursery at Ash Mountain that provided seedlings for both parks during the next decade and a half.[54]

In wildlife management, the NPS's programs were inconsistent throughout the national park system. At Sequoia and General Grant, Colonel White halted the use of steel traps for the control of predators—particularly for coyote and mountain lion—but only in response to emotional condemnation of the cruelty of their use. The superintendent lectured Horace Albright about the improper destruction of predators within national parks, but he occasionally resorted to those actions himself, when it seemed necessary and propitious. In 1920, legislation gave the NPS permission to destroy "dangerous animals," when it was necessary to save human lives or prevent injury to visitors or employees. At Sequoia, this act spurred various aggressive measures, particularly against rattlesnakes, which were virtually eliminated from some areas of the parks. Throughout the Mather years, the NPS also accelerated a program of poisoning rodents. Unfortunately, one of the side effects of this effort in Sequoia was elimination of the native black-tailed jackrabbit, which also ate the poisoned bait. The original target of the poison campaign, the common ground squirrel, easily survived and continued to plague the parks' housing and concession areas, at least in part due to reduction of one of its chief predators, the rattlesnake.[55]

Perhaps in no area has the clash of human emotion and ecological principles been quite so harsh as with the management of bears. By the time the new NPS took over Sequoia and General Grant, the state's emblem, the grizzly bear, was nearly extinct in the parks' areas. The last certain sighting of a grizzly was at Horse Corral Meadow in 1922 by Jesse Agnew, who promptly shot and killed the creature.[56] Black bears had fared much better, due, perhaps, to the perception that they were less dangerous, but they had proven troublesome in the parks as marauding vandals, even during the military period when the first bear was officially killed as a pest by army rifles in 1912. But, by 1922 and possibly two or three years earlier, destruction of problem bears had become standard procedure. Between 1922 and 1931, fifteen black bears were killed, while several others were relocated within the park or to zoos.[57]

While this desperate and aggressive measure became policy, the NPS ironically increased visitors' contact with these large and potentially dangerous animals. For years, visitors had enjoyed the spectacle of bears pawing through garbage at the park's dumping area in the Giant Forest. By 1921, "Bear Hill," slightly southeast of the future Giant Forest Village site, had become a regular evening attraction. In time, park rangers erected bleachers, where several hundred visitors at one time would sit and surround the garbage dump, while up to two-dozen bears foraged through the piles. Even though the black bear is relatively docile by comparison to the grizzly, problems were inevitable. Rangers waded through the refuse, trying to keep bears and visitors apart, not always successfully. This resembled a circus, a sideshow, and many tourists forgot that these were still wild animals. Although no deaths or serious injuries occurred, many frightening and occasionally harmful encounters befell those tourists who got in the way of a bear intent upon its cubs, its food, or making its way out of the ring.[58]

Amid the general confusion and groping that characterized resource management and preservation by NPS administrators, a grave threat arose during World War I, when the agency and preservationists found themselves hard pressed to defend the position of excluding cattle from the parks' lands. The U.S. had assumed the role not only of supplying its own war effort, but also its war-weary allies. Added to the problem were several successive years of drought in many parts of the West. The federal Food Administration, congressional members from the West, and, of course, ranchers clamored for access to the only lands in the nation deliberately withheld from use for food production. Mather and Albright were torn between the dangerous precedent that would be set if the parks were opened to cattle again and the potentially disastrous results of having the young and fragile NPS appear unpatriotic at this time of national emergency.

The response by Mather again showed his political acumen and diplomatic skills. He granted small, token permits to park neighbors who did not intend to use the land heavily. Meanwhile, he and Albright circulated among congressmen the idea that ranchers in the West had far less concern for the war effort than they did for recovering access to lands they had lost when the parks were created. Preservationist and civic groups helped out by publishing highly visible reports on the threats to the parks and by courting reticent members of Congress. In retrospect, by granting token permits the NPS managed to resist the most serious damage to the parks and to park policy.[59] But there was a hitch: Once the ranchers and their cattle got onto park lands, it proved a devil of a job getting them off again.

One of the parks most attractive to western cattlemen was Sequoia. Accordingly, in June 1918, Superintendent Fry conducted a series of meetings with the local cattlemen's association that resulted in a plan to allow 2,675 cattle to graze the park's backcountry. With the conclusion of the war, the emergency ended and with it the excuse for using the parks' lands. But cattlemen claimed they had adjusted their herding and cropping practices to include this range and would be financially hurt without access to the park. Director Mather agreed, and, for the entire decade of the 1920s, cattle roamed the areas around Hockett Meadow, Kern Canyon, and the foothills north of Ash Mountain. Through those years, many more requests were received for access. Despite Colonel White's intercession on behalf of some individuals whom he knew and respected, the director rejected all further applications. Approximately 1,300 cattle grazed the park each year, not enough to do serious damage but enough to prevent regeneration from past excesses and to give credence to claims by other cattlemen that they, too, should have fair access to the park, especially during dry years. Finally, in 1930, White and Albright suspended the few remaining permits, citing four decades of park policy and philosophy. Although protests were immediate and applications to resume frequent, the NPS has managed to resist further interruptions of this oldest and most basic founding policy of the national park system.[60]

In sum, the period 1916 to 1931 marked a nadir in resource management. The return of cattle grazing threatened to tear down the philosophical walls that carefully preserved the parks' resources and provided the underpinning of the entire national park system. In matters of vegetation and wildlife, the NPS experimented with active controls but for all the wrong reasons. Fortunately, the weight of scientific inquiry and evidence accumulated during the years to force some grudging moves toward more responsible management. In 1931, Walter Fry released a twenty-five-year survey of the status of wildlife in Sequoia National Park. His statistical report was alarming and caught not only the NPS's attention, but that of zoologists outside the agency as well:

> Of the 63 known species that inhabited the park in 1906, two have increased, 35 have held their own, 21 have been greatly reduced, three are verging on extinction, and two have disappeared. One animal has been added, the opossum . . .[61]

Later that same year, Director Albright published a new predator-control policy that recognized predators as integral parts of the parks' protected ecosystems. He ordered discontinuance of control programs that used steel traps and poison with a few emergency exceptions.[62] In 1930 and 1931, there was a great expansion of the Ash Mountain Nursery, initiation of studies of the insect-control policy, and a rise in scientific investigation of both vegetation and wildlife. The reactions and reversal of philosophy exemplified by these steps were a harbinger of efforts to come in the management of visitors and their interaction with the limited area and resources of the two fragile parks.

PRESERVATION: THE CONFLICT FOR THE GIANT FOREST BEGINS

Dr. Emilio Meinecke's report on the status of the giant sequoias and their susceptibility to human-caused damage came during an important year for the two parks. In 1926, the park's acreage more than doubled, the new road to the Giant Forest opened, and Howard Hays brought stability to the parks' concessions. Meinecke's report was like a bucket of cold water thrown on the cheery scene. He demonstrated that the giant sequoia suffered serious root damage when confronted with roads, buildings, and extensive human traffic. Its shallow roots seemed particularly susceptible to soil compaction and the danger of severing during construction. With a badly damaged root system inhibiting the intake of water and nutrients, how long would it be before the tree died? As an added matter of concern to Colonel White and his staff, the scenery and serenity of the Giant Forest, in particular, was being gravely harmed. Subsumed under scores of buildings and up to several thousand cars at a time, appreciation of nature was nearly impossible on busy summer days and evenings. It went against the superintendent's nature to interfere with visitors' enjoyment of the park's primary resource, but there was no ignoring the serious breach of quality that beset the grove.[63]

For Colonel White, the solution was always some measure that would encourage people to go elsewhere in the big park. Construction of the High Sierra Trail as well as limits on cabins, recreation buildings, services, and amenities in the Giant Forest were actions aimed at dispersing use and focusing attention on the park's spiritually uplifting qualities. Meinecke's report added fuel to the fire of these thoughts by simply stating that the best solution to the damage caused by construction among sequoias was to stop building.[64] Much harm had already been done by the new Generals Highway; prevention of further damage was paramount.

The superintendent fired the opening shot on May 26, 1927, in a letter to Director Mather. He wrote that, after careful consideration, he believed that limits should be placed on the concessioner's housing capacity in the Giant Forest. White suggested limits of 600 guests at Giant Forest Lodge and 600 more at Camp Kaweah for the 1927 season. Further, he suggested that, at the end of the season, the Giant Forest Lodge's cabins be removed from under the sequoias to some unspecified location—possibly near Beetle Rock and Camp Kaweah or, perhaps even, to Lodgepole.[65] Mather initially agreed but recommended they wait a month until their scheduled meeting with Hays, during which time the concessioner would submit his plans. There is no record of that meeting, but whatever Howard Hays told his old friend worked, because no more was heard of White's recommendations for several years.[66] A few years later, in 1929, White did gain one victory by blocking Hays's request to build a new auto camp at Round Meadow. The NPS had just cleared the ramshackle litter of campsites that had covered the area for the previous twenty summers. It sharply opposed building a new camp there. Hays was forced to develop the auto camp at Pinewood instead.[67]

On July 4, 1930, a disturbing and increasingly familiar scene unfolded before Colonel White and his staff. Cars crowded around Giant Forest Village, honking and jostling for parking places in the lot and along the road. Over at Giant Forest Lodge, more cars clogged the sprawling complex of housekeeping cabins. People coursed this way and that between their cars and cabins and from the dining room to the museum. At Camp Kaweah, the scene was repeated. There were traffic jams at the Moro Rock road junction, at the new Giant Forest Village gas station, and at the access roads to Giant Forest Lodge and Camp Kaweah. More cars and more people packed into the four campgrounds and Pinewood Auto Camp. In all, nearly 1,200 cars brought almost 4,300 people into the Giant Forest that day. A few years earlier, that would have been more than a month's total.[68]

On that Independence Day of 1930, White worried about what he saw and a few months later put those worries to paper in his report to the director:

> The problem of handling such numbers (of visitors) in the congested central Big Tree area at Giant Forest is a serious one; and much study and planning must be given to developing new areas for hotels, housekeeping camps, public camps etc. in order to accommodate the increasing crowds. If we do not plan carefully and transfer the major part of the present activity away from the heart of Giant Forest, the beauties of that area—already badly tarnished—will be further impaired.[69]

It was a desperate situation that threatened to leave the world's greatest forest anything but "unimpaired for future generations." In the Giant Forest, something drastic was required—something that would restore the grove and make sure that its beauty and inspirational qualities were never again tarnished. That something was the complete evacuation of concession facilities from among the Big Trees.

The opening of this battle came in 1931, with Hays's request to add five new redwood cabins to Giant Forest Lodge. It was a simple and modest request; Hays believed it was scarcely more than a formality before construction began. To his amazement, Colonel White rejected his proposal and answered that Hays ought to be planning instead to move the entire lodge complex to another site. White's idea was nearly five years old, but this time he meant it. To Hays and his manager, George Mauger, the rejection threatened the viability of their operation. They believed that visitors came to the park to stay among the Big Trees, not to pay short visits from their lodgings in a mundane pine forest. Removal of the facilities from the Giant Forest might spell

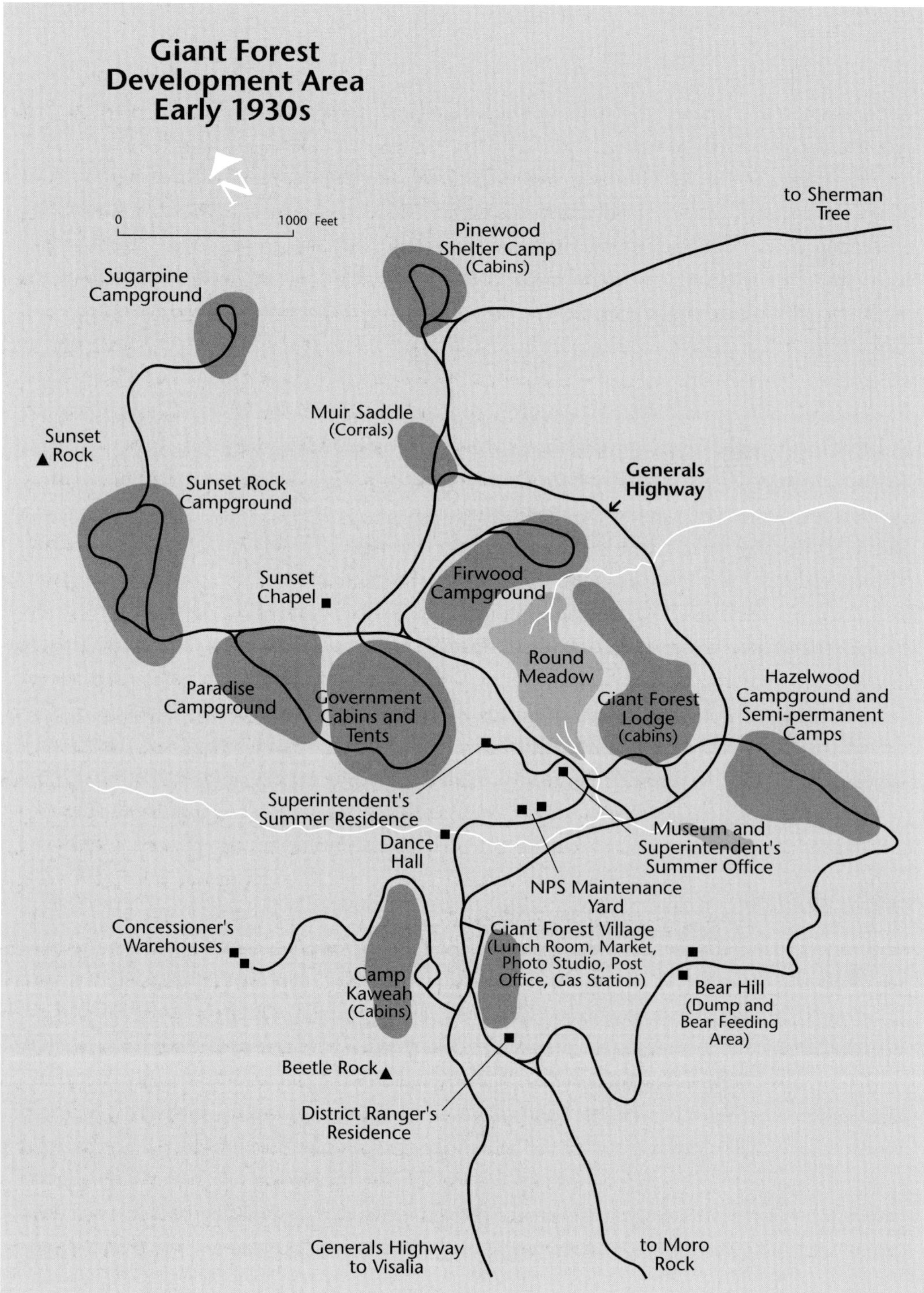
Giant Forest
Development Area
Early 1930s
N
0
1000 Feet
to Sherman Tree
Pinewood Shelter Camp (Cabins)
Sugarpine Campground
Muir Saddle (Corrals)
Sunset Rock
Sunset Rock Campground
Generals Highway
Sunset Chapel
Firwood Campground
Round Meadow
Paradise Campground
Government Cabins and Tents
Giant Forest Lodge (cabins)
Hazelwood Campground and Semi-permanent Camps
Superintendent's Summer Residence
Dance Hall
Museum and Superintendent's Summer Office
NPS Maintenance Yard
Concessioner's Warehouses
Giant Forest Village (Lunch Room, Market, Photo Studio, Post Office, Gas Station)
Camp Kaweah (Cabins)
Bear Hill (Dump and Bear Feeding Area)
Beetle Rock
District Ranger's Residence
Generals Highway to Visalia
to Moro Rock

a serious fall in concession-customer numbers. In addition, they believed that whatever damage might befall the "half-dozen" sequoias on their grounds (a considerable underestimate) would be minimal compared to the damage done by "hundreds of thousands of sightseers and campers who will be motoring through and picnicking under the Big Trees." Hays concluded his response by writing:

> No money payment as damages or expense could compensate us for the moving of our Hotel from our present site out to (say) Lodgepole. There is no National Park feeling at Lodgepole. Among the finest pages of John Muir are those where he writes of his poignant sorrow because the venerable Emerson was restrained from joining him (Muir) for a night under the Big Trees.[70]

The lines were drawn, and two resolute, erudite, and savvy men—John R. White and Howard Hays—faced off over the future of the concessioner's major investment and the park's principal resource.[71]

For Hays, the next step was obvious. Whenever he had problems with his concession operations in Sequoia and General Grant, he simply went to his old friend Horace Albright, now the second director of the NPS. This practice infuriated Colonel White, who believed that only the superintendent could make such decisions based on fact, observation, and the best interests of the park, uninfluenced by outside concerns. Left unsaid were White's increasingly proprietary feelings about his two charges. White had begun to see Sequoia and General Grant as his fiefdoms and resented any activity in them that was not directly under his control. He fired off letters to Albright, to members of the director's Washington, D.C., staff, and to friends in the Sierra Club, bitterly complaining about the concessioner's penchant for going over his head.[72]

In the end, Hays's tactic worked. Albright overruled White and flatly stated that he would never insist that the Giant Forest Lodge be removed from the sequoia belt. Indeed, if some reason was found why they should move from the site they occupied, then they should move to another site under the Big Trees. That settled the matter of moving the lodge out of the Giant Forest, at least for the time being. In addition, the director approved the construction of the five redwood cabins that had triggered the whole conflict.[73] It was a crushing defeat for Colonel White and those who would protect the sequoias.

Nevertheless, it was not a total victory for Hays and his company either. Albright, like his predecessor, was gravely concerned about the protection of the sequoias and of the parks' values in the Giant Forest. He recognized that limits had to be placed somewhere, lest the magnificent grove be turned into a residential neighborhood with rather large, backyard trees. Thus, on November 23, 1931, Albright ordered that the Giant Forest Lodge's capacity henceforth would be limited to 200 guests or "pillows" and a number of still-to-be-determined quarters for employees. This pinned the concession company to a total only slightly higher than they already had. A few months later, the director expanded the "pillow limit" concept to cover Camp Kaweah, where up to 500 guests could be housed, and Pinewood Auto Camp, which would be limited to 300. Both complexes were well below those totals, and Albright's decree thus allowed the concessioner considerable further expansion within the Giant Forest. The areas most directly among the major sequoias, however, those of the lodge, were virtually closed to further construction.[74]

The magnitude of this decision can scarcely be overestimated. It was the first time the NPS placed a limit on tourism development in any of its parks. It was a revolution of sorts in policy and philosophy and arose from men who had campaigned vigorously for recreational development. Mather had been leaning toward control; Albright had implemented it. Some of the evidence to back the latest decisions came from Walter Fry's observations of nature. But it was Colonel White, the increasingly dominant and preservation-oriented superintendent, who drove the NPS to the decision and who was far from finished in his efforts to force the concessioner out from among the sequoias.

1916–1931: DEVELOPMENT AND RECONSIDERATION

During the first fifteen years of NPS's management of Sequoia and General Grant National Parks, there were significant human impacts on the environments of the two parks. Before 1916, for twenty-five years, the parks had been run mostly as strict preserves, not necessarily because of a strong philosophical commitment to preservation but largely because pressure for tourist-based development and congressional appropriations for visitor facilities were limited. All this changed with the successful establishment of the Mather-Albright program in the years immediately following World War I.

Determined to build and maintain public support for the national parks and their new NPS, Mather and Albright found successful ways to publicize the parks and succeeded in obtaining increasing amounts of money for development. The result was a nearly logarithmic increase in parks' visitation and an equal increase in the impact of visitors on natural resources. When combined with a visually based philosophy of national park management, which allowed almost no consideration of what little was known then of ecology, the unsurprising outcome was a significant setback in the biological health of the two parks.

The damage done during the 1920s unevenly affected the parks and their resources. In the Giant Forest and, to a lesser extent, in General Grant, the sheer physical impact of heavy visitation was unmistakable. In these geographically limited areas, nearly all resources suffered. Unrestricted heavy camping trampled and destroyed the forest's undergrowth and meadows' vegetation, while animals suffered disruption of habitat and destruction of predators. Most severely affected were large animals such as bears, which were strongly attracted to human food sources, and mountain lions, which were regularly killed throughout the decade. Smaller species suffered, too, and never again would it be possible to describe the Giant Forest's fauna as natural or undisturbed.

Impacts were not limited to areas of heavy development, however. The resumption of cattle grazing in Sequoia was a setback that undid a quarter-century of military protection, as did the increasing effectiveness of the NPS's fire-suppression activities. Serious support from Congress for fire suppression arrived in the two parks during the late 1920s, just as three decades of fire suppression began finally to allow the dangerous accumulation of fuels. This coincidence would bear increasingly significant results, as the next several decades passed.

In the surrounding Sierra and Sequoia National Forests during the same period, there was much less change in the state of the natural environment, for the USFS during these years, did little more than continue the policies defined during its first decade of existence. Grazing remained widespread throughout the forests, and limited development in the form of road building, logging, and recreational settlement took place mostly along the accessible western fringes of the forests. The USFS, at the time, shared many resource-management programs with the NPS, including suppression of fire and control of predators, but the immense size of the national forests and their relative inaccessibility rendered them less susceptible to quick change. In many ways, the wilderness resources of the national forests of the southern Sierra were protected better than those of the national parks of the same region during the 1920s.

In 1926, Sequoia National Park doubled in size by absorbing the USFS lands at the headwaters of the North Fork of the Kern River. These lands were little different than they had been in 1910, shortly after the USFS had finally succeeded in controlling unpermitted grazing of sheep. In comparison, many resources in the national parks had suffered significantly since 1916. (The USFS had its plans, though: In the extensive high country of the Kings River drainage, the USFS, true to its mission, allowed studies to proceed that were intended to lead eventually to massive development of hydroelectric power.) As the decade ended, though, the wilderness in the national forests of the southern Sierra remained almost completely intact, except for the continuing impacts of grazing.

During the last years of the 1920s, Superintendent White, whose understanding of his parks had grown considerably, began to realize what the NPS's programs had wrought. He and others were beginning to note human impacts on the landscape and even on ecosystems and were pondering the implications. Two more major waves of development would have to be weathered, however, before concerns about the parks' resources would come to dominate the NPS's management of its southern Sierra national parks.

John Roberts White was born in England, served in the U.S. Army in the Philippines, reaching the rank of colonel, and became Superintendent of Sequoia and General Grant National Parks in 1920. He brought vision, discipline, and a strong determination to block overdevelopment in the parks, which led to clashes with the concessioners. Except for a brief period as a regional director for the National Park Service in San Francisco during the early 1940s, he served at Sequoia until 1947. Photographer and date unknown.

CHAPTER SIX

Colonel John White and Preservation in Sequoia National Park (1931–1947)

In February 1936, Colonel John R. White delivered an address to a group of national park superintendents meeting in Washington, D.C. With nearly seventeen years at Sequoia National Park, White was one of the senior spokesmen, a man with experience, ranging from the early days of Stephen Mather's directorship of the National Park Service (NPS) to the Depression and its drastic governmental changes. He had seen the parks' visitation multiply sixfold and auto use twelvefold. And he had seen it all from the perspective of his home park—Sequoia. With the benefit of those years of experience had come changes in the superintendent's philosophy and interpretation of the NPS's 1916 charter—to use and preserve national parks. In his address, Colonel White expounded on that philosophy derived from his years in Sequoia:

> To preserve the national park atmosphere we must curb the human desire to develop the parks quickly to compete in popularity with other resorts, or even State or other parks or national forest areas. When a new project is proposed, the first question should be, 'how will it affect the park atmosphere which we desire to maintain or restore?'
>
> We should boldly ask ourselves whether we want the national parks to duplicate the features and entertainments of other resorts, or whether we want them to stand for something distinct, and we hope better in our national life.
>
> We are a restless people, mechanically minded, and proud of doing constructive work. Our factories, railroads, roads and buildings are admired by the world. We have in the parks a host of technicians, each anxious to leave his mark. But in all this energy and ambition there is danger unless all plans are subordinated to that atmosphere which though unseen, is no less surely felt by all who visit those eternal masterpieces of the Great Architect which we little men are temporarily protecting.[1]

This viewpoint represents one of the earliest expressions of systemic preservation, even as it is, from today's perspective, immature and unscientific. What White wanted to protect and saw as the paramount value was preserving a semblance of the natural world and creating a nearly intangible feeling of a "national park atmosphere," not the preservation of selected objects and scenery as curious and isolated treasures within a much-paved and adorned visitor complex. He still wanted heavy visitor use but for education and enrichment. He still encouraged or accepted many types of use incompatible with today's NPS values, but he discouraged many others of common acceptance in his time. He believed that encouragement of the proper "atmosphere" in national parks had to be the province of the superintendent, as did the power to control and implement whatever policies and actions were necessary toward that end.

White had developed these ideas by the late 1920s and simply refined and strengthened them as time passed. The situation at the Giant Forest, where eighty percent of the visitors and seemingly even more of the problems were concentrated, had forged in him strong likes and dislikes about NPS's policies and practices. The 1931 pillow limit, as applied to concessions in the Giant Forest, represented a partial victory in his ongoing war to make Sequoia fit the image later described in his address to the superintendents.

White, however, would face constant battles to protect and restore his ideas of a national park atmosphere in Sequoia. In some areas, serious pressure arose for the first time, such as the designs of road builders upon the backcountry. In other cases, constant agitation for new development demanded unceasing vigilance and diplomacy, particularly concerning popular amusements of dubious propriety. And in one area, the Giant Forest, development clearly had already gone too far. The problem there would bedevil the NPS throughout the entire system and throughout its history—how to remove facilities and suspend activities that had already become established. Having achieved the questionable adjective "traditional," almost no practice with any adherents, no matter how offensive to administrators, could easily be halted.

Thus, in 1931, Colonel White faced an increasingly complex task: to control escalating development and reduce it in some areas. For the next seventeen years, White, his staff at Sequoia, and the NPS would dramatically reassess priorities and policies. No longer was it imperative to scramble for visitors to justify a park's existence. The early generation of development-minded NPS officials such as Horace Albright gave way to a second generation. Colonel White's spirit and philosophy of preservation of a "national park atmosphere" replaced that of preserving specific objects and isolated scenery, first at Sequoia and, later, nationally. In the process, the foundations of scientific inquiry and ecological preservation were laid as well. At Sequoia, White's experience, seniority, and personality would create a unique situation whereby initiation of policy and impetus for change came from the local administration. This marked the only time in the park's post-1916 history when the Washington, D.C., office was reduced to the role of reviewer rather than originator of policy. Nevertheless, despite the shift of initiative, the NPS's head office in Washington always maintained the ultimate veto, and this would eventually bring an end to Colonel White's reign and a retreat from many of the standards he pursued and the difficult changes he demanded.

THE CCC: ALMOST TOO MUCH OF A GOOD THING

Long before that final battle, White faced a potentially grave challenge to his principles and to his control of the parks' development. In the early years of his superintendency, he had complained endlessly about the dismal lack of funds and manpower available to accomplish the many necessary improvements to the park. Later, although he continued to press for more money and employees, his tone and subject had shifted to controlling development in the park. Ironically, beginning in 1933, White's earliest priorities were satisfied to such a remarkable extent that his later preservation ones could have been seriously jeopardized. The crash of the stock market on October 29, 1929, and resulting Great Depression had created a desperate situation for the American economy and people. A full one-quarter of the work force was idle, while another thirty percent struggled to eke out a living with part-time jobs. Through the remainder President Herbert Hoover's term in the White House, the nation wallowed in misery and unemployment. Following his sweeping presidential victory in 1933 and that of his Democratic party, Franklin D. Roosevelt and his administration ramrodded a massive collection of federal aid and social programs through Congress, changing forever American society and government.

One of the bills in this spate of legislation created the Emergency Conservation Work program, popularly called and later officially renamed the Civilian Conservation Corps (CCC). The CCC would employ young men in quasi-military camps to carry out primarily manual-labor projects on federal lands, including national parks. Suddenly, as Colonel White wrestled with controlling the concessioner, limiting and redirecting development, and allocating meager funds toward maintenance and resource protection, several thousand men per year and the money to pay and support them arrived in the parks. During the next nine years, the CCC would accomplish more labor-intensive and landscaping work than the military and NPS administrations had in the previous forty-three years. Colonel White's intimidating task became the moderation of this unwieldy development machine to preserve the parks from construction on a scale and at a pace completely out of proportion and out of the NPS's control.[2] Fortunately, White's power and skill prevented excesses and turned the CCC into the most valuable development tool in the parks' history.

The CCC operation was an ambitious project, the likes of which has never been matched in U.S. history. During its years of operation, from 1933 to 1942, more than 2,000,000 young men performed work in nearly 900 camps located in ninety-four national parks and monuments and 881 state, county, and municipal areas. Starting from scratch with no model or experience to draw upon, its directors and personnel forged a program still ranked among the most successful in the history of the federal government. Some credit for the success in the national parks went to Robert Fechner, Director of the CCC, to Conrad Wirth, the coordinator of the CCC program in national parks and future NPS Director, and to President Roosevelt. The reason for success, however, lay more in the organization and allocation of responsibility. Administration of the camps themselves and the day-to-day activities of the men fell to the army, as befitted the military form and approach to camp operation and projects. Selection and supervision of projects, hiring of specialists, allocation of crews to specific duties, and compilation of progress reports were carried out by park superintendents. Finally, the Washington, D.C., office of the NPS approved projects and exercised quality control through a system of regional directors and skilled specialists who became the framework for later reorganization of the NPS into regions and specialized branches.[3]

At times, there was friction between the camp commanders and park superintendents, largely owing to the attempts of one to interfere with the duties of the other. Sequoia had up to five camps operating at a time, and each army officer in charge naturally tended to extend his authority to the projects of his men. On the other side, Colonel White sought ways to dominate further the day-to-day camp operation as well as the choice of projects upon which the enrollees worked. In his reports on the CCC's progress as well as his annual superintendent's reports and general correspondence, White complained about being deprived of direct control over the thousands of young men living and working in his park. He thought the only way to assure that the park's values were preserved from youthful exuberance and ill-placed recreational desires was for the superintendent to control those activities. White found particularly obnoxious some of the movies shown at CCC camps as well as the boxing matches and vaudeville shows. He agitated for greater emphasis on educational, "park appropriate" activities. Still, as an old military man, White accepted and understood the way camps were run, and he limited most of his protestations to what he deemed offensive activities.[4]

Over the years, eleven different CCC camps operated in Sequoia National Park, while Grant Grove and, later, Kings Canyon were sites of three others. In most years, five base camps were occupied at once, their crews alternating between high-altitude summer work and winter work in the foothills. Among the most important summer camps were Potwisha, at the present-day campground; Atwell Mill along the Mineral King Road; Marble Fork on the Crystal Cave Road; Yucca Creek on the North Fork of the Kaweah River; and Buckeye, near Ash Mountain. Each camp as well as other less-popular sites became temporary homes for up to 200 men. A standard camp consisted of a rough, U-shaped formation of wooden buildings, including barracks, a mess hall, a recreation hall, officers' quarters, a lavatory and bathhouse, an educational building, and various storage, maintenance, and special-function structures such as a dispensary, blacksmith's shop, generator house, and pump house.[5]

The men were generally eighteen to twenty-five years of age, in good health, unemployed, unmarried, and U.S. citizens. They were paid thirty dollars a month, of which half went directly to dependents and another seven dollars into a savings account to be turned over to the enrollee upon his discharge. Six months was the normal enrollment period, and, at the end of each period,

Colonel White greets the military commander and crew of the Civilian Conservation Corps (CCC) at the Potwisha camp in May 1933. The CCC was a program of President Franklin D. Roosevelt's New Deal designed to employ out-of-work young men during the Great Depression. White determined which projects the crews accomplished in the twin parks, but he resisted the money and labor that accompanied projects such as the Sierra Way Road, which he judged to be overdevelopment. Photographer unknown.

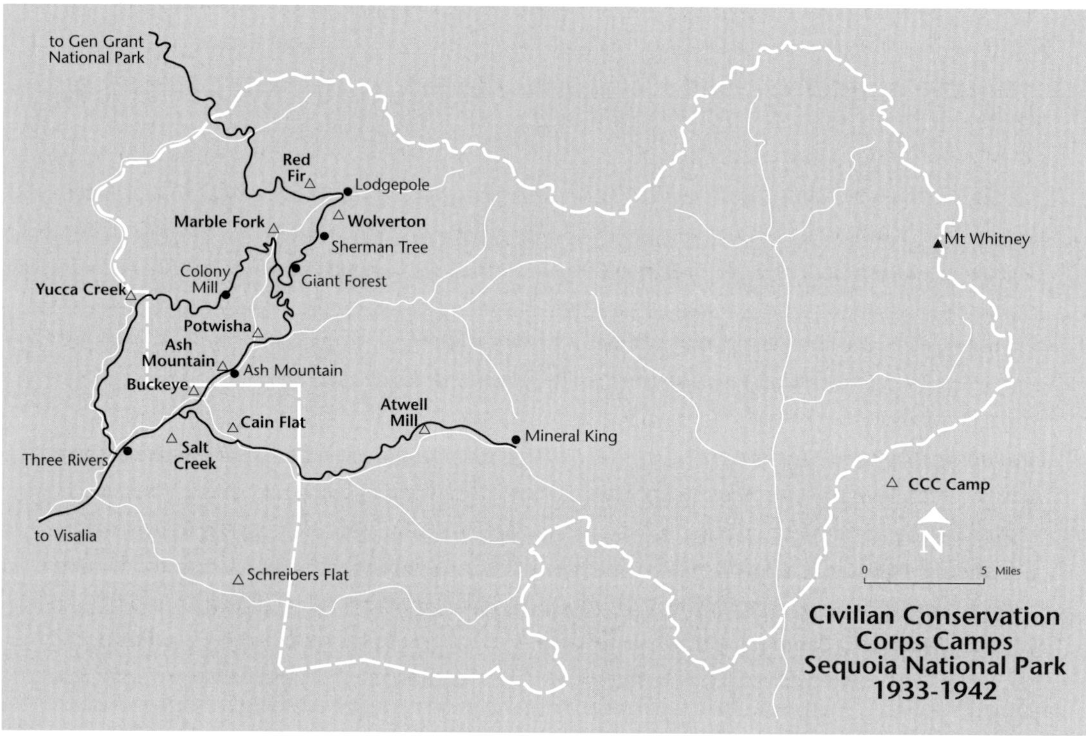
to Gen Grant
National Park
Red
Fir
Lodgepole
Marble Fork
Wolverton
Sherman Tree
Colony
Mill
Giant Forest
Yucca Creek
Potwisha
Ash
Mountain
Ash Mountain
Buckeye
Atwell
Mill
Cain Flat
Mineral King
Salt
Creek
Three Rivers
to Visalia
Schreibers Flat
Mt Whitney
CCC Camp
N
0
5 Miles
Civilian Conservation
Corps Camps
Sequoia National Park
1933-1942

capable enrollees were encouraged to reenlist. The men wore military-style uniforms, attended a "boot camp" of sorts for two weeks prior to assignment, and were expected to finish their volunteer assignments. Desertion remained a small but nagging problem throughout the CCC program. In addition to their meager salaries, the enrollees received full room and board as well as access to education and recreation. It was an attractive option both for young out-of-work men and their desperate and hungry families.

The work conducted by the CCC men in the national parks primarily consisted of the construction of roads, maintenance of trails, construction and razing of buildings and campsites, fighting fires, controlling insects and fungus, and replanting and landscaping. Those who were so trained conducted specialized activities such as surveying, resource planning, and even participation in natural-history programs for visitors. Each day began at 6:00 a.m. with reveille followed by calisthenics, breakfast, and a general policing of the camp. Work began at 8:00 a.m. and generally concluded between 4:00 and 5:00 p.m., with a one-hour lunch. The maximum work week was forty hours. On evenings and weekends, enrollees engaged in sports or games with equipment procured by local park officials. It was a well-ordered life disrupted only by inclement weather or forest fire.[6]

The experiences of two CCC men at Sequoia National Park exemplify the work done in the park under that program. Filmore Criss, a West Virginia native, joined the CCC at age sixteen, and, after working near Phoenix, Arizona, for a short time, came with his company to Ash Mountain in 1936 to work on the Mineral King Road. Later, he and some of his co-workers were assigned to clear part of the High Sierra Trail that had been damaged by severe storms the previous winter. During their time in the high country, the men stayed near Bearpaw Meadow in a temporary camp of four-man tents dating from the Spanish-American War. Despite substandard accommodations, Criss much preferred trail work to the hot and dusty labor on the Mineral King Road. He participated in several fire-fighting assignments, some of which were as far away as the Coast Range.[7]

In contrast to the typical duties of Filmore Criss, Roy DeVoe, of Welden, California, enjoyed several unusual and more intellectually demanding tasks. Transferred from Lassen Volcanic National Park in northeastern California, early in the CCC days, DeVoe was one of only a few young men with any surveying experience. Although his expertise was limited, he secured a position as surveyor for CCC projects in Sequoia and studied nights to keep up with his job. Among his accomplishments were surveying a road to Muir Grove and the layout of Dorst Campground. When not surveying, DeVoe participated in several other noteworthy jobs. When a sequoia fell across the Moro Rock Road, it was he and his crew who suggested cutting a tunnel in the huge log. With torches and adzes, they chopped out Tunnel Log much as native Indians had made their log canoes. Colonel White was pleased with their suggestion and encouraged them to think about other such improvements. DeVoe also assisted with filming a movie at Beetle Rock. Living at Lodgepole or Wolverton during most of his assignment, DeVoe guided visitors on Sundays, chiefly at Moro Rock. He even claimed to have discovered an unclassified and unnamed fly at Red Fir that a biologist from the University of California in Berkeley purchased from him. For Roy DeVoe, the CCC was an opportunity to participate in many activities that would have been denied him as an unemployed and undereducated youth in the Depression.[8]

The results of the CCC's work in Sequoia National Park form a legacy that still shines today. From 1933 to 1942, the NPS added ninety buildings and renovated another sixteen with CCC labor. At the same time, enrollees razed dozens of old and dilapidated structures. In those nine years, the park's road mileage doubled from seventy-five to 138 miles. No new major trails were added, but the CCC assumed annual maintenance of the 625 miles of backcountry paths and oiled several miles within the Giant Forest. Enrollees installed 2.7 miles of underground electric cable, built more than fifty comfort stations, designed 200 new campsites, and helped install new water systems, five sewage plants, and several electric generators. Under the direction of Colonel White's landscape architects, CCC men put in several miles of fence, four dozen benches, and eight corrals. They graded and landscaped 243 acres in visitor areas and cleared and cleaned hundreds more acres; they planted 50,000 shrubs and trees and forty-one acres of lawn, supplied all the firewood for the park, and constructed countless retaining walls, stone-lined gutters, and parapets along the roads. In addition to these tangible results of their labor, CCC workers fought dozens of fires; cleared tons of brush in presuppression programs; collected refuse from trails, campgrounds, and roadsides; and acted as surveyors, guides, and safety officers.[9]

One final project of note that CCC men completed was construction of infrastructure for visitors at Crystal Cave. The cave was first discovered in 1918 by A. C. Medley and C. M. Webster, two NPS employees who happened upon it while fishing. Initial exploration showed that the new cave's beauty far surpassed that of two other oft-visited caverns in the park, Clough and Paradise Caves. In addition, the two well-known caves had been severely damaged by vandals and trophy seekers. With this destruction in mind and with no funds for proper development, the NPS decided to close Crystal Cave. More than twenty years passed before the NPS devoted money and men to Crystal Cave. Finally, during the seasons of 1939 through 1941, CCC men paved more than 1,000 feet of trail within the cave, installed electric lights, and built a road connection to Generals Highway, a parking lot, and a steep trail to the cave's entrance. Within weeks of its opening in 1940, the cave became one of the most popular visitor attractions in the park.[10]

During the first six years of this era of construction and development, Colonel White maintained iron control of the progress and projects in his park. Picking and choosing tasks, coordinating plans, and allocating work crews, White continued his rule of Sequoia's development and prevented the abuse that too much labor and too much money threatened to bring. By late 1938, President

Roosevelt and his administration had scaled back the CCC, and soon Sequoia and other parks found the workforce inadequate to meet their demands, inflated by six years of rich supply. When White accepted, without much enthusiasm, the first of two and one-half years of jobs away from his beloved park, much of the danger of exorbitant and irresponsible construction had passed. His successor, Eivind Scoyen, continued White's use of the CCC for conservation projects and careful, limited development. Thus, when the colonel returned to oversee the last half year of CCC activity, the program had tremendously improved access for visitors and helped to maintain his increasingly staunch policy of resource preservation.

In the history of Sequoia National Park, the CCC ranks as one of the most important factors in promotion of NPS's goals and values. Carefully controlled and operating within the rigid philosophical confines of Colonel White's preservation-oriented policies, the CCC gave a huge boost to infrastructural improvement while avoiding the pitfalls of sudden, uncontrolled development. Visitors today who file through Crystal Cave, lean on the parapet at Amphitheater Point, camp at Lodgepole Campground, drive through Tunnel Log, run their hands along the Moro Rock handrail, hike the trails and drive the roads of Sequoia, and enjoy a thousand other little benefits can thank the young men of the CCC for their effort and labor.

THE PRESERVATION OF A "NATURAL ATMOSPHERE": HOLDING THE LINE

As Colonel White wielded the powerful CCC-development machine, he assumed an ever-greater role in determining which projects could be adopted and which should be abandoned. At least part of the reason for his waxing personal control derived from a transition in administration within the NPS. Prior to 1933, the NPS was a small, centralized organization with a tight chain of command in Washington, D.C. The director approved nearly every significant decision. During the CCC period, organization of the NPS evolved into a system of regional officers and well-staffed divisions within those regions and within the headquarters in Washington. When this system became fully established with its various officers in well-defined roles, it distanced the Washington office from many decisions and diminished the power of each park superintendent. During this hectic transition period, however, and with the added impetus of local direction of each park's CCC program, superintendents gained great power to originate development and interpret policy.[11]

Colonel White's senior and honored status, his strong convictions and forceful personality, and the growing suspicion that he might be right in his increasingly preservationist ideals combined to lend him extra authority. White took advantage of the situation to imprint his views on Sequoia National Park to a greater extent, perhaps, than any other superintendent has done. And nowhere were his views in the mid-1930s better expressed than in his landmark address to his fellow superintendents, entitled "Atmosphere in the National Parks." White proposed that there were four parties who had interests in a national park: (1) future generations of Americans; (2) the people who visited and supported the parks; (3) the government, principally represented by a park unit's superintendent; and (4) the concessioners. While all four had rights in the parks according to their legally specified roles, there was no question in White's mind that future generations—a group with no power and no voice save that of the park staff—should have paramount rights. Hence, he endorsed a policy of erring on the side of preservation.[12]

After defining the situation and the interested parties, White went on to comment on specific practices and developments and their propriety for national parks. He supported campfire programs and nature hikes as well as educational films, natural areas for winter sports, and widely dispersed facilities for camping and lodging. He opposed radios, loudspeakers, stages and shows, dances and dance halls, tennis courts, golf courses, swimming pools, bands, electric lighting, movies for entertainment, convention business, sporting competitions, concession-operated sightseeing buses, tacky curio sales, and most of the kinds of entertainment typical resorts of the day provided. To promote the "proper" park uses and forestall "improper" ones, he believed that a superintendent needed to be an "obstructionist." He suggested that people using and supporting the park would, often in ignorance, desire these negative additions. Meanwhile, the concessioner could be counted upon to press for such amusements at every turn to maximize business and profits. In White's mind, only the superintendent—the lead obstructionist—stood between the park for future generations and the agitators clamoring for ever greater development.[13]

From 1931 through 1941, visitation to Sequoia National Park continued a meteoric annual increase, jumping from 143,573 to 300,012.[14] In addition, after 1935, most of the nearly equal numbers of entrants to General Grant National Park were able to journey into Sequoia on the completed Generals Highway. Virtually all these visitors poured into the Giant Forest, creating massive traffic problems. The chaos and racket that attended a holiday weekend often obliterated the "atmosphere" that White sought to promote. Thus, while directing the vast development actions of the CCC, the superintendent also conducted his campaign of "obstructionism," concentrating on three courses of action: control and exclusion of improper uses of the park, dispersal of activities and infrastructure, and careful regulation of the concessioner.

Every year, Colonel White received requests that forced reappraisal of the park's resources and the NPS charter. Many of these he rejected outright, while others called for consultation with his staff and superiors. In most cases, his decisions reflected a will to preserve the atmosphere by direct exclusion or tight control. Even before the end of Stephen Mather's directorship in 1929, White squared off against the concession company and most public opinion by rejecting funds to install electricity lines to the Giant Forest. Despite incessant pressure and insistent pleading, he rejected appropriations, turned back offers from power companies, and repeatedly turned down Mauger and Hays.[15] He allowed small, isolated generators but only in a few concession areas and for limited purposes. During the 1930s, White turned down applications from the Sequoia and General Grant National Parks Company to build a commercial movie theater, a miniature golf course, tennis courts, and a croquet field. Independent operators who proposed placing telescopes on Moro Rock and conducting pony rides in the Giant Forest also met swift rejection. Other suggestions such as a system of sightseeing buses with loud speakers, a cable lift to Moro Rock, and hay rides never even reached full proposal status before the colonel shot them down. He had mixed feelings on the notion of airplanes and landing fields in or near the park. While he disapproved of such interference, he felt that construction of a small field at the edge of the park and strict enforcement of a narrow flying corridor over the park offered a better chance of controlling intrusion by airplanes than outright exclusion, which he felt would be ignored by pilots. In this rare instance, then NPS Director Arno Cammerer overruled White and established the more stringent policy of exclusion, with predictably mixed results.[16]

While fending off these obnoxious suggestions, Colonel White also tackled the problem of dispersing the activities and visitation that placed so much pressure on the Giant Forest. One measure was to encourage visitors to come to Sequoia at times other than the busy peak season. Winter use in the Giant Forest had begun in 1921 and become institutionalized when the concessioner took over winter accommodations in 1927. After the completion of the Generals Highway, most of the activity concentrated at Lodgepole and Wolverton, which dovetailed nicely with White's plan to shift use away from the sequoias to nearby valleys and meadows. It soon became apparent, however, that visitors did not come in winter instead of summer but in addition to it. By 1936, White was forced to reject pleas from the concessioner for a ski lift and other artificial facilities. So many people crowded Wolverton Meadow and its gentle surrounding slopes that traffic again became a problem, exacerbated by snow and the much higher incidence of injury to visitors from various winter activities. At least it gave White the excuse to move the hospital and doctor out of the Giant Forest to nearby Lodgepole.[17]

Of greater promise were White's plans to disperse various functions and facilities from the Giant Forest to other sites in the park. He had already shifted camping from the center of the grove to its rim, but Hazelwood, Firwood, and other campgrounds had become serious problems. Part of the troubles arose from some campers' five- or six-month stays. Many were victims of the Depression, while others simply intended to enjoy extended vacations and cheap accommodations at the government's expense. By 1933, park forester Lawrence Cook suggested that limits be placed on the duration of camping in the park. He believed that a rigorous one-night limit at Hazelwood and two- or four-week limits at the other campgrounds in the Giant Forest would suffice. As a concession to demand and a ploy to shift visitors out of the grove, Lodgepole could remain limitless, and the Dorst Creek campground should be developed rapidly.[18] The following year, White implemented a modified plan that placed a thirty-day limit on all areas in the Giant Forest, left Lodgepole open, and started development of Dorst Campground. Between 1936 and 1939, the NPS completed Dorst and enlarged Lodgepole, while closing Hazelwood to overnight use and greatly reducing the size of the other Giant Forest camps. With less infrastructure and lower cost of replacement, camping was an easy target for the reform-minded NPS.[19]

Colonel White also decided to shift as many NPS structures as possible out of the Giant Forest. In 1931 and 1932, park officials removed corrals and barns and all maintenance facilities, returning several hundred acres to relatively natural conditions and public use. The maintenance facilities went to Lodgepole, near the burgeoning main campground, while the corrals went to Wolverton.[20] During the late 1920s and early 1930s, considerable discussion had revolved around a large museum and administrative center at Giant Forest Village. Although many supporters of the evacuation of facilities at the Giant Forest urged White to make an exception in this case, the superintendent convinced his superiors to dispense with a museum and build a smaller summer headquarters at Lodgepole. At the same time, White gained approval to improve housing for the park's employees in Lodgepole near the new administrative center. Although the government still maintained a number of facilities in the grove, including ranger cabins, visitor contact stations, the superintendent's house, and assorted support buildings, the trend and progress of removal advanced sharply during the CCC era. The availability of CCC labor allowed White to designate each cleared zone for cleanup, landscaping, and replanting, until a semblance of "natural atmosphere" and appearance returned to the forest.[21]

In controlling unwanted practices in the park and removing NPS features from the Giant Forest, Colonel White achieved considerable success and branded Sequoia with his philosophy and actions. When it came to the concession company, however, White's control was small. Throughout his career, the superintendent had problems with company executives Howard Hays and George Mauger. In the case of Hays, White met his intellectual and expository equal. Their often friction-filled correspondence bristled with neat turns of phrase and eloquent defenses of their respective positions. Fortunately for Sequoia and for White, Hays was a fairly restrained and responsible man who had a genuine interest in preserving the Big Trees, while operating his business among them. Still, his ideas of appropriate level and character of visitor use of the grove differed widely from those of White. For more than two decades, from the arrival of his company in 1926 until Colonel White's departure in 1947, Hays battled with the superintendent over seemingly every issue of building and expansion. At least part of the problem stemmed from Hays's continuing penchant for going over White's head. Often this worked, particularly during the years of Albright's directorship. White would later write to William Colby, of the Sierra Club, "during my 28 years in the national parks the concessioner problem was the only really difficult one, largely insoluble by a superintendent because the concessioner had such constant access to higher ups of the Department and the Service and could afford to disregard a superintendent."[22]

After White's plan to oust Giant Forest Lodge was rejected in 1931, several years of tense relations followed between White and Hays and between White and Albright. When White continued to complain about the lodge and block moves to upgrade and expand to the new pillow limit, Albright upbraided him for his "attitude" problem. In March 1932, Albright wrote to White:

> We are extremely fortunate to have the facilities that are now available in the Giant Forest and in General Grant Park. The pity of it is that we had to lose the General Grant Lodge (destroyed by fire) which the company cannot well afford to rebuild. Your attitude toward the operator is of course known to the company officers and is very discouraging. It seems to me to reflect a feeling which I have felt that you have had for a long time, that there ought to be some other way of providing facilities in national parks besides through our present concession system. I hope I am mistaken in this impression, for there is no hope of Congress changing the present policy and as long as we have to operate under the present general policy we should do so wholeheartedly, giving our operators who are serving the public in just the same way as we are, full encouragement and support.[23]

To this challenge a deeply offended White briskly responded. Hays had convinced Albright that the company was barely squeaking by, but White showed that the concessioner had enjoyed steady profits of nearly ten percent over the previous three years. To Hays's admonition that concession customers were the true park visitors, because they stayed longer, White charged elitism and violently disagreed. Finally, to the charge that he had an attitude problem, White reiterated the financial success of the concession company and added:

> I submit that if the operator has obtained these results despite my covert or expressed hostility, he is either a financial genius or I am singularly unfortunate in my objectives. I cannot but believe, however, that my supervision of the operator's activities has been beneficial to all three of the interested parties: the Government, the people and the operators. . . . We are building as we go, and the Service is young. But I had hoped that I was contributing to the solution of operator problems, and regret that my protection of the park and the public should have been interpreted into hostility to the operator, which I do not in any way feel. I rather like him, or them; but I like the Big Trees even better.[24]

Amid this acrimonious atmosphere and the continued increase of visitors and their demands, the decade 1931 to 1941 unfolded as a recurring war of nerves and influence between White and the company. After establishment of the pillow limits, Hays and Mauger quickly assembled more cabins, reaching the guest limit of 200 for Giant Forest Lodge by 1932, 500 for Camp Kaweah by 1936, and 300 at Pinewood, the last to be established, by 1938.[25] At the same time, the concessioner gained approval to enlarge the lodge's office, the gas station, and most of the buildings at Giant Forest Village. An example of one technique used by the company was provided by the Giant Forest's lunchroom, which later became the Giant Forest's studio gift shop and today is a museum. Mauger requested permission to erect a temporary tent addition, in May 1933, to handle the summer season overflow. After meeting some resistance from White, he secured approval from Director Albright on the condition that the structure was "definitely temporary."[26] Later that year, after a successful tourist season, Mauger requested that the structure remain in use during the winter. White responded by agreeing, with the understanding that he could demand its removal at any time.[27] Apparently, Mauger was persuasive, for the "temporary addition" remained in use into the late 1990s.

Use of Giant Forest Village's facilities continued to grow, and, in 1935, Mauger convinced the NPS of the need to add onto the village in some fashion. The solution was replacement of the dance area of the coffee shop with expanded restaurant facilities and an addition, several years later, of a separate assembly-dance hall across the road in Camp Kaweah. Time and again, Hays and Mauger gained approval for little "temporary additions" and jockeyed them into permanent features in the face of stiff opposition from the superintendent.[28]

The Sequoia and General Grant National Parks Company did not always emerge victorious, however. White categorically refused to allow construction of a gift shop at the General Sherman Tree, a decision that the Washington office upheld.[29] Upon receiving permission to build an assembly hall, Hays and Mauger submitted plans for both the recreational structure and an additional dormitory for employees behind and slightly upslope from Giant Forest Village near Bear Hill. This would have placed structures amid sequoia trees in a previously undeveloped area and would have considerably increased traffic and parking problems in the village. White launched a campaign to block this location and enlisted the aid of regional and Washington-office landscape architects to support his position against an expected appeal to the director by Hays. In the end, White succeeded in getting the assembly hall built in Camp Kaweah near Beetle Rock, in reducing employee housing capacity, and in shifting it, likewise, to Kaweah. In addition, when the assembly hall opened in August 1940, conspicuously absent from its name and designated purposes were dancing and conventions, although both activities persisted in limited form for some years.[30]

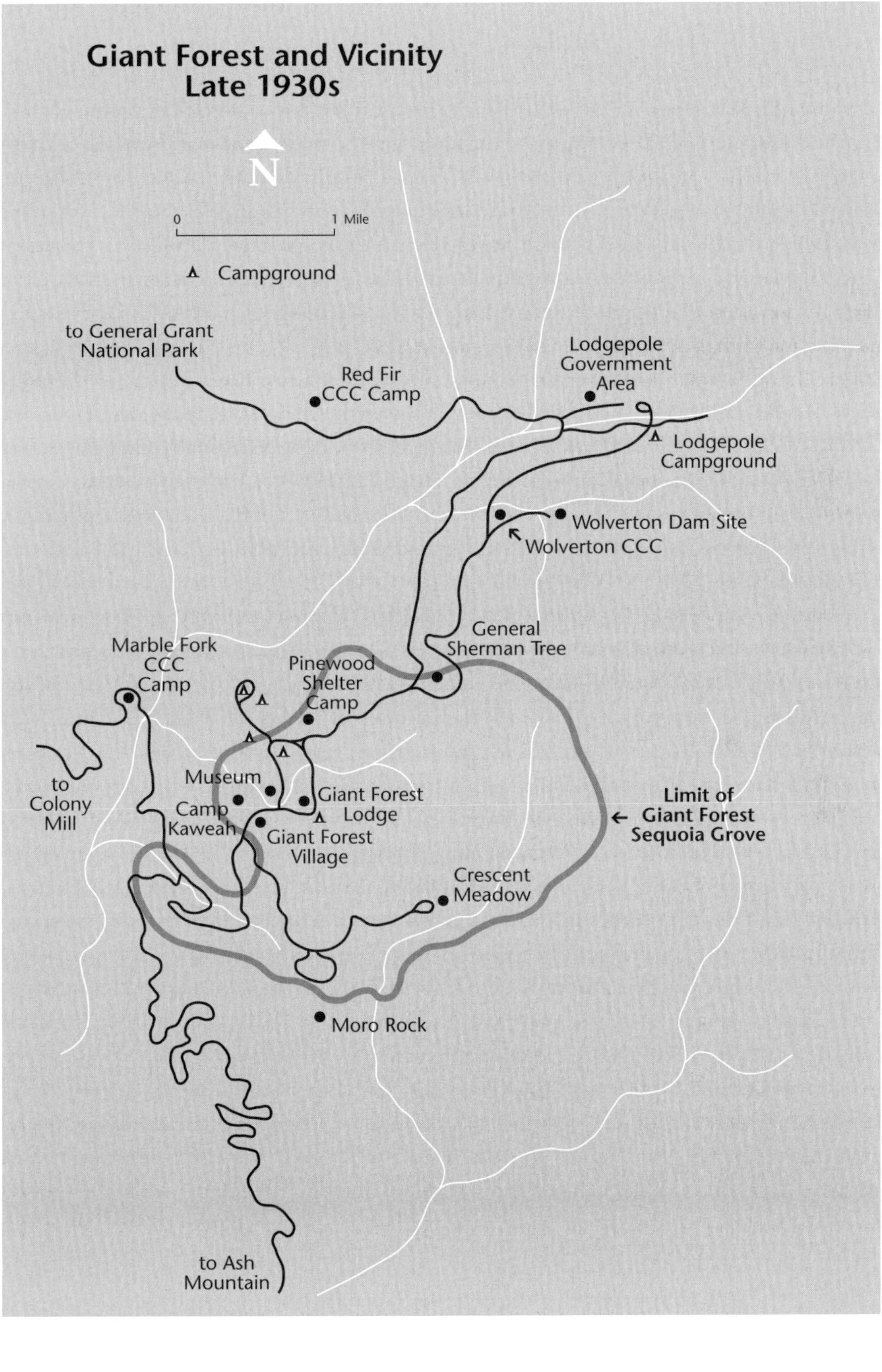
Giant Forest and Vicinity
Late 1930s
N
0
1 Mile
Campground
to General Grant
National Park
Red Fir
CCC Camp
Lodgepole
Government
Area
Lodgepole
Campground
Wolverton Dam Site
Wolverton CCC
General
Sherman Tree
Marble Fork
CCC
Camp
Pinewood
Shelter
Camp
to
Colony
Mill
Museum
Camp
Kaweah
Giant Forest
Lodge
Giant Forest
Village
Limit of
Giant Forest
Sequoia Grove
Crescent
Meadow
Moro Rock
to Ash
Mountain

For a decade, Colonel White lived with the reality of the concessioner's indefinite presence in Giant Forest and, at the same time, battled to control its expansion and remove whatever facilities he could. With scientific evidence of harm to the Big Trees and widespread disruption of the national park atmosphere, Albright's rejection of White's attempted ouster of concessions from the grove had been a bitter pill for the superintendent to swallow. White never gave up on the idea, however, and, by 1940, while assigned to the NPS's regional office in San Francisco as its director, he succeeded in resurrecting the concept before the Washington office, at least in theory. Then, in January 1941, as White entered his last six months in San Francisco, his replacement in Sequoia, Eivind Scoyen, wrote to inform him that a falling sequoia had crushed the superintendent's summer cabin. White had spent many a happy season there, hosting dignitaries, meeting the public, and conducting the business of Sequoia National Park. He sympathized with Scoyen's desire to reconstruct the cabin and continue its pleasant occupation. He believed, however, that the campaign against building in the Giant Forest precluded rebuilding a government structure in the grove. Instead, he suggested it be built at Lodgepole, alongside the other offices and residences of the NPS.[31]

Some months later, in July 1941, White returned to Sequoia to resume his role as superintendent. Although his return meant relinquishing his promotion and any chance of further career advancement, White had never been happy away from his beloved park. His disaffection for both San Francisco and Washington led to health problems and depression. When he returned, one of the first duties he faced was solution of the superintendent's cabin question. To White, the presence of the park's principal public officer within the grove was far more important than the cabins, stores, and cafeterias of the concessioner. So he reversed his former stance and requested that his cabin be rebuilt at its old site, pending removal of the fallen tree, or at a similar site within 100 yards. After due consideration, the Washington office refused but, in so doing, was forced to hear again White's vigorous and righteous arguments on behalf of the total evacuation of facilities from the Giant Forest. If the NPS's major officer could not be in the grove, he argued, then why should the concessioner?[32]

Thus, after ten years of relative quiescence, the big question for Sequoia National Park reared again. The catalyst of the superintendent's cabin, fueled by White's return and the return of his strident philosophical program, once again threatened to wrench Hays, Mauger, and their company out of the so-called "sacred area." Much of the reason for the resurgence was a more widespread acceptance of Colonel White's ideas of a national park atmosphere, particularly among landscape architects whose voices still carried great power at all levels of the NPS. Additionally, the tiny seed of science and ecology had begun to sprout. It was still weak and applied more to the management of the park's backcountry and wildlife, but its paradigms were gaining power. The growth of scientific management, during the 1930s, would lay the foundation for a revolution in the NPS's philosophy and purpose two decades later.

SCIENCE AND RESOURCE MANAGEMENT: REVERSING BAD HABITS

As we have seen, the years prior to 1931 were bleak ones for ecology and scientific management in the national park system and in Sequoia. Nevertheless, the roots of ecological preservation and the organizational wing of the NPS set up to carry it out go back nearly three decades earlier. In 1905 and 1908, Dr. Charles C. Adams began his long association with wildlife and ecological management in national parks with a pair of classic studies of Isle Royale in Michigan. Two decades later, he devoted a considerable portion of his lengthy article, "Ecological Conditions in the National Parks and National Forests," to Sequoia National Park. Although he lauded efforts to protect individual Big Trees, Adams decried existing wildlife policies and the overdevelopment of the Giant Forest. He also noted the usefulness of "light burning" of the forest floor but concluded it would cost too much to carry out.[33]

At the same time that Adams was compiling his retrospective analysis for *The Scientific Monthly* and Emilio Meinecke was conducting his study on sequoias in the Giant Forest, two other men began laying the groundwork for change. Aldo Leopold developed a theory and philosophy of human-park interaction based on careful stewardship and specific ecological principles that he outlined in his pioneering book *Game Management* (1933), which helped to establish Leopold as a founder of "wildlife ecology." Nearly thirty-five years later, park biologist Lowell Sumner would conclude that Leopold's philosophy and recommendations still formed the backbone of NPS's program for resource management.[34] The other pioneer was Joseph Grinnell, who, in his classic studies of Yosemite and Lassen Volcanic National Parks, eloquently presented his concepts of ecological interdependence and stated the importance of non-interference with natural process. As important as Grinnell's research and writings were for the NPS, his most important contribution came in training NPS biologists at the University of California in Berkeley. Students such as Harold C. Bryant, Ben Thompson, and Joseph Dixon would found the NPS's biology program. Two other Grinnell students deserve particular attention for their monumental impact on Sequoia: George M. Wright, who became the first chief of the system-wide wildlife division, and Lowell Sumner, whose name became synonymous with resource management at Sequoia for some three decades.[35]

Independently wealthy and deeply committed to inducing ecological responsibility in the NPS, George Wright, in his first major action, personally financed a classic evaluation of wildlife policy and status in the national parks. With the assistance of Joseph Dixon and Ben Thompson, he compiled, from 1929 to 1931, a historic volume entitled *Fauna of the National Parks of the United States* (1932).[36] In it, he proposed twenty policy statements that became forerunners of the resource-management program adopted thirty years later. Among his recommendations were establishment of an organized research program to include environmental impact studies, bans on artificial feeding, predator control and automatic destruction of problem animals, elimination of exotic species and reintroduction of extirpated ones, and extension of each park's boundaries to include the natural ranges of its wildlife. Although not all of his policy suggestions were immediately adopted, they led to creation of the wildlife division that he would head. Wright immediately began to imprint on the NPS his ideas, along with those of Grinnell and Leopold. He wrote that protection of resources was not enough. It was necessary "to restore and perpetuate" by combating the harmful effects of human use. Wright was tragically killed in an automobile accident in February 1936, and his engaging personality and consummate scholarship were sorely missed. With him went much of the momentum of scientific advancement of NPS policy, further devastated by World War II and drastic cuts in funds and manpower. But Wright had sown the seeds of an organization that would later spring to life to become the divisions of research and resource management and revolutionize environmental management in all national parks.[37]

In Sequoia, the NPS benefited from the industry and dedication of Lowell Sumner, one of Wright's earliest colleagues who began conducting research at Sequoia in 1935 and continued there or at the Western Region Office for most of the next thirty-three years. Although Colonel White listened primarily to landscape architects, he gave increasing attention to the scientist's opinions. Sumner was instrumental in planting ecology in the management program at Sequoia in three specific programs: wildlife management; vegetation management, including that of sequoias; and protection of the backcountry.

The program where Wright, Sumner, and other biologists had their greatest impact was that of wildlife management, logical in view of their initial appointments in a "wildlife division." One of the most troublesome and much-discussed issues was the management of deer. Rigorous protection of deer and wholesale slaughter of predators had allowed herds to multiply well beyond the capacity of the park's forage. In 1934, CCC laborers replanted browse to bring back the natural appearance of the Giant Forest and other grossly over-browsed areas, but, in the face of several thousand voracious deer, it was a paltry effort. At the same time, park officials constructed an enclosure to test the impact on vegetation of denying access to deer. Results were little short of spectacular and corroborated the opinion that drastic action must be taken. Still, old ideas die hard, and although browse was estimated to be down by seventy-five percent in 1935, it was five

Each afternoon at Bear Hill, behind the Giant Forest Village, the National Park Service (NPS) allowed black bears to rummage through the garbage before burning the inedible portions. It soon drew so many visitors that bleachers had to be erected. The popular attraction demonstrated the lack of scientific knowledge in the management of the bears during the 1920s and 1930s. After wildlife ecologists such as the NPS's own George M. Wright decried the policy, the agency stopped the practice at Sequoia in 1940 as well as at other national parks. Unfortunately, the bears turned to campgrounds to search for substitute human food. Photographer and date unknown.

more years before the NPS experimented with capturing and moving some deer to less sensitive areas. From 1940 to 1943, rangers moved approximately eighty deer, but the impact was negligible, since the park's deer population numbered in the thousands. From 1943 to 1947, park officials killed a few deer, primarily for study. The results showed disease and stress, presumably resulting, in part, from overpopulation. By the time of Colonel White's departure, the deer problem was far from solved or even systematically attacked, but these tentative experiments in management were already a considerable advance over the anthropogenic practices of earlier years.[38]

Of equal concern to park biologists was the delicate issue of management of black bears. The garbage pit and bear-feeding station atop Bear Hill was one of the park's principal attractions, yet the bears, now concentrated in the area of greatest human population, rendered them at least partially dependent on human food and wholly familiar with people and their practices. Occasionally, bears were not content with the organized feeding area and foraged through campgrounds and concession areas in almost nightly searches. In 1938, park officials began trapping and transporting bears, even as they continued to kill them in larger numbers. That same year, biologists convinced a favorably predisposed Colonel White to order the closure of the Bear Hill facility and to explore the options of tagging problem bears and bringing in bear-proof garbage cans. Neither of the latter two measures was adopted, but, after a two-decade show, Superintendent Scoyen closed Bear Hill in 1940, with the blessing of White and the Washington, D.C., office. Thereafter, the park experienced a severe rise in bear problems, as the destructive animals rambled through visitor accommodations seeking a replacement for their traditional garbage diet. Finally, in 1947, evening collection of garbage was instituted, and human-bear contacts were reduced to an endurable level.[39]

Other accomplishments in wildlife management included Joseph Dixon's study on bighorn sheep, in which he suggested establishing a sanctuary east of Mt. Baxter, reducing aggressive rodent-control measures, especially with poison, and beginning a series of wildlife-status reports for the park in 1939. World War II and the flagging influence of the wildlife division, when deprived of Wright's leadership, diminished these studies, but they continued at least as statistical reports. As such, they form a link between early, exciting, and important years of the NPS's early embrace of ecology to the science's grand resurgence, during the late-1950s, that revolutionized NPS's management priorities.[40]

Management of vegetation also received greater attention from 1931 to 1947, especially before the war. A spate of studies on the bark beetle, control of blister rust, and techniques for controlling insects in Sequoia and other national parks in the West were undertaken during the early 1930s. The Ash Mountain Nursery expanded tremendously with the addition of CCC labor, and most of the park's areas of visitor access were vigorously replanted with tree and browse species. Organized programs to implement the recommendations of earlier studies began with blister rust, in 1938, and insect control, in 1941.[41] Attention to the management of sequoias, still the park's primary purpose, occupied a pivotal position in the questions of ecological investigation and policy. The policies of Wright—attested to and carried out by Sumner, Dixon, and others—unquestionably influenced the decision to reopen the question of removing buildings at the Giant Forest. To address that question, the NPS, in 1944, brought back a then-aged and retired Emilio Meinecke to restudy human impact upon the giant sequoias. Meinecke's recommendations added fuel to the fires for an ouster of the concessions from the Giant Forest already being stoked by Colonel White.[42] That same year, NPS Director Newton Drury met with regional directors and questioned the right of the NPS to tamper with natural succession and other environmental processes to improve visitor experiences. The specific question was forest growth in Yosemite Valley, which threatened to block many popular vistas of waterfalls and cliffs. The issue had particular import to Sequoia and to Grant Grove, where views of the largest sequoias could often only be obtained by removing surrounding trees. The very consideration of abandoning this time-honored policy of enhancement for visitors marked a minor revolution in NPS resource management.[43]

One byproduct of the vegetation-management work was increased interest in the huge, alpine, and largely roadless majority of the park known as the backcountry. With far less pressure from visitors, the backcountry had received only sufficient attention to establish a trail network and protect it from grazing, the latter task having lapsed somewhat from 1918 to 1930. The addition of Lowell Sumner to the park's staff, along with evidence of rapidly increasing use of the backcountry, led to research that later resulted in the management of meadows and livestock. Shortly after Sumner arrived in Sequoia, he conducted extensive field investigations of the backcountry and submitted a summary of conditions arising from the recently suspended use by cattle and the continued grazing by stock. He found serious erosion in many meadows and suggested the closure of some areas to stock. In 1940, the NPS received a huge new park—Kings Canyon—which more than doubled the backcountry's acreage of what would soon be a single administrative unit. This land had been in the hands of the USFS for nearly fifty years. Forest Service policy had allowed extensive grazing, and, consequently, much of the damage incurred before 1893 had never healed. Park scientist John Armstrong conducted the first of what would become a series of in-depth studies of the Roaring River Grazing District during 1941 and 1942. That study and follow-ups established a basis for monitoring meadows as a standard resource-management procedure. After the hiatus of the war and postwar years, the backcountry was destined to become one of the principal targets of resurging scientific concern.[44]

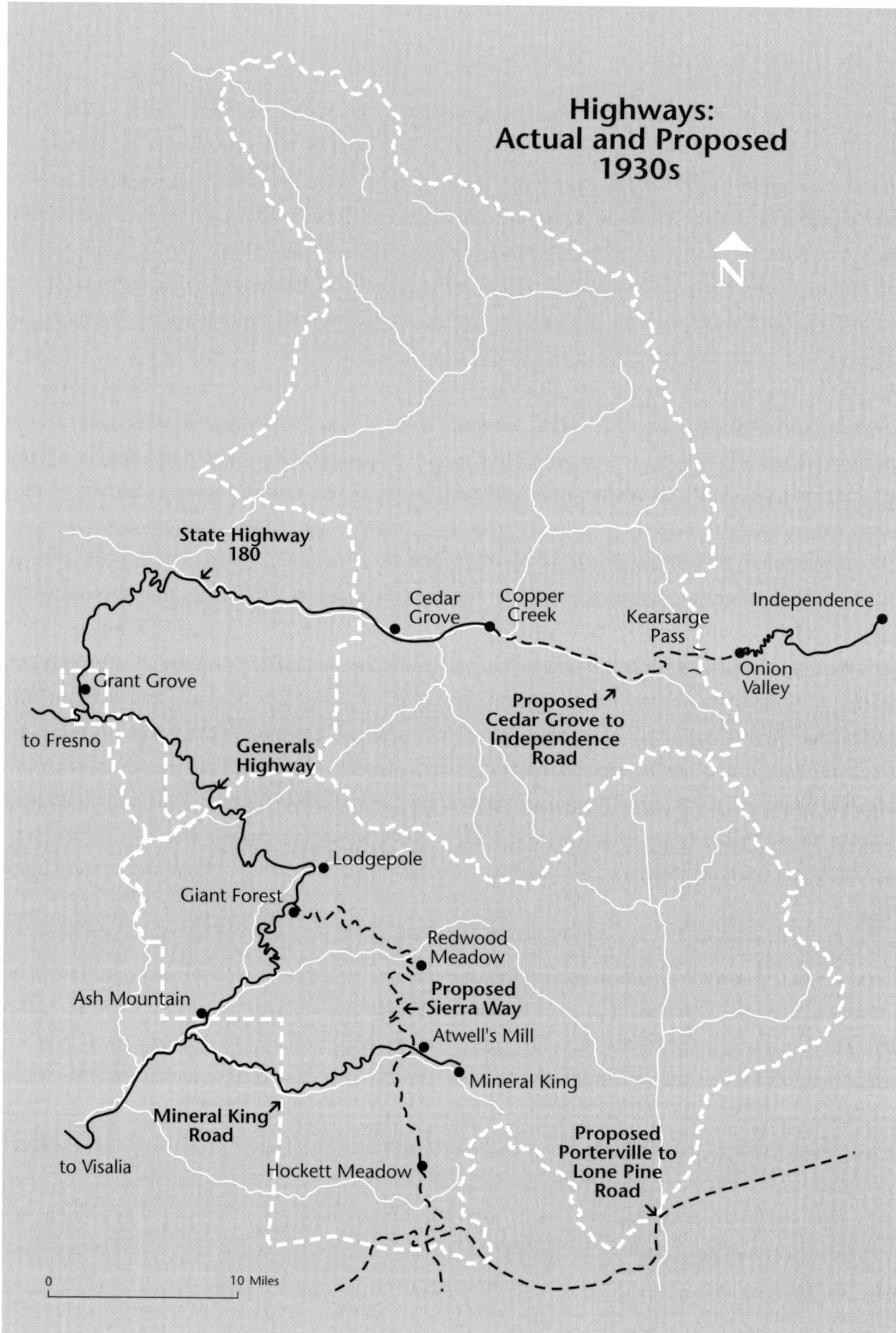
Highways:
Actual and Proposed
1930s
N
State Highway
180
Cedar
Grove
Copper
Creek
Kearsarge
Pass
Independence
Onion
Valley
Grant Grove
to Fresno
Proposed
Cedar Grove to
Independence
Road
Generals
Highway
Lodgepole
Giant Forest
Redwood
Meadow
Proposed
Sierra Way
Ash Mountain
Atwell's Mill
Mineral King
Mineral King
Road
to Visalia
Hockett Meadow
Proposed
Porterville to
Lone Pine
Road
0
10 Miles

INTO THE BACKCOUNTRY: THE THREAT OF ROADS

Although management of the backcountry usually ranked low on the list of priorities in Colonel White's park, there was one topic over which the NPS and the public had widely varying and deeply held beliefs: the matter of access by roads. During the first four decades of Sequoia National Park, many roads were discussed, but few could be afforded. Hence, the Generals Highway remained the NPS's major commitment. By the late 1920s, however, several other projects had been proposed by enthusiastic businessmen in the San Joaquin and Owens Valleys. The largest, most expensive, and potentially most threatening of those projects was known as the Sierra Nevada National Parks Highway, or "The Sierra Way." It would have been one of the great mountain highways of the world, both from engineering and scenic standpoints. But it ran into an agency and a superintendent, John White, who both had come to believe that preservation of roadless areas was a moral responsibility.

Sequoia had just been enlarged to include Mt. Whitney and Kern Canyon when, in January 1927, an association of businessmen, city and county officials, engineers, and others from the San Joaquin Valley formed to promote a road from Lake Isabella in Kern County to Yosemite National Park. The Generals Highway portion from Sequoia to General Grant, still in the planning stages, would compose a portion of the highway. By 1931, the scheme had been expanded to include Lassen Volcanic National Park and Mt. Shasta, the fifth-highest peak in Califonia. Later, Colonel White speculated that it was the Generals Highway connection between his two parks that had suggested the whole road. The highway would maintain an elevation of 6,000 feet or more over nearly all the route and handle traffic at speeds averaging forty miles per hour. Most of the road would pass through federal lands, including four national parks and a half-dozen national forests, but seven counties also joined in the project.[45]

Initially, the NPS's response to the project was mixed. Although the road in general seemed a worthy idea, portions of it bothered then Director Mather. Chief among those troublesome sections was the piece running from the Giant Forest to the southern boundary of Sequoia. The earliest plans from the San Joaquin Valley suggested a route through the Kern Canyon, a region Mather had envisioned for some time as a permanently roadless. In response to his objections, road planners shifted the route to one that brought the road through Hockett Meadow, over Tar Gap to Mineral King, then over Paradise Ridge to Redwood Meadow. From there, the road was planned to veer westward and link with the Generals Highway near the General Sherman Tree. Colonel White initially favored this route, because it would provide a new destination and relieve the Giant Forest. As an added benefit, it would allow easy penetration of much of the park's backcountry for fire control. White's attitude toward the entire Sierra Way project changed, however, as his preservationist philosophy deepened. By 1932, White was one of the project's most powerful opponents, at least insofar as it affected his park.

From 1928 to 1931, the Sierra Nevada National Parks Highway Association continued to meet and plan. Existing roads were incorporated into the plan, while engineers commenced construction of other portions. A few spots, particularly those associated with national parks, remained sources of contention, including the route out of the southeastern corner of Lassen and the segment from Yosemite Valley to the northern boundary of that park. But, by far, the most acrimonious debate centered on the southern part of Sequoia.[46]

Colonel White had many friends among the backers of the project, and their support was necessary to Sequoia and General Grant National Parks as well as for ambitious designs such as the creation of a huge new Kings Canyon Park. Thus, the superintendent urged the NPS to support the larger project in principle but with a route that would cross into the park over Farewell Gap to Mineral King and then follow the Mineral King Road to Three Rivers and link with the Generals Highway at Ash Mountain. This route strayed widely from the alpine nature of the proposed project but still linked the parks in the overall project. In 1931, the NPS financed a survey of the potential routes to answer mounting pressure and criticism from businesses in the San Joaquin Valley. Engineer W. P. Webber concluded that the so-called "high route" over Paradise Ridge was undesirable, largely due to difficulty of construction and cost. The combination of this negative report and the deepening Great Depression served to table the project for several years.[47]

In late 1934, with CCC labor and funds available and economic hope springing from President Roosevelt administration's sweeping reforms, the Sierra Way issue arose once again. Led by valuable park allies such as Fresno lawyer Chester Warlow, the highway association convinced the USFS, California State Legislature, and many local governments to push the project, including the "high route" in Sequoia. In the evolving attitude of the NPS, however, the concept of roadless wilderness had been enjoying ever-increasing popularity. In part, this arose from rapidly amassing evidence of scenic disruption by auto traffic in the accessible portions of parks like Sequoia. In part, it arose from strong statements by groups such as the Sierra Club and Commonwealth Club of California in opposition to mountain roads.[48] And, in part, it arose from the success of trails such as the High Sierra Trail and evidence of public need for wilderness areas. In sum, these attitudes erased nearly every vestige of support for the Redwood Meadow-Paradise Ridge route among NPS planners. Even old road engineers like Frank Kittredge vehemently opposed the concept.[49]

Their antagonism focused on two results the road would bring. First, the "high route" would slash across the western slopes of the Great Western Divide, creating a road scar visible from Moro Rock. This type of unacceptable scenic disruption had already led to abandonment of the

Middle Fork Road. The NPS's landscape architects bitterly opposed what they saw as vicious destruction of the park's principal vista.[50] In addition, park officials did not want the backcountry opened to a highway for fear of the secondary development that would accompany it. Although San Joaquin Valley businessmen passed resolutions promising that no roads would be built eastward and that this would serve as a "boundary" to development, park planners envisioned inevitable pressure to extend a small, scenic road here, build a campground there, and so forth, which would turn the highway into a full-blown development corridor. Not a small part of the justification for the NPS's opposition came from the park's biologists, who feared the intrusion would devastate wildlife and alpine vegetation.[51]

Finally, after continued argument, the federal Bureau of Public Roads, as a theoretically nonpartisan group, agreed to survey the various routes from Giant Forest to Lake Isabella. Its conclusion was not popular with anyone. The bureau found the "high route" practical and promising of exhilarating scenery for any who drove it, but it also found the route terribly expensive, requiring an enormous amount of blasting and rock clearing to hug the cliff faces and cross the difficult passes. To the NPS, the bureau's recommendations added official fuel to the threatening fire of the Sierra Way. But, to proponents of the road in the San Joaquin Valley, it tagged the project with a backbreaking price.[52]

In answer to mounting criticism, the NPS finally pledged some $15,000,000 to Colonel White for sections of the road within Sequoia, although he remained adamant in his opposition to the project. The exact sequence of political events at this stage remains clouded in partial secrecy and closed negotiations. Nevertheless, several events transpired to finally defeat the Sierra Way. First, the Commonwealth Club released a widely published and highly touted booklet entitled "Should We Stop Building New Roads into California's High Mountains?"[53] The influential club decried several road projects, including the Sierra Way. At the same time, Colonel White flatly refused the money provided for construction of the high-altitude road. Finally, NPS Director Cammerer dismissed the entire Sierra Way scheme as something that "might be appropriate in 25 or 50 years." Cost was cited by White and Cammerer as the deciding factor, although neither lost an opportunity to mention the Commonwealth Club's booklet, similar releases by the Sierra Club, and their own beliefs about an inviolate backcountry.[54]

By the end of 1936, the Sierra Way was dead. Northward, many portions of the road had been completed and, today, form a series of popular links in the still-incomplete chain. During the 1960s, the Sierra Way project surfaced again as a route predominantly in the foothills to connect CA 49 with Isabella via the Generals Highway, but it, too, failed to gain sufficient official backing and funding. The Sierra Way was by far the most serious potential threat to befall Sequoia's backcountry. Its defeat marked another turning point in the shift of the NPS's policies from development and public use to restriction and preservation.[55]

While enthusiasts of an alpine highway pushed the Sierra Way, they also boosted several trans-Sierra road projects. Communities in the Owens Valley, particularly Independence and Lone Pine, were the major proponents. Their support of a trans-Sierra road was understandable. Access to the San Joaquin Valley and through it to the San Francisco Bay area would dramatically improve their situation for goods, services, and tourists. In addition, they would benefit from another connection to southern California. Two distinct projects became popular, both of which were peripheral but threatening to Sequoia National Park. One route from the San Joaquin Valley to Independence was planned for Kearsarge Pass in the Kings Canyon area. This project called for extension of the highway that was being built into the canyon of the South Fork of the Kings River and would have provided access to spectacular scenery for nearly its entire distance. The other road would have affected the southern edge of Sequoia, as it joined Porterville to Lone Pine. A variety of exact routes were suggested, some entirely outside the park and some routed so as to open up the sequoia groves of Dennison Ridge and other portions of the park's southern townships.[56]

During the 1930s, the NPS opposed both concepts, even if both roads remained outside the park. The Kings Canyon area was a long-sought addition to Sequoia, specifically for its magnificent backcountry. Proponents of the park believed that a road such as the Kearsarge-Independence Highway would dramatically reduce the quality of the proposed addition and its primary justification. Meanwhile, the southern crossing threatened to deliver auto-tourists to Hockett Meadow and other delicate areas of the backcountry. According to the park's officials, even if the road itself remained outside these areas, its proximity would lead to inevitable trail development and public pressure. Ironically, the commitment by powerful San Joaquin Valley groups to the Sierra Way as an eastern boundary to auto traffic placed them in direct opposition to their Owens Valley counterparts. By the time the Sierra Way project died, public support for major road incursions into the southern Sierra Nevada had also waned. A few years later, creation of Kings Canyon National Park as a "wilderness park" and improvement of a trans-Sierra road well south of Sequoia National Park removed the threat of these mountain highways.[57]

Defeat of these three road projects—the Sierra Way, the Porterville to Lone Pine Highway, and the Kearsarge-Independence Road—allowed the NPS to keep the backcountry as a zone of low use. The frontcountry's problems in the Giant Forest existed because development for roads and mass traffic had occurred before planning and before any semblance of resource preservation. In rescuing the backcountry from similar auto access, the NPS assured itself of easier conversion to limits on use and to preservationist policies two decades later.

WORLD WAR II

In late 1941, Colonel White returned from the Western Regional Office in San Francisco to superintend Sequoia National Park once again. Studies of the backcountry showed that vigorous protection and repair would be needed for mountain meadows. Whimpers of protest from the Owens Valley reminded him that proposals for trans-Sierra roads could again reappear. Resource management was building scientific expertise, and expensive programs of managing deer, revegetation, and protecting sequoias were poised on the drawing board. Most exciting, the Washington, D.C., office appeared willing to reconsider the question of removing buildings from the Giant Forest. CCC labor, although much diminished from the halcyon days of 1933 and 1934, still gave White a workforce to perform desperately needed protection and maintenance. After fifty-one years as a national park, Sequoia appeared to be entering a dramatic and crucial time, a time of great accomplishment and profound execution of philosophy. The colonel was determined to see his reforms brought about and the park further shaped to his ideals.

Then came World War II. The effects were immediate and profound. Within six months, the NPS in Sequoia lost more than half its rangers, laborers, and administrators. The CCC operation came to an abrupt halt, and its men disappeared into the ranks of the military or the civilian war machine. Funding for development, maintenance, and resource protection dried to a trickle. And, in the first year of the war, the number of park visitors fell from more than 300,000 to fewer than 167,000. Visitation to Sequoia would barely reach 54,000 in 1944. With that continued decrease came deepening paralysis of all the park's programs. Trails washed out under loads of snow, violent storms, and avalanches. Maintenance of roads and the spectacular improvements of the CCC subsided to the barest minimum for safe travel. All resource, research, and management programs halted, as the much-reduced staff struggled to provide protection and some interpretation for those visitors who did arrive.[58]

Traditional visitors to the parks, along with the CCC and NPS's employees who worked to accommodate them, were replaced by two very different groups: visiting soldiers and conscientious objectors. Sequoia National Park itself became part of the war effort. One of its roles became that of a rest-and-recuperation site for soldiers and sailors. A trip to the wonders of the Sierra park served as a patriotic reminder of America's beauty as well as an uplifting and soothing interruption of the war. In addition, Wolverton and other former CCC camps became temporary sites for training exercises. The park also became a location for the storage of weapons and ammunition. On at least one occasion, this had potentially tragi-comic results, when a marauding bear tore the door off an ammunition storage shed in search of food.[59]

While troops replaced the average family as park visitors, conscientious objectors operating from several former CCC camps assumed many of the maintenance duties of the CCC and NPS laborers. Colonel White initially found the prospect of employing such men a dubious one. As a former military man, he questioned their ability to carry out hard work, yet they ultimately became the only force available to maintain the Generals Highway and other roads as well as the many park structures under annual winter stress. In some cases, the objectors, chiefly Mennonites, continued CCC construction projects. Some of the attractive stone walls and parapets in the park date not from the CCC era, as is usually supposed, but from the conscientious objectors of World War II. The chief problems that White faced with these crews came from a few rebellions against this virtual forced labor and from public reaction to the objectors, when they took recreation in nearby towns. Residents of Exeter and Porterville found their presence offensive, accusing them of paying unwelcome attention to the local girls. Colonel White received a number of complaints that he answered by extolling the objectors' value to the park. In total, the conscientious objectors proved to be a valuable, albeit small labor force that prevented the worst kinds of resource and infrastructure damage during their nearly four-year stint at the park.[60]

While Colonel White and his much-diminished staff struggled to cope with shortages in labor and funding, decay of resources, and the park's new role as a military-training area, a familiar hard-times threat reappeared. Almost before the last bomb fell on Pearl Harbor in Hawaii on December 7, 1941, western ranchers appealed to open the parks to cattle grazing. The NPS was able to resist such intrusions, despite the greater severity and danger to America of this world war that now involved both Europe and the Pacific. New NPS Director Newton Drury undertook a widely publicized campaign of radio addresses and articles, suggesting that the parks contained insufficient forage to make any difference, that the grazing damage to meadows was so severe that some areas had not recovered from World War I, much less the terrible depredations of the pre-park days, and that protection of the park's resources "unimpaired" was one of the fondest values for which America's military men were fighting and dying. Letters from soldiers and sailors recalling fondly the parks and their beauty were systematically published as evidence against potential grazing users.

A much stronger NPS, sure of itself and its popularity with the general public, waged the campaign as if from a lofty moral standard. Although cattlemen were never harshly criticized, they were portrayed as shortsighted, opportunistic, and more interested in setting a precedent than in providing some great advantage to the war effort. At Sequoia, Colonel White vigorously joined in this effort both through publicity and by rejecting whatever applications for grazing permits came his way. Preservation organizations, biologists, and even some tourism organizations joined in supporting the NPS's position. These combined efforts were successful at Sequoia in preventing any cattle or sheep from grazing the park's delicate and overtaxed alpine country. It was another success that clearly demonstrated the altered attitudes of the NPS toward its preservation duties and of the public toward its precious parks.[61]

THE GIANT FOREST: THE LAST BATTLE FOR COLONEL WHITE

World War II dramatically affected the national parks with its elimination of visitors, funds, and labor and its suspension of almost all existing programs. Research and planning became academic exercises, because no funds were available to carry them out. As such, the war allowed a reassessment of priorities and a reconsideration of values. Thus, while nearly everything else came to a halt in Sequoia, discussion of removal of facilities from the Giant Forest area actually accelerated. The concessioner, too, had suffered losses of customers, money, and employees, while operations were reduced to a limited summer program. Under such circumstances, the question of concession activities in Sequoia became a natural topic. With Colonel White's unyielding position, with evidence from both biologists and landscape architects, with apparent support from the Washington, D.C., office and with the public preoccupied elsewhere, the time appeared right to solve the problem of the Giant Forest. Also promising was the forthcoming conclusion of Hays's twenty-year contract, which gave the NPS some much-needed leverage. Colonel White believed he could finally see light at the end of the tunnel in the long struggle to evacuate facilities from the Giant Forest.

Even before World War II, White's persistent campaign for either reconstruction of the superintendent's cabin in the Giant Forest or some fair and ordered resolution of the concession's presence there had forced the NPS to make hard policy choices. Accordingly, on September 5, 1941, Director Newton Drury ordered regional and park officers to operate, henceforth, on the premise of imminent and orderly removal of all facilities from the grove.[62] Drury further ordered that this new policy be incorporated into the park's master plan, then under preparation, and into contract negotiations with the concession company. Although their twenty-year contract still had five years to run, Hays and Mauger had already begun to discuss its renewal. As it would turn out, five years was not nearly enough time.

The newly renamed Sequoia and Kings Canyon National Parks Company owned some 180 structures in the Giant Forest, compared to thirty-four owned by the NPS. The company's complex was divided into three areas, each of which presented its own set of problems and each of which became the focus of separate but related debates. The largest complex was Camp Kaweah, which contained more than 120 structures. Ironically, this huge complex received the greatest NPS support to stay in the Giant Forest. Even Colonel White had mixed feelings about evicting Camp Kaweah's structures, because the area contained no significant stands of sequoia. The oldest area, Giant Forest Lodge, was another matter. With fifty-three structures crowding some of the park's finest sequoia forest, the lodge had, of course, been the focus of controversy for years. Here, the NPS and concession company had their greatest differences. White and his staff took the position that the lodge's cabins both damaged the trees and detracted from the scenery and serenity of the grove. On ecological grounds, they offered evidence from Emilio Meinecke and others in the growing biology movement within the NPS. Their argument about destruction was backed by a host of landscape architects. Meanwhile, Hays and Mauger maintained that the NPS had overstated its evidence and ignored the fact that this was the heart of the concession operation for both parks. Without a lodge under the sequoias, they had grave doubts whether the company could even survive. The third area, Giant Forest Village, was the smallest with only five structures, but each was a commercial center. Traffic congestion from pedestrians and cars, noise and air pollution, and the ease with which this tiny complex could be shifted made it the first and easiest target of the NPS and the one for which the concessioner offered the poorest defense.[63]

Howard Hays and George Mauger reacted immediately to renewed discussion of removal. Hays wrote Director Drury, bitterly complaining that Albright's decision in 1931 to permit continued occupancy and expansion to the pillow limits had been a commitment to him and the company. He stated that, in acting upon that commitment, they had completely replaced their existing infrastructure with new structures as well as expensive water and power modifications. He argued that it was dishonorable and unfair for the NPS to discuss removal after all that investment. Further, Hays found Colonel White's arguments to be weak and biased. For evidence, he cited company-commissioned studies by three forest pathologists that disputed the NPS's evidence of damage to sequoias from the company's buildings. He argued that his structures gave visitors an opportunity to truly experience the Big Trees, by sleeping amongst them. Finally, he suggested that the company had nowhere near the funds necessary to carry out the move.[64]

During World War II, the NPS conducted a variety of planning investigations and continued to negotiate with the concessioner. Plans submitted in 1943, 1944, and 1945 each pursued Drury's mandate and developed contingencies for concession relocation to Lodgepole, Wolverton, and various combinations of both. In 1944, reacting to Hays's stepped-up criticism of its evidence, the NPS brought in various experts to study conditions at the Giant Forest. Included were Dr. Meinecke, NPS landscape architects Thomas Vint and Ernest Davidson, Regional Chief Ranger Lawrence Cook, and eminent consulting landscape architect Frederick Law Olmsted, Jr. Each submitted a separate, detailed report of his investigation. Each recommended that the structures be cleared from the grove. It began to look as if, this time, the Giant Forest really would be restored.[65]

As the war wound down, negotiations for a new contract between the concession company and the government intensified. The principal points of contention were inclusion of a stipulation guaranteeing the company's evacuation of the Giant Forest and the government's belief that it did not owe proprietary-interest payments to the company. In addition, Colonel White injected a bit of confusion and disharmony by vigorously pushing for a five- or ten-year contract, rather than twenty years, and for an end to monopoly status. White sought nothing less than to alter the basic structure of the NPS's relations with the concessioner established and modified by Congress decades earlier.[66]

The end of the war increased the tension and acrimony that had begun to exacerbate government-concession relations. Only a few months remained until the end of the company's contract on the last day of 1945, and there still appeared to be no solution in sight to the points of disagreement. White became consumed with the issues and infuriated with Hays and Mauger. He bombarded the Washington office and the regional director with long memoranda, sometimes up to fifteen single-spaced pages, reiterating his position and assailing the company and its officers. He became more strident about doing away with monopolistic concessions, gaining leverage by using short contracts, and placing preservation values over company profits. It was during this period that the colonel began to complain to old non-NPS friends about the concession company as the only real problem and unpleasant feature of his job.[67]

In some desperation, Howard Hays resisted these moves and carried on his negotiations, but he had to admit things looked bleak. There were, however, two points on which he would not budge. First, he insisted on receiving proprietary payment for any structures damaged or destroyed, and the NPS finally gave in on that point. Negotiations then turned to the specific dollar value of each of the 180 buildings. Second, Hays would not sign any contract that legally committed him to removal from the Giant Forest. With Director Drury's stipulation that this be mandatory, the battle lines were clearly drawn. In 1946, Hays finally agreed to a contract that would include a stipulation for removal of Giant Forest Village only. This was a major concession on Hays's part and still left open the door for removal of the lodge and Camp Kaweah. Other matters, however, particularly the proprietary interest of various structures, the timetable for removal, and a clause insisting on concession investment in Kings Canyon, led to another breakdown in negotiations.[68]

As Colonel White watched the contract negotiations proceed, the bitter and frustrated superintendent wrote to Regional Director Owen Tomlinson:

> It is evident that the policy of Mr. Hays will be to stall and postpone action on any physical changes at Giant Forest as long as possible. He may reasonably hope that with a change of

> Superintendent, Regional Director and Director, there may be an opportunity for the Company to continue business at the same old stand and in the same old way; that the concessioners go on forever, while the Park Service and Department administration changes.[69]

It was a startlingly prophetic statement. At the end of 1945, the contract lapsed, yet Hays and Mauger continued to conduct business and to negotiate. After six months of confusion, the NPS granted a short-term extension until September of 1946. At the end of that extension, ten weeks of confusion passed before another extension was granted. With evidence that the NPS would continue to grant extensions of the old contract, the company hardened its position. It backed away from Hays's commitment to move Giant Forest Village and continued to resist inclusion of any contract clause that even mentioned removal from the Giant Forest.[70]

Meanwhile, the NPS subtly signaled a change in its posture. The bulwark of idealistic, domineering, and preservationist NPS control in Sequoia National Park had always been Colonel White. At age sixty-seven, he was as tireless and skilled as ever, yet he had become overzealous, strident, and somewhat uncontrollable in the eyes of his superiors. His insistence on a new concession policy with competition and short contracts disturbed the status quo of a system most officials approved. His increasingly virulent attacks on the concessioner complicated the negotiations.

And so an increasingly bureaucratic NPS decided to dispense with the nagging problem of John White. The reason given was his age. Although he was as erudite and vigorous in his defense and management of the park as ever, he was declared to be beyond retirement age. The order came: Retire to a well-deserved pension, and let a younger man take over. Angry, hurt, and feeling betrayed, Colonel John R. White, master of Sequoia National Park for nearly a quarter-century, left in the midst of its greatest battle. He had taken over two parks with no regular concession, few roads or trails, a confused and development-oriented policy, and barely 50,000 visitors a year. He left two vastly enlarged parks with a big concession monopoly, a breathtaking park-to-park highway, nearly 1,000 miles of trail, a staunch preservation policy implemented by naturalists, biologists, landscape architects, and engineers, and more than 600,000 visitors a year. White's legacy is present in every feature of the twin parks' development and in every wild place where he prevented it. His devotion and skill have been a hard act to follow for subsequent superintendents.[71]

THE CONTRIBUTION OF JOHN ROBERTS WHITE

The state of Sequoia National Park's resources in 1947 reflected unmistakably the imprint of Colonel White and his full quarter-century of responsibility. The colonel had worked hard in his early years to create a national park for the use of the people, and he had succeeded so well in that task that all his later efforts to control and even undo his early successes were largely ineffective. Nowhere is this better represented than in the endless failures of the 1930s and 1940s to control the concessioner in the Giant Forest.

The battles of Giant Forest were not total defeats, however, for they sensitized the park's officials to the concept of too many visitors and brought the beginning of formal limits on development. Critical as these accomplishments were in the long run, they did little to reduce the continuing damage to the Big Trees. The state of Giant Forest in 1947 was better than it had been during the early 1920s but not much better. Physical limits had been placed on development, it is true, and camping had been organized and confined to certain areas, but congestion in those areas remained as bad as it had ever been. On an average summer night during the late 1940s, several thousand people slept in the Giant Forest Village, a densely structured enclave in a fragile forest and a settlement with only marginally adequate infrastructure.

Yet if, during the 1930s and 1940s, White saw no improvement in the protection of Sequoia National Park's best-known single feature, other portions of the park benefited from stunningly significant victories by the stubborn superintendent. Of these victories, by far the greatest was White's successful containment of the road-building urge that swept over America during the 1930s. Once the Generals Highway was completed in 1935, the colonel held the line successfully, preventing construction of the new Middle Fork Highway to the Giant Forest and the Sierra Way south from the Giant Forest to Mineral King. Had these roads been built, the entire future character of Sequoia National Park would have been drastically altered.

In his anti-roads campaign for the backcountry, Colonel White prevented a full third of Sequoia National Park's later formal wilderness from being lost. Yet he was not opposed to appropriate, low-level development, even in the backcountry. We have already documented his trail-building efforts, and it was in 1933, while he was still smarting from his first serious attempts to remove facilities from the Giant Forest, when Colonel White and George Mauger rode together out the new High Sierra Trail to choose a location for the park's first concessioner-operated High Sierra Camp at Bearpaw Meadow.

Ultimately, Colonel White was no scientist. When given the chance, in 1936, to summarize his ideas to his peers, he spoke not of resources but of "atmosphere." In this he was very much a man of his times. The 1930s were the great era of NPS visual management: If a park looked good, it must be successful in its goal of resource protection. Often in that decade, the colonel railed against landscape architects, but ultimately he thought much as they did. And so, during the two final decades of Colonel White's reign, the true resources of the park—the forests, the wildlife, and the natural systems that connect them into functional patterns–suffered locally in areas of out-of-control development. Yet they survived generally, because the Colonel had come to see the critical necessity of limiting the geographical spread of visitor congestion with its inescapable impacts. This was Colonel White's greatest contribution to the generations that have since come to the parks. John Roberts White did not understand, in twenty-first-century terms, what was critically important in Sequoia National Park, but he knew instinctively, after his early experiences in the Giant Forest, that visitors were best sustained as small, widely dispersed groups.

Later, it would be apparent that Sequoia National Park's greatest feature was its grand and spacious backcountry. Other national parks started with equally grand wilderness resources, but projects such as Going-to-the-Sun Highway in Montana's Glacier National Park and Trail Ridge Road in Colorado's Rocky Mountain National Park drastically limited future options for wilderness. In Sequoia, the Generals Highway avoided the high country, and the Middle Fork Highway and Sierra Way were never built. For these reasons and many others, Colonel White deserves grateful remembrance.

CHAPTER SEVEN

Two Battles for Kings Canyon (1931–1947)

In the vast Sierra wilderness, far to the southward of the famous Yosemite Valley, there is yet a grander valley of the same kind. It is situated on the south fork of the Kings River, above the most extensive groves and forests of the giant sequoia, and beneath the shadows of the highest mountains in the range, where canyons are the deepest and the snow-laden peaks are crowded most closely together.[1]

So wrote John Muir, in 1891, about an area he had come to love and admire in nearly two decades of exploration. Muir was not the earliest to explore the region or to pen its praises, but it was Muir, poet and scientist of the Sierra Nevada, and after him his beloved Sierra Club who would inextricably link their goals and philosophy with the future parkland.[2]

Thus began one of the longest and ultimately most cantankerous struggles to create a national park. Historians of the national park movement in America have long suggested that national parks were created from lands deemed "worthless" for traditional resources such as minerals, timber, agriculture, and water.[3] The problem of Kings Canyon and its ultimate solution, however, were quite the opposite. Contestants so perceived the presence of such valuable resources, especially irrigation and hydroelectric potential, that they fought one another to a developmental standstill for more than sixty years. In so doing, they allowed recreational and preservation factions to gain power, divide their enemies, and negotiate a compromise that allowed the eventual formation of one of the nation's earliest "wilderness" parks.

THE EARLY BATTLES

Although grazing and timber interests had deflected previous attempts to establish a park in the Kings River watershed, the worth of pasture and timber resources was recognized as relatively low. In 1902, however, the U.S. Geological Survey published an evaluation of the water-storage capacity of the Kings River.[4] It suggested four major dam sites with associated irrigation canals and power plants. Two sites were in the spectacular canyons of Tehipite Valley and Kings Canyon. More than half the financial support for this study had come from local irrigation associations.

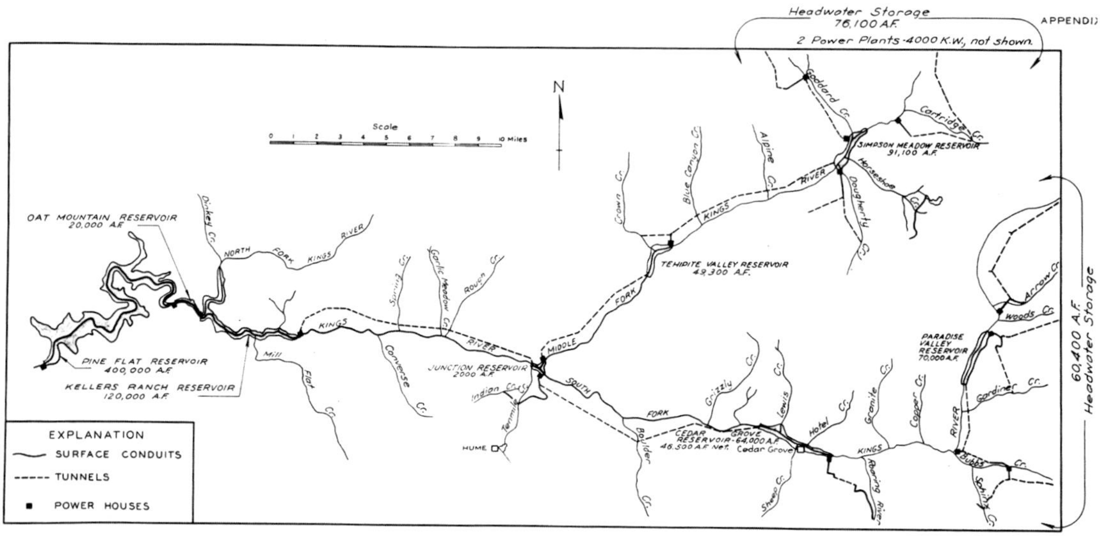

COMPLETE DEVELOPMENT

Proposals to develop the watershed of the Kings River for hydroelectric power generation played a major role in the decades-long debate over whether to create a Kings Canyon National Park. This map, prepared by the Federal Power Commission in 1930, analyzes how the rugged canyons could have been filled with a series of reservoirs and power plants.

Although groundwater and surface sources within the San Joaquin Valley had proven adequate to date, the future of the district's agriculture appeared to depend upon the rugged watershed of the Kings River. With this favorable report, local farmers and businessmen commenced long-range planning in an atmosphere of comfortable confidence.

Meanwhile, fresh from its water-diversion victory in the Owens Valley and mindful of San Francisco's water-and-power triumph on the Tuolumne River, the City of Los Angeles cast an interested eye toward the Kings River. In 1919, the Los Angeles Bureau of Power and Light released a study showing the watershed's considerable potential for power generation.[5] Contemporary rumors suggested that Los Angeles had struck a deal with Southern California Edison to sell its surplus power to the utility company for a healthy addition of revenue to the city's budget.[6]

In June 1920, the Federal Power Act touched off the real action by creating a commission to be headed by the Secretaries of Agriculture, Interior, and War, which could license water and power projects on government lands, including lands in national forests. Several months later, Los Angeles seized the initiative by applying to the commission to construct an elaborate water-control and power-generation system on the Kings River. Principal dams were to be located at Cedar Grove and Tehipite Valley, with other units on tributaries above the canyons and on the main channel below. The fledgling Federal Power Commission took the plan under study, and Los Angeles dug in to fight the expected opponents.[7]

The city did not have long to wait. Residents of the San Joaquin Valley were angered by what they perceived to be a territorial intrusion by money-hungry urban business interests. They also feared a repeat of the Owens Valley debacle that had all but destroyed a bustling agricultural industry in that distant valley. Before the Federal Power Commission was entirely sure of its duties and limits, the San Joaquin Light and Power Corporation filed a proposal to develop the same sites Los Angeles desired but for local consumption.

While the power contestants froze the commission, proponents of both tourism and the park gained steam. Increasingly during the 1920s, businessmen from Fresno and other nearby towns and cities looked favorably on the potential revenue from tourism of another Yosemite Valley. Although still overshadowed by proponents of reclamation, talk of a major resort complex began to circulate at businessmen's socials and in the halls of local government. The U.S. Forest Service (USFS), which had administered the area since 1905, seemed favorable to recreation as part of its portfolio of activities for the Kings River watershed.[8]

Still, from 1881 through the 1920s, pressure for a national park encompassing the Kings River country continued to mount. A succession of Department of the Interior secretaries vocally supported park status. Conservation groups, led by the Sierra Club, kept up a continuous drumbeat through pamphlets, editorials, and letters to members of the U.S. Congress. The legislators responded with a dozen bills, between 1911 and 1926, aimed at creating a new park or enlarging nearby Sequoia National Park to protect the Kings River drainage. Establishment of Sequoia and General Grant National Parks, in 1890, and the vast expansion of Sequoia, in 1926, both represented compromises in drives that had set out to save the Kings River country. Agitation by preservationists and other supporters consistently kept the Kings River watershed in the public eye.[9]

The result of these conflicting proposals by proponents of water, power, tourism, and the parks was an atmosphere of such confusion and desperate antagonism that those politicians and government officials not directly involved avoided the controversy. Politicians who were involved moved slowly and cautiously, weighing each decision for political as well as legal and economic consequences. Hence, the Federal Power Commission took nearly three years to reject the 1920 power application of Los Angeles. The city immediately refiled, so the controversy continued. And Congress simply found the Kings River issue too hot to handle. The campaign to enlarge Sequoia was extremely well organized, lasted seven long years, and succeeded in adding Kern Canyon and the Mt. Whitney country to the park in 1926. The original proposal to include the Kings River watershed, however, brought such diverse, rapid, and boisterous opposition that the legislators opted to ignore the entire region.[10]

By 1930, a harried Federal Power Commission, stinging from criticism of its apparent inactivity and indecisiveness, released its own report on Kings River water resources. Challenges by opponents to reclamation and power development had increasingly taken the form of disputing the very feasibility of damming the Kings River in the mountains. The commission's so-called Randell Report aimed to settle the matter of water-storage and power-generation capacities once and for all. Senior engineer Ralph Randell concluded that nineteen dam sites were feasible. One, at Pine Flat in the lower foothills, would be a huge structure, intercepting the main valley-bound flow of the combined forks of the Kings River. Included among the other sites were both Cedar Grove (Kings Canyon) and Tehipite Valley as well as the rugged junction of the Middle and South Forks. Eastward and upward, smaller dams could flood more than a dozen alpine basins. Power enthusiasts from the San Joaquin Valley and Los Angeles gleefully noted Randell's healthy figures for potential electricity from the network of structures.[11]

The report momentarily stunned proponents of the parks and tourism, as the potential benefits of such a reclamation project appeared insurmountable. Soon, however, controversy again surfaced to cloud the issue. Opponents of reclamation discovered that Randell's "extensive field survey" actually consisted of an eight-day horseback circuit of part of the watershed and a one-day flyover of the larger area he could not reach. Based on this circumscribed fieldwork, Randell not only recommended nineteen sites, but also provided a cost estimate for construction of $130,000,000. When pressed for an explanation of this figure, the engineer admitted that three small dams in the Mineral King Valley formed the basis of his cost figures on the nineteen proposed dams. Opponents quickly pointed out that the Mineral King dams lay three miles from a road, while some of the dams proposed for the Kings River watershed were more than twenty-five miles from a road, and some dams were in remarkably rugged terrain. The expense of packing workers, supplies, and construction materials to such sites would far inflate the project's total figure. Several months of debate and defense ensued, as an embarrassed Federal Power Commission tried to salvage parts of the report. By the end of 1931, the Randell Report was virtually discredited, and confusion again reigned in the battle for the Kings River country.[12]

THE U.S. FOREST SERVICE IN KINGS CANYON

The Forest Service watched the controversy with considerable but detached interest. Perhaps in the minds of forestry officials the entire conflict was a tempest in a teapot, particularly that between proponents of tourism and reclamation. The philosophy and policy of multiple use would surely allow some combination of these features to be established. Accordingly, the USFS's regional office began planning to develop recreational facilities along both the South and Middle Forks of the Kings River, regardless of whether dams and reservoirs were to be established. The key to any comprehensive development was Cedar Grove. Here, the USFS intended to build a grand resort complex that would cater to the recreational desires of a broad cross-section of the population. Tehipite Valley was to be approached by road for possible later development.

The earliest planning efforts culminated with a lengthy document prepared by USFS landscape architect George Gibbs. His plan proposed an enormous infrastructure, so large that his supervisor angrily rejected the report and forced Gibbs to redo it. That first report called for camping facilities for more than 6,000 people; up to six fairly large hotels and numerous other structures; access roads from the west, south, and over the High Sierra from the east; and even an airstrip. His second report, completed one year later, reduced the camping capacity and road plans, particularly eliminating the trans-Sierra component. Nevertheless, this plan, too, was apparently beyond the immediate designs or desires of Gibbs's supervisors.[13]

The USFS, like the National Park Service (NPS), was much affected by pressure groups, persuasive popular movements, and infiltration by proponents of different conservation strategies and philosophies. All of these had combined, by the 1930s, to create a USFS anxious to please both development and preservation interests. While the USFS has often been accused of catering only to resource developers and users, it has long responded to groups such as the Sierra Club and the Wilderness Society. Hence, despite the magnitude of the plans for Cedar Grove and even after Gibbs's proposals were scaled down, the 1935 master plan of Sequoia National Forest also called for a "primitive area," including the upper canyon of the South Fork from the Roaring River eastward. It also suggested eventual inclusion of the entire Middle Fork area. This area was to be closed to roads and summer homes, and grazing was to be halted. The only development in the area would be an expanded trail network, principally for hikers.[14] How long this novel idea had been brewing and its exact relationship to the almost concurrent proposal from the Department of the Interior for a wilderness park may never be known. What is clear, however, was the waxing power of the preservation lobby on the national scene and in the southern Sierra.

While debate continued on the nature and magnitude of development, the USFS, in cooperation with the State of California, set out, in 1933, to build a spectacular mountain road from General Grant National Park to Cedar Grove, a distance of some thirty miles. Not until 1939 was the project complete. Meanwhile, in Kings Canyon, beginning in 1937, four large and comfortable campgrounds with a combined capacity of 335 sites were built near a tiny, existing ranger station. Plans for Cedar Grove, however, were delayed, as the USFS cautiously watched the intensifying controversy. Not only the threat of inundation, but also the possible loss of the area to the NPS made this a delicate arena in which to spend limited monies and manpower. And that possibility appeared to be growing ever stronger as the decade waned. Meanwhile, road plans for Tehipite Valley foundered after being incorporated into the Sierra Way proposal, in time for that entire road project to collapse.[15]

HAROLD ICKES AND THE FINAL BATTLE

In 1933, as George Gibbs released his grand development plan for Kings Canyon and as the USFS began the road into Kings Canyon, another event occurred with profound consequences for the future park. Newly elected President Franklin D. Roosevelt appointed as secretary of the interior a Chicago lawyer named Harold Ickes. In Ickes, Roosevelt had one of the most strong-willed, heartily disliked, and powerfully effective appointees in the Department of the Interior's history.[16] The secretary took particular interest in the NPS, actively promoting, some say interfering in, decisions on the creation, funding, and management of parks. Among his accomplishments, during his dozen years at the helm, were absorption of national battlefield sites from the U.S. Department of War and of national monuments from the U.S. Department of Agriculture (USDA). In 1934, Ickes came close to adding the entire USFS to Interior, even as the Secretary of Agriculture campaigned to take over the NPS. These political maneuvers created a healthy distrust and dislike of Ickes by many both in and out of government but particularly within the USFS and the forestry and ranching communities.[17]

Ickes also incurred the wrath of corporations for his anti-trust stance, all segregationist groups for his incipient pro-civil rights actions, and many politicians for his acerbic, perhaps even brutal, verbal and written assaults. He was dictatorial, suspicious, petty, and vindictive to employees and absolutely merciless with enemies. USFS Regional Forester S. B. Show later described Ickes as "overambitious, ignorant, egocentric, ruthless, unethical and highly effective."[18] The last adjective conveys part of the positive side of Harold Ickes. He was highly principled and even righteous, and he was as tenacious a fighter as Washington, D.C., has ever seen.

Ickes had long cultivated strong ideas on conservation, initially those espoused by Gifford Pinchot and later those of Stephen Mather.[19] The secretary had become interested in the Hetch Hetchy conflict two decades earlier and, through his subsequent relationships with Mather and Albright, had taken an interest in preserving wilderness.[20] Indeed, by the time of his appointment as Secretary of the Interior, Ickes had developed a preservationist philosophy that went well beyond that espoused by most NPS personnel. In May 1933, he declared, "If I had my way about national parks, I would create one without a road in it. I would have it impenetrable forever to automobiles, a place where man would not try to improve upon God."[21]

In the Kings Canyon conflict, Ickes had a chance to put those words into action. In 1935, he persuaded California Senator Hiram Johnson to propose a bill to create a John Muir-Kings Canyon National Park and, further, to make it a wilderness preserve. As noted, this proposal came at the same time as the USFS's plan for a "primitive area." In any case, the confusion and counterproposals of the previous fifty years had so long stalled development that the concept of a roadless wilderness remained a viable one. In Johnson's bill, horse trails, footpaths, controlled use by commercial packers, and simple camping facilities were to be encouraged. Roads, hotels, and other large-scale developments would be banned—including those within Kings Canyon itself.[22]

If nothing else could unify the development claimants, this bill and the presence of Harold Ickes in the conflict did. A storm of protest from power, reclamation, tourism, grazing, and timber interests drowned Johnson's bill in committee. Thereupon, with the immediate threat of park status averted, the various claimants retired to continue maneuvering for control of the watershed, its lands and water. Los Angeles, its power needs temporarily satisfied by the huge, new Boulder Dam (later renamed Hoover Dam) on the Colorado River, dropped out, but the battle between irrigation and tourism factions continued unabated.

In this atmosphere, Secretary Ickes, NPS Regional Director Frank Kittredge, and members of the Sierra Club decided on a plan of concerted action. After lengthy discussions with the park's proponents around the state and a careful survey of the opponents among the local residents and businessmen, two things became clear. First, the NPS had a poor reputation. Despite the nearly universal respect for Colonel White and his staff, locals perceived the NPS as an agency opposed to development, unconcerned about the economic fates of local farmers and communities, dictatorial and restrictive in the management of their lands and resources, largely under the control of wealthy, urban pleasure-seekers, and, finally, extraordinarily land hungry. Almost to a person, they preferred the USFS, whose personnel espoused a freer use of lands and resources, seemed ready and anxious to promote the economic welfare of farmers in the San Joaquin Valley, and allowed much easier access to hunting, fishing, and travel within their mountain territories. Ickes and Kittredge discovered that much of this damaging sentiment was fostered by local and regional USFS officials. From Regional Forester Show on down, the USFS's men lost no opportunity to reinforce these perceptions and, indeed, cultivate no small fear of the consequences of expanding the park in the southern Sierra Nevada.[23]

The second thing that became clear was the confusion among opponents to the park, as they bickered over different proposals for the watershed's future. Some wanted extensive reclamation, some wanted roads and tourism, some even wanted a wilderness preserve, but all wanted it under the USFS's control. The one other view all locals shared, whether for or against a park, was a deep antagonism toward and fear of Los Angeles. Neither San Francisco nor Los Angeles had shown any compunction in recent history about stripping a watershed of its water and power resources, regardless of the consequences for those who might depend for their very economic existence on those resources. Los Angeles had destroyed the Owens Valley, bled water from the Colorado River, and convinced the State of California to implement a vast plan aimed at shifting water southward from rivers in the Sacramento Valley toward the huge city. What chance did the Fresno Irrigation District have in blocking this imperialistic juggernaut?

Here was the opening and the opportunity backers of the park had needed. Ickes, Kittredge, and members of the Sierra Club such as William Colby conceived a plan to improve the NPS's reputation and garner some critical support for a Kings Canyon park by dividing their enemies and playing on this fear of Los Angeles.[24] The campaign began in earnest during the early months of 1938. Both Ickes and Kittredge commenced a series of radio addresses and speaking engagements aimed at newspaper publishers, outdoor-recreation groups, influential women's and businessmen's groups, state and local legislators, and nearly anyone else who would listen. Most talks were in San Francisco or Los Angeles, although both men appeared in Fresno and other San Joaquin Valley towns during the next two years. Superintendent White also stumped about the state promoting the idea that Sequoia National Park was everyone's park and that they should support it and the NPS.

The real job of diplomacy, however, fell to Assistant Regional Director B. F. Manbey. Through the spring and summer of 1938, Manbey met dozens of times with civic officials, sportsmen's groups, publishers, businessmen's clubs, farmers, irrigation associations, and even timber and grazing interests to sell both Kings Canyon National Park and the NPS. His seventeen reports back to Frank Kittredge, in fact, went to Harold Ickes, from whom Manbey took direct orders. Those reports show a vigorous, tiring schedule, a veritable whirlwind of speeches and panel discussions, and as neat a piece of diplomatic negotiation as the San Joaquin Valley had ever seen.

Manbey's orders from Ickes were strict and, given the source, surprising. He was not to challenge, insult, or in any way conflict with the USFS; rather, he was to strive for an image of calm, concerned reasonableness, exactly the opposite of how the USFS had portrayed the NPS. Manbey told farmers and proponents of irrigation that the NPS understood and sympathized with their needs. Certainly, the very fate of the nation depended on assuring the success of agriculture, particularly in a breadbasket such as the San Joaquin Valley. He reassured the locals that Harold Ickes would see that their water needs were not ignored or usurped. And he was in a position to make good on that promise, for, in addition to the NPS, Secretary Ickes had control of the U.S. Bureau of Reclamation.

Concerning the proposed new national park, Manbey promoted the health, educational, and spiritual benefits of saving the wilderness. More and more people who were tired, dispirited, and aching from the chaos and pressures of urban life would come to mend themselves along the paths, lakes, and canyons of the mountain park. The approaches to this fountain of salubrity would pass directly through Fresno and other valley towns, where recreational staging areas, auto and camping supply services, and other businesses would cater to increasing numbers of tourists. As for hunting and other activities, there still existed around the proposed park a huge national forest area on all but the south side to accommodate sportsmen.[25]

Many, of course, remained unconvinced by the combined persuasive assaults of Ickes, Kittredge, White, and, especially, Manbey—unconvinced, at least, to back the park proposal. Still, the NPS as an organization fared rather better. Bitter enemies, including local USFS officials, were nonplussed. At the occasional meeting where both agencies were represented, NPS officials invariably complimented their Forest Service counterparts graciously, even effusively. Thus, the USFS's rancorous criticism was blunted for a time, and stories of an arrogant, aloof, and power-hungry NPS faded.[26]

Slowly but surely through this media and personal campaign, a compromise developed between Ickes and local civic officials, businessmen, and ultimately most farmers and irrigation groups. That compromise became the basis for the final successful push for park status, for the organization and operation of the future park, and for a series of promises the NPS made, which came back to haunt it later.

Three conditions were to be met by the Department of Interior. First, immediate water and power needs were to be met with construction of a large facility at Pine Flat. The Bureau of Reclamation, under Harold Ickes, was to undertake construction, with the brunt of the cost being borne by the federal government and the bulk of the benefit going to local water users. In addition, reclamation projects on the North Fork of the Kings River, well outside any proposed park, were to be sanctioned by Interior.

Second, Tehipite Valley and Kings Canyon were to be excluded from the park proposal. Both sites had been the core of the 1902 U.S. Geological Survey Report, the 1920 Los Angeles proposal, and the Randell Report. Although local farmers saw no immediate need for construction of dams at these sites, they were loath to give them up for inclusion in the park. One thing still clear after all the negotiations was that, once in the park, these canyons would be forever lost to reclamation. Hence, both had to be withheld until future demand determined their importance. Exclusion of these magnificent canyons, the very heart of the proposed park, was a bitter pill for the NPS to swallow but one absolutely necessary to placate local water users.

Finally, the third condition set by locals was that the NPS would see that a major tourism development would be constructed in the canyon of the South Fork. The preferred sites were at Kanawyer's Camp adjacent to Copper Creek, just within the boundary of the proposed wilderness park, or at Cedar Grove, where the USFS had begun development. This was a curious provision for both the NPS and the Fresno community, because if the canyon was excluded from the new park, the USFS, not the NPS, would still control Cedar Grove and its development. Nevertheless, a verbal agreement was concluded, and the much-bolstered park lobby geared up again to tackle Congress with the Kings Canyon issue.[27]

Despite depleting the ranks of the opposition with diplomacy and promises, the road ahead for the NPS remained a difficult one. When Representative Bertrand "Bud" Gearhart proposed a new bill to create a John Muir-Kings Canyon National Park, opponents were still many, strong, and loud. Several irrigation associations had not been lured into the pro-park camp, chief among them the California Mutual Water Companies Association that represented forty-eight irrigation companies. Sportsmen's associations to a member opposed the NPS's administration of any more territory. Several influential state newspapers, the California State Legislature, and the California Chamber of Commerce also went on record against the park.[28]

Among the most vocal anti-park groups was the USFS in California. This is noteworthy, because Secretary of Agriculture Henry Wallace, under strict orders from President Roosevelt, had already firmly stated his own and his department's support for the new park. Reasons for the local USFS revolt were many: widespread enmity toward Harold Ickes, his recent attempt to take over the USFS, the ardent belief among California members of the USFS in the superiority of their multiple-use philosophy, and the deep-seated mistrust and dislike of their conservation competitor, the NPS. That orders from Secretary Wallace had come to support the park proposal is clear;

that Show, his assistants, and field men ignored them is equally clear. As the spring of 1939 rolled by and the bill came closer to consideration by the House of Representatives, the verbal attacks on Ickes and the NPS by Show and others became strident and frenzied.[29]

Meanwhile, a new issue entered the fray. For many years, Redwood Mountain, one of the largest and most impressive giant sequoia groves, had remained in private hands. The park's officials often worried about the future of this huge grove of magnificent trees. Fortunately, the owners had seemed ill-disposed to cut the trees, and, hence, for decades the forest had remained intact. In 1939, the owners of the grove found themselves in a precarious situation. With no income from the land and with taxes mounting, they tried to sell the area to the government for inclusion in a national park. Typically, the government could not make up its mind how or even whether to buy the forest. As the taxes mounted and the owners prepared to default on their payment, it became clear that the land would have to be sold to someone soon, and logging of the Redwood Mountain Grove was a virtual certainty thereafter. The grove had been included in Representative Gearhart's bill, yet time was running out.[30]

With this impetus, the campaign for Kings Canyon further intensified. In the process, so did the antagonism between the two agencies involved. Subsequently, NPS officials accused USFS representatives of poisoning local sentiment with distortion and slander. To be sure, Show and his assistants were now working full time to marshal support for their position and to convince fence sitters of the USFS's superior moral and economic position. In this, he was ably assisted by Charles Dunwoody, a local member of the California Chamber of Commerce, and several other local officials, whose interests would apparently be damaged by creation of the park.[31]

Meanwhile, the USFS reacted with even stronger charges. Among the actions of which the NPS was accused were wire-tapping, which is likely, given Ickes's predilection for that sort of thing, bullying of USFS personnel, which seems unlikely, since their own boss could not control them, and burglary of the USFS office in Porterville. The burglary charge was tricky, because park officials had obtained the USDA's permission to enter the offices and seemed unconcerned when caught red-handed by USFS personnel. Thereafter, Show claimed he hid all his records, so they could not be summoned by his boss, who was acting under orders from the President. What is perhaps the greatest wonder throughout this campaign is that Show and his assistants managed to keep their jobs.[32]

A curious rift had also developed in the preservationist camp. Several organizations, notably the National Parks Association and The Wilderness Society, opposed Gearhart's bill on the grounds that a park without the two canyons was unworthy. They insisted on holding out for a proposal that would include the canyons and perhaps some additional territory along the road from Grant Park to Cedar Grove. The Sierra Club and the Emergency Conservation Committee supported the bill, taking the pragmatic approach that a park without the canyons was better than no park at all. Besides, the threat to the canyons was not imminent, and they might be added later.

As the campaign developed, the National Parks Association, in particular, became very active in opposition, publishing pamphlets and frequently going on public record against the park. Two years earlier, this same group had equally loudly opposed creation of Olympic National Park in Washington. Roosevelt aide Irving Brant subsequently suggested that a fairly dim William Wharton, who headed and formed the financial backbone of the National Parks Association, had been duped by his friend William Greeley, a lumberman and recognized advocate of resource development. The Wilderness Society finally agreed to support the bill, freeing it from the insulting label "The Be-wildered Society," which had been applied by other preservationist organizations.[33]

The outcome of the park bill and this latest and most organized Kings Canyon campaign was by no means clear when an unexpected and startling event occurred to demoralize and destroy organized opposition to the park. A busy Congress, preoccupied with continuing economic recovery and ominous events overseas, looked to local representatives for guidance on domestic issues such as the John Muir-Kings Canyon National Park bill. The two local congressmen were Bud Gearhart, of Fresno, author of the bill, and Alfred Elliot, of Visalia. Elliott was deeply and emotionally opposed to it. He was also well known and respected, and his frequent antagonistic pronouncements about the bill, the NPS, and Secretary Ickes had an effect. Despite the compromise, the combination of Elliott's opposition and that of the state legislature still made passage difficult.

Then, on March 4, 1939, an elderly Sierra Club member and park supporter, Mrs. Gertrude Achilles, of Morgan Hill, California, wrote both Gearhart and Elliott, urging passage of the park bill. In addition, she wrote a check to Gearhart for $100 and instructed him to apply it to the cause. She inadvertently, however, enclosed the check to Gearhart in the envelope to Elliott.

Upon receiving his letter and the check to Gearhart, Elliott envisioned a bribery scandal and saw a way to defeat the pesky conservation bill. He notified the Federal Bureau of Investigation, made a copy of the check typed a new letter and envelope, and had an ally mail the check to Gearhart from San Jose, near Morgan Hill. Gearhart received the check, but returned it to the woman, thanked her for her endorsement, and suggested she send the money to the Sierra Club.

The trap had not worked, yet Elliott plunged ahead anyway, showing a photostat of the check to prominent men in the San Joaquin Valley and to several other congressmen. Gearhart first learned of the plot, when he received an anonymous phone call from a man who had been at one of the meetings where Elliott showed the check and implied corruption on the part of his Fresno colleague. In his tipoff, the speaker concluded, "He is out to frame you, Buddy, and I would not be a party to it. I had to tell you. Be on your guard."[34]

Over the next few days, three congressmen approached Gearhart with the same news. Gearhart, a former district attorney, then set about collecting the evidence to protect himself and show Elliott's misconduct. He had an affidavit prepared from Mrs. Achilles and reassembled the pertinent steps in the plot with evidence of motive and actions taken.

During April 1939, Elliott compounded the problem by again suggesting to San Joaquin Valley men that Gearhart only wanted the park created because he would personally profit from it. The two men proceeded on a collision course.

Finally, on May 2, Representative Gearhart rose before the House on a question of personal privilege. He was, he stated, shocked and dismayed that a congressional colleague would stoop to flagrantly false character assassination to get a bill defeated. He reported the entire sequence to a packed House and gallery and then refused to demand Elliott's expulsion. In his concluding remarks, Gearhart showed his oratorical skills, stating:

> I have searched the precedents of this body, searched them down through the last 150 years of the history of this body, and I fail to find one case referred to in those proceedings that even approaches that which I have been compelled to lay before you.
>
> I ask no action. There was a time when I thought of expulsion. There was a time when I thought of disciplinary action. But all that is past now. The record is made. I am content.[35]

To thunderous applause, Gearhart sat down, and the House turned an expectant eye toward Elliott, whose futile defense consisted chiefly of an attack on the park bill and on Secretary Ickes. Frequently interrupted, peppered with questions on his actions and laughed at, Elliott finally blurted in frustration, ". . . some of you might think you are making a monkey out of me, but that cannot be done." Roars of derisive laughter followed, and Elliott sat down shortly thereafter, an embarrassed and lonely figure.[36]

The representatives were aghast at the thought of this sort of character assassination and frustrated by Gearhart's unwillingness to demand ouster of Elliott. In August, as the vote on the bill approached, Gearhart read into the record a number of accounts of the scandal in San Joaquin Valley newspapers to refresh the minds of his colleagues.[37] When the vote came up, opponents attempted one last sabotage by attaching a rider, allowing unlimited reclamation in the new park. In the ensuing arguments, the rider was excised but with it went the John Muir portion of the park name. Once this last shot failed, the bill passed easily. After a relatively easy passage in the Senate, President Roosevelt, on March 4, 1940, signed the bill creating Kings Canyon National Park.[38]

Thus ended a sixty-year conservation struggle, one nearly unrivaled for rancorous debate, emotional character assassination, and political wheeling and dealing. Three factors were important

Sequoia and Kings Canyon National Parks after Act of March 4, 1940 and Presidential Proclamation of June 21, 1940
N
Evolution Valley
SIERRA NATIONAL FOREST
KINGS CANYON NATIONAL PARK
Tehipite Valley
SEQUOIA NATIONAL FOREST
Cedar Grove
Zumwalt Meadows
Grant Grove
Kings Canyon National Park
Lodgepole
Giant Forest
Mt Whitney
Mt Kaweah
SEQUOIA NATIONAL PARK
Ash Mountain
Mineral King
Three Rivers
0
10 Miles
SEQUOIA NATIONAL FOREST

in the creation of Kings Canyon National Park over the objections of numerous and vociferous groups. First, the opposition was unable to unite, which allowed proponents of the park to divide and conquer them. Second, this same disunity prevented development of other forms of land and resource use that would have doomed the prospects of a park in the region. Finally, an amazing and egregious political blunder eliminated the last stumbling block by infuriating both Congress and the public to righteous and convenient indignation.

PLANNING A NEW KINGS CANYON NATIONAL PARK

Once the dust had settled from the successful congressional battle and the park's creation was a certainty, the NPS established a local administration and began to run its newest acquisition. The new park covered more than 454,000 acres of territory, the vast majority being above the tree line, and included the fifty-year-old General Grant area. The act also authorized the President, by proclamation, to add lands within Redwood Mountain to the park, an action President Roosevelt soon took. In subsequent meetings, Sierra and Sequoia National Forest supervisors reported that the new park contained approximately 350 miles of trails, including access trails from both the eastern and western slopes and the John Muir Trail from the north. In addition, the NPS inherited a few fire lookout stations near the two excluded canyons, a few inconsequential mineral exclusions, and nine lifetime grazing permittees. The grazing permits, resulting from the compromise negotiations, were located chiefly in the Roaring River and Sugarloaf Creek areas. Secretary Ickes and NPS Director Cammerer initially appointed Guy Hopping, the superintendent of tiny General Grant National Park, as acting head of the huge new unit, but when Colonel White returned to Sequoia, his long-time associate and friend Eivind Scoyen took over at Kings Canyon. Meanwhile, the administration of Sequoia National Park loaned several personnel and some equipment to assist in early operations, particularly at what was now called the Grant Grove area, a well-established visitor destination. A few months later, on June 9, Sequoia personnel again assisted as the Redwood Mountain Grove was officially dedicated.[39]

It is understandable that the Kings Canyon staff would rely on its fifty-year-old neighbor park, and it illustrated the close relationship the two staffs maintained during the new unit's short tenure as a separate administration. In 1943, in the midst of World War II, the government suspended independent administration of Kings Canyon. After only three years, the new park united with Sequoia under Colonel White, and the two parks continue today as a single administrative unit.

Amid the flush of victory and excitement over the new wilderness park, problems had to be addressed. Ironically, these problems did not come with the 450,000 acres of wilderness in the High Sierra. They did not come with the great grove of giant sequoias so near to Generals

Highway in Redwood Mountain. They did not even come with the heavily developed, fifty-year-old property at Grant Grove. Rather, they came with a 2,879-acre piece of land the NPS did not officially control, and therein lay part of those problems. For the next twenty-five years, the canyon floor of the South Fork at Cedar Grove was to bedevil the NPS. It was a spectacular area, accessible by road to tourists, controlled by the USFS, but an area the NPS had solemnly vowed to develop and maintain. On top of all that, it still lay under the heavy threat of potential inundation by reservoir waters. Who would administer the canyon's development? How large would that development be? Where in the canyon would it be located? These were the questions surrounding Kings Canyon National Park.

THE MATTER OF JURISDICTION

The first issue, and the one on which all the others ultimately hinged, revolved around jurisdiction and administration. Congress had left no doubt about who had ultimate legal jurisdiction—the USFS. Yet the canyon was virtually surrounded by national park land at the far end of a dead-end road. Before the ink had dried on the act of March 4, the NPS approached Agriculture Secretary Wallace and Acting Chief Forester Granger with a proposal for NPS administration of Cedar Grove. A week later, on March 11, representatives of the two agencies met for the first time in what was to become a long and confusing process. Regional Forester Show attended, and his mood was anything but cooperative. Frank Kittredge subsequently reported that Show believed the exclusion of Cedar Grove from the park indicated a congressional mandate for development by the USFS, a mandate he fully intended to carry out. Kittredge summed up the situation some weeks later: "no arguments by Park Service participants seemed to appeal to Mr. Show, who stood staunchly for Forest Service administration and operation of the Cedar Grove area."[40]

Once again, Show was overruled by his superiors. Granger saw the issue as one of cost. Despite the feelings of his subordinates and, perhaps, his own ideas as well, Granger believed the USFS could better spend its limited capital on larger areas under complete USFS control, those not threatened with destruction by reclamation development. In July 1940, he instructed Show to make the necessary arrangements for NPS administration of Cedar Grove in Kings Canyon to keep "uniformity of planning and administration of recreation facilities on this and the adjacent areas of similar character within the Kings Canyon National Park."[41] The USFS also readily agreed to protect the road on USFS land between Grant Grove and Cedar Grove.

Despite this reasonably quick and amicable settlement, problems of definition and decision still cropped up during the next decade. Congress did not allocate money for NPS's development of other federal lands until August 1946. The matter of entry fees to the park and acreage allowances for concessions still needed to be settled. In these cases, the decisions went with USFS fees, which were zero, and NPS's regulations regarding concessions. Meanwhile, the concession company, led by George Mauger, looked suspiciously at this unusual agreement and, as we discuss in the next chapter, used it to delay construction of visitor facilities at Cedar Grove.[42]

Perhaps to NPS personnel, the most trying issue of jurisdiction concerned regulations and law enforcement. Basically, it was understood that this remained a USFS holding, with appropriate USFS regulations. Park rangers were deputized by the USFS to enforce those statutes. This necessitated learning just what those regulations were and then retraining park rangers. A most significant issue with this arrangement arose, however, when visitors questioned the regulations. Cedar Grove was an area ostensibly under NPS's management, which, according to law, was open to USFS regulations that allowed firearms, hunting, and uncontrolled camping. Time and again during the 1940s and 1950s, rangers and superintendents questioned this "difficult" arrangement. Throughout the period, they insisted that visitors behave as if Cedar Grove were part of the national park. Fortunately, no visitors ever legally challenged the NPS's right to insist upon their own regulations, however inappropriately.[43]

HOW MUCH TOURISM AND WHERE WILL IT BE?

While the Park Service struggled to resolve these persistent questions of regulation and jurisdiction in Kings Canyon, a larger and more critical question arose: What form and extent would development along the South Fork take? In resolving this issue, the NPS faced unusually heavy pressure from outside interest groups that had participated in formation of the park and, thus, held some proprietary feelings. There were many opinions on specific development decisions, but three basic groups evolved to represent distinctly different overall plans.

First, there was the Fresno Chamber of Commerce led by lawyer and former chamber president Chester Warlow. A tireless benefactor of the parks, he had been instrumental in hammering out the great compromise between Ickes and the San Joaquin Valley's citizens. The Fresno group favored extensive development and incessantly reminded the NPS of its promises to do so.[44] At the other end of the development spectrum was the Sierra Club. Its members, including highly respected figures such as William Colby and Francis Farquhar, had feverishly campaigned on behalf of the park for more than a half century. Sierra Club members favored minimum construction, preferring to leave the bulk of the canyon floor for hiking and horseback exploration.[45] Finally, in the middle, was the NPS. For the next quarter century, in every decision affecting the Kings Canyon, park officials were pulled from either side and were themselves much divided on the issues.

Colonel White, oddly enough, leaned heavily toward the opinion of the Fresno group. Although indefatigable in his campaign to control and reduce tourism in the Giant Forest, he nonetheless favored fairly extensive operations in Kings Canyon. His reasons were, first, because the area should be seen by as many people as possible; second, because it would draw people away from the Giant Forest, giving it a chance to recover; and, third and most important, because the NPS had promised extensive development to the Fresno people.[46] NPS naturalist-scientists such as Lowell Sumner and Joseph Dixon strongly favored minimum development, citing ecological reasons such as preserving meadows and marshes and protecting wildlife. NPS landscape architects such as Ernest Davidson and Sanford Hill ranged somewhere in the middle.[47]

Three basic packages of development decisions formed the substance over which these groups disagreed. The first concerned how far and by what route a road should extend into the canyon. Initially, the NPS verbally agreed to build the road as far as the old Kanawyer's site east of Copper Creek. Yet, by December 1938, well before the park's creation could be confidently assured, the Sierra Club and other preservationists began to press for a road terminus at Roaring River, where the USFS had plotted its "wilderness" boundary.[48] Word of this pressure leaked to backers of the park in Fresno, and an angry Chester Warlow challenged the NPS to honor its agreement or suffer the abandonment of any local support for the park.[49]

On January 20, 1939, NPS Associate Director Demaray responded in writing to Warlow that the park would definitely extend the road to Copper Creek.[50] Then, in May 1940, a few weeks after the park bill passed, another angry letter from Warlow to Demaray complained that younger members of the Sierra Club were agitating for a shorter road:

> The activities of the Sierra Club stopped the old 1908 canyon road at Lookout Point. They are attempting to do the same thing now at Cedar Grove. We were generous enough to allow 2-1/2 miles of the upper canyon for their altruistic wilderness theories, but we do insist that a portion of the beautiful portion of the canyon be available to the 'softies.' It seems a shame that a small group of individuals would want to lock this place up so that it will be used only by 100 or so people a year when it is entitled to be enjoyed by thousands.[51]

Warlow finished by warning that the betrayal of supporters in Fresno and the dishonor of breaking their promises would destroy any chance the NPS might have for credibility and for further cooperation from the citizens of the San Joaquin Valley.

During the next few months, hasty and placating negotiations culminated in a decision to plan for a road terminus at Copper Creek, regardless of any designs or ideas to the contrary. To the dismay of the Sierra Club, rumors then began circulating about a new drive to push the road through the park, over Kearsarge Pass, and on to the Owens Valley. Warlow and other Fresno people, however, assured NPS officials that no support for road development across the Sierra would come from their community. Congress, in 1946, further buried such rumors by passing an appropriations bill that outlawed any funding for road construction within Kings Canyon National Park, except for the short distance from the park's boundary near Zumwalt Meadow to Copper Creek. Thus, by the end of 1946, the Copper Creek vicinity became the accepted area for road's end. Despite grumbling from some in the Sierra Club, most members contented themselves with trying to influence other development plans for the park.[52]

Having established Copper Creek as the general area of the road's terminus, NPS landscape architects discussed whether the road should end with a loop on the east or west side of the creek. Despite the need to build two bridges over Copper Creek, the architects and park engineers preferred a gradual road loop east of the creek.[53] At the same time, the NPS struggled with the issue of where the road should terminate, and the matter of its route through the canyon also begged solution. Citizens from Fresno and some NPS officials favored a road along the south side of the river through the beautiful but ecologically delicate Zumwalt Meadow. The Sierra Club and other NPS planners maintained that the road should proceed past the existing campgrounds on the southern side as far as Roaring River, then cross to the northern side, hugging the talus slope along the north wall to Copper Creek. For a period of time in the late war years, a few planners and engineers promoted a dual road system—eastbound along the south side of the river through Zumwalt Meadow and then a westbound return on the north side.[54]

As World War II wound down, the NPS geared up for an expected infusion of development capital. Hot debate continued to swirl about the issues of the route and terminus, and the Sierra Club decided to play its trump card. Although it could not prevent the road from reaching the Copper Creek vicinity, it could influence these detail decisions. In 1924, the daughter of Jesse Agnew, an early Kings Canyon settler, had deeded to the Sierra Club eighty acres of land, extending across the canyon and including Zumwalt Meadow. As early as 1938, the NPS requested that the club donate its easement land to the forthcoming park or, short of that, grant an easement for a NPS road. Although sentiment favored turning the land over to the NPS, Sierra Club representatives made it clear to the government that they were unprepared to do so, until certain guarantees were made. Specifically, they wanted assurances that the road would end very near Copper Creek and that it would follow a route against the base of the northern wall of the canyon. Indeed, they would not even grant an easement for any other road route.[55]

The effect of these stipulations was substantial. Zumwalt Meadow formed the very heart of the scenic and ecological treasures of the upper canyon, so many park officials were only too ready to push for its unspoiled, roadless preservation. Because an easement from the Sierra Club was politically necessary if a road were even to approach Copper Creek, by 1947 a north-side route was a matter of policy. As for the exact spot of a road loop, the plans still called for crossing Copper Creek but with a dramatically diminished road loop on the eastern side.[56]

A second major development issue in the canyon consisted of the proper location for visitor facilities. All parties agreed that some lodgings and other infrastructure should be built at Cedar Grove. Logic seemed to dictate some development near the existing ranger contact station and the four big campgrounds. Beyond that obvious point, however, opinion diverged drastically. Representatives from Fresno insisted that the NPS had promised to build a hotel, cabins, and a large pack station at the old Kanawyer's site, east of Copper Creek. Colonel White again concurred and frequently reminded his superiors of their promises and commitments. The Sierra Club, conversely, wanted the developments concentrated down-canyon at Cedar Grove, with no more than a small outlying pack station, rather than the main base, at Copper Creek. Again, a frustrated Chester Warlow blistered the NPS with complaints, oral and written.[57]

Here, the NPS found itself in the middle and again deeply divided internally. At various times from 1939 to 1947, park planners considered developing Cedar Grove, Lewis Creek, Hotel Creek, Roaring River, Copper Creek (both sides), and various combinations of all of these. By the end of the war, however, the only serious issue was the extent of facilities to be imposed at Copper Creek. Nearly all planners favored retaining visitor lodgings, food services, and a main visitor center at Cedar Grove. At Copper Creek, the focus became the main pack station for the entire national park. This was to be a substantial complex, covering at least six or seven acres. In addition to the corrals, storage barns, sheds, work yards, and feed lots, the packers would need housing for up to thirty employees, recreational facilities, and possibly a store, a snack bar, and a few visitor amenities.[58]

The Sierra Club, once again, strongly influenced the final decision. Preliminary plans for development in the canyon became available, in the early months of 1946. The club then convinced one of its foremost members, Frederick Law Olmsted, Jr., to review those plans, visit the sites, and make recommendations. Olmsted was a nationally renowned landscape architect whose father, with architect Calvert Vaux, had designed Central Park in New York City, contributed considerably to the foundation of the national park movement, and was considered the "father of landscape architecture in America." Both the USFS, whose planners had consulted Olmsted about Cedar Grove during the 1930s, and the NPS deeply respected his abilities and opinion. He was, coincidentally, Vice-President of the Sierra Club.[59]

Olmsted dove into the project with all his considerable skill and energy. In late September 1946, he released his report, which was subsequently published in the *Sierra Club Bulletin* in the spring of 1947. The landscape architect favored a north-side road, a road terminus west of Copper Creek, and reduction of any pack-station facilities there to the "least extensive and least conspicuous things that will permit reasonably good service to the public." The effect of this report by so eminent a commentator on park design and development was pronounced. Immediately, the NPS concluded that construction of two small pack stations, one at Copper Creek and the other at Cedar Grove, followed by further study, would be a safer course of action.[60]

The third and final development issue in the canyon was the scope of visitor facilities to be constructed, wherever they might be located. Businessmen from Fresno and other towns and cities in the San Joaquin Valley envisioned a major development on the scale the USFS had proposed. That meant cabins or hotel space for between 700 and 1,500 people, an elaborate cafeteria and retail complex, a large visitor center, and an expanded camping area. The Sierra Club favored a smaller infrastructure, although it was not adamant, provided the facilities were kept at Cedar Grove. Here, the NPS fully intended to honor its promises, perhaps because there seemed to be little contention. In 1947, the agency's "Kings Canyon Development Plan" called for the design of overnight facilities at Cedar Grove to include an expanded camping capacity of 400 sites for 1,500 people, a picnic area for up to forty groups, 200 housekeeping cabins (500 people), an inn with fifty overnight cabins (another 200 people), a store, post office, visitor center, cafeteria, and pack station. A second pack station was proposed for Copper Creek and housing for employees for the Lewis Creek area. Further study of the issues of visitor facilities at Copper Creek, further expansion of campgrounds, and a larger picnic capacity would commence immediately.[61]

Thus, it seemed, by the summer of 1947, that the NPS could look forward to development of major visitor facilities in the Kings River Canyon. The road would cross the river at Roaring River, proceed along the northern wall, and execute a tight loop just to the west of Copper Creek. A large tourism infrastructure would be established at Cedar Grove, with a small pack station at Copper Creek. Finally, the park could attract thousands of scenery-hungry visitors and fulfill promises to the San Joaquin Valley's businessmen. Development of trails would proceed for the greater enjoyment of the Sierra Club's members and other wilderness enthusiasts. New Regional Director O. A. Tomlinson confidently assured Warlow and others that the road to Copper Canyon would be completed by late 1948.[62] Major visitor facilities and concession lodgings would be available shortly to accept the anticipated boom of visitors to the nation's great new wilderness park.

The NPS, however, had not predicted three final factors that were to delay construction in the canyon for another two and one-half decades. One was the fault of the government itself, which, by its niggardly appropriations, dragged out construction of the road to Copper Creek

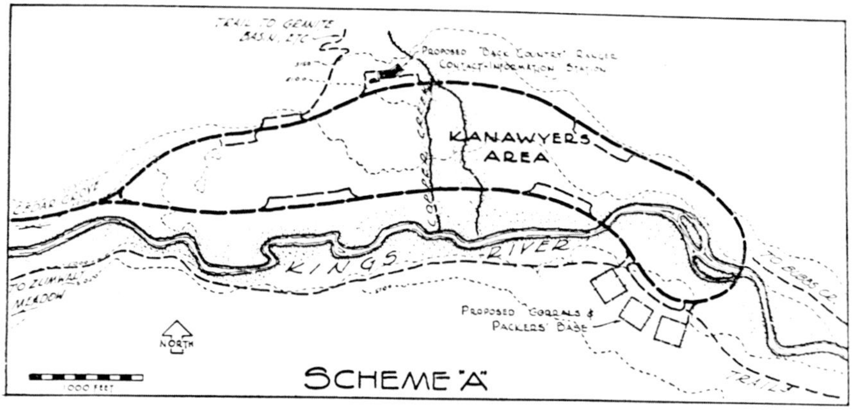

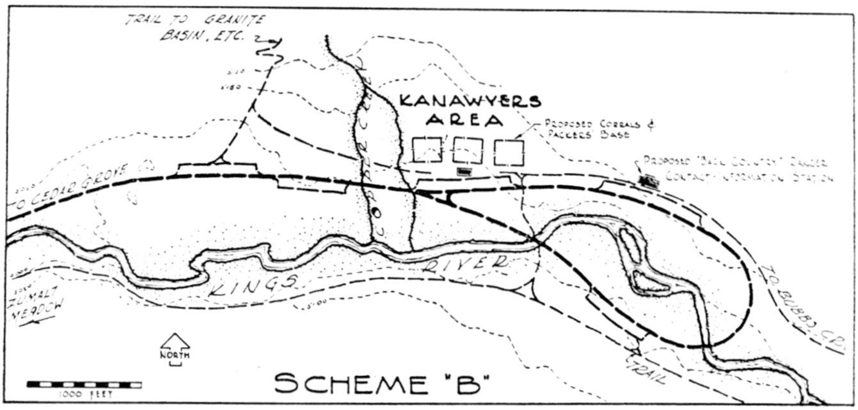

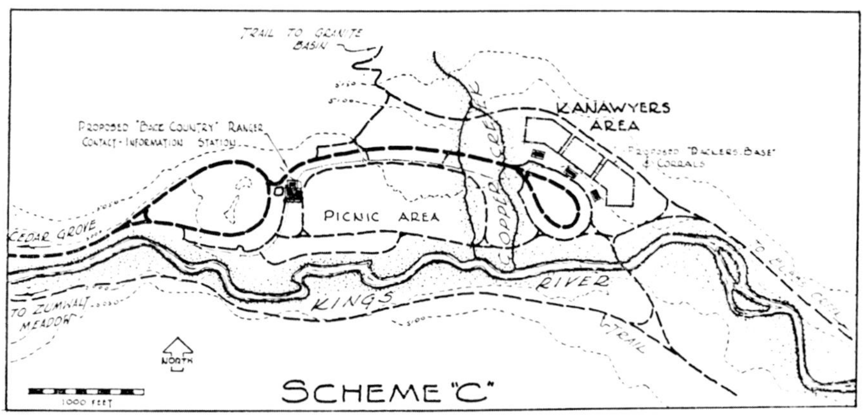

In 1947, the National Park Service honored promises it had made during the campaign to create Kings Canyon National Park by offering to the public multiple visions (such as those above) for the large-scale development of visitor facilities near Copper Creek on the floor of the Kings Canyon. In the end, none of these would be constructed.

for another ten years. Another was the unwillingness of concessioners Howard Hays and George Mauger to spend any money or effort developing Cedar Grove. And the third was the stunning reapplication by Los Angeles to build dams on the Kings River watershed both outside and inside the young park.

RETROSPECT ON KINGS CANYON

The battles fought during the 1930s and 1940s over the creation and proper development of Kings Canyon National Park represented a full collision between two equally valid but completely incompatible concepts of federal land use, each with its own view of what constituted a valuable resource. During the nineteenth century, despite considerable searching, only a few shepherds had found resources of significant value in the rugged maze of canyons forming the Kings River watershed. By the turn of the century, another value had been established— recreation areas in wilderness—but its practitioners remained small in number, if not always in visibility.

By the early 1920s, the resource value of the region had risen significantly. Two sets of perceived resources, only barely related, were clearly defined; two sets of resource users awaited the opportunity to implement their schemes; and two sets of potential managers sought either to maintain or obtain control of the region. The USFS, together with competing irrigation and hydroelectric interests, defined their resources through a utilitarian worldview. Kings Canyon would best serve America by being tamed, by sharing its water and power with the nation's economic mainstream. Opposed to this utilitarian vision were the intellectual descendants of its ultimate critic—John Muir. The Sierra Club, after several decades of organized and individual recreational use of the Kings River country, saw the region's resources not as potential contributors to industrial America but rather as an antidote. To the club and others who loved the wild Sierra, the valuable resources of the region were not waterpower and grazing potential but wild surging rivers and fields of alpine wildflowers. Sharing the view of the Sierra Club was the NPS.

To the true physical resources of Kings Canyon, the ecosystems and their natural inhabitants, the decisions of the Kings Canyon political wars were of paramount importance. Ultimately, the preservationists won most of their goals, despite the initial handicap of the USFS's management of the area. Passage of the Kings Canyon Park Act seems, in hindsight, as much a political accident as a carefully moderated political decision. Without Congressman Elliot's decisive blunder, Kings Canyon National Park might never have come to be. Had the park not been created, the alternative vision of conservation would have altered the landscape and its inhabitants severely and permanently.

More than either Sequoia or Yosemite, both of which were created before the twentieth-century resource values of the Sierra Nevada had become apparent, Kings Canyon National

Park was a commitment of valuable resources. That commitment came out of a half-century of wilderness recreation, and, at the same time, it facilitated a partial recovery from the impacts of early grazing and trapping. Although many individuals and organizations helped to create Kings Canyon National Park and to determine its destiny once it was established, the membership of the Sierra Club, during nearly five decades of exploration, publicity, and lobbying, played the single biggest role and deserves ultimate credit.

CHAPTER EIGHT

Controlling Development: How Much Is Too Much (1947–1972)

During the first sixty-five years of their existence, Sequoia and Kings Canyon as well as the remainder of the national park system evolved through three stages. The early years were difficult and confused, as goals and policies remained unclear. The parks had received little money and few employees to define and defend the reserves. The establishment of the National Park Service (NPS) in 1916, under the directorships of Stephen Tyng Mather and then Horace Albright, initiated a second phase that emphasized development of recreational and visitor amenities. That phase lasted through the decades of the 1920s and 1930s, culminating in the spectacular achievements of the Civilian Conservation Corps (CCC). The third stage overlapped with this period of development and resulted from it. Questions of the propriety of recreational activities and their infrastructure began to crop up, even as newer and more ambitious plans were submitted. Were park managers living up to their congressional charge of preserving the resources unimpaired for the future? These thoughts heralded a series of moves aimed at both studying and controlling use and abuse.

This might have stimulated an uninterrupted evolution toward improved funding, more scientific management, and a philosophy that emphasized preservation. World War II, however, brought the parks and their management to a catastrophic decline, which, in turn, sparked a virtual repetition of these three stages. The NPS's budget had been cut more than seventy-five percent, and, during and after the war, the national park system wallowed in low funding and grudging congressional attention for more than a decade and a half. To correct these problems, the NPS undertook a dramatic, highly publicized program of infrastructural development. Once this program had caught attention from the public and dollars from lawmakers, the NPS revived questions of philosophy and resource management. This cycle of retreat, renewal, and reappraisal further strengthened the NPS within the mass of government agencies competing for funds and again moved it toward the more scientific, ecology-oriented management that prevails today.

RETREAT: HARD TIMES AND TOUGH QUESTIONS

The post-World War II era began for the NPS with a flood of optimistic enthusiasm. Park planners expected a speedy return of visitors and with them funding at prewar levels. Thousands of structures built by the CCC as well as many more built during earlier years desperately needed renovation or reconstruction. Miles of roads and trails also demanded major repairs. Most postwar park planners hoped for a return of CCC-type work camps, from which they could draw labor to continue the parks' progress. It was time to get on with plans and dreams, time to reevaluate the park's resources, redesign facilities, and redouble efforts to make each visitor's experience educational and fulfilling.[1]

In Sequoia and Kings Canyon National Parks, the staff shared this service-wide optimism. Cedar Grove promised to be a new and exciting area to develop, a second Yosemite Valley. The Giant Forest might finally be freed from its half-century of crowds and clutter to become again the spiritually and emotionally uplifting reserve park planners knew it could be. Elaborate remodeling of structures at Grant Grove, Lodgepole, and Ash Mountain awaited attention, as did hundreds of miles of winter-ravaged backcountry trails. Along with all this development, Colonel White and his successor Eivind Scoyen hoped to reassess park management and study the problems of resource use and concomitant preservation.

To the dismay of the NPS, its allies in the preservation movement, and the public that visited and used the parks, these hopes were dashed for more than a decade after the war. Although the number of visitors to the national park system rose more than 250 percent between 1940 and 1955, funding lagged far behind, with an increase of only fifty-six percent.[2] Throughout the nation, superintendents reported decaying structures, potholed roads, tawdry visitor displays, and gross understaffing of popular areas. Laws and regulations went unenforced in backcountry areas. Virtually all acquisition of inholdings ceased, as did negotiations for elimination of grazing permits. By 1955, noted historian and popular author Bernard DeVoto, in one of his monthly columns ("The Easy Chair") for *Harpers Magazine*, called for a drastic solution to these problems. Specifically, he suggested closing some of the larger parks, because "they have the largest staffs in the system but neither those staffs nor the budgets allotted them are large enough to maintain the areas at a proper level of safety, attractiveness, comfort, or efficiency. They are unable to do the job in full and so it had better not be attempted at all."[3]

Back in the two southern Sierra parks, the problems of insufficient funds and manpower were keenly felt. During the decade and a half after 1940, annual visitation rose from 483,743 to 1,074,134, or 122 percent, but funding failed to increase even half that percentage. Colonel White complained in 1947:

> Despite our best efforts, our public camps are run down, our scenic spots improperly protected, our park buildings and all facilities inadequately maintained, and the public neither protected nor advised, or educated, as should be possible in these great heritages and builders of national pride and morale.[4]

His successor, Superintendent Scoyen, reiterated such sentiments in succeeding years and added that a doubling of appropriations would not overcome the years of neglect.

One example of the irksome effects of diminished funding occurred with the road from Cedar Grove to Copper Creek. Even as San Joaquin Valley newspapers reported a promised completion time of late 1948, actual construction bogged down, due to paltry funding and contractor problems. By 1952, annoyed citizens in Fresno demanded that the NPS fulfill its promise. Yet, four years later, the winter of 1955–1956 brought flood damage to a still-incomplete road. Work on a bridge over the Kings River dragged into late 1956, and, six months later, the contractor suffered bankruptcy. Finally, in September 1957, the road was completed, ending a decade of frustration and confusion arising from what had begun as a relatively simple one-year project.[5]

Elsewhere in Sequoia and Kings Canyon, conditions were equally worrisome. The Giant Forest and other visitor areas suffered from overuse and a lack of vegetative regeneration. The replanting program and the Ash Mountain Nursery had been early casualties of wartime and postwar cuts in funding. Crying for repair were tumbled-down visitor contact stations, dirty and undersized amphitheaters, and campgrounds sporting tire-damaged sites, wrecked camp facilities, and nearly denuded forests. In the backcountry, some trails became impassible, and meadows turned to muddy bogs, as a few overtaxed work crews and rangers tried to care for more than 1,100 square miles of territory. Park employees, many of them recent veterans of World War II and Korea, crammed into grubby and substandard tent-top cabins.[6]

RENEWAL: MISSION 66

By the mid-1950s, everyone in the Park Service and an increasing number of outside observers knew that the system was in trouble. The U.S. Congress had chosen to neglect the nation's parklands; facilities and structures were seriously declining, yet visitors continued to pour in at alarming rates. Hamstrung by budget constraints, the administration of a single park or, for that matter, of an entire region was powerless to reverse the decay. Any recovery would have to come from Washington, D.C.[7]

New NPS Director Conrad Wirth and his associates had been focusing on these problems. But anger and frustration continued to mount, as senior officials repeatedly met with polite but aloof response from a Congress consumed with other issues. In 1955, in an article published in *The Reader's Digest,* a worried Director Wirth complained:

> It is not possible to provide essential services. Visitor concentration points can't be kept in sanitary condition. Comfort stations can't be kept clean and serviced. Water, sewer and electrical systems are taxed to the utmost. Protective services to safeguard the public and preserve park values are far short of requirements. Physical facilities are deteriorating or are inadequate to meet public needs. Some of the camps are approaching rural slums.

The article went on to warn prospective visitors that "your trip is likely to be fraught with discomfort, disappointment, and even danger."[8]

The problem, as Wirth saw it, lay in the budgeting procedure. The NPS had a series of discrete, short-term projects in individual parks that could be, and often were, trimmed at budget time. Wirth hit upon an idea, based on the funding successes of agencies such as the Bureau of Reclamation, of presenting Congress with a grand, multi-year project aimed at capturing more funds to halt the degeneration of facilities. The resulting plan—Mission 66—was a masterpiece of emotional appeal, hard sell, and clever maneuvering worthy of the NPS's founding director Stephen Mather.[9]

A full year's preparation went into the proposal. To the annoyance of the Sierra Club and other preservationists, the NPS publicized the process but kept details secret. At last, in the winter of 1956, the NPS presented its overall plans to President Dwight D. Eisenhower and Congress. Mission 66 contained a series of basic points that upheld the NPS's traditional preservation goals, but two specific statements embodied the project: (1) "Substantial and appropriate use of the National Park System is the best means by which its basic purpose is realized and is the best guarantee of perpetuating the system"; and (2) "Adequate and appropriate developments are required for public use and appreciation of an area, and for prevention of overuse." Mission 66 was to be, first and foremost, a program aimed at redressing the decline of the NPS's structures used by visitors and employees. Although other points in the guidelines addressed issues such as wilderness areas and resource preservation, these were philosophical and cautionary advisements, not the guts of the proposed plan. Mission 66 would last ten years and carry a whopping price tag of nearly $800,000,000. It would conclude in 1966, on the fiftieth anniversary of the founding of the NPS, and would reverse the physical and spiritual decline that had beset the parks for more than fifteen years.[10]

The Mission 66 plan had vision, scope, emotional appeal, grand design, and historical precedent. It combined the charisma and political charm that Stephen Mather's programs had so successfully displayed. After a hasty endorsement by President Eisenhower, Congress got its chance to study the proposal. Here, the scope of the project had its real impact. With 168 units scattered across the nation, there was something for everyone in Mission 66. Likewise, the publicized planning process had already had a profound effect. As planning had proceeded, an intrigued Congress boosted funding for 1956 by fifty percent. When lawmakers finally received the proposal, they quickly approved it and attached another thirty-nine percent hike in appropriations to inaugurate the program. Ultimately Congress appropriated more than $1,000,000,000 for Mission 66 projects and quadrupled the NPS's annual budget to $128,000,000 by 1966.[11]

The staff of Sequoia and Kings Canyon greeted the Mission 66 concept with enthusiasm and optimism. Superintendent Scoyen's men scrambled to assimilate data, inventory and field check facilities, and provide their ten-year plan for renewal of the parks' physical resources. The resulting proposal embodied the plans and ideas of the previous two decades of park management. Included were provisions for developing Cedar Grove, rerouting Generals Highway, acquiring inholdings and eliminating grazing permits, redesigning structures at all the parks' developed areas, and studying ways to remove the concessioner from the Giant Forest. The proposals were broken into three priority lists and totaled nearly $19,000,000 for the decade-long program.[12]

One benefit of a multi-year, established program soon became apparent at Sequoia and Kings Canyon. A few weeks before Mission 66 received congressional approval, Eivind Scoyen departed to become NPS's associate director. The appointment of George A. Walker as acting superintendent commenced a sequence of relatively frequent top-level changes at the parks. Walker was followed by Thomas J. Allen, John M. Davis, and Frank F. Kowski as superintendents during the Mission 66 decade. Yet, despite the potential confusion such personnel changes could have brought, the projects proceeded toward specified goals at a measured and largely successful pace.

The program designed by Scoyen's team and incorporated into Mission 66's legislation proposed an ambitious agenda for construction. Major projects included four new visitor centers at the Giant Forest, Lodgepole, Grant Grove, and Cedar Grove; a new administration complex at Ash Mountain; replacement or erection of new water, sewage, and trash facilities; electrification at the Giant Forest and Cedar Grove; construction of additional employee housing; and partial relocation of Generals Highway, especially around the Giant Forest. Lesser projects included expansion and redesign of some campgrounds; construction of additional comfort stations, amphitheaters, and entrance stations; and repair of assorted roads, fences, and overlooks.[13]

For a time, though, it appeared that Sequoia and Kings Canyon would be among the failures of Mission 66. Superintendent Allen wrote, in his 1959 annual report, that the vaunted program had gotten off to a slow start, accomplished little, and had not impressed the public.[14] But, during the 1960s, there was a rapid acceleration, culminating in the completion of nearly all of the parks' Mission 66 goals. Employee housing was added along with a big, new administration complex at Ash Mountain. The Giant Forest and Cedar Grove areas received new water and sewage systems as well as new garbage incinerators. Electric power lines reached the Giant Forest in 1956. New comfort stations, entrance stations, interpretive displays, trails, and parking areas served visitors. Perhaps most significant for the public, the NPS completed new visitor centers at Ash Mountain in 1963, Grant Grove in 1965, and Lodgepole in 1966. George Mauger's concession company also contributed to the revamped infrastructure for visitors, with a large new coffee shop and store complex at Grant Grove, bringing that neglected area up to standard for the first time, along with construction of new cabins to replace some of the miserable, substandard shacks in both the Giant Forest and Grant Grove. [15]

Despite all the gains of Mission 66 in Sequoia and Kings Canyon, three major NPS goals were not fulfilled: development of Cedar Grove, construction of a visitor center at the Giant Forest, and relocation of Generals Highway. In each case, lack of funds was not the problem. At Cedar Grove, the stubborn unwillingness of the concessioner to participate threatened to sabotage all development in the spectacular canyon. Meanwhile, projects in the Giant Forest were among the earliest casualties in a dramatic, pervasive, and hitherto unchecked rise of ecological science and preservationist philosophy.

CEDAR GROVE: THE ONE BIG FAILURE OF MISSION 66

In 1947, with the release of the "Kings Canyon Development Plan," the NPS confidently expected imminent completion of major visitor facilities at Cedar Grove. The Fresno Chamber of Commerce and other local business groups had abandoned their efforts to force construction of the infrastructure at Copper Creek and had expressed satisfaction with the scale of the plans for Cedar Grove. The Sierra Club, despite the grumblings of younger members, accepted the location and scale of the planned development as the least of all evils. Although government funds for completion of the road to Copper Creek were slow in coming, there was no reason to believe that this delay would affect development at Cedar Grove. At long last, the NPS hoped to see the canyon brought into full use and the completion of the government's side of the great compromise.

Park officials, however, had not bargained on Howard Hays, George Mauger, and their Sequoia and Kings Canyon National Parks Company. For the next two decades, Hays and Mauger resisted every effort of the NPS to force investment in and expansion of concession operations in the canyon. With the deliberate destruction of company records by later executives in the 1960s, the reflections

The most troubling issue for Superintendent (Colonel) John R. White and many of his successors in managing Sequoia National Park was the relationship with the Sequoia and Kings Canyon National Parks Company. Howard Hays owned the company, but the man who ran the operations and faced the superintendents daily was George Mauger, shown here cooking alongside an employee. Mauger managed the concession from 1926 until he sold the company in 1965. Photographer and date unknown.

and confidential preferences of the men are unavailable. Yet their record on all matters regarding construction, expanded operations, and longer seasons of operation point to a pair of men who simply did not want to invest in Cedar Grove. Indeed, in a rare glimpse of true feelings, Hays wrote in 1955:

> I do not feel that Kings Canyon is a second Yosemite by a long shot. It is a delightful Sierra Valley and will have many attractions for visitors, but I do not think it will attract the resort type who enjoy a vacation in the cool area of the Giant Forest.

It was in that resort crowd and in the Giant Forest that Mauger and Hays saw their priorities. They had no interest in what they saw as a distant, seasonally snowbound, and presumably doomed canyon far from the main park highway.[16]

The company had seemed interested during the early days of the park. Shortly after successful passage of the Kings Canyon park bill in 1940, Mauger officially applied for permission to develop the canyon's tourism resources. That enthusiasm seemed to evaporate once the park began operations, to be replaced with protestations that conditions made investment unsafe and unwise. The earliest reasons arose from the odd status of the canyon's jurisdiction. Under the laws of the time, concessions on U.S. Forest Service (USFS) lands could only receive five-year contracts, compared to the twenty-year contracts signed with the NPS. In addition, USFS permits only allowed five acres to each concession company for its operations. Throughout Kings Canyon's first decade, Department of Interior representatives, along with friendly members of Congress, struggled and successfully overcame these problems by special legislation and brought Cedar Grove into line with the rest of the parks.[17]

World War II was a second issue that obviously hindered investment. The scarcity of equipment, supplies, funds, manpower, and visitors combined to squash all construction plans for nearly four years. By 1945, however, with visitation on the rise and the war moving toward its conclusion, Colonel White suggested resumption of limited operations in the canyon and of planning for postwar development. The concessioners responded by writing that they were shocked at this suggestion and that, "when the casualties affect every neighborhood, as they will by next summer, our people (Americans) are going to be on edge about undue emphasis on non-essentials." Colonel White reacted with immediate and typical scorn by writing to Director Drury:

> The point is that I have for years been trying to discuss plans with Mr. Mauger, but find that he must always refer them to Mr. Hays. And when I suggest an appointment with Mr. Hays, he is too busy on important matters or he cannot stand the arduous drive up the frightful Giant Forest road, or there is some other excuse. . . . I fully realize the difficulties

> under which all park operators now labor with regard to employment and OPA and other regulations. But the fact remains that, as good businessmen, the officers of the Sequoia and Kings Canyon National Parks Company desire to serve the public only when the cream is cheap and plentiful. I do not mind that natural attitude but object to the insinuations that they are virtuously refraining from stimulating travel while park officers are viciously disregarding the national interest and all regulations.[18]

With World War II over and the jurisdictional and planning problems almost solved, Mauger and Hays presented three new and ultimately far more obstructive reasons for delay. The first was the inadequacy of infrastructure, particularly the lack of a water system for fire protection and the undersized sewage-treatment facility. Available systems dated from the early days of the USFS in Kings Canyon and were wholly inadequate for existing demand, much less any grand expansion. The government did improve both systems by 1954 with further enlargement in 1957, but the concessioners had managed to win an agreement, allowing them to delay construction until five years after completion of improved water and sewage lines. Hence, it was late in the decade before Mauger and company were required to uphold their agreement. These delays in government installation of infrastructure arose from the same funding and development woes that plagued the road to Copper Creek and blunted programs throughout the national park system.[19]

A second reason for resistance to investment in Cedar Grove sprang from the issue of power, specifically electrification. Commencing in the late 1950s, negotiations for construction of a power line to the canyon by the Pacific Gas and Electric Company (PG&E) snagged on the matter of the concessioner's share of the costs. Initially, Mauger tried to coax the government into bearing the entire charge. As negotiations proceeded through and beyond Mission 66, the company's representatives held out for government payment of two-thirds of the $37,000 annual maintenance fee, even though the concession facilities would use more than half the power. Finally, the government and PG&E split nearly the entire cost of construction and early maintenance, allowing completion of lines into the canyon in early 1972.[20]

Despite the importance to Mauger and Hays of such issues as water, sewage, and power, they paled in contrast to the threat of inundation from reclamation and power development in the canyon. In 1947, that issue had seemed a distant and unlikely prospect. Downstream, in the foothills, construction was underway on an enormous structure at Pine Flat. The reservoir would hold approximately 1,000,000 acre-feet of water, or two-thirds of the total annual runoff from the entire Kings River system. In addition, negotiations had begun for further projects on the North Fork of the river. Most Department of Interior people and many in the San Joaquin Valley expected there never to be a need for reservoirs at Cedar Grove or Tehipite Valley.[21]

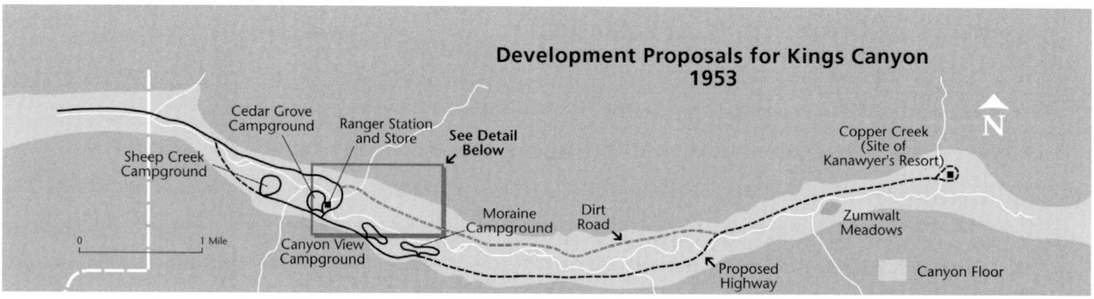
Development Proposals for Kings Canyon
1953
Cedar Grove Campground
Ranger Station and Store
See Detail Below
Sheep Creek Campground
Copper Creek (Site of Kanawyer's Resort)
Moraine Campground
Dirt Road
Zumwalt Meadows
Canyon View Campground
Proposed Highway
Canyon Floor
0
1 Mile

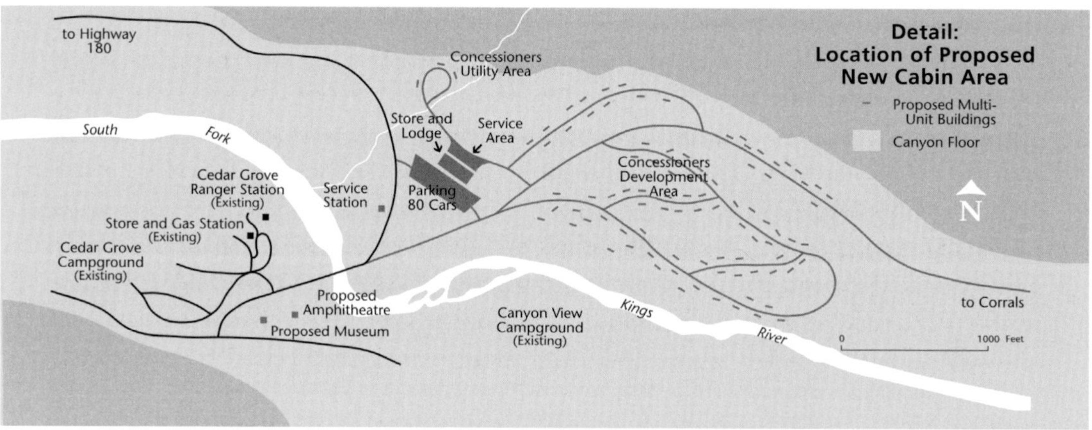
to Highway 180
Detail: Location of Proposed New Cabin Area
Proposed Multi-Unit Buildings
Canyon Floor
Concessioners Utility Area
South
Fork
Store and Lodge
Service Area
Concessioners Development Area
Cedar Grove Ranger Station (Existing)
Service Station
Parking 80 Cars
Store and Gas Station (Existing)
Cedar Grove Campground (Existing)
Proposed Amphitheatre
Proposed Museum
Canyon View Campground (Existing)
Kings
River
to Corrals
0
1000 Feet

Then, to the consternation of everyone, on May 4, 1948, Los Angeles re-filed petitions with both the Federal Power Commission and the State Water Board to build dams and power stations at both canyon sites as well as at several other locations within the young park. For several reasons, the Kings River Conservation District filed immediately on the same sites. One of their reasons was to block Los Angeles. Rumors had begun to surface that the city did not need the power but simply meant to sell it for profit. In such a development, local communities would receive no benefit. Another story suggested that City of Los Angeles engineers meant to drill a tunnel fourteen miles under the Sierra Nevada and add Kings River water to their Owens Valley aqueduct. Although most reasonable men discounted that suggestion, the old fears of Los Angeles's water piracy had re-surfaced.[22]

In addition to the threat from Los Angeles, locals had fallen into bitter disagreement with the Bureau of Reclamation over development of the North Fork. The Kings River Water Association wanted development of combined water-storage and power-generation facilities by PG&E. This would allow the water to be kept entirely for local irrigation districts. The bureau, on the other hand, wanted to design similar structures but make the river part of the Central Valley Project, a huge federal program principally aimed at shifting water southward from the Sacramento Valley to the San Joaquin Valley. As a byproduct, some extra water went, once again, to Los Angeles. If the North Fork waters became part of the Central Valley Project, local farmers would lose control of the water and, as they saw it, suffer during California's periodic drought years.[23]

The Federal Power Commission took both issues under study, while NPS officials, civic leaders from Fresno, and representatives of the Sierra Club hurriedly conferred. The problem of development along the North Fork was settled relatively quickly, with the nod going to the locals and PG&E, on November 5, 1949. Thereafter, construction began on the Courtwright and Wishon Dams and on associated power stations. The two projects were completed in 1962, ten years after the Pine Flat Dam, and gave locals control of storage facilities capable of holding more than three-fourth's of the annual runoff from the Kings River Basin. [24]

The defeat of Los Angeles, on the other hand, took somewhat longer. Despite continued rejections of their applications, the city re-filed in 1952, 1954, and 1959. After settlement of the North Fork issue, local irrigation officials felt secure, yet they re-filed each time on the same sites, confiding to the NPS that they only meant to block Los Angeles. Finally, in 1963, the State Water Board, following the lead of the federal government by three years, rejected Los Angeles's last proposal for the Kings River.[25] And with the Los Angeles threat finally removed, most local politicians and citizens joined the quarter-century-old movement to give the canyons to the national park. The Kings River Water Association, loath to lose control of any potential resource, still opposed inclusion, but, nevertheless, the bill passed easily. On August 6, 1965, Cedar Grove and Tehipite Valley became parts of Kings Canyon National Park, some eighty-four years after Senator Miller made the first proposal to protect the two scenic canyons.

This persistent, uncertain status of Cedar Grove gave George Mauger and Howard Hays all the reason they needed to balk at spending money for construction. Always a miserly sort, Mauger complained that his company could barely hold its own and could scarcely be expected to invest in such a large construction project in such a threatened locale. He and Hays consulted with an attorney, in 1954, and, based on his recommendations, offered three solutions to the problem. First, the canyon could be incorporated into the national park, thus eliminating the threat, or, second, the federal government could build concession facilities and lease them to the Sequoia and Kings Canyon National Parks Company. This would place the investment risk on the government rather than on Mauger and Hays. Finally, the NPS could allow construction of facilities near Copper Creek, within the existing park and well east of the reservoir's reach.[26]

The NPS declined the last two options and could not unilaterally implement a takeover of Cedar Grove, but it assured Mauger that, if he built visitor facilities that were later flooded, he would be recompensed. Mauger, however, took a dim view of such promises, and, secretly, so did some NPS personnel. This attitude may have arisen because, in two and one-half decades of arguing with George Mauger and despite the prominent inclusion of the Cedar Grove development in Mission 66's plans, the NPS never invested in any substantial structures either. Here, at the nub of the issue, the official record becomes nebulous, but Mauger's reticent attitude seemed to be infectious. Repeatedly, Mauger pointed to the threat of a withdrawal of power and pleaded that his limited resources were needed elsewhere—now for repairs at the Giant Forest, later a new Grant Grove coffee shop, and, still later, additions to visitor facilities at Lodgepole. Again and again, he made the case stand up and resisted efforts to build more than a few miserable tent cabins at Cedar Grove.[27] As long as Mauger delayed, the NPS seemed equally unwilling to build beyond the water and sewage infrastructure. Plans for a major visitor center with a museum simply lay dormant, while the parks' planners reallocated funds and priorities elsewhere.

In 1965, as Mission 66 drew to a close, the NPS finally fulfilled the first of Mauger's options—incorporation of the canyon into the park and its automatic protection from inundation. But before the issue could again be broached, George Mauger, who had earlier taken over Hays's interests, sold the company and, shortly thereafter, retired. This began a lengthy, confusing process of sellouts and mergers that combined to freeze any further progress for another seven years. The new owner was the Fred Harvey Company, a major concessioner, especially in the national parks of the Southwest. In Cedar Grove, the Harvey Company exhibited the same unwillingness as Mauger to make any improvements. Indeed, during its short tenure operating the Sequoia and Kings Canyon National Parks Company, it allowed much of the maintenance to lapse. In 1968, the company merged with the huge Amfac conglomerate, a corporation so diverse and so large that a puny operation such as the Sequoia and Kings Canyon concession received only enough attention to assure that it was not a strong moneymaker. Accordingly, in 1972, Amfac sold the concession rights to Government Services, Incorporated (GSI), a concessioner for the national capital parks in Washington, D.C., that later changed its name to Guest Services, Inc.[28]

In GSI, the parks finally had a concessioner with substantial resources devoted to the business of national park concessions. The company had been founded as a nonprofit organization to bring better quality to tourism operations in the parks. GSI approached Sequoia and Kings Canyon National Parks, in general, and Cedar Grove, in particular, with a will to develop and the money to back it up. The coincident arrival of PG&E electric lines seemed finally to clear the way for the kind of development in the canyon that had been sought since the early 1930s.

During the years of negotiating with Mauger and Company, the NPS had scaled back its plans for Cedar Grove, in reaction to continued pressure from the Sierra Club and its own increasingly preservationist officials. In 1957, the NPS dropped the proposed pillow count for cabins from 700 to 260.[29] Gone, too, were ideas of expanding campgrounds beyond the 370 sites in existence. Nevertheless, the plans released by the NPS, in 1972, with GSI's blessings, still called for a substantial buildup of facilities for visitors. New lodges and cabins would house 260 people, and a new 11,000-square-foot store and cafeteria complex would complement an equal-sized new visitor center now well overdue from Mission 66. Parking for more than 500 cars in the canyon was anticipated as well as enlarged facilities for picnicking.[30] The main pack station would also remain at Cedar Grove, but a small branch station would be built at Copper Creek. The long years of delay, argument, and stingy investment were over. With these plans amicably approved by the new concessioner, a confident NPS sat back to wait for the reaction from the public on what finally was to be done with the beautiful canyon of the South Fork.

REAPPRAISAL: THE GIANT FOREST

From 1930 through 1947, assaults on the scenery and serenity of Sequoia and Kings Canyon had continued to mount and with them concern about the future of the parks. These fears for resource conservation and the park administration's ability to carry out its founding charter were fueled principally by landscape architects. Although scientists such as Emilio Meinecke, George Wright, and Lowell Sumner contributed important and respected research that further demonstrated ecological decline from human impact, theirs was a tiny voice in the management chorus. Quite simply, ecological science was too immature and under-supported in the parks to contribute strong factual data and, thus, shape management's opinion. Landscape architects tackled visible problems with visible solutions aimed at creating visual pleasure. To an agency still concerned with preserving isolated objects and scenery and entertaining visitors, the voice of landscape architecture remained the star player.[31]

During the 1950s, however, science began to assume a stronger role. Not only had botany, zoology, conservation, and ecology made tremendous strides in methodology and in the sophistication of their conclusions, but more science-trained people were joining the NPS, both in the Sierra Nevada's parks and nationwide. From 1947 to 1972, the NPS would see a revolution in management priorities in the national parks, as the voice of science replaced that of landscape architecture in management decisions. In Sequoia and Kings Canyon, this role reversal both caused and resulted from a reappraisal of resource management in the two parks. In the Giant Forest, in the alpine backcountry, and with animals and vegetation, the NPS scrutinized past policies, gauged their results, and began a profound shift toward preserving ecosystems and a new interpretation of the 1916 charter that tilted ever more toward preservation and away from visitor use.

Nowhere in the two parks had resource threats and concerns gone deeper than in the Giant Forest. In 1947, when an embattled and embittered Colonel White retired, the struggle to control human use in the grove was already twenty years old, but the forced retirement of the powerful superintendent signaled a change in the tone of contract negotiations between the concessioner and those who would evict his company from the forest. Superintendent Scoyen, who replaced White for the second time, had long served with and respected his old boss, but he had his own ideas and agenda for the parks. Scoyen was younger, more flexible, and apparently less proprietary in his administration than the colonel had been. In addition, he held somewhat different ideas about the development of concessions and the proper balance between use and preservation. He announced his new administrative philosophy with small changes such as adding a second lane to the Generals Highway between the Four Guardsmen, four spectacular sequoias that Colonel White had long protected, even though they were an obvious bottleneck. And, within a few months of assuming the superintendency, Scoyen went on record in favor of allowing all concession facilities, except Giant Forest Village to remain in the grove. Although the Washington, D.C., office was actually responsible for contract negotiations with concessions, they listened carefully to the opinion of the superintendent on site. Following Scoyen's advice and recalling Howard Hays's similar plan of a few years earlier, the NPS approached the concessioners with such a plan. All too quickly the stringent efforts of Colonel White fell to a new philosophy and an expedient solution.[32]

At the same time, however, Hays and Mauger had also reconsidered their position and replied that they would be happier if the NPS would simply forget about any notion of evacuating the Giant Forest. More than seventy-five percent of the revenue from their operations through the two parks derived from the Giant Forest. Neither believed that Lodgepole or any other site could replace the experience of being beneath the Big Trees or that many people would pay for a substitute. Bolstered by an apparent governmental willingness to grant indefinitely short extensions of the old contract, the two men commenced a series of objections and stall tactics. First, they balked at a provision that would allow complete evacuation to be reconsidered after a ten-year hiatus. Then, there was the matter of how much the government should reimburse them for moving the village's structures. The Korean War provided another excuse, as everyone tried to measure the seriousness of the conflict and whether it heralded another period of austerity and low visitation. Finally, for nearly a year, the company negotiated to sell the business to a nonprofit organization formed by former NPS employees. With each new problem and each nine- or twelve-month contract extension, Mauger and Hays backed further away from the notion of leaving the Giant Forest.[33]

Finally, in 1952, the issue came to a head. Negotiations with the potential buyer broke down, and the concessioners suggested that a new contract was now long overdue. They would not budge from their stand to remain in the grove, with one exception. That was a concession from Hays, allowing reconsideration of removal of Giant Forest Village in ten years. NPS's Interim Director Arthur Demaray signaled the weariness and frustration of the government by summarily ordering that the concessioner be allowed to remain in the grove and that contract negotiations should conclude as soon as possible. In August 1952, both parties inked a new contract, specifying the conditions Hays had recently suggested and consigning to the scrap heap twenty years of effort by Colonel White and his allies. The former superintendent's prediction of concessioner tactics and their eventual results proved to be exactly accurate.[34]

The conclusion of contract negotiations between the NPS and Sequoia and Kings Canyon National Parks Company seemed to settle the issue of evacuation from the grove once and for all. With a twenty-year contract in hand and further written approval from the director, Mauger and Hays resumed normal operations. The NPS, too, turned its attention to managing the Giant Forest under existing conditions and doing the best job possible to provide quality experiences for visitors, while preserving the delicate sequoias. True, conditions were distressing, but the issue was settled, and there was no alternative but to forge ahead.[35]

As the years passed and annual visitation nearly doubled pre-World War II totals, conditions in the Giant Forest continued to deteriorate. The concessioner had more than 400 structures in the area, including 303 cabins for guests, forty-seven cabins for employees, assorted bathing and rest facilities, entertainment and office buildings, stores, a gas station, dining facilities, and storage sheds. A number of those buildings cramped giant sequoias in the lodge area at the heart of the grove.[36] The NPS itself owned several dozen or so structures as well as four large and rapidly

The popularity of the "frontcountry" of Sequoia and Kings Canyon National Parks drew record numbers of visitors that reached 1,000,000 in 1953 and doubled during the next two decades. The increase in visitation resulted in worrisome congestion, especially in the Giant Forest and Grant Grove. Drivers often searched fruitlessly for parking at the village. To cope, the National Park Service first removed the gas station and much later almost all of the government and concession facilities from the grove. Ironically, the only portion to stay is the large building shown here, which originally held a restaurant and store and now houses a museum. Photographer and date unknown.

deteriorating campgrounds, a picnic area at Hazelwood, and associated features such as sewage plants, cisterns, and an amphitheater. Traffic along the Generals Highway competed with cars leaving Camp Kaweah, Giant Forest Lodge, Giant Forest Village, Moro Rock Road, four campgrounds, a picnic area, and a variety of scenic turnouts.[37] In addition, on crowded weekends and holidays, long lines of cars waiting at Sequoia's only gas station in the Village spilled onto the road. Driving to the peaceful and edifying serenity of the Giant Forest often became a chaotic and frustrating experience. Within the Village, pedestrian traffic at the post office, village market, and gift shops became equally disturbing. To any park administrator, these alarming conditions begged for solution. To the park's resource managers and visiting scientists, such conditions boded poorly for the future of the grove itself.[38]

George Mauger offered a simple solution: enlarge and expand operations in the Giant Forest. Throughout the remainder of his tenure in the parks, Mauger pressed for a higher pillow limit, newer and larger guest cabins, expansion of the gas station, coffee shop, and gift shops, and oiling of footpaths in the concession areas to control the dust generated by thousands of tourist feet.[39] In a few cases, Mauger succeeded. The NPS oiled several miles of footpaths, despite worries about the effect on the root systems of the sequoias. He also received permission to replace many of the ramshackle tent-top cabins with more permanent and comfortable units. Although park officials rejected most of his other requests, Mauger remained, until the day he retired, unceasing in his efforts to enlarge the Giant Forest's operation.[40]

Even before the frustrating contract negotiations ended and as summer traffic became increasingly congested, a disquieting incident further focused attention on human activity amid the sequoias. In the spring of 1950, park rangers observed a sequoia near Giant Forest Lodge that appeared to be leaning toward a number of concession cabins. The big tree, eighteen feet in diameter and more than 240 feet high, had always exhibited a lean. Subsequent measurements, however, showed that lean to have increased slightly in the previous year to a point where the top was twenty-eight feet out of plumb. For sixty years, the preservation of giant sequoias had been the one incontrovertible policy of the park's management, the one thing that all agreed upon. Here, however, a tree leaned dangerously toward more than a dozen concession cabins. The thought of the giant crashing to the ground onto hapless visitors in the cabins gave both NPS officials and George Mauger many worried nights.[41]

Throughout the summer, park officers and various forestry experts consulted over the fate of the Big Tree. Among the scientists to study the tree on site were Emilio Meinecke, recently retired, and Professor Emanuel Fritz, of the University of California, Berkeley. USFS officials, park foresters from other units, and Director Drury himself traveled to the Giant Forest to view the problem tree. Throughout the process, an anxious George Mauger pressed to have the tree cut down. To suggestions that he move the dozen or so cabins in danger, Mauger said he could not afford that. Yet park officials found it distressing to consider the destruction of one of the "objects" they had promised to protect, particularly since some sequoias had persisted at a tilt for longer than anyone could remember.[42]

At last, the NPS agreed to have the tree felled. The concessioner could move his cabins, but at what cost and to what new area? Superintendent Scoyen favored felling the tree, because if it later fell and killed or injured someone, he would be "on a very lofty and exposed pinnacle of personal responsibility." A subsequent flurry of correspondence between the Washington, D.C., office and Sequoia National Park confirmed the fate of the first giant sequoia to be cut deliberately in the sixty-year history of the park.

The actual job of bringing down the giant went to two brothers, Marshall and Leonard Brown. On November 8, they made a deep, horizontal cut on the side facing a prearranged direction, where the tree could fall and do no appreciable damage. Through the day with axes and a twelve-foot power saw, the brothers worked as a crowd of more than 100 employees and their families gathered. Telegrams from Scoyen to Regional Director Tomlinson reported the progress every few hours. Finally, at 4:15 p.m., the huge tree toppled with a tremendous crash, spraying cabins up to 350 feet away with mud and clots of dirt. With the aid of modern tools, including a block-and-tackle connected to a jeep via another sequoia, the Brown brothers successfully laid the tree exactly on target between permanent structures of Giant Forest Lodge. Subsequent investigation showed the tree to be an estimated 2,222 years of age. It lies today where it fell, minus only a few sections of the trunk that were later taken as museum displays.[43]

The cabins were safe, no visitors had even been inconvenienced, and the cutting had been an impressive feat; nevertheless, the entire episode badly disturbed park officials. Even George Mauger reported the deep sense of sadness that swept the crowd of onlookers, when the task was done. It had been a blow to the deepest loyalties of the parks' administrators, an action none had ever envisioned taking. Even before the tree came down, Mauger pointed out another leaning tree near Beetle Rock, which threatened cabins at Camp Kaweah. Scoyen, however, brusquely refused his request that it be cut at the same time, on the grounds that no shift in its lean had been observed.[44]

Failure to remove the concession company from the Giant Forest renewed pressure from Mauger and Hays to expand operations in the grove. At the same time, the deeply disturbing incident with the leaning sequoia and distressingly crowded conditions motivated the NPS to search frantically for options to ameliorate the situation. In the minds of Scoyen and his aides, neither of the parks' purposes was being fulfilled. Visitors were so crowded, jostled, and stressed that they could find little enjoyment or inspiration on busy days. And the scenery and serenity of the grand trees was being despoiled by the sheer numbers of tourists.

In 1950, a 240-foot giant sequoia that had always leaned toward some of the cabins of the Giant Forest Lodge shifted enough to alarm both National Park Service and concession officials. After worried consultations, the agency hired two brothers to cut down the tree that threatened multiple cabins. They successfully laid the tree between the structures on November 8, after which foresters determined it was more than 2,200 years old. Photographer and date unknown.

Mission 66 gave park officials an opportunity to address the situation. The landscape architects who designed the program chose two options aimed at relieving traffic congestion and compressing the NPS's operations in the grove. First, they would reroute Generals Highway around the Giant Forest as Frederick Law Olmsted, Jr. had suggested more than a decade earlier. Among several routes, Olmsted favored looping the road below and to the west of the plateau, tunneling below Sunset Rock, and rejoining the old highway somewhere near Lodgepole or the General Sherman Tree. Engineers with the NPS and the Bureau of Public Roads supported the project for traffic considerations, although most considered the notion of a tunnel under Sunset Rock to be dubious at best. Most park officials strongly supported the plan as a desperate measure to control crowding. Under the scheme, the Giant Forest and all its camping and lodging facilities would remain on a spur road leading ultimately to Crescent Meadow.[45]

The second option incorporated into Mission 66 was construction of a large new visitor center in Giant Forest Village, within which the functions of a half-dozen existing structures could be concentrated. Not only would this plan replace a scattering of buildings with one unit, but it would take some of those functions away from one of the densest areas of the Big Trees and put them in Giant Forest Village, where only a few trees could be affected. Suggestion of this plan marked one of the first times that landscape architects recommended a single, large structure in place of several, smaller, rustically "appropriate" ones.[46]

While businessmen, landscape architects, and rangers versed in people-management debated how to improve conditions in the Giant Forest, alarming scientific evidence continued to accumulate. That evidence suggested that all ideas proposed to date, with one exception, would fall short of preserving the Giant Forest's ecosystem. That exception was Colonel White's old notion of completely removing from the grove all visitor facilities of the concessioner and the NPS.

One of the earliest research studies to influence management of giant sequoias ironically came from Yosemite National Park. In January 1954, a committee appointed by the superintendent there released its "Report on the Effects of Human Impact Upon the Giant Sequoias of the Mariposa and Tuolumne Groves—Yosemite National Park." The chief conclusion of the "Yosemite Report" was that roads, buildings, sewage and power lines, and human compaction of soil all harmed the delicate root systems of the Big Trees. The committee could offer no solution to preserve the trees, except to remove the offending structures and paths. Although the report was widely read and respected in Sequoia and Kings Canyon, it alone did not sway management's opinion. It did, however, lay the foundation by bringing ecological concerns to the forefront and by calling for a large-scale, continuing program of research on sequoias.[47]

The name most associated with research on sequoias, in Sequoia and Kings Canyon and elsewhere in the species' range, was Richard Hartesveldt. A doctoral candidate at the University of Michigan when he began his studies, the native of Grand Rapids continued his work throughout the next two decades, later as a member of the faculty at San Jose State University. Much of Hartesveldt's early research took place in the Mariposa Grove of Yosemite National Park. There, he found evidence that not only corroborated the conclusions in the "Yosemite Report" and those of Emilio Meinecke back in 1944, but also suggested that the peril of the Big Trees was much more serious.[48] Steps would have to be taken, if the species were to continue in the grove and if the existing old giants were to survive.[49]

Hartesveldt's evidence, when added to that of the "Yosemite Report" and Meinecke's research, presented the NPS with stark choices. The gravity of the problem appeared irrefutable. Partial solutions and half-hearted attempts would doom the giant sequoias. In response, in 1960, Superintendent John M. Davis called for a high-level conference of park officials to consider the evidence, review the options, and decide on the management future for the Giant Forest. In attendance at the "summit meeting" were NPS Chief Ranger Lawrence Cook, Chief Landscape Architect Merel Sager, and Chief Naturalist Howard Stagner from the Washington, D.C., office, their counterparts at the Western Region Office, all the senior officials from Sequoia and Kings Canyon, Regional Research Biologist Lowell Sumner, and several landscape architects from the Washington Office Development Center. The ostensible purpose of the meeting, held from May 31 to June 2, was to choose the exact site for a visitor center in the Giant Forest, but, in reality, it was to decide the fate of developments, both existing and future, in the sequoia grove.[50]

The committee released its report and recommendations a few weeks later. The ominous evidence presented by Meinecke, the Yosemite Committee, and Hartesveldt was cited to underline the urgency and seriousness of the problem. In answer to the specific question of locating a visitor center, the committee recommended that it be located in or near Giant Forest Village, if the Generals Highway remained where it was. If, on the other hand, the road were to be rerouted around the Giant Forest, then the visitor center should be built at Lodgepole. Having settled the nominal topic of the conference, the committee then addressed the weightier issue of the grove's future development and made several recommendations, specifically: (1) all commercial activities (retail and food services) should ultimately be moved to Lodgepole or some other nearby site; (2) the Giant Forest should be allowed to recover its "natural aspects"; (3) the gas station, ice house, and grocery store in the Village should be given first and immediate priority in the move to Lodgepole; (4) a continuous program of research and observation of human impact on giant sequoias should be established; (5) walkways, parking areas, and other blacktop features should be moved or eliminated near sequoias; and (6) "the questions of the relocation of all overnight accommodations and campgrounds from Giant Forest to Lodgepole or elsewhere, as a long-term objective, should be reopened."[51]

The final, albeit understated, recommendation resurrected, after a decade of relative quiet, the most complex and divisive issue in the history of Sequoia and Kings Canyon. From such a blue-ribbon panel, relying on hard scientific data from a variety of sources and with such stakes at risk, Colonel White's old proposal packed a lot more potential punch this time around. Superintendent Davis supported all the recommendations with virtually no alterations, but Director Wirth still remained unconvinced on the matter of removing all facilities from the Giant Forest. Instead, he suggested restudying a bypass road, an option that had gotten bogged down in the early days of Mission 66.[52]

Although the Bureau of Public Roads had conducted a bypass study in 1957, Wirth now wanted a more in-depth analysis by the same agency. In late October and early November 1961, road engineers conducted field reconnaissance and, a few months later, released a second report. The bureau offered two routes around the Giant Forest, both of which veered from the existing road south and west of Beetle Rock, wound below the plateau to a point near Sunset Rock, and then curved northeastward to rejoin the highway near Lodgepole. There was no mention of a tunnel. In subsequent studies, NPS engineers modified the routes to form a third option that combined elements of the first two. In all three cases, the price tag hovered at between five and five and one-half million dollars, and in all three cases the Giant Forest remained on a spur road.[53]

Almost immediately, problems with the routes and, indeed, the very concept of a bypass road began to surface. The routes proposed by the Bureau of Public Roads required removal of a few sequoia trees. Superintendent Davis called this suggestion "a dead duck from the beginning." Thereafter, questions arose about the level of decrease in traffic that could be expected from such a move and how much protection the giant sequoias would receive if the spur road remained. Eventually, in 1969, the NPS commissioned a traffic study for the parks as part of a new master plan. In the resulting report, engineer D. Jackson Faustman suggested that construction of a bypass for traffic reasons alone was unjustified. If facilities remained in the Giant Forest, especially at the Village, they would continue to create "congestion and hazard," he wrote. Thus, it seemed from both traffic and ecological standpoints that a bypass road would be ineffectual.[54]

Even before these doubts torpedoed the bypass road project, the NPS turned its attention once again to the more controversial measure: evacuation of infrastructure from the Giant Forest. If the NPS were to implement this "ultimate solution," it faced the same issues as before: the concessioner, who owned some 400 buildings, and the government's own structures, four sizeable campgrounds, and picnic area at Hazelwood. The public enjoyed all these services, despite the overcrowding, while the concessioner remained adamant about staying in the forest.

Taking the easiest job first, the government indefinitely deferred action on building a new visitor center in the Giant Forest and accelerated construction of the one at Lodgepole. In addition, in 1962, it closed the smallest of the four campgrounds, Firwood. Park officers wanted to close the remaining three campgrounds—Paradise, Sunset Rock, and Sugar Pine, which totaled 152 sites—but felt obliged first to replace the sites elsewhere. This they eventually accomplished by doubling the size of Dorst Campground some twelve miles north of the Giant Forest. Finally, in 1971, over protestations from some visitors who decried park policy as favoring the concession-housed "rich," the NPS closed the remaining campgrounds in the Giant Forest. It was not lost on campers that the concessioner needed space for a new sewage-treatment facility and that Sugar Pine had provided a remarkably perfect site for such an installation.[55]

At the Hazelwood Picnic Area, the NPS also faced an uneasy prospect in eliminating a popular feature. In this case, however, a tragic occurrence provided the excuse it needed. On August 9, 1969, a 240-foot sequoia tree, partially damaged by fire and by carpenter ants, fell against another sequoia, toppling the upper 130 feet of the second tree onto a picnic table. An elderly woman was killed instantly. In the days that followed, Superintendent John McLaughlin proposed that the picnic area be closed for safety reasons. The regional director approved, and park workers hastily removed all the sites, leaving only a hiking trail behind in what had once been a popular campground and later a favorite lunchtime stop.[56]

Thus, by 1971, the government's public presence in the Giant Forest consisted of only one building—a tiny information station in Giant Forest Village—and restrooms. But the other side of the NPS's plan—removal of concession facilities—continued to be an entirely different matter. NPS planners remained divided on the issue, despite the growing scientific evidence and an increased acceptance by the public. Some officials favored complete evacuation, some only the removal of Giant Forest Village, and a few still accepted George Mauger's contentions that damage from his structures was minimal and that there were plenty of other sequoia groves for those aesthetes who insisted on freedom from humans in their experience of nature. With each passing year, the balance of administrative opinion tipped further toward complete removal of facilities. By 1970, the two features that all park planners had agreed to oust, the gas station and post office, were moved to Lodgepole. They were the first significant non–NPS facilities ever to be removed to another site.[57] At the same time, ironically, the concessioner gained permission to replace a dozen tent-top cabins at Giant Forest Lodge with modern units, to rebuild and enlarge the lodge dining room, and even to erect a new gift shop on the site of the just-removed post office.

While debate continued about the Village and its retail and food structures, the matter of housing for visitors continued to be the major source of contention and negotiations between the government and the company. In a startling and unheralded move, the NPS raised the pillow limit in 1964, from 1,000 to 1,240. There is no record of what debate or agreement led to this action nor of how, after forty-three years, George Mauger convinced the government to accede

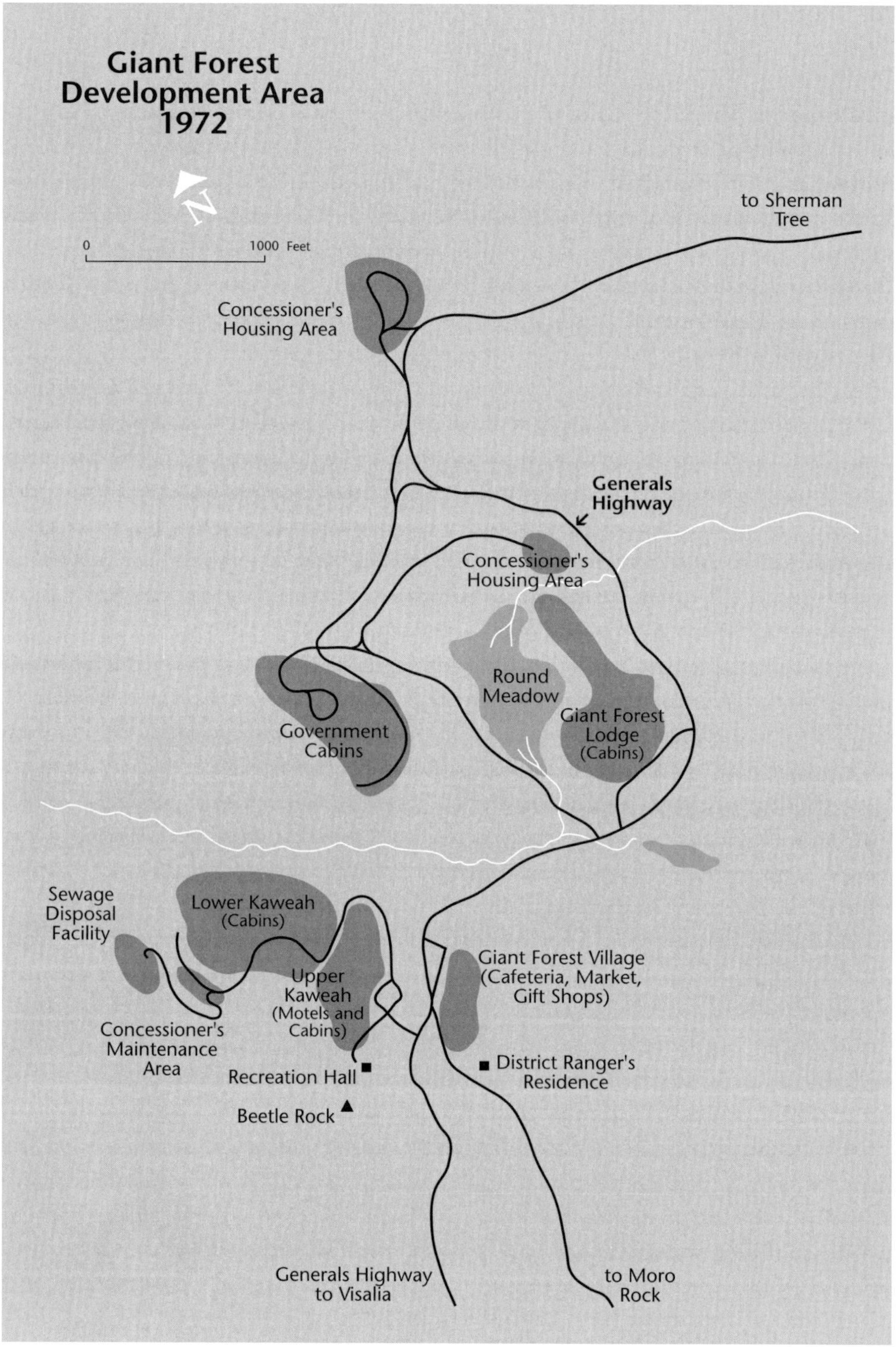
Giant Forest Development Area 1972
N
0
1000 Feet
to Sherman Tree
Concessioner's Housing Area
Generals Highway
Concessioner's Housing Area
Round Meadow
Giant Forest Lodge (Cabins)
Government Cabins
Sewage Disposal Facility
Lower Kaweah (Cabins)
Upper Kaweah (Motels and Cabins)
Giant Forest Village (Cafeteria, Market, Gift Shops)
Concessioner's Maintenance Area
Recreation Hall
District Ranger's Residence
Beetle Rock
Generals Highway to Visalia
to Moro Rock

to his long-held wishes.[58] It may have been done to facilitate Mauger's negotiations for sale of the concession company. Less than a year later, Mauger sold to the legendary Fred Harvey Company, which immediately took up the cudgels for further expansion of facilities in the grove. In 1967, the leaning tree at Beetle Rock exhibited new cracks at its base and threatened rustic guest cabins at Camp Kaweah. Park foresters felled their second giant sequoia in the history of the park, on January 13, 1967. This series of events—raising the pillow limit, continued aggravating pressure for more development, and destruction of a second sequoia tree—strengthened the resolve of those park employees committed to the evacuation of facilities from the grove and intensified negotiations toward that end.[59]

As noted, however, the period 1965 to 1972 was one of confusion and inaction due to repeated corporate changes. In addition, the approaching termination of the twenty-year contract with the concessioner exacerbated the situation. Hence, both sides were tentative in their efforts to change the status quo. In January 1972, GSI assumed operations and accelerated negotiations for a new long-term contract. Owing to the confusion of the preceding decade, the NPS made no drastic demands but satisfied itself with a contractual stipulation that the concessioner would build a large market, gift shop, and snack bar facility at Lodgepole. Although this left both concession housing and the Giant Forest Village in place, park officials fervently hoped that the concessioner could later be convinced to move, once superior visitor services were in place at Lodgepole.[60]

Thus, in 1971, as the government removed the last campgrounds, hailed the new gas station at Lodgepole, and negotiated for a new contract with a concessioner, it backed down again from a commitment to remove the concessioner's structures from the Giant Forest. The park's 1971 master plan allowed that concession housing in the grove was appropriate and merely called for further investigation of alternative sites by the NPS.[61] On August 22, 1972, the NPS signed a twenty-year contract with the new concessioner, which required no additional removals from the Giant Forest. In the closing decades of the park's first century, the subject would continue to be the biggest in a portfolio of ecological problems put under the spotlight by resurging ecological research.

REAPPRAISAL: THE LEOPOLD REPORT

The shift toward management for ecological reasons was part of a much larger shift both in the Sierra Nevada's parks and throughout the national park system. The death of George Wright and onset of World War II had all but eliminated biological research in the parks nationwide, and postwar funding left the program in shambles. Occasional efforts such as the "Yosemite Report" were noteworthy exceptions to a pattern of general disinterest in science.[62]

It was during the late 1950s, however, when the NPS saw the beginning of a recovery in resource management and research programs, spurred by critical appraisals from outside. The Sierra Club and National Parks Association both decried the lack of research and of the funding and organization to begin it. In 1959, Dr. Stanley Cain, of the University of Michigan (and one of Richard Hartesveldt's mentors), reported to the Sixth Biennial Wilderness Conference: "the National Park Service does not have a program of basic ecological research. . . . [What is being done] fails to approach at all closely to the fundamental need of the Service itself . . . [and] the service is missing a bet by not having an adequate natural history (ecological) research program."[63]

As a result of this prodding by Cain as well as by other ecologists and by the always powerful preservationist groups, both the NPS and its parent Department of Interior again began to look seriously at the needs for ecological research and for more scientific and ecologically sensitive park management. Several important studies and analyses of the park's resources thus appeared in the next few years, including one funded by The Conservation Foundation. which employed two internationally renowned scholars, F. Fraser Darling and Noel Eichhorn, to survey the status of ecological management, park by park.[64] The study that would have, perhaps, the most profound effect since Secretary Lane's letter of 1918 was the so-called Leopold Report.[65]

Secretary of Interior Stewart Udall was especially sensitive to the criticism of Cain and other observers. Both Udall and President John F. Kennedy cared about matters of conservation, and the news from the parks troubled the secretary. In response to the need for a general appraisal of ecosystem management in the national parks and, in particular, to desperate problems of overgrazing by elk in Yellowstone, Udall appointed a blue-ribbon advisory board. The members, a veritable who's who of fish and wildlife management, included Stanley Cain; Dr. Clarence Cottam, Director of the Welder Wildlife Foundation and former Assistant Director of the U.S. Fish and Wildlife Service (USFWS); Dr. Ira Gabrielson, President of the Wildlife Management Institute and former Director of the USFWS; Thomas Kimball, Executive Director of the National Wildlife Federation and former Director of the Colorado Game and Fish Department; and Dr. A. Starker Leopold, a professor of zoology, Assistant to the Chancellor at University of California, Berkeley, and a former President of The Wildlife Society.[66] Leopold, who chaired the Advisory Board on Wildlife Management in National Parks, came from what might be called America's first family of conservation. His father, ecologist Aldo Leopold, author of the still-influential book *A Sand County Almanac: And Sketches Here and There* (1949), was the man who so deeply influenced George Wright and the early ecologists of the NPS. Two brothers and a sister also achieved fame for their research and writings in ecology and conservation in North America.[67] The composition of the board was widely lauded by the Sierra Club and other preservation organizations, and few critics could challenge the members' impressive credentials.

On March 4, 1963, the advisory board transmitted its report to Udall, and, subsequently, the Sierra Club and several other groups published it in full in their respective journals. Board members characterized the report as conceptual rather than statistical and intended it to "enhance the aesthetic, historical, and scientific values of the parks to the American public, vis-a-vis the mass recreational values."[68] Thus, Leopold and other members went well beyond the tasks prescribed by Udall and launched an attempt to alter the basic management philosophy of the NPS toward biological preservation, even at the cost of the objects of the scenery, upon which preservation values of the past had been placed. In a now-familiar statement, the board suggested that the primary goal of the parks was maintenance of the biotic associations within each unit, or restoration of them, to the "condition that prevailed when the area was first visited by the white man."[69] (This would later call into question the impact of Native Americans, particularly in an area such as Sequoia and Kings Canyon, where aboriginal burning was widely reported.) In 1963, the report essentially called for maintaining, or restoring, natural park environments to the greatest extent possible.

Board members offered specific recommendations about specific problems in various parks in order to demonstrate their principal point—the necessity of a return to "naturalness." In the matter of habitat protection, they recommended a research-based policy that would protect climax communities but allow successional ones to change naturally. In terms of faunal management, the board recommended elimination of introduced species (exotics), reintroduction of locally extinct native species, and maintenance of natural ecological relationships, including protection of native insects, despite their damage to some attractive species and of predators such as coyote, wolf, and mountain lion. It recommended prescribed burning to return forests overgrown by understory vegetation to the open character displayed when first viewed by whites. In this instance, they referred specifically to the groves of sequoia in Sequoia and Kings Canyon, where Cain's former student Hartesveldt busily continued his research. In addition, the advisory board recommended sweeping changes in the research and resource-management situations throughout the NPS. Specifically, it called for (1) a large, full-time, permanent staff of ecologists to conduct a broad spectrum of research, (2) establishment of research reserves within various park environments from which visitors might be excluded, and (3) flexible management of the parks responsive to the findings of these scientists. Finally, in a strong statement applauded by those who would see the parks turned from recreational grounds to biological reserves, Leopold and his committee wrote, "If too many tourists crowd the roadways then we should ration the tourists rather than expand the roadways."[70]

The impact of the "Leopold Report" was immediate and profound. Preservation organizations heralded it as a new dawn of intelligent and responsible management of the national parks. Secretary Udall accepted the report and issued an order that its recommendations be followed. The slow recovery of biological research in the parks received a huge boost, as each unit scrambled to review its ecological situation, establish research programs, and, in many cases, hire new scientists to implement them. The report has subsequently been called the "Bible" of modern management of the national parks. The board's recommendations institutionalized a philosophy in the NPS and provided a framework for the organized expansion of science as a management tool. Before the Leopold Report, ecological data formed a relatively minor part of decision-making information. After acceptance of the Leopold Report, the goal of park management shifted from strict protection of scenic objects found desirable by the public to an aggressive attempt to re-establish past ecosystems and unhindered natural processes. Gone was the philosophy of environmental manipulation toward human ideals of beauty, comfort, or anthropocentric value. In place came a structured attempt to re-create past scenes and situations, regardless of implications for visitor appreciation. Although this did not happen overnight, the speed with which the NPS shifted shocked many visitors, older park employees, and more than a few superintendents.[71]

In Sequoia and Kings Canyon, a resurgence of research and ecology-oriented management was already underway, albeit grudgingly. The reports and studies of human impact on the Giant Forest and other sequoia groves, such as those of Hartesveldt and the Yosemite Committee, were only part of a gradual reawakening of interest in scientific data for parks administration. In 1954, Lowell Sumner had returned to assume a re-created position as the park's biologist. Once in place, he instituted several programs such as reduction of the population of mule deer, increased research on beavers and other exotics, investigations of bighorn sheep and other species with ranges that were threatened, and review of the always controversial issue of managing bears. Just two months before release of the Leopold Report, Superintendent John Davis received permission and funding for a wildlife ranger position to assist the park biologist.[72]

The Leopold Report gave both real and psychological support to this growing agenda by providing funds and organizational backing as well as spotlighting the role of scientific research in the parks' resource management. New positions were created, and academically trained scientists quickly filled them, bringing a newer and louder voice of idealism based on ecological tenets. By the time of the 1971 *Master Plan*, Sequoia and Kings Canyon had a chief scientist, a research botanist, several wildlife ranger positions, plus assorted permanent and temporary research positions within a division of natural sciences. In addition, the parks had an ambitious research plan extending to all its resources and life zones, cooperative interagency projects with the USFS, Bureau of Land Management (BLM), and various state groups, and liaisons with university researchers for exchange of information. The parks had truly become part of the rapidly expanding research frontiers of the natural sciences.[73]

The direct impact of the Leopold Report on resource-management practice within Sequoia and Kings Canyon varied, depending on the program. Dr. Leopold and his colleagues confirmed many existing policies, while recommending that others be initiated. And, in some cases, their recommendations overturned more than a century of resource-management practice, dating to pre-park days in the American West. With amazing alacrity, however, it charted the very basis of resource management for parks to the singular goals of re-establishing the ecological scene that existed when "the forty-niners poured over the Sierra Nevada into California . . . ," complete with original flora, fauna, and ecological dynamism.[74]

One example of a program in place in Sequoia and Kings Canyon that coordinated well with the advisory board's recommendations was the deer-management program. The problem of over-grazing by deer, first addressed during the 1930s, had been exacerbated in the ensuing decades by visitors who encouraged unnaturally high populations by constantly feeding the nearly tame deer that entered the campgrounds. During the low-visitation seasons thereafter, those hungry deer obliterated the native vegetation, in some cases eliminating brush entirely from large sections of the two parks.[75] In 1943, Field Naturalist Joseph Dixon found the Giant Forest browse badly over-used and implemented a plan to trap and remove deer to other ranges. That plan was ineffectual, taking only an average of twenty-five to thirty deer a year from a herd that probably exceeded 6,000 for the parks with possibly 1,000 in the Giant Forest area. Between 1947 and 1952, some fifty-two deer were killed by park officials upon orders of Acting Director Hilary Tolson, but even this drastic step was far too circumscribed to have any effect.[76]

Park Biologist Sumner took up the challenge upon his return to Sequoia and Kings Canyon, implementing a much more ambitious program of "direct reduction." From 1955 to 1965, park rangers shot almost 900 deer, primarily pregnant does.[77] As expected, the program received some criticism from the public for two reasons. First, hunters in the surrounding communities were annoyed that the parks' administration often discarded the venison. The other criticism came from park visitors who, on rare occasions, stumbled across a park ranger in the act of killing a deer. The emotional letters that resulted from these incidents served to remind the NPS of the resistance of the public to programs that ignored their fervently held and well-entrenched beliefs in park management for human ideals.[78]

With the release of the Leopold Report, Sumner and Dr. Bruce Kilgore, the parks' "research scientist," had been handed independent and prominent support for this aggressive program. This was precisely the management technique suggested by the advisory board for Yellowstone's

Many campers in the backcountry followed a tradition of burying cans, paper, and other waste material before leaving a campsite. This reflected the mindset of "out of sight, out of mind"; that is, if a place in the park looks pristine, then all is well. Unfortunately, erosion occasionally uncovered the buried dumps. In this case, Lowell Sumner, a National Park Service scientist, views a site in which the camper did not even bother to bury the trash, necessitating its removal by a park crew. This type of careless behavior spawned the "leave-no-trace" policy now promoted by land managers nationwide. Photographer and date unknown.

elk and for other cases of ungulate overpopulation. Ironically, as money and personnel became more easily available, the program waned, due to a combination of its own success and conditions outside the parks. From 1965 to 1970, the NPS decreased annual deer kills by eighty percent to an average of fifteen animals a year. The program was discontinued thereafter, owing to a marked drop in the statewide population of mule deer. The deer-management program, brutal though it may have seemed, accomplished its purpose by reducing the herd to a level that allowed substantial recovery of the browse vegetation in the two parks. Still, it relied on excessive and unpopular manipulation. The advisory board had planned on this as an acceptable technique, but park officials nevertheless continued to search for a way to emphasize natural controls rather than human ones. To that end, consistent as it was with the ultimate goal of management according to the Leopold Report, the NPS beefed up programs of research and resource management aimed at fostering populations of mountain lion and other predators. The deer-reduction program had been a scientifically established administrative plan that predated and fully implemented the Leopold proposals. Despite that, the zeal of the parks' resource managers led them to look for better and more natural ways to approach a pioneer ecosystem.[79]

Numerous other research programs for wildlife management began as a result of the increased attention and funding brought about by the Leopold Report. Although most of the problems had been recognized and given cursory research attention in the past, they could now be tackled in a serious and systematic way. For example, the diminishing population of bighorn sheep had been recognized and charted since 1948. A large part of the problem arose from the fact that the native ungulate only spent summers in the parks' territory, wintering on USFS and BLM lands, where they were exposed to domestic sheep grazing and associated diseases. Increased research and a vigorous effort to promote cooperative interagency management led to agreements, by 1970, to conduct research and, by 1973, to manage the habitat for protection of the species, regardless of an agency's jurisdiction.[80]

For the management of bears, the NPS continued to face its most complicated animal-management problem. After the closing of the bear pit, bears deprived of their easy nightly handouts had foraged through campgrounds and concession areas in often fruitful, nocturnal forays. In 1947, the NPS had initiated evening garbage pickup that seemed to suppress the scavenging for a while, but the problem continued to result in human contact with bears, leading to damage of property and an occasional injury. Throughout the 1950s, park rangers experimented with bear-resistant garbage facilities, education of the public, and destruction of offensive bears. The last measure became so institutionalized and simple a solution that, during a three-year period from 1959 to 1961, sixty-one bears were killed. A drought occurred during those same years and contributed to a sudden and sharp decrease in the bear population.

After the Leopold Report, park biologists prepared a bear-management plan. It authorized destruction of up to ten bears a year, thus placing a limit on the zeal of rangers to protect visitor property at the expense of wildlife. In addition, the plan proposed use of bear-proof garbage cans and an expanded program to educate park visitors, and it mandated systematic and ongoing research on bears. Although bear problems persist to this day, the NPS continues, with few modifications, to follow those management techniques.[81]

Yet another wildlife management program in the years after the Leopold Report focused on elimination of exotic species, many of which had been introduced deliberately by the NPS during the early years. Park scientists, however, found these tasks easier to plan than to implement. Efforts to halt fish stocking, particularly of nonnative varieties of rainbow trout, were met with loud and immediate choruses of anger from sport fishermen, so the efforts were abandoned temporarily. Studies of ways to remove alien bird species such as the brown-headed cowbird indicated that the task was probably beyond anyone's control by that time. In the case of the beaver, a major attempt to eradicate the species was attempted. Beaver had been introduced to the lower Kern River from 1949 to 1952 and subsequently had spread northward into the parks. A 1966 study estimated the population in the Kern drainage to be between 100 and 200 animals. Park biologists and rangers attempted to eradicate the beaver, in 1969 and 1970, trapping some fifty of the rodents. Yet the effort was not sustained, and the population quickly reestablished itself. Although none of these practices in wildlife management was particularly successful, they further demonstrated the commitment of the NPS to the philosophy and policies of the Leopold Report.[82]

Of all the programs in resource management fostered by the advisory board's recommendations, none represented a more dramatic policy reversal or a more fundamental commitment to ecological dynamism than that of NPS's management of fire. In deriving his conclusions on the harmful effects of humans and their structures on sequoia root systems, Richard Hartesveldt also found groves of sequoia to be choked with dead and decaying fuel, the product of generations of vegetation rigorously preserved from natural fire. White fir and other understory trees crowded the sequoias and strangled their offspring. Past solutions to the mysterious lack of regeneration of sequoias, such as the Ash Mountain Nursery and its associated planting program, would never overcome the problem. What Hartesveldt found and communicated to the advisory board was that suppression of fire had flatly halted the sequoias' regrowth. In this case, supposed protection of the parks' primary resource, in a classic case of object preservation, actually had hindered protection of the species.[83]

The advisory board spent no small percentage of its short report commenting on the sequoia situation and, in fact, used it as a prime example of how overprotection of individuals had created a grossly unnatural scene, one that carried its own seeds of destruction. By the time of the Leopold Report, Hartesveldt had continued and expanded his research, compiling mounting evidence of the relationship between fire suppression and a lack of regeneration. As a byproduct, he showed the catastrophic results that would eventually occur because of the huge, unnatural fuel level below the Big Trees. By the end of 1963, his research had led to a plan to set fire deliberately to a small patch of sequoia-mixed conifer forest to test his hypotheses.[84]

The area chosen by Hartesveldt and his colleague Thomas Harvey was the Redwood Mountain Grove, part of the area brought into the national park system in 1940. After carefully measuring the existing vegetation by biomass, species populations, fuel load, and other criteria and carefully preparing to control the fire's extent, the team set the first purposeful fire in a sequoia grove in nearly seventy-five years. The results were startling. The fire reduced fuel concentrations by more than fifty percent and, months later, dazzled the scientists with a veritable thicket of new, tiny sequoia seedlings. Most, of course, soon fell to various rigors of the environment, but the relatively hot fire established, beyond doubt, its role in the regeneration of sequoias and in keeping the sequoia forest open and "natural."[85]

With this success to bolster their research conclusions, park scientists recommended an ambitious program of returning fire to the parks: natural if possible, prescribed if necessary. Beginning in 1968, park rangers allowed fires in the high-altitude lodgepole pine and subalpine forest communities, generally above 8,000 feet, to burn themselves out naturally but under close supervision. Because individual trees in these communities are widely spaced, uncontrollable and destructive conflagrations were highly unlikely. Also, in 1968, rangers successfully experimented with an 800-acre prescribed burn in a community of red fir. Once again, they achieved spectacular results in reduction of fuel and invigoration of the community. A year later, officials fired more than 6,300 acres of fuel breaks in oak woodland, chaparral, ponderosa pine, and mixed conifer forests. In each case, regeneration and reduced danger from subsequent larger fires were equally positive. In 1970, rangers brought fire to Cedar Grove to reduce downed limbs and duff in campgrounds and other developed areas. Finally, in 1972, they set up the first fully scheduled, long-term prescribed burn program in Redwood Mountain, still an experiment but now in full-scale management proportions. Thus, in a single decade, that most ardently held and rigorously enforced of all government forest-management beliefs was reversed on the basis of scientific data and the overwhelming impact of a single panel's report.[86]

REAPPRAISAL: WILDERNESS IN THE BACKCOUNTRY

Of all the portions of Sequoia and Kings Canyon National Parks subject to a reappraisal of resource management, perhaps the most profound changes occurred in the backcountry. This enormous area, almost ninety-eight percent of the parks' total acreage, had suffered from an unfortunate combination of its own ecological fragility and severe abuse by pre-park settlers and agriculturalists from adjacent lowlands. Early graphic descriptions of destruction and virtual defoliation were followed, during the 1930s and 1940s, by studies by Sumner, Armstrong, and others. They drew a bleak picture of a loss of meadows, pollution of alpine lakes, and erosion along trails. Yet, in spite of some continued grazing by cattle and pack stock and a dramatic post-war rise in visitors' use in the backcountry, the decades of inaccessibility to the teeming masses of auto-bound public had allowed the backcountry to survive, gravely injured in spots but not mortally. A follow-up study of the Roaring River Grazing District in Kings Canyon, during 1947, showed that the meadows and woodlands could recover, if managed carefully with as little human and animal traffic as possible.[87]

During the next twenty-five years, the rise of science and shift in management goals and policies would come earliest to the backcountry and go furthest there toward the ideals expressed in the Leopold Report. There were four types of issues that faced backcountry rangers and park biologists: controlling the numbers and impact of people in the backcountry; reconciling structures, campsites, and other paraphernalia in an area of officially avowed "wilderness"; managing the effects of use by stock and some cattle grazing on the delicate and still-damaged meadows; and achieving official designation of the backcountry as a legal wilderness area. Management began with tentative research and a search for ways to control human and stock use. By 1960, it had evolved to active management controls that, nevertheless, still allowed unlimited access by visitors and, thereafter, responded to a flood of new enthusiasts of the backcountry by turning rapidly to strict controls, including quotas on visitor use.

Despite the meager funds available, several important studies of backcountry status were conducted between 1947 and 1952. Their importance in turning the NPS's attention to problems in the backcountry far outweighed the actual value of their scientific conclusions. First, in 1948, biologist Lowell Sumner, then working from the regional office, conducted a review of damage by tourists to mountain meadows since his earlier 1936 report.[88] Sumner found conditions largely unimproved and recommended immediate action, lest the deterioration of some meadows reach an irreversible stage. Four years later, Ranger Bruce Black submitted a second follow-up study of the Roaring River Grazing District.[89] In comparing the region over a decade, Black found that, while some meadows had remained static and a few had even improved, in most instances serious and easily observable decline had continued. Although Black's immediate supervisor took issue with the degree of pessimism in his report, its conclusions were widely read and discussed among the park's administrators.[90]

Hard on the heels of the Roaring River study came a much more extensive *Back Country Use Report* (1953) compiled by Black, Assistant Chief Ranger John Rutter, and others.[91] The report had required three years of field study in Sequoia and Kings Canyon and addressed grazing, camping, maintenance of trails, use of stock, and many other concerns. In total, the report was not excessively negative. The authors called sanitation and camping issues irritations rather than serious problems. In both parks, damage to meadows was not yet severe, although invasion by weeds and trees was widespread, thought to be the result of overgrazing. To control camping, Black and his colleagues suggested constructing campgrounds at six backcountry sites and removing the dozens of visitor-built sites scattered through the parks. They also proposed a detailed annual program for maintenance of trails; construction of six new high-country trails, ranging in length from three to more than twenty miles, to absorb increased visitor usage; and establishment of nine new ranger stations to house a larger backcountry staff who could better patrol the region.

Although the tone of the *Back Country Use Report* was generally optimistic, the authors were explicit in their proposals and cautionary in their conclusion:

> There is no reason to believe that we cannot stop all damaging practices; that meadows cannot be restored; that camps cannot be clean and appropriate; that fisheries cannot be maintained; and that the Wilderness Atmosphere cannot be preserved. A start has been made and if aggressively pursued, the end product will be gratifying to everyone concerned.[92]

Understated and between the lines of this conclusion were the increasingly obvious facts that damaging practices were occurring, meadows needed restoration, camps were not clean or appropriate, and the wilderness atmosphere was in jeopardy. Park Biologist Lowell Sumner urged caution and deliberation in constructing camps and ranger stations, but he enthusiastically supported the rest of the report.[93]

Even before Black's two reports joined those of Sumner and Armstrong, park officials had begun to look for ways to ameliorate damage and crowding in the backcountry. One way park rangers could control use by stock was by limiting the number of concession packers and their horses in the backcountry. Because they were concession operators, making a profit on the parks' resources, they could be controlled, where individual stock users could not. Park officials exercised this power on an organization known as the Three Corners Round Outfit. This group, founded by employees of the Cleveland (Ohio) Museum of Natural History, brought teenage boys into the mountains each summer to teach them skills in stock riding and care, camping and wilderness practices, trail building, shooting, and, incidentally, natural history, all at a cost of about $400 per boy. In 1951, Superintendent Scoyen received a number of complaints that this group, consisting of fourteen boys and two men, had more than forty burros that had virtually eliminated the forage in the Sixty-Lakes area. This was not the first time complaints had been received about this group,

During the first six decades of the twentieth century, most travel in the alpine backcountry of the two national parks depended on horses and mules for riding and packing. Here, strings of mules ascend the north side of Forester Pass (13,153 feet highest elevation) on the Kings-Kern Divide. Equestrian use of the high country had some negative impacts on the habitat, especially where clusters of animals congregated. After the boom in backpacking during the late 1960s and 1970s, hikers challenged the use of pack animals, thereby creating a controversy that continues today. Photographer and date unknown.

and, after consultation with the regional office in San Francisco, local packers, and the Sierra Club, Scoyen declared the group to be a concession and slapped a limit on its operation. Two years later, the Three Corners Round Outfit would again fall foul of park rangers, for refusing to stop building their own trails in the Kings Canyon high country, for stocking fish in park lakes, for shooting firearms in the parks, and for indiscriminate collection of animals and plants. The owners of Three Corners Round had been operating in this fashion for more than twenty years and were deeply aggrieved, but nonetheless they complied when ordered to desist.[94]

At the same time that the Three Corners Round Outfit was confronted, the NPS began to look for ways to improve or close one of the more deteriorated of the backcountry's camps. Located just inside the park's southeastern boundary on the Kern River, Camp Lewis (or Coterno Camp) consisted of six tent-top cabins, a tent-top dining room, and a log structure housing a store and a kitchen. Its condition was variously reported as "flimsy," "unsightly," and "beyond repair." Park officials insisted that the owner, as a concessioner, clean and repair his camp, whereupon, in 1952, he cheerfully gave up any claim to the camp. Park officials razed and removed most of the facilities the following spring.[95]

Controlling the Three Corners Round Outfit and eliminating Camp Lewis were steps in the right direction, but they were small steps in what rangers recognized as a long journey. By 1950, intense discussions among park officials centered on the concept of placing restrictions on the backcountry that would go well beyond those already in place in the frontcountry. Although use of the parks by pack stock had fallen by forty percent between 1947 and 1952, the reports by Black served further notice on damage to meadows as well as other problems related to people and horses. In 1952, Park Naturalist Howard Stagner proposed regulation of the number of stock per visitor, the size of an individual party and length of stay, plus stipulations against building trails, planting fish, and dirty camps. He also proposed indefinite closing of certain meadows to use by stock. Some of these proposals were new, many were not. They mirrored the concerns and ideas of most rangers who worked and studied the backcountry.[96]

The problem with implementing these recommendations arose from two sources. First, commercial stock-user associations resented and feared any control on their activity. The backcountry had persisted as an area of free activity, a virtual frontier, well beyond the settled low country and road-accessible portions of the mountains. Any type of restriction on use of the backcountry was viewed as another attempt to box in and regulate to death the last vestiges of pioneer America. The East Side and West Side Packers Associations numbered, in their membership, important and often powerful individuals, including several members of Congress, assorted state and local legislators, and many wealthy businessmen and landowners. The NPS could ill afford to anger these vocal and powerful groups.[97]

At the same time and of even greater concern, there was a general lack of funds in this pre-Mission 66 administration to enforce any regulations. For years, while visitors and park employees bemoaned the decay of the frontcountry's structures, roads, and visitor-contact facilities, rangers, likewise, worried about maintenance of trails and law enforcement in the backcountry. Chief Ranger Irwin Kerr sent a stream of memoranda and letters through channels seconding the need for regulation but wondering who would patrol these new campgrounds, restricted lakes and meadows, and miles of new trails. After release of the *Back Country Use Report,* Superintendent Scoyen sent it on to Director Wirth, in the hope that increases in funding and labor allotments might be forthcoming. In November 1953, however, Assistant Director Thomas Allen responded with an all-too-familiar recommendation:

> It will probably not be feasible to carry out...all of the recommendations that we may agree are necessary. . . . Some of the proposals, however, can be put into execution without additional funds or personnel by giving them greater emphasis in the overall Park program.[98]

In the face of deterioration of the parks' natural resources as well as its visitor and government facilities, the NPS could do no more than encourage stretching overtaxed labor and insufficient funds even further.

After 1953, a hiatus set in, although park rangers continued to compile status reports on the backcountry's resources and problems. Park officials did close a few severely damaged meadows, yet, at the same time, a steady rise of visitors increased pressure on the remainder. By 1955, Kerr estimated that visitors to the backcountry had more than doubled in the previous decade, due, in part, to a new high-speed highway connecting Los Angeles with Owens Valley and its eastern and shortest approaches to the high country. He further estimated that nearly all that increase came in the form of backpackers. Questions about policy, about purpose, and about the quality of the wilderness experience repeatedly arose from visitors and organizations, particularly the Sierra Club.[99]

The year 1958 marked a shift into higher gear for resolution of the parks' backcountry problems. Former concession packer Hugh Traweek applied for a permit to re-establish his business in Kings Canyon. He had sold his former operation, and the new owner was happily making a profit. Traweek was a popular and able packer, well-liked by other stock users, the public, and park officials. Yet their appraisal of resource quality and carrying capacity caused those officials to reject his application. For the next three years, Traweek engaged in a test of wills by calling in every ally and potential friend he could find to force the NPS to capitulate. Senators and representatives of Congress, a governor, assorted wealthy nabobs, and a host of former customers besieged the park with letters of support for Traweek. Through it all, with the backing of the regional office, local NPS officers stood fast in rejecting his application. They had no beef with Traweek but could neither morally justify stripping another packer of his concession nor sanction an increase of pack-stock business in the most delicate and damaged portion of the backcountry.[100]

Also, during 1958, the Sierra Club conducted a highly touted and publicized drive to remove trash from two popular lakes in the Kings Canyon backcountry. In a few days, they collected more than three tons of trash from the two lakeshores. Throughout the 1950s, the Sierra Club had taken an ever-greater interest in the backcountry's management and ecology. The club instituted a series of discussions and studies aimed at determining whether its own large pack trips were excessively harmful. Although initial results indicated that the effect per person was lower in a large party, the club continued to sponsor these studies during the next fifteen years. In the case of this trash collection, the club performed a valuable and symbolic gesture. Within weeks, the NPS began to study ways to collect the trash accumulated over the entire 840,000-plus-acre backcountry and initiated a campaign to have visitors carry out their own bottles and cans. For decades, the policy had been to burn and bury trash, flattening the cans and breaking bottles if possible. In many cases, this trash resurfaced at popular camping areas a few months or years later.[101]

Finally, also in 1958, the NPS commissioned biologist Dr. Carl W Sharsmith, of San Jose State University, to conduct a major study of the status of the backcountry's meadows. Once again, the NPS appealed to a trained scientist to help determine management policy. In his study, released the following year, Sharsmith reported that meadows were undergoing serious decline or change throughout the parks but particularly in the area known as the Rae Lakes Loop that encompasses the Paradise and Bubbs Creek trails from Kearsarge Pass to Kings Canyon.[102] Bullfrog Lake, one of the nearest to the easily accessible pass, was a virtual catastrophe. Almost every meadow from 6,000 to 8,500 feet was being invaded by weeds, lodgepole pine, or both. Sharsmith recommended revolutionary steps, including complete exclusion of camping and other activities at Bullfrog Lake, restrictions on the size of stock parties, construction of camp and latrine facilities to concentrate human impact, prohibition of "base camps," encouragement of the practice of packing out one's trash, and, finally, loose herding of stock. Loose herding meant allowing horses or mules to wander in a general direction over a broad area rather than confining them in single or double file along a narrow trail where they would damage trails and overgraze forage.[103]

Sharsmith's report convinced the NPS to take more assertive steps to redress the backcountry's problems. The following season, 1960, marked the first time park officials restricted campers from an area. Campers were to avoid not only Bullfrog Lake, but also the nearby Kearsarge Lakes. Rangers in the backcountry estimated that, during the previous seven seasons, annual visitor use of these areas had averaged 26,000 camper days and 2,100 stock-use days, all on about thirty

A high-level inspection team for the National Park Service (NPS) views the rugged Kings Canyon backcountry from Windy Point on August 20, 1951. The viewers, from left to right, are: Harold Bradley, of the Sierra Club; Eivind Scoyen, Superintendent of Sequoia National Park; a man with the last name of Crow; Conrad Wirth, Associate Director of the NPS who, a few months later, would become the sixth director of the NPS; and Regional Director Lawrence C. Merriam. Photographer unknown.

acres.[104] As reports of a major Inyo County program to repave and extend mountain access roads reached the parks, NPS administrators restricted stock use in six meadows in Kings Canyon National Park, commenced an annual trash cleanup drive for the backcountry, and initiated a study to devise a comprehensive management plan for the backcountry. The study would not only direct Sequoia and Kings Canyon, but also serve as a model for all the national parks with extensive wilderness areas.[105]

The *Backcountry Management Plan* for Sequoia and Kings Canyon National Parks was released a year later.[106] NPS scientists Maurice Thede and Lowell Sumner and ranger William Briggle completed an exhaustive literature review and three lengthy field trips in composing what became a major philosophical and practical guide to the backcountry's management. The scientists began with the basics. They defined wilderness, conservation, and carrying capacity and discussed such concepts as the ultimate goal of conservation, what type of people used the wilderness, and wilderness protection versus personal freedom. Thereafter, they launched into specific recommendations, many of which echoed Sharsmith's proposals. Additionally, they suggested an increased ranger force, a vigorous program of exclusions in meadows and camping areas, an interagency approach to tourist management in the backcountry, and construction of seven relatively large and permanent "rustic camps," each with a fireplace, tables, hitching rack, and pit toilet. They also suggested that the NPS use helicopters rather than pack stock as the least disruptive management tools.

The *Backcountry Management Plan* became the blueprint for Sequoia and Kings Canyon for the next decade. Park rangers restricted the meadows that Thede and company had proposed for exclusion and instituted a program of regular monitoring of meadows for future management decisions. In 1961, two new ranger positions were created that allowed the parks to undertake a systematic cleanup of the backcountry. Employees and volunteers removed fourteen tons of tin cans and buried six tons of other trash in the first year alone. The cleanup program continued until 1967, when it was deemed a success. Annual reports on the backcountry apprised the parks' administration of problem areas, trail maintenance requirements, and ecological recovery or degeneration. Until 1965, park foresters removed lodgepole pines that encroached on damaged meadows. Park biologists, however, responding to the Leopold Report, halted this action to conduct studies of succession and find out if this was a natural process.[107] In 1969, the NPS dropped plans for shelters in the backcountry and, the following year, removed most of the backcountry's remaining telephone lines. Although the number of maintained trail miles fluctuated periodically with budget constraints, it was allowed to fall from 952 to 755 during the decade. Piece by piece, area by area, the NPS edged toward a truer but more regulated "wilderness" backcountry.[108]

The environmental consciousness-raising of the 1960s paid off for Sequoia and Kings Canyon, with a concerted and steady shift of management's attitude toward regulation, exclusion, and whatever other policies were necessary to foster ecological viability of the backcountry's resources. The *Backcountry Management Plan*, Leopold Report, and passage of the federal Wilderness Act in 1964 assisted that philosophical evolution. That same environmental movement, however, propelled thousands of new backpackers, hungry for the wilderness experience, into the fragile alpine reaches of the two parks. From 1962 to 1971, the number of people who officially entered the backcountry each summer jumped from slightly over 8,000 to more than 44,000, while visitor days increased from 57,000 to well over 200,000.[109] By 1970, it was clear that even the recommendations of the 1961 management plan were out of date. Research for a new management plan for the backcountry commenced amidst discussion of a variety of relatively extreme measures.

The next year of decision came in 1972. Research for the new plan was well underway. In addition, an in-depth study by Richard Hartesveldt, Thomas Harvey, and J. T. Stanley, on behalf of the Sierra Club, recommended stronger action, including regulations for using kerosene cookery instead of wood stoves, for carrying out all trash, including organic matter, and for designating outing itineraries to avoid overuse of popular areas.[110] A few months later, Regional Director Howard Chapman suggested study of a newly published NPS report on regulations for carrying capacity in wilderness areas.[111] But the local parks administration had already taken some of these steps by the time the corroborating correspondence and interim research reports had reached them. In July 1972, at the start of the main backcountry season, the NPS and USFS began issuing interagency wilderness permits in place of the old campfire permits—an effort to control all access to the parks' backcountry from both eastern and western sides. The heavily traveled Rae Lakes Loop was declared a control zone, and limits were placed on the number of permits issued to that popular area. This was a test of procedure and public reaction that would be followed by more extensive permit regulations if successful. To the pleasure of park officials, the new plan was accepted with few complaints. The public, by and large, seemed to understand the need for controls in the interest of protecting the resource.[112]

As the NPS edged toward total control of visitors in its backcountry wilderness, a related issue unfolded during the 1960s. In 1964, after years of urging by preservationist groups and some sportsmen's societies, Congress passed the Wilderness Act.[113] By this act, legislators could designate portions of federal lands that exhibited "wilderness" character as so-named areas. Wilderness was defined in the act as "an area where the earth and its community of life are untrammeled by man, where man himself is a visitor who does not remain . . . " Within these "wilderness areas," the act banned any form of development such as timber cutting, mining, quarrying, and all roads.[114] But, to qualify for wilderness status, a proposed area had to be free of these features at the start. Of course, the vast majority of Sequoia and Kings Canyon met these criteria easily.

Under instructions from the Washington, D.C., office, park officials began to formulate specific recommendations for how much of the parks' lands should be designated as wilderness and, thus, be legally immune from any future development.

Given the evolving attitude within the parks toward the backcountry's preservation, it would seem that the matter could have been settled easily and quickly. The act, however, in addition to its definition of wilderness and the regulations against development, also provided for the public's participation in the planning procedure. Since this legislation rigidly proscribed economic use of large tracts of public land, legislators wanted to make sure everyone had a chance to offer his or her comments on how large an area should be so designated. The procedure for public review could be lengthy and the debate intense. The USFS moved rapidly on its lands, designating, by 1966, a large alpine portion of the adjacent Sierra and Inyo National Forests as the John Muir Wilderness Area. The NPS, however, was an agency far more committed to absolute preservation than its rival, and it seemed to have problems with the process.

Initial hearings for the proposed wilderness area of the two parks took place on November 21 and 22, 1966. Fifty people testified, and 477 letters and documents were accepted. The NPS had proposed an area of 740,165 acres, or eighty-seven percent of the parks' then total 847,194 acres. Conspicuously absent from the proposed area were Redwood Mountain, classified as a scientific reserve for the continuing prescribed-burn experimentation, and the Yucca Mountain region, in the foothills of Sequoia National Park. The Sierra Club and other preservation organizations favored up to ninety-eight percent of the parks' land to be designated as wilderness, and, in all, more than nine of every ten respondents wanted more land in the wilderness area than the NPS had proposed. Some two percent wanted less or no land in wilderness, and the rest went along with the NPS's plan. A few organizations interested in a planned ski development at Mineral King resisted wilderness designation for park lands surrounding that valley and adjacent to its only access route, the Mineral King Road through Sequoia. They were perfectly content, however, to increase designations of wilderness areas elsewhere in the two parks. Despite the overwhelming response in favor of greater wilderness acreage, the confusion over details temporarily shelved the whole proposal.[115]

After some rethinking, further discussion with interested groups, and more detailed planning, local park officials forwarded a new proposal to the regional office in San Francisco, in March 1967. In this proposal, Redwood Mountain (also called Redwood Canyon) and Yucca Mountain were included as wilderness, but a buffer strip along the Mineral King Road and around the proposed ski development was removed. The new proposal totaled 768,515 acres, or ninety-one percent of the parks. Local officials confidently awaited approval, but, a few months

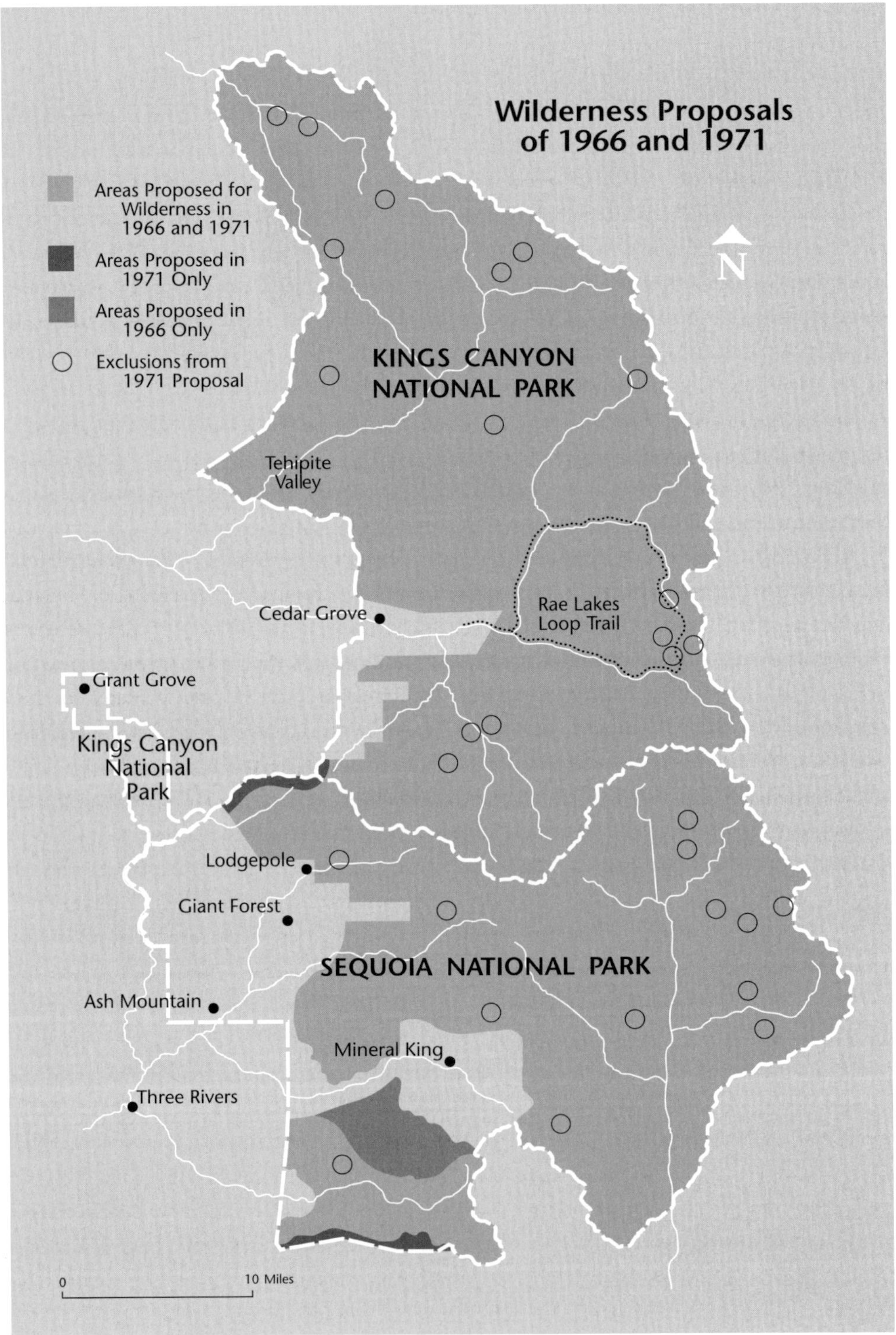
Wilderness Proposals of 1966 and 1971
Areas Proposed for Wilderness in 1966 and 1971
Areas Proposed in 1971 Only
Areas Proposed in 1966 Only
Exclusions from 1971 Proposal
N
KINGS CANYON NATIONAL PARK
Tehipite Valley
Cedar Grove
Rae Lakes Loop Trail
Grant Grove
Kings Canyon National Park
Lodgepole
Giant Forest
SEQUOIA NATIONAL PARK
Ash Mountain
Mineral King
Three Rivers
0
10 Miles

later, objections to the Mineral King exclusions and initiation of study for a new master plan once again postponed further action.[116]

With the release of the parks' master plan in 1971, the public began to review yet a third proposal for wilderness in Sequoia and Kings Canyon National Parks. During the master plan study, park officials had become extremely rigid about their interpretation of the Wilderness Act. In this latest proposal, planners had excluded small areas surrounding any and all visitor facilities, including overnight shelters and sanitation facilities. On the map, this created a wilderness region with so-called "Swiss-cheese holes" of development. In addition, planners excluded a strip along the Mineral King Road and an area around Alta Peak, where a tramway was being considered. The total acreage of the new proposal was 721,970 acres, or eighty-five percent of the parks' land, the lowest total up to that time. The NPS then began another round of public hearings and correspondence, which met with savage attack by preservation organizations. Each area excluded from wilderness status was an area that could potentially be developed further. The "Swiss-cheese" look of this latest plan left opportunity for development to be scattered throughout the parks. Soon, it became apparent to the NPS that this round of simple hearings was going to take much longer and be much more acrimonious than it had hoped. By the end of 1972, the debate still raged. As the NPS continued to shift its management priorities for the backcountry toward the preservation of wilderness, its proposals for the legalization of that "wilderness" status continued to arouse impassioned conflict among the backcountry's enthusiasts.[117] In 1984, Congress would settle the issue with much less political turmoil, as will be revealed in the next chapter.

The profound changes witnessed during these twenty-five years of resource management for the backcountry gave fitting evidence of the full implications of the rise of science in the NPS's philosophy. Because the region had hitherto escaped severe use, its resource policies were the easiest to change. Because its users were unusually preservation-oriented, they would tolerate the constraints of exclusion and permits. Because the resource so easily showed stress, the evidence favoring ecological management was patently obvious. In the backcountry, the revolution personified by Sumner, Armstrong, Hartesveldt, and Cain, codified by the Leopold Report, and bolstered by hundreds of smaller studies and reports sent the first shock waves that would seek to freeze the parks as ecological islands in their time.

THE NATIONAL FORESTS AND MINERAL KING

The fundamental reassessment of policy and direction that occurred in Sequoia and Kings Canyon National Parks, during the 1960s and 1970s, was paralleled by an equally dramatic change in the management of the surrounding national forests. This change was not so much in policy or direction as in scale of operation and impact. As late as 1950, the Sierra and Sequoia National Forests remained much as they had been when first set aside in 1893 and 1908, respectively. Hydroelectric development had begun in some areas, and logging was increasing in its scale in the western portions of the two forests, but large expanses of the two reservations remained largely pristine, except for low levels of trapping, sport hunting, and permitted grazing. South of Sequoia National Park and east of the main stem of the Kern River there stretched, in 1950, an extensive de facto wilderness known as the Kern Plateau. This roadless area, more than twenty miles wide and seventy-five miles long, spanned the Sierra Crest and included miles of subalpine meadowland and foxtail pine forest. Included in this region was the Horseshoe Meadow Plateau, a 10,000-foot-high basin that dominated natural access to the southeastern corner of Sequoia National Park. Another large tract of relatively pristine land, known to the USFS as the Hume Lake District, filled the triangular wedge of land between Sequoia and Kings Canyon National Parks along Generals Highway. A few roads entered this region, one extending as far as Horse Corral Meadow, only a few miles short of the boundary of the main portion of Kings Canyon National Park. The forests, however, remained almost entirely uncut.

All of this changed during the two following decades. In the 1960s, enormous tracts of previously little-used national forest were opened to roads and logging, much of it by clear-cutting. By the 1970s, roads pierced the southern half of the Kern Plateau as well as the Horseshoe Meadow Plateau, where plans were underway to construct a large ski area on Trail Peak. To the north, lumbering in the Hume Lake District produced several tens of millions of board feet annually. These changes represented no shift whatsoever in the USFS's plans or philosophy. The development of the Sequoia and Sierra National Forests represented nothing more than the faithful execution of the utilitarian goals the USFS had set for itself from its founding in 1905. What had changed was the need for the forests' resources and the ability of the USFS to implement schemes for development.

Perhaps the best example of the controversies that rocked national forest lands surrounding Sequoia and Kings Canyon National Parks occurred in Mineral King, the subalpine valley where Tom Fowler had lost his fortune back in 1880. In 1926, Mineral King had been omitted from Sequoia National Park, even though the park was expanded that year in a way that left Mineral King jutting as a peninsula of national forest land into the national park. The river that flowed from the area went into the park, and the only access road, the same road miners had built in 1879, passed through the park. Mineral King had been left out of the park on purpose, in 1926, because the NPS perceived the area as having too many compromised land titles, resulting from the never-successful mines, and too many small development blemishes in the form of cabins, reservoirs, and pack stations. Recognizing the inseparable geographical relationship that tied the area to park lands, however, Congress did, in 1926, declare the 16,000-acre Mineral King basin as the "Sequoia Game Refuge," under the jurisdiction of Sequoia National Forest.

For several decades after 1926, Mineral King slumbered under its game-refuge status, enjoyed mostly by residents of Tulare County who came up to the mountains during the summer to camp or to live in simple, rustic cabins. By the late 1940s, a new group was prospecting in the area, however, seeking not silver but a new form of wealth—ski terrain. Following national trends, commercial downhill skiing had begun in the Sierra during the late 1930s, with the introduction of rope tows in several locations in the Donner-Tahoe region. By the beginning of World War II, small ski resorts had been installed at Wolverton in Sequoia National Park and Badger Pass at Yosemite. After the war, as the same recreation boom that eventually required Mission 66 accelerated, a search began for appropriate terrain for large-scale commercial ski development. As early as 1946, the name of Mineral King Valley showed up on lists of potential ski areas.

In 1949, Sequoia National Forest, carrying out its perceived recreational mandate, called for bids for ski development in Mineral King. The sole bidder, however, was unable to meet the USFS's conditions, so nothing happened. At that time, however, the Sierra Club supported the concept of skiing in Mineral King, a concept that seemed unlikely ever to lead to much more than a small lodge and a few lifts in the remote valley. Critical to the club's thoughts at that time was protection of the San Gorgonio Primitive Area in southern California. In 1949, Mineral King seemed far less important to the club than one of southern California's very limited subalpine areas.

Early in the 1960s, the idea surfaced again but this time with a much stronger interested party—Walt Disney and his entertainment company. For several years, rumors quietly floated over the valley that Disney was interested in the area, a fact that became fully apparent only after his company purchased two tracts of private land in Mineral King Valley in January 1965. The following month, the supervisor of Sequoia National Forest began openly to discuss reopening the area to ski-development proposals. Finally, in late February, the USFS issued its call for development bids, and the die was cast: The Mineral King area would be developed under the USFS's mandate for multiple-use land management. Bids were due at the Sequoia National Forest headquarters no later than August 31, 1965. During the spring and summer of 1965, Mineral King was on many tongues and minds. In early May, with the large scale of the potential development becoming obvious, the Sierra Club reversed its 1949 position and announced its opposition to massive recreational development in the small subalpine valley. By the end of August, six separate development bids were in the USFS's hands, with the most expansive proposal calling for more than $40,000,000 in investment for facilities.

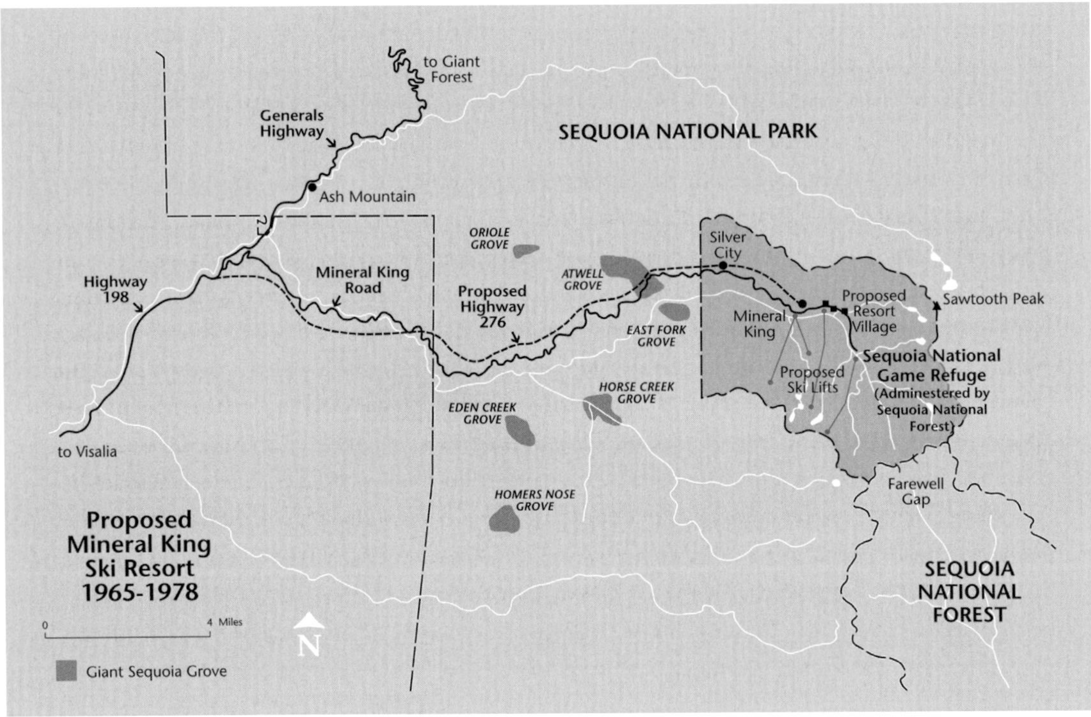

to Giant Forest
Generals Highway
SEQUOIA NATIONAL PARK
Ash Mountain
ORIOLE GROVE
Silver City
Highway 198
Mineral King Road
Proposed Highway 276
ATWELL GROVE
Proposed Resort Village
Sawtooth Peak
Mineral King
EAST FORK GROVE
Proposed Ski Lifts
Sequoia National Game Refuge
(Administered by Sequoia National Forest)
HORSE CREEK GROVE
EDEN CREEK GROVE
to Visalia
Farewell Gap
HOMERS NOSE GROVE
Proposed Mineral King Ski Resort 1965-1978
SEQUOIA NATIONAL FOREST
0
4 Miles
N
Giant Sequoia Grove

In January 1966, Walt Disney Productions, the top bidder, signed a three-year development contract with the USFS that allowed the company to begin planning for the Mineral King ski resort. By October 1967, the State of California had adopted a final route for the new state highway to Mineral King, a route that began in Three Rivers and crossed some ten miles of Sequoia National Park. This direct impact on the park was not well received by park officials, but, as realists, they sensed that the project was already too big to stop. Ironically, Secretary of Interior Stewart Udall himself made his department's only significant resistance to the road development project, but, by December 1967, he, too, had lapsed into defeated silence. Mineral King seemed on its way to development. According to the Disney proposal, Mineral King would soon have fourteen ski lifts, two large hotels, and a parking garage for 2,500 vehicles.

And yet, as the NPS caved in, significant opposition came from another source: the Sierra Club, which filed suit against the proposed development on June 5, 1969. In the suit, which named both the USFS and NPS as defendants, the club asserted that the two agencies had broken a number of federal statutes, including the law that established the Sequoia National Game Refuge in 1926, the law that limited recreational leases in the national forest to eighty acres, and laws that established and required the protection of Sequoia National Park. In July, a federal judge issued a temporary injunction forbidding development until the issues were resolved, and a new decade-long chapter in the Mineral King story began. For the first time in a generation in the southern Sierra, the Forest Service faced a major challenge to the implementation of its multiple-use mandate. As explained in the following chapter, a protracted legal and political battle over Mineral King ensued, which preservationists eventually won.[118]

HOW MUCH IS TOO MUCH?

In the quarter-century following the end of World War II, Sequoia and Kings Canyon National Parks repeated the same cycles of development and concern that had occurred during the two decades before the war. Again, as recreational use of the parks grew rapidly, the NPS found itself with inadequate funds to meet the demand. Again, when funds were finally forthcoming, this time through Mission 66, they were invested almost entirely in visitor facilities, and, again, as the period drew to a close, the realization grew that preservation of the critical features of the two parks would require far more than just new and better bathrooms and campgrounds.

Nowhere was this cycle of retreat, renewal, and reappraisal more apparent than in the developed sequoia groves. During the early 1950s, tight budgets and continued resistance from the Sequoia and Kings Canyon National Parks Company forced abandonment of the two-decade dreams of restoring the Giant Forest to a more pristine state. When the NPS allowed the felling of the leaning tree at Giant Forest Lodge in 1950, it, in effect, also felled its own efforts to limit additional human impacts within the grove. Accepting all the problems that had been unacceptable to park planners and managers during the 1940s, the NPS learned once again to live with Giant Forest's congestion and mediocrity. Not until after the concession company finally changed hands in 1966 did the NPS succeed in making even the smallest improvements in what everyone agreed was a deplorable situation. And, even then, improvements made during the late 1960s and early 1970s—closing campgrounds and removing of the post office, gas station, and old Giant Forest Museum—only cleared the way for another wave of investment by the concessioner in upgraded dining facilities and new motel rooms.

The only bright spot in the management of sequoias during this period came from the long-needed initiation of sustained ecological research into the status of the Big Trees. Within a few years, work begun in the mid-1960s by Richard Hartesveldt revolutionized the NPS's understanding of what was necessary for the long-term preservation of the groves. Ultimately, Hartesveldt's research on fire ecology would synergize with the NPS's acceptance of the Leopold Report, in addition to changing perceptions by the public on environmental priorities, lead the NPS in completely new directions. In 1971, however, as the NPS completed a new and very cautious *Master Plan* for Sequoia and Kings Canyon, the biggest changes remained in the future.

In the backcountry during the postwar years, there was a recreational revolution unprecedented in the history of the two parks. In a few short years beginning in the mid-1960s, fifty years of management schemes for the backcountry were rendered almost useless by the arrival of the backpacking, baby-boom generation. In the years after the war, the NPS focused largely on controlling the impacts of past and present grazing and on undoing the old habits of burying garbage and the like. Suddenly, as the 1970s began and use of the backcountry skyrocketed, the NPS rushed to respond to new and different problems, carrying out experiments with limiting people—something it never had the nerve to try elsewhere in the parks. At the same time, the NPS wrestled with how much of its backcountry to designate formally as wilderness, which Congress required and that the NPS met with hesitation and vagueness. Here was a chance to clarify the agency's management directions toward wilderness and reconcile once and for all how the remaining backcountry of the twin parks would be developed or preserved. But, the final recommendations represented merely a cautious mixture of Colonel White's prewar land management decisions and the input of numerous interest groups.

In the postwar era, the world surrounding the two parks also changed quickly. Nowhere was this more evident than in the three surrounding national forests. During the postwar decades, Sequoia National Forest began, at last, to execute the full mission that had been identified for it decades earlier. In the lands surrounding the parks, this largely took the form of logging, especially on the Sequoia Forest's Hume Lake District. By 1970, logging had begun to approach the parks' boundary for the first time since the turn of the century. Perhaps even more threatening to the biological integrity of Sequoia was the proposed ski-resort development in Mineral King Valley. As endorsed by the Sequoia National Forest during the late 1960s, this development would have placed as many annual visitors in tiny Mineral King Valley as were then visiting all of Sequoia and Kings Canyon National Parks. And nearly all of those visitors would have come to Mineral King by crossing the park on a modern highway cut through a major grove of sequoias. How these visitors would affect the park, in both winter and summer, the NPS had just begun, quietly, to consider. In public, the agency had nothing whatsoever to say, exactly the instructions it had received from President Richard M. Nixon's administration. The protection of the parks' interests instead fell largely to political groups such as the Sierra Club.

Only in the true high country, it seemed, were the boundaries of the parks relatively safe from threat—a situation confirmed by the creation of the John Muir Wilderness, which bordered Sequoia and Kings Canyon on the east and wrapped around the northern end of Kings Canyon. Elsewhere, in the Hume Lake country, along the foothill western border of Sequoia, in the Mineral King region, and eastward across the southern side of Sequoia, the NPS watched silently, as the modern world crept ever closer.

It is possible to suggest that, during the two and a half decades following World War II, the NPS lost its way, as it attempted to protect the two parks. Certainly, none of the numerous superintendents of Sequoia and Kings Canyon National Parks showed the vision or strength of Colonel White. In a larger sense, of course, the NPS of the 1950s and 1960s reflected accurately the temper of its times, in its commitment to the development of facilities and in its hesitancy to upset resolved situations. But nagging at the NPS throughout the period and increasingly as the 1960s ended was the realization that the status quo, ultimately, would not succeed. In the groves of sequoia, increasing scientific evidence clearly pointed out the consequences of overdevelopment and fire suppression. In the backcountry, with the onset of the 1970s, some limits on use were beginning to be set. And on the surrounding lands? Well, that would need to be someone else's battle, perhaps the public's. Luckily, as the 1970s commenced, Americans began to show a shift in attitude that would revolutionize its expectations of national parks and allow the resolution of many of Sequoia and Kings Canyon's most pressing issues.

Tehipite Dome, at 7,708 feet elevation, rises more than 3,500 feet above the Middle Fork of the Kings River. It is the largest dome in the Sierra Nevada and towers over another glacially carved canyon that is similar to the South Fork of the Kings River and Yosemite Valley. Tehipite Dome is located well within the official wilderness area of Kings Canyon National Park and is approachable only by hikers, climbers, and equestrian parties. The exposed North Ridge is a Class 3 ascent to the summit, compared with a technical rating of 5.9 and higher for ascents from the south. Photographer and date unknown.

CHAPTER NINE

New Directions (1972–1990)

In early 1973, the management of Sequoia and Kings Canyon National Parks found itself attempting to overcome a growing list of difficult planning and resource problems. The new *Master Plan* for the parks, completed in early 1971, identified many of these issues, including congestion in developed areas, aging and inadequate facilities, understaffed programs in resource management, research, and interpretion, and a lack of broad-based planning in and around the parks. Issues not specifically mentioned in the plan but directly threatening the two parks in the same year included the ongoing effort by the U.S. Forest Service (USFS) to develop Mineral King, increasing intensive use of adjacent USFS lands, enormous growth in travel to the backcountry, and the rapid population increase of both California, in general, and Tulare and Fresno Counties, in particular. For these problems, the National Park Service (NPS) had no bold solutions. The *Master Plan* did not call for major changes in the parks' facilities or for removal of facilities from the Giant Forest. Instead, the plan conservatively suggested a highway bypass around the Giant Forest area, a bus system, and relocation of the Giant Forest Lodge to a nearby site with fewer sequoias.[1]

About Mineral King the agency had almost nothing to say. With the top of the federal executive branch committed to the project, neither the Department of Interior nor the NPS was in a position to object. Some other problems had proven more amenable to change, however. The experimental limiting of use of the backcountry along the Rae Lakes Loop had worked out well during the summer of 1972, and, as the following year began, park managers seriously discussed extending entry quotas into the backcountry to the remainder of the two parks. The staffing shortfalls identified in the *Master Plan* also showed promise of improvement. In many ways, calls for new programs and additional staffing were easier for the parks to present than initiatives that threatened existing facilities or uses or challenged incompatible uses on adjacent lands.

During the last two decades of the first century, Sequoia and Kings Canyon would see rapidly intensifying debate over proper use and management of the two parks. For the first time, the public would be invited to join the planning process, a change that would have large consequences because of the enormous shift in the public's awareness of environmental issues. During the period, this same shift would become apparent in the NPS itself, as a new generation of science-trained and environmentally aware personnel entered management levels within the agency. This new generation of park managers would take the recommendations of the 1963 Leopold Report to heart and seriously pursue their implementation. In the process, the veracity and attainability of the Leopold Report's goals would ultimately fall into question. The final chapter of the parks' first century would also see vastly exacerbated threats from outside the parks' boundaries—threats of a magnitude never before faced by the Sierra parks' managers. Against all these changes, the haunting legacy of tradition—traditional uses and traditional attitudes—would prove to be a formidable obstacle. As Sequoia and Kings Canyon moved toward their second century, questions of management philosophy and technique, questions of public and personal values, and questions of human/land interaction loomed larger than ever.

Inside the front cover of the 1971 *Master Plan* could be found a note informing readers that the document was "based on plans presented at the Public Discussions held in conjunction with the Wilderness hearings in 1966."[2] This simple note, quite unlike anything that had previously appeared in NPS planning documents for the parks, marked the opening wedge of a new era. In 1969, the U.S. Congress passed the National Environmental Policy Act (NEPA), an elaborate statute that resulted in revolutionary changes in the federal planning process. NEPA required that the environmental consequences of all major federal actions be evaluated and that those consequences be mitigated to the greatest degree possible. The statute also required public input as a part of the evaluation and consideration process. Henceforth, the resolution of any park-management question that affected the natural or human environment would require some form of public disclosure and participation. One of the unintended consequences of NEPA and the formalization of the planning procedure would be to minimize the delays and confusion of personnel changes. During the 1970s, Sequoia and Kings Canyon would have no less than five superintendents, but a combination of NEPA regulations and a stable upper-level management team kept planning and management on a relatively steady course.

THE GIANT FOREST RECONSIDERED

Public involvement in the planning process soon had an unexpected and startling impact. In response to planning problems raised about the Giant Forest in the *Master Plan,* the NPS decided to produce a development concept plan (DCP) for the Giant Forest/Lodgepole area. Preparation of this document fell to a private contractor: Sasaki, Walker Associates, a well-known landscape architecture firm that worked in conjunction with the NPS's system-wide planning staff at the agency's new Denver Service Center (DSC). During preparation of the DCP, Sasaki, Walker Associates rediscovered what others had known for several decades—that the preservation of the

Giant Forest required significant reductions in development within the grove. The new DCP described the visitors' experiences at the Giant Forest in starkly unflattering terms:

> Upon cresting the hill . . . the visual impression in Giant Forest Village and Kaweah is that of old dilapidated buildings bounding a rather large, disorderly area of asphalt paving—cars everywhere—some at a standstill . . . with occupants reading signs. . . . This anticlimactic, confusing and disorderly arrival brings traffic to a standstill and prolongs the frustration caused by the climb into the Giant Forest.[3]

To correct the dismal situation, the first public draft of the new DCP called not just for the relocation of a portion of the accommodations, as had the recent master plan, but instead for the full removal of all commercial facilities from the grove. Once again, Colonel White's grand plan resurfaced, this time with a variety of complicated new twists. New structures at Lodgepole would replace the hundreds of small concessioner cabins in the Giant Forest. Near Wolverton, on the site of the existing pack station, the draft DCP proposed the construction of a large "staging area," which would serve as the terminal for interpretive bus tours of the Giant Forest. The tours would make use not only of the existing Generals Highway between the General Sherman Tree and the Village and the existing Moro Rock/Crescent Meadow Road, but also of a new interpretive roadway to be constructed across the northeastern portion of the grove, connecting Crescent Meadow with Wolverton. Thus, the draft DCP went well beyond previous plans for removing traffic from the grove by attempting to replace auto touring with public transportation.

On the issue of camping, the plan remained vague. The 1971 *Master Plan* called for maintaining existing campsite capacity and relocating the Giant Forest's campgrounds to the "Clover Creek-Willow Meadow" area north of Lodgepole. By August 1974, however, after the three remaining Giant Forest campgrounds had been closed, the draft DCP itself made no specific allowance for any camping construction at all, except to note: "All camping at Lodgepole may eventually be phased out, allowing room for the village development with the balance of open space to be returned to a more natural state."[4] On several other issues mentioned in the *Master Plan*, including the proposed tramway up Alta Peak, the draft DCP remained silent.

In August 1974, a confident NPS released the draft DCP to the public and held public hearings in Visalia, Fresno, and Ash Mountain. At the hearings, required by NEPA, the NPS ran directly into a shocking crossfire. Frustrated campers complained bitterly that, first, they had lost the Giant Forest's campgrounds and, now, the NPS wanted to phase out camping at Lodgepole, too, with only a vague promise of additional development in the undefined future. To the park's many longtime campers, the proposal to move the Giant Forest's accommodations to Lodgepole was offensive and biased in favor of visitors to the lodge. Significantly, while critics angrily attacked the use of Lodgepole for accommodations construction and others questioned the need and potential impact of an additional road through the Giant Forest, the commenting public generally supported the concept of removing commercial facilities from the grove.

The NPS's first public hearing under the new NEPA procedures had not gone well. Few on the park's staff had expected such a vigorous and negative public response. But, through the cloud of criticism, park planners and managers saw the bright light of opportunity. With apparent public support for removal of commercial facilities from the Giant Forest, perhaps it would at last be possible to break the generation-long stalemate that continued to threaten Sequoia National Park's most cherished feature. Quickly, the NPS moved to exploit the limited mandate it had received during the summer hearings. In November, Superintendent Henry Schmidt announced that, since the public agreed with the concept of relocating facilities to less fragile sites and objected only to the designation of Lodgepole as the new hotel site, the park would revise the draft DCP and seek alternative locations for development.[5]

In a November 1974 news release, Superintendent Schmidt promised to have a revised plan for the Giant Forest available for public review by early summer 1975. What came out instead, in May, was a set of four "planning alternatives," together with a "response booklet." Stung by the response to the Sasaki, Walker proposal yet encouraged by the public's general support for the removal of facilities from the Giant Forest, the NPS now proceeded cautiously. The four alternatives included a "no action" option, which left Giant Forest's facilities largely intact, and three possible patterns of relocation. One option followed closely the Sasaki, Walker plan of 1974, while the remaining two proposed either centralizing most visitor accommodations at Clover Creek, two miles north of Lodgepole, or scattering the accommodations through the Lodgepole/Wolverton/Clover Creek region. All the facility-relocation options included proposals for a public transportation system, using only existing roads, and all four proposals carefully spelled out provisions for maintaining a substantial number of campsites.[6]

In July 1975, a chastened but quietly optimistic NPS held another series of public workshops to accept comments on the four planning alternatives. Trying to avoid the camping problems that had blown up so badly the previous summer, these workshops occurred not only in Visalia and Fresno, but also at Lodgepole Campground. NPS officials also took their workshop format to six local service clubs. Again, several themes came through clearly in the public response. Generally, most of those who responded supported converting the Giant Forest to a day-use-only area and did not object to a public transportation system, as long as accommodations and camping were maintained in the Lodgepole/Clover Creek area and the number of campsites did not drop below the existing level. Conspicuous in its absence was any strong criticism of the removal alternatives from Government Services, Incorporated (GSI), the company that had purchased the Fred Harvey concession operations within the park in 1972. For decades, Howard Hays and George Mauger had vigorously opposed removal, insisting that the public would never accept accommodations that did not stand beneath the Big Trees. Now, with visible public support for removal, the new concessioner remained essentially silent, tacitly accepting at least the concept of change.

Two years passed while planners at the agency's DSC analyzed the public comment received in 1975 and converted it into a viable redevelopment concept. Finally, in December 1977, the NPS announced the availability of a new draft plan for the Giant Forest/Lodgepole area.[7] The package the NPS now presented to the public differed markedly from that first experiment of three years earlier. No longer did the plan set out boldly to solve every problem once and for all. Indeed, the first words inside the document set a cautious tone: "This plan has not yet been approved. Its purpose is to provide planning information for further consideration and discussion, and it may undergo considerable revision." In content, the new plan drew mostly from elements evaluated during the 1975 public review. It called for the redesign of the Giant Forest as a day-use-only area, with public transportation access from near Wolverton. At Clover Creek, two miles north of Lodgepole, the concessioner would build its new lodges, keeping to the pillow limit of 1,240, established in 1964. Camping would remain at Lodgepole, with no significant change in the number of sites. Additional provisions included interim improvement of wastewater processing in the Giant Forest and major changes in housing for NPS employees and maintenance.[8] To meet the requirements of NEPA, an additional public document supported the new draft DCP, the *Draft Environmental Statement*. This 280-page document discussed in detail the possible environmental impacts of the proposed action.[9] Altogether, the 1977 package, based on public reaction to the four alternatives of 1975 and supported by a detailed environmental assessment, reflected how thoroughly NEPA had changed park planning in Sequoia during the 1970s. Never again would the NPS have the luxury of planning the park's development without having to explain its actions to the public.

On December 21, 1977, new Superintendent David D. Thompson, Jr. announced public meetings to discuss the new plan. Several months later, a majority of the public attending hearings in Fresno and Visalia voiced support for the central tenets of the scheme, and, again, the concessioner did not object. During the public comment period that followed the meetings, however, GSI President Walter Williams clarified the concessioner's stance with an ominous warning: "in our past comments we have not suggested that it was within the concessioner's purview to argue against the relocation of visitor facilities from the Giant Forest Village area." Yet, Williams continued, "the scope of concessions activities at Sequoia/Kings Canyon National Parks is not sufficient to finance, either through debt or revenue . . . a capital investment approaching $11 million."[10] Williams had picked that figure from the total costs of the project's construction estimated in the

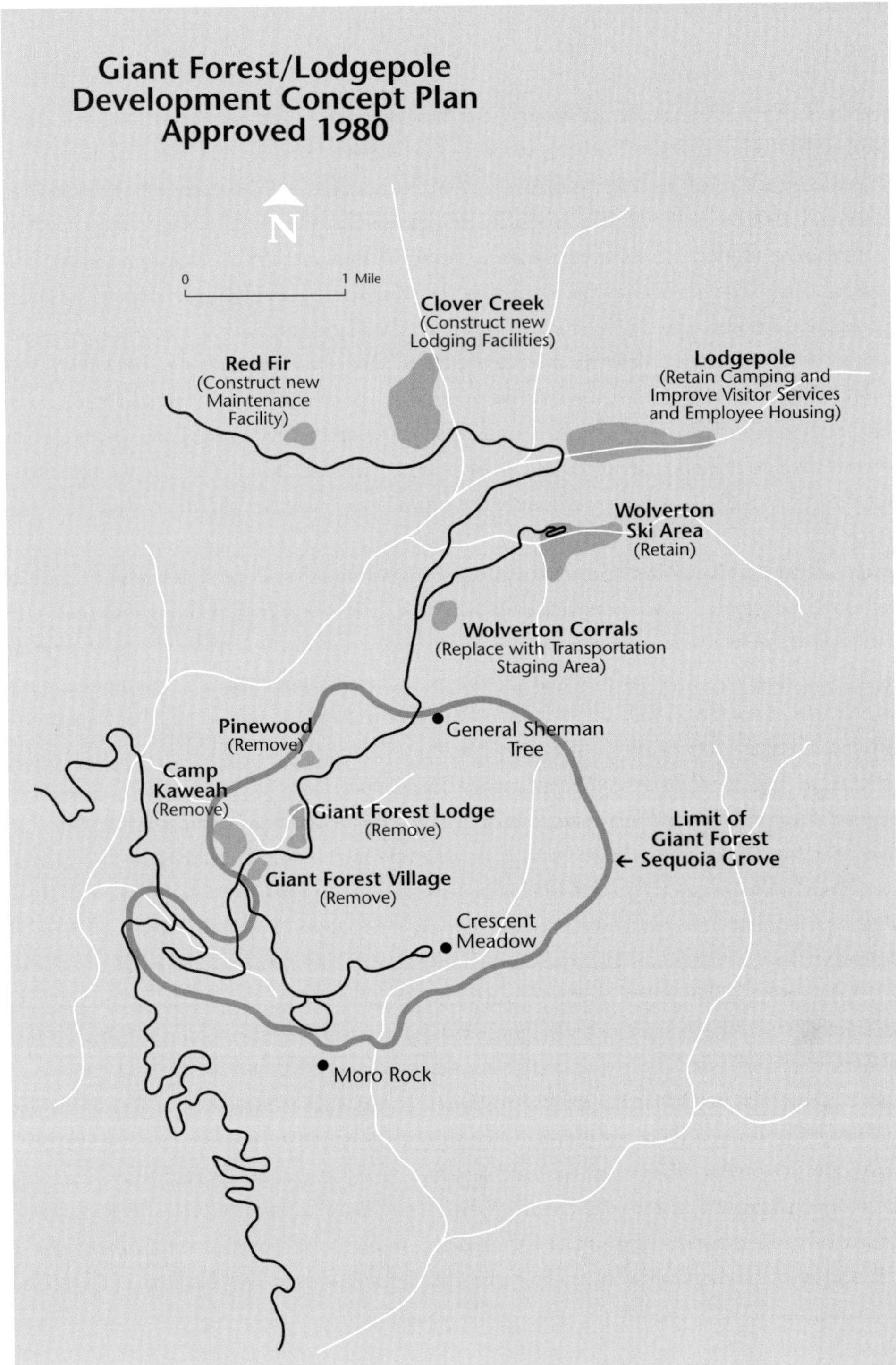
Giant Forest/Lodgepole
Development Concept Plan
Approved 1980
N
0
1 Mile
Clover Creek
(Construct new
Lodging Facilities)
Red Fir
(Construct new
Maintenance
Facility)
Lodgepole
(Retain Camping and
Improve Visitor Services
and Employee Housing)
Wolverton
Ski Area
(Retain)
Wolverton Corrals
(Replace with Transportation
Staging Area)
Pinewood
(Remove)
General Sherman
Tree
Camp
Kaweah
(Remove)
Giant Forest Lodge
(Remove)
Limit of
Giant Forest
← Sequoia Grove
Giant Forest Village
(Remove)
Crescent
Meadow
Moro Rock

new draft DCP, which called for almost $20,000,000 of NPS work and more than $11,000,000 of "concessioner-related costs." During subsequent years, the issue of economic feasibility for the concessioner would prove to be a continuing stumbling block in the ongoing effort to restore the Giant Forest.

In November 1979, still moving slowly and deliberately, the NPS issued the final environmental assessment for the project, and, on December 31, 1979, the last public comment period for that plan passed without additional surprises. NPS Regional Director Howard Chapman quietly approved the *Development Concept Plan* for Giant Forest/Lodgepole on January 17, 1980. The final plan differed little from the second draft released in 1977. For the first time since 1952, when the removal effort instigated by Colonel White collapsed, the NPS had a formal plan to restore the Giant Forest and correct the development mistakes of the 1920s. It had taken nearly a decade to secure the new plan, starting from the vague 1971 *Master Plan* and persevering through a seemingly endless cycle of planning documents and public meetings. Those meetings proved crucial, however, for they allowed the public, an interest group whose views had long been assumed by both the NPS and the concessioner, to speak for itself about development in the Giant Forest and to show its willingness to accept change. With public support, the other necessary aspects of the plan, including acceptance by the concessioner, followed in due time.

IMPLEMENTING THE NEW PLAN

With the *Development Concept Plan* in place, restoration of the Giant Forest moved from the arena of policy to the challenge of implementation. During the early 1980s, the fight to restore the Giant Forest became a battle for money, a conflict intensified by a new round of federal budget cutting under President Ronald Reagan that began in the same year the final Giant Forest plan was approved. By 1982, park managers perceived the funding shortage to be so acute that they feared the removal of facilities from the Giant Forest might be delayed indefinitely. In response to this fear and under pressure from the concessioner to upgrade worn-out facilities, the NPS reluctantly granted permission to replace fifty 1920s-era housekeeping cabins in the Upper Kaweah area near Giant Forest Village with fifty new motel units. Park planners retained enough faith in their plan, however, to insist that the new buildings be constructed modularly, so they could be relocated at some future date. At the same time, the concessioner also constructed a new market and food-service building at Lodgepole and installed a Poma (T-bar) ski lift at Wolverton. The NPS matched these investments with several of its own, including roads and parking at Lodgepole to support the new market and a waste-water treatment plant at Clover Creek that would accept effluent from the enlarged facilities at Lodgepole and perhaps someday also support hotels at Clover Creek. Despite these investments, many park employees were openly skeptical that the move to Clover Creek would ever happen.

Meanwhile, Superintendent Boyd Evison worked hard behind the scenes to convince the NPS to begin funding the huge project defined by the 1980 *Giant Forest/Lodgepole Development Concept Plan*. All involved knew that the project would entail one of the most extensive remodeling efforts ever undertaken in an old-line national park. Regional Director Howard Chapman supported the plan, and, by the time the NPS's budget for fiscal year 1984 was confirmed by Congress, Evison's lobbying effort had borne fruit. The appropriation contained funding for the first phase of work at Clover Creek. Money flowed annually for the remainder of the decade, and, during the next several years, the NPS constructed an access road into the new site, a new water-treatment plant at Wolverton, and a new government maintenance yard at nearby Red Fir. Almost none of this work occurred within the Clover Creek site, however, for the simple reason that the NPS did not yet know exactly what would be built there.

Moving forward at Clover Creek required that the NPS engage GSI, the parks concessioner, and here the NPS found itself with a commercial partner every bit as independent as Howard Hays had been during the 1930s. Founded in 1917 to provide food service within federal facilities in the District of Columbia, GSI had evolved by the 1980s into a national hospitality company with a new name: Guest Services, Inc. Headed by Sebastian J. DiMeglio, who had come to GSI after a career with the famous Fred Harvey Company, the Virginia-based company soon made it clear that its primary goal in any remodeling of commercial facilities within Sequoia National Park was to protect its own financial health.

Operating under a 1974 concessions contract that would run until the end of 1991, the concessioner indicated soon after the approval of the 1980 *DCP* that the immediate issue at the top of its work list was the protection of its existing investment in Sequoia National Park. For GSI, this involved protecting the company's "possessory interest," a legal concept contained within the concessioner's contract that gave it a compensable financial interest in the facilities it operated within the parks. Put simply, if the government wanted to close and remove the commercial facilities within the Giant Forest, it would have to pay GSI for the right to do so. Howard Hays and John White had argued about this issue decades earlier, but now the concessioner's contract clearly defined its rights. The government would have to pay GSI to close down the company's facilities in the Giant Forest.

Buying out GSI's possessory interest in the Giant Forest required that the "sound value" of the facilities be defined, an effort that began in 1983 and stretched out over five contentious years. Unsurprisingly, initial appraisals commissioned independently by GSI and the NPS differed significantly, and the two parties eventually agreed to a third appraisal. By late 1986, general agreement had been achieved regarding the value of what was to be torn down within the grove, but the *DCP* also called for moving a number of buildings from the Giant Forest to the new site at Clover Creek, and this raised additional questions. The fifty new motel units at Upper Kaweah, constructed in 1983–1984, topped this relocation list, but it also included twelve "Boise Cascade" cabins at the Giant Forest Lodge built by Fred Harvey in 1969 and a replacement registration office at Giant Forest Lodge that had been erected in 1983 after a falling tree destroyed the old office. Since these buildings were to be relocated, the NPS did not need to purchase GSI's possessory interest in them. GSI argued, however, that the NPS needed to cover the cost of the physical transfer of the buildings. Estimating that the relocation of the fifty motel units alone could cost $1,000,000, the NPS balked at guaranteeing to underwrite this expenditure. GSI responded by refusing to sign the already negotiated agreement that defined the value of the structures to be torn down in the Giant Forest. After much back and forth, the two sparring partners finally reached a settlement in late 1988. The NPS would pay GSI $3,678,118 for the buildings in the Giant Forest that would be torn down, and the agency also gave in and agreed to cover unspecified relocation costs for the building relocation.[11]

During the five years that the NPS and GSI argued about possessory interest, the concessioner repeatedly used the issue to postpone making a final commitment to the move to Clover Creek. Early in this period, in the spring of 1984, NPS officials met with GSI, with the goal of gaining more cooperation from the concessioner. At the meeting, the NPS asked GSI to make several commitments, including the building of 244 units at Clover Creek, providing design input regarding the mix and phasing of new lodging units, and working with the NPS to resolve, within the next year, the possessory interest issues related to the facilities at the Giant Forest.[12] GSI did not make formal commitments to any of these propositions, but, in the months following the spring 1984 meeting, the company cooperated sufficiently to raise the government's hopes. By the end of the year, the concessioner had provided the NPS with architectural concepts for the proposed new development. These had been developed by architect Clay Wardle, of the Thompson Architectural Group in Fresno.

With this material in hand, the NPS design team at the DSC was able to prepare a draft "comprehensive design plan" for Clover Creek that showed how the site could be developed. Incorporating GSI's suggestions, the plan called for a "grand lodge" and also defined locations for the buildings to be relocated from the Giant Forest. Following GSI's lead, the site plan also identified an area for new tent-top cabins at Clover Creek and even a site for a seasonal tent-roofed dining room.

In March, Superintendent Jack Davis signed the parks' review comments on the Clover Creek Comprehensive Design Plan and noted that, although many details would need revision and the tent dining room was not a good idea, the general design concept was acceptable.[13]

At this point, GSI again pulled back from the project. Since GSI's contract was to end in 1991, the concessioner now began to argue that any commitment to Clover Creek needed to be based on a new long-term contract. Under NPS policy, a new concessions contract could not be negotiated until the agency could demonstrate that its plans were economically feasible. So the agency went to work on an economic-feasibility analysis. This required input from GSI, and, in February 1988, the company estimated that it would require $12,000,000 to build a new central lodge and ninety rustic cabins at Clover Creek. The figure, which also covered support facilities such as housing for employees, assumed that the government would pay for relocating the fifty motel units and twelve individual cabins.[14] Beyond providing these numbers, however, GSI would not go. As GSI President DiMeglio put it to NPS Regional Director in December 1989, the company was "being asked to spend money for the design process without having a contract in hand," and that was not a prudent thing for the concessioner to do[15]

At least for the NPS, there were opportunities in this situation. GSI's continuing refusal to commit to Clover Creek allowed the agency to reconsider the architectural character of new construction. During the early 1980s, at both the Giant Forest, where GSI built the fifty motel units, and at Lodgepole, where the company had erected a large market and food-service facility, park managers had been exposed to the "national-park-modern" design style that GSI preferred. With simple, boxy lines, exterior plywood paneling, and extensive metal roofs, the new buildings represented a major shift away from traditional national park design pioneered by landscape architects decades ago. The more the NPS lived with these new buildings, the less it liked their appearance, and, since GSI had not formally committed to the Clover Creek project, the NPS had the leeway to define a new direction.

In mid-1988, the NPS signed a contract with the San Francisco architectural firm of Esherick, Homsey, Dodge, and Davis to prepare architectural-character guidelines for future development at Sequoia and Kings Canyon National Parks. The effort began with an in-house inventory of "significant" existing structures carried out by architectural historian Laura Soulliere Harrison. Architect George Homsey built on this inventory, as he drafted the final document, which proposed that new buildings in the park should be contemporary interpretations of the rustic design ethic of times past. Park management accepted the *Guidelines* as presented, and subsequent architectural design at Sequoia and Kings Canyon took on a more traditional bent. There would be no more modern box buildings in the twin national parks of the southern Sierra.[16]

As Sequoia National Park approached its centennial in 1990, the effort to remove commercial visitor facilities from the Giant Forest had begun but was nowhere near completion. After six years of annual funding, nearly $20,000,000 had been invested in the project, most of which had gone into purchasing the concessioner's possessory interest and constructing new utility and maintenance facilities. Nothing had been removed from the Giant Forest, and the NPS did not yet have a workable plan for Clover Creek or a commitment from GSI that it would build there. Yet a substantial investment had now been made, and park management remained optimistic that the project would keep moving forward.

A DEVELOPMENT PLAN FOR THE KINGS CANYON

In Kings Canyon National Park, at Cedar Grove, the NPS attempted, during the 1970s, to implement the same lessons it was learning in the Giant Forest/Lodgepole area of Sequoia. The 1971 *Master Plan* for the two parks called for continued camping and lodging at Cedar Grove but offered no guidance as to appropriate size, except to note that camping would not be enlarged beyond the existing 370 sites. In mid-1972, an internal draft statement suggested that the area would support accommodations for up to 260 people. The advent of NEPA mandated a fresh start with public input, however, and this effort began during the summer of 1975, using the format developed that same summer for use in the Giant Forest/Lodgepole area. Again, the NPS issued a planning alternatives workbook and encouraged comments. Six alternatives ranged from closing the area to the public for use as a scientific-research area on one extreme to intensive tourist development on the other end of the spectrum. Only two alternatives called for overnight use. Of these, one called for no more than twenty motel rooms and no more than 400 campsites, while the other allowed 160 rooms and up to 750 campsites.[17]

Compared to the situation at Giant Forest/Lodgepole, the planning effort for Kings Canyon and Cedar Grove Village proceeded rapidly. Surprisingly, considering the emotions the issue had evoked three decades earlier, public interest in Kings Canyon remained muted this time. Largely absent were the Fresno boosters, who had held such high hopes for Kings Canyon development during the 1940s and 1950s. The generation of businessmen from the nearby San Joaquin Valley, who had supported creation of the park but demanded a resort at Cedar Grove in return, had passed. Gone were Chester Warlow and others who had dreamed of a Yosemite-like complex and the thousands who would pass through Fresno to reach it. A new generation of Fresnans lived in a far larger metropolis, a self-focused one less concerned about economic developments in the nearby mountains.

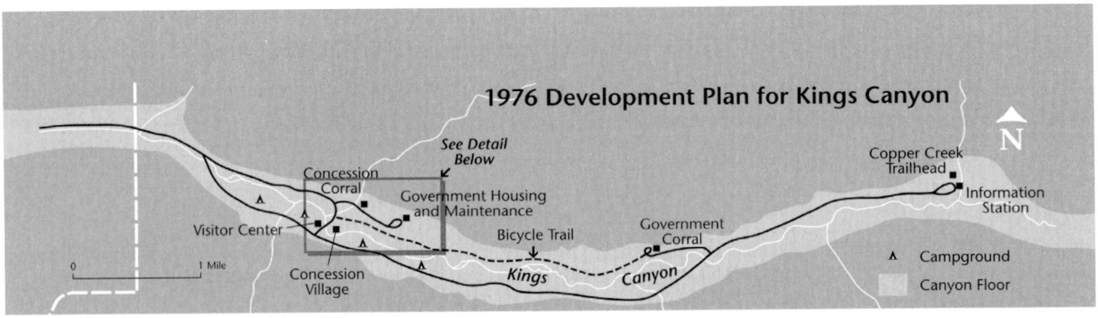
1976 Development Plan for Kings Canyon
See Detail Below
Concession Corral
Government Housing and Maintenance
Visitor Center
Concession Village
Bicycle Trail
Government Corral
Kings Canyon
Copper Creek Trailhead
Information Station
Campground
Canyon Floor
0
1 Mile
N

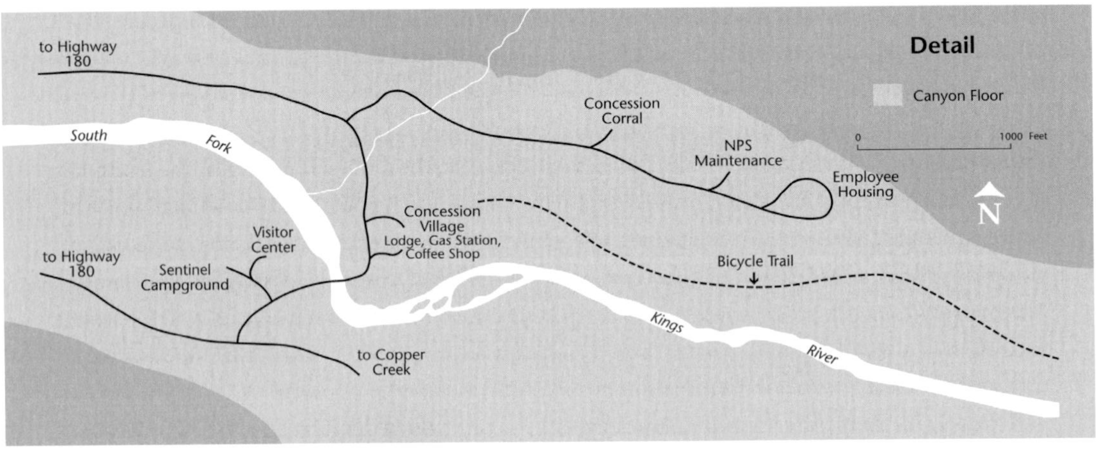
Detail
Canyon Floor
to Highway 180
South Fork
Concession Corral
NPS Maintenance
Employee Housing
Concession Village
Lodge, Gas Station, Coffee Shop
Visitor Center
Sentinel Campground
to Highway 180
Bicycle Trail
Kings River
to Copper Creek
0
1000 Feet
N

During the summer of 1975, most public comment at the Cedar Grove hearings came not from outside parties hoping to develop the area but from groups and individuals already using the area's facilities—people who enjoyed the canyon as it was. From these visitors came a simple message: Limit development in the canyon. The highest level of new development that most participants would support was adding a small lodge, while retaining the existing camping. In May 1976, the NPS issued a draft DCP for the area, supplemented by an *Environmental Review.*[18] The preferred option identified in the two documents allowed a new, twenty-room lodge but no enlargement of camping or other visitor facilities in the canyon. Superintendent Stanley Albright announced the draft plan, on June 10, 1976, as well as a comment period ending July 12. Public comment on the plan was so positive that Albright signed it with no changes. In less than a year, a quiet resolution had been achieved, bringing an anti-climactic end to more than three decades of bitter argument over the future of Kings Canyon. Two years later, during the summer of 1978, GSI constructed a new Cedar Grove Lodge, with eighteen rental rooms upstairs and a market and snack bar downstairs.

MINERAL KING ENTERS THE PARK

Nowhere during the 1970s did the public play a larger role in decision making in the southern Sierra than in Mineral King. The court's temporary injunction, issued in July 1969, had blocked implementation of the USFS/Disney ski-development plan for the basin for three full years, before the U S. Supreme Court finally addressed the Sierra Club's lawsuit. In an April 1972 decision, the Court rejected the suit, which challenged the legality of the entire resort-development scheme, on the grounds that the Sierra Club had not established that its members were suffering direct harm as a result of the USFS's actions. The Supreme Court also made it obvious that the club could refile the suit with certain modifications and gain a serious hearing.[19] Almost before the pro-resort faction could savor this victory, however, a new obstacle to development arose, when the California State Assembly voted to remove the proposed new road to Mineral King from the state highway system. In June, the Sierra Club filed an amended suit, and, in August, the State Senate joined the Assembly in pulling back the state's commitment for highway access to the mountain valley. Public opposition to development at Mineral King had begun to increase, as the Sierra Club carried its campaign against the project to a population in the midst of an environmental awakening unparalleled in American history. By the early 1970s, the battle for Mineral King was no longer a one-sided affair, in which a few environmentalists attempted to stave off a popular development scheme. Taking advantage of the increasing urban sensitivity to wilderness preservation that was sweeping across California, the Sierra Club had become a formidable adversary.

Increasingly, with legal and political issues at a stalemate, the two sides fought in the arena of public opinion. In May 1972, Walt Disney Productions took out a full-page advertisement in *The San Francisco Chronicle*, defending its plans for development as both environmentally sensitive and fully legal. To give the project a better environmental image, Disney Productions assembled a prestigious advisory committee for the project. Among its members were former NPS Director Horace Albright, former Sequoia and Kings Canyon Superintendent Eivind Scoyen, and former Sierra Club President Bestor Robinson.[20] Leading the opposition was the Mineral King Task Force of the Sierra Club, which used its newsletter, *The Optimist*, to spread the word. Among the task force's tactics were "Save Mineral King" T-shirts, public workshops, and even a march on Disneyland in Anaheim, staged on April 14, 1973.

Slowly, the situation shifted to the advantage of the project's opponents. In November 1974, political newcomer John Krebs defeated Tulare County's long-time U.S. Representative Bob Mathias, who had consistently supported the project. Momentum faded further during 1973 and 1974, while the USFS, in an effort to comply with NEPA requirements, prepared a massive *Draft Environmental Statement* for the Mineral King project. As completed in December 1974 by Sasaki, Walker Associates, the same design firm that prepared the 1974 DCP for the Giant Forest, the 300-page document opened entire new areas for discussion, argument, and public comment.[21] In early 1976, after sifting through an enormous amount of highly partisan public comment, the USFS issued a *Final Environmental Statement* for the project. Significantly, in this document, the USFS scaled down the maximum size of the proposed development, reducing winter use by twenty percent and summer use by forty percent. In the report, the USFS listed five development alternatives, ranging from no action to development for 20,000 skiers a day. As its preferred alternative, the agency chose the latter, with its highest possible level of the development.[22]

Even as the USFS downsized its development plans, the tide continued to turn against the agency. In March 1976, Tulare County Representative John Krebs announced that he would introduce a bill to transfer the disputed area to Sequoia National Park. Previous bills to effect this transfer had already been introduced but never before with local political support. Responding to those earlier bills, the NPS had quietly undertaken an analysis of the suitability of the area for addition to the park. In March 1976, the NPS concluded:

> The outstanding natural resources of the Mineral King valley argue for its inclusion in the National Park System, and there is still a considerable segment of public opinion that believes that Mineral King should be given this status. None of the former problems now appear to be insurmountable . . . [23]

With the election of President Jimmy Carter in November 1976 and the re-election at the same time of John Krebs, the battle for Mineral King entered its final phase. Criticism of the USFS had begun to take its toll on the agency. In February 1977, Representative Krebs angrily challenged the chief of the USFS to explain the presence of two USFS officials, apparently on official duty, at a pro-development and anti-John Krebs political meeting.[24] In early January 1978, the USFS further scaled down the size of the proposed development, this time to 6,000 skiers and 4,000 daily summer visitors, but it was too late. Late in the same month, after a meeting of the White House Domestic Policy Council, the Carter administration reversed the decade-long executive branch policy of support for the development and announced it would instead support addition of the 16,000-acre area to Sequoia National Park.[25] On November 10, 1978, President Jimmy Carter signed the Omnibus Parks Bill sponsored by Representative Philip Burton, of San Francisco. Among its many provisions was the addition of Mineral King to Sequoia National Park. To settle any remaining doubts, the bill also prohibited construction of any downhill-skiing facilities in the area.

The thirteen-year battle for Mineral King between developers, who perceived themselves as conservationists, and the rapidly growing preservationist branch of the same historic tree left deep scars. To Sequoia National Forest, the final outcome represented a public rejection of its basic management philosophies. After all, the USFS had done nothing more in Mineral King than attempt to execute its long-standing multiple-use policies. To the Disney Company, the whole affair had been a public-relations debacle, an effort that made enemies and squandered a good deal of the organization's money and positive public reputation. To the people of Tulare County, many of whom saw opportunities for economic growth in the proposal, the death of the project marked yet another occasion in which "outsiders" decided the fate of local mountain resources. In November 1978, local voters soundly rejected John Krebs in his bid for a third term, selecting instead a conservative Republican, who publicly announced his continued support for development of the area.

On the winning side of the Mineral King battle was the Sierra Club, which grew immensely in prestige and power during the years of the conflict, as well as the larger preservationist/national park public. Ultimately, it was this last group that prevailed, just as it did during the contemporary planning efforts in the Giant Forest and Kings Canyon. In Mineral King, the USFS attempted to sell to the public a large, intensive recreational development at exactly the same time that such ideas were being soundly rejected by the public in adjacent national parks. It is thus not all that surprising that, in the end, proposed development of Mineral King sold no better than the rejected options of enlarged facility development in Sequoia and Kings Canyon National Parks.

In the Omnibus Parks Act of 1978, Congress called not only for the addition of Mineral King to Sequoia National Park, but also for the preparation of a comprehensive management plan for the area within two years. Following now-familiar procedures, the NPS assembled a planning team and sought public opinion. Again, as had been the case at Cedar Grove, resolution came easily, because only those who had supported national park status for the area chose to participate. The completed plan announced its intentions clearly enough: "The actions detailed in this plan are intended to maintain the current pattern, density, and level of public use—both in summer and in winter—and to retain the traditional character of Mineral King."[26]

As the 1980s began, however, one Mineral King issue remained only partially resolved. The legislation in 1978 that transferred the area to the national park also allowed the USFS's special-use permit sites to continue to be occupied by summer cabins. Many of these simple structures were occupied seasonally by extended families with multi-generation ties to Mineral King. The legislation authorized indefinite five-year renewals of cabin permits but, critically, only to permittees of record at the time of the transfer. Eventually, the legislation implied, the cabins would all disappear. Thus, in a spirit of compromise, the 1978 act accepted into the national park yet another body of traditional users with a deeply personal as well as potentially incompatible relationship with what were now national park resources. The ultimate fate of these cabins would continue to be a subject of controversy for decades to come.

A NEW PLAN FOR GRANT GROVE

By the beginning of the 1980s, with for new DCPs in place for Giant Forest/Lodgepole and Mineral King in Sequoia National Park and Cedar Grove in Kings Canyon, park planners turned their attention to the other remaining major developed area in the two parks—the Grant Grove Section of Kings Canyon. At Grant Grove, the concessioner still operated a tourist camp left over from the 1930s. Only nine cabins, all built before 1930, offered private baths. Forty-three additional rustic cabins completed the available accommodations, many of them with canvas tent-style roofs and no electricity. This situation satisfied neither the NPS nor the management of GSI.

By early 1982, as a part of the same effort that resulted in the new motel units in the Giant Forest, GSI began pushing actively for permission to construct fifty new motel units at General Grant. In 1983, again following NEPA procedures, the NPS issued a draft DCP for Grant Grove. In addition to the required "no action" option, the draft contained two alternatives, one for enlarging accommodations from fifty-two units to 150 units and another for maintaining the level of development at fifty-two units but replacing the existing substandard cabins with new facilities. The plan's "preferred alternative" was the facility-enlargement option.[27] The proposal to triple visitor

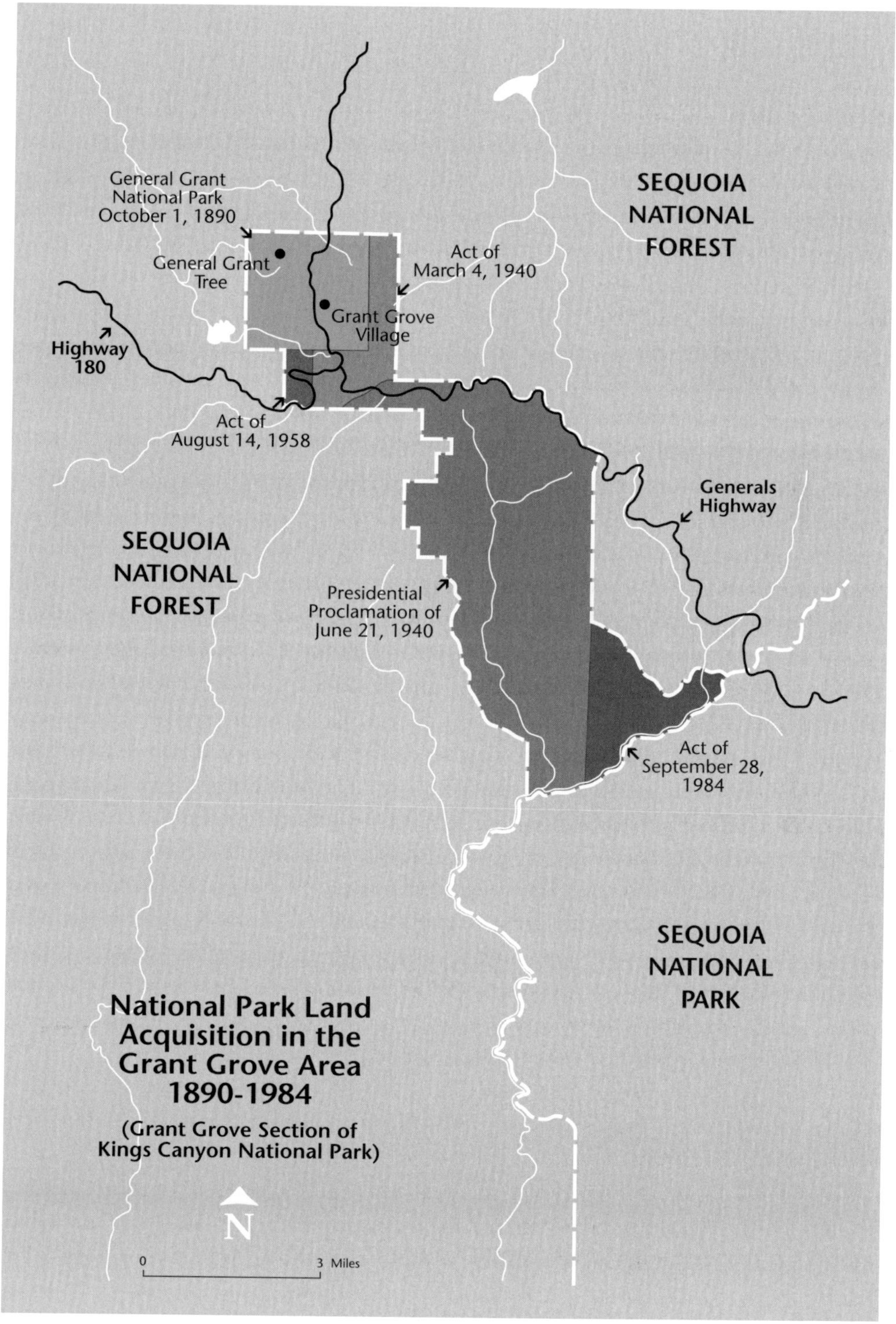
General Grant
National Park
October 1, 1890
General Grant
Tree
Grant Grove
Village
Act of
March 4, 1940
Highway
180
Act of
August 14, 1958
SEQUOIA
NATIONAL
FOREST
SEQUOIA
NATIONAL
FOREST
Generals
Highway
Presidential
Proclamation of
June 21, 1940
Act of
September 28,
1984
SEQUOIA
NATIONAL
PARK
National Park Land
Acquisition in the
Grant Grove Area
1890-1984
(Grant Grove Section of
Kings Canyon National Park)
N
0
3 Miles

accommodations at Grant Grove resulted largely from the parks' long-time commitment to the concessioner to allow accommodations for up to 2,000 persons within Sequoia and Kings Canyon National Parks. With a limit of 1,240 set for Clover Creek and with fewer than 100 allocated to the small lodge at Cedar Grove, the only remaining location for facility enlargement was at Grant Grove.

Once released, the draft plan generated public comment similar to that received in response to the proposals for Cedar Grove and Mineral King. Most comments came from existing users, who wrote that they liked Grant Grove's low-key, old-fashioned atmosphere. Only limited support appeared for enlargement of facilities, and some found the prospect completely unsatisfactory. The Sierra Club, in particular, objected to facility expansion on this scale and demanded that the government prepare a full environmental impact statement (EIS) before it proceeded with any facility replacement or enlargement. Ultimately, the NPS acceded to this demand and prepared the more-thorough document, retaining as its preferred alternative the plan to expand facilities but now in a dispersed arrangement. The NPS released the draft EIS in August 1986, allowing more than two months for comment. A tabulation of the comments received showed a nearly even division between the preferred alternative for dispersed facility enlargement and no action whatsoever. When the time came for a decision, the NPS retained nearly all elements of its preferred alternative.[28]

The decision in the mid-1980s to enlarge visitor facilities at Grant Grove and the muted public response to the plan stood in interesting contrast to the events of the previous decade in the Giant Forest, Mineral King, and Cedar Grove. In part, the situation may have been explained by the truly miserable condition of the existing facilities at Grant Grove and, perhaps also, by the fact that the proposed enlargements in accommodations had only minimal effect on other uses of the area. Many park users may even have accepted the premise that it did not make sense to focus development in the two parks so heavily towards Sequoia, which had long had nearly five times as many visitor cabins for rent as Kings Canyon. Ultimately, the NPS pushed through its plan for Grant Grove, compromising only in the form of a promise to disperse the new facilities rather than concentrate them in over-large buildings. In this way, the 2,000-person accommodations target set in the *Master Plan* was finally achieved, at least on paper. As of the end of the 1980s, however, no action had yet been taken to implement the plan at Grant Grove, and none seemed likely until completion of work on the Clover Creek project.

PUBLIC PLANNING: WHO AND WHY

Between 1976 and 1987, the Park Service succeeded in developing politically acceptable development plans for every major facility area in Sequoia and Kings Canyon National Parks. These plans resolved many long-standing conflicts between concessioners, area boosters, preservationists, and the managing agency. And, repeatedly, involvement of the public forced decisions much more sensitive to national park values than those reached in previous decades by NPS planners working alone. In the Giant Forest, the planning process resulted in a recommitment to restore Sequoia National Park's best-known sequoia grove to a more natural state, an idea that had become a crusade in earlier times, only to be abandoned in frustration during the 1950s. At Cedar Grove, the public-planning process clearly rejected the schemes for major development that had haunted Kings Canyon since creation of the northern park. The eighteen-room lodge that finally opened there in 1979 bore little resemblance to the dream structures of earlier boosters and planners. In Mineral King, too, the public imposed a conservative direction on the planning process. Only at Grant Grove, during the mid-1980s, did the pattern shift. There, where nearly everyone agreed that the existing facilities had to be replaced, the NPS successfully sold a scheme for enlarging facilities. Even in that case, however, the public exercised a conservative role, pushing for careful consideration of the impacts of enlargement and a more dispersed physical layout.

The significance of public input in the development of these plans cannot be ignored. In each case, a majority of the commenting public either supported the NPS, when it took a preservationist stance, or criticized the NPS, when it strayed. In this process, of course, everything depended less on public input in general and more on those who took the time to get involved. Repeatedly, it turned out, those who cared enough to do so were existing park users—individuals with the deepest involvement in the status quo. On the other extreme, the developers and boosters, who had played such a major role in the early days of both parks, often perceived themselves so far outside the NEPA planning process that they ceased to comment at all. To the extent that this happened, the new plans incorporated a fundamental bias toward limited use, but, in the larger sense, the plans also reflected the protective instincts of a substantial portion of the general public toward the national parks. By 1980, few Americans still believed that growth could occur without costs, and nowhere was the citizenry less inclined to accept those costs than in their federal parklands.

THE BABY BOOMERS AND THE BACKCOUNTRY

During the early years of the 1970s, the demographics of the postwar "baby boom" led to an extraordinary period of intense use of the backcountry of Sequoia and Kings Canyon National Parks. The combination of unprecedented numbers of young people, increasing environmental awareness, and great strides in the quality of backpacking equipment resulted in one of the most dramatic short-term use increases witnessed by the two parks during their first century. In 1962, 8,054 people entered the backcountry of the two parks; thirteen years later, the comparable figure totaled 48,207, an increase of nearly 600 percent.

By 1973, a decade of rapid growth in such use had made the trend fully obvious to the parks' management. Already, in July 1972, park officials had imposed quotas on daily use on the popular Rae Lakes Loop in Kings Canyon National Park. During the winter of 1972–1973, they worked rapidly on a supplement to the existing *Backcountry Management Plan* intended to address these changes and otherwise update the pioneering 1963 plan. In May 1973, the NPS released the new document, and with it came bold new regulations aimed at tighter control of use by both people and stock.[29] The plan established limits for both seasonal and daily wilderness permits along with limits on total group size, length of stay per person, and the number of stock per party. New rules excluded campers from within 100 feet of water sources and the same distance from meadows and the grassy margins of lakes, prohibited open use of soap or detergents, and required that only dead and downed wood be burned. Backpackers thenceforth were required to pack out all their trash. Park managers closed a number of areas to camping entirely and restricted access in the areas of bighorn sheep near Sawmill, Baxter, and Shepherd passes to all but scientists or those with special permits. Stock use remained more loosely controlled, but several additional meadows were ruled off limits. Of greatest significance, the new Backcountry Management Plan extended the permit/quota system to all of Kings Canyon National Park during 1973 and to both parks in 1974. Through these actions, the agency achieved there what it had shied away from in the frontcountry—limits on the number of visitors allowed on the park's land.

During the following decade, managers of the backcountry continued to expand controls, as particular problems became apparent. The issue of campfires grew to be an issue, because the number of users remained high. In alpine areas, wood grew so slowly that, once consumed by campers, it might take centuries to replace. As the 1970s proceeded, the NPS closed one area after another to campfires. Finally, the agency imposed broad-based restrictions that prohibited all fires above certain altitudes. Other new problems demanded the addition of physical facilities, a fact that worried park officials, as they attempted to maintain a wilderness atmosphere in the backcountry. The problem of bears, in particular, fueled debates about management of the wilderness within the NPS. The great increase in human activity in the backcountry eventually attracted to the wilderness the same sort of bear activity that had long plagued the frontcountry's campgrounds in the two parks. As adaptable and intelligent animals, bears recognized that backpackers' food justified summer forays into areas that previously had not supported them. NPS's responses, none of them fully successful, included seemingly endless attempts to teach the public how to hang food, so that bears could not reach it, experiments with the design and manufacture of portable bear-proof canisters, and installation of bear cables and ultimately bear boxes, both designed to separate bears from human food. Each of these tactics had its flaws, however. Efforts

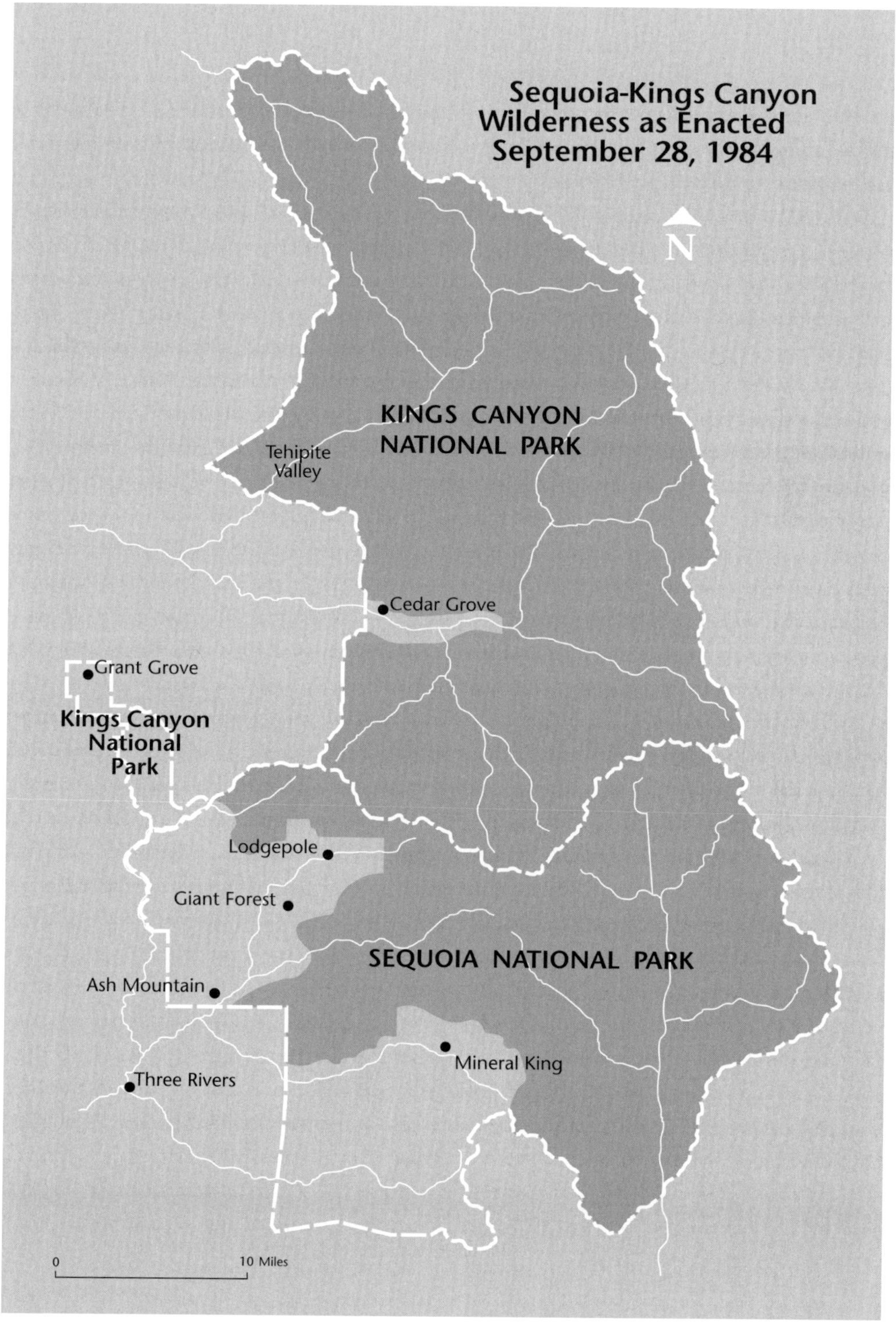

Sequoia-Kings Canyon
Wilderness as Enacted
September 28, 1984
N
KINGS CANYON
NATIONAL PARK
Tehipite
Valley
Cedar Grove
Grant Grove
Kings Canyon
National
Park
Lodgepole
Giant Forest
SEQUOIA NATIONAL PARK
Ash Mountain
Mineral King
Three Rivers
0
10 Miles

to train visitors were inconsistent in their results to defeat hungry bears, and the introduction of physical measures like bear boxes led to such heavy use at designated campsites that sanitation and congestion problems developed.

Not all of the backcountry's needs could be resolved locally. In 1984, Congress finally took up again the long-standing question of formal wilderness status for the backcountry of Sequoia and Kings Canyon National Parks and, on September 28, Congress legislatively placed eighty-five percent of the acreage of the two parks within the national wilderness system. This figure matched that proposed in the 1971 *Master Plan*, which had been savagely attacked at the time by the Sierra Club and other preservation groups as insufficient. Their acceptance of the final proposal, a dozen years later, was due to several changes and factors. First, the final 1980 NPS recommendation eliminated the "Swiss-cheese holes," which could, in theory, be developed later. In addition, the wilderness status of the two parks had really ceased to be a significant political issue, because the NPS managed the lands in question as de facto wilderness and would have to consult the public through the NEPA process, if it ever decided to develop an area. Finally, the proposed designation had been attached to the much larger and more complex California Wilderness Bill of 1984. This both delayed passage and defused potential challenge of individual parts of the legislation. Thus, the NPS and preservationists opted not to object when the final bill omitted several areas of Sequoia National Park that had been parts of previous wilderness proposals, including the Yucca Mountain/North Fork area west of the Generals Highway, the Hockett Meadow country, and all alpine basins in the Mineral King addition. On the other hand, with the exception of the floor of Kings Canyon from Cedar Grove to Copper Creek, the entire main section of Kings Canyon National Park received wilderness designation.

Ironically, the most intense backcountry-management controversies of the 1980s in the two parks did not come from backpackers but from stock users, a group that represented barely five percent of use in the backcountry. During the early 1980s, the NPS initiated a new planning effort for the parks' backcountry that stirred up a great deal of controversy by attempting to place additional limits on stock. In reality, the attempt reflected not a change in perceived resource impacts but a change in park standards. Prior to the 1960s, when use in the backcountry remained below 10,000 people a year and stock use comprised a major percentage of that use, the NPS received few complaints about the impacts of horses and mules on trails and meadows. All this changed, however, in the 1970s, with the arrival of tens of thousands of backpackers. Trail hikers responded angrily to dusty or muddy, stock-disturbed trails. Additional impetus came from the increasing realization that preservation of the backcountry's resources required careful attention to the impacts of exotic animals such as horses and mules on fragile alpine vegetation.

The controversy arose from the efforts of the NPS to update the parks' management plans for the backcountry. As the 1980s began, the 1963 *Backcountry Management Plan* remained technically in effect, together with its 1976 supplement. Patterns of visitor use and expectations in the backcountry had changed so much during the 1970s, however, that the need for a complete new plan had become obvious. In February 1984, the NPS released draft environmental assessments of new management plans for the backcountry regarding both stock use and meadows. In a news release about the two new complementary plans, Superintendent Boyd Evison announced a thirty-day public comment period.[30] Instead of quiet public support for the plans, which planners had come to expect in recent years, the NPS received strong protests from an organization of private stock users known as the High Sierra Stock Users Association, which demanded more time to study and evaluate the NPS's proposals. Evison, under political pressure and sensing that public review of the two plans would not be as simple as previously hoped, announced, on March 29, that the review period would remain open for the remainder of the calendar year. No steps to implement the new plans would be made during that period.[31]

During the summer, distrust of the proposed plans mounted. Particularly upsetting to private stock users were proposed new controls on when stock could be used in the backcountry and which of the parks' many meadows would be closed completely to grazing. Then, in the fall, rumors began circulating among stock users that animal use would be phased out of the parks altogether, and they responded furiously, with letters and calls of protest. Critical among their complaints was the apparent lack of a connection between regulations or closure, on one hand, and demonstrated actual damage, on the other.

By March 1986, when Regional Director Howard Chapman finally approved the two plans, two full years had passed since the NPS initiated what it had intended to be a mere thirty-day comment period. As finally authorized, the *Stock Use and Meadow Management Plan*, in particular, reflected a great deal of input from both private stock users and commercial packers. Through careful negotiations with user groups, the NPS eventually gained most of what it originally thought important, but the agency had suffered much negative criticism and substantial political pressure on behalf of the stock users. For the first time since the public meetings in 1974 about the Giant Forest, the NPS had received significant public criticism of its plans. Several times during the previous decade, the parks successfully resolved difficult problems through public input from limited interest groups. When it issued drafts of the *Backcountry Management Plan* and accompanying *Stock Use and Meadow Management Plan*, the NPS was reminded that, sometimes, the public that chose to pursue an issue could be critical and unsupportive of the government's position. Another important issue came to light during the controversies of the 1980s regarding use in backcountry. Park management realized that backpackers, the user group expected to dominate the planning process, did not involve themselves to any significant degree. Several possible explanations were advanced, but, perhaps, the most significant was that the baby-boom generation had begun to age. Use of the backcountry dropped significantly during the mid-1980s. Following the peak year of 1975, when more than 48,000 people entered the backcountry, annual use stabilized for a decade in the lower 40,000 range. Then, beginning in 1985, backcountry entries dropped off. In 1988, barely 32,000 people entered the Sequoia-Kings Wilderness. As the decade ended, the demographic implications of wilderness management in an aging America were just beginning to sink in.

RESOURCES MANAGEMENT AND RESEARCH COME OF AGE

The 1971 *Master Plan* listed as a goal the expansion of the parks' resource-management program. Barely a decade earlier, the concept had barely existed, but the 1963 Leopold Report committed the NPS to a fundamental change of direction in managing natural resources: the preservation of natural scenes and systems in as near a state as possible to that found at the time of Euro-American entry.

As noted previously, the NPS's early response to the Leopold Report at Sequoia and Kings Canyon focused principally on the ecology of the giant sequoias and, especially, on the trees' relationship to natural fire. By the mid-1970s, as a ten-year research effort drew to a close, the challenge became how to implement what had been learned. In the light of the policies espoused in the report, much of the parks' first century of management now appeared to be seriously misguided. The suppression of essentially all natural fire represented the greatest of these mistakes. Other obvious problems included the clash of bears and campers in developed areas, the effects of intense human recreation on forests, and the ominous and increasing specter of air pollution.

In 1976, in accordance with the *Master Plan*, Sequoia and Kings Canyon National Parks separated several employees and programs from the parks' various work units and reconstituted them as the "Division of Natural Resources Management." Resource officers were directed to manage the physical interaction between visitors and natural resources. At the end of the year, Sequoia and Kings Canyon published the *Natural Resources Management Plan and Environmental Assessment*, the parks' first comprehensive plan for limiting and mitigating human damage to the park's resources.[32] This plan called for a wide variety of overdue actions, including a full inventory of the giant sequoias in the parks, implementation of a natural-fire program, abatement of hazardous trees, management of bears, control of exotic animals, monitoring of water quality, and revegetation of campgrounds. Another part of the plan identified necessary natural-science research projects. Responsibility for this last program fell largely to the parks' research scientist, a position first filled in 1968 with fire ecologist Bruce Kilgore. Completion of an integrated resources-management plan marked the final shift at Sequoia and Kings Canyon from visual to ecological management, a change that had tentatively begun several decades earlier, with the Meinecke studies of the Big Trees and was formally chartered by the Leopold Report's board in 1963.

During the following decade, the parks' natural-resource management program and its smaller companion, the natural-science research program, faced rapidly increasing workloads. During the 1970s, management of natural and human-made fire dominated the resource-management program. Before they ended in 1974, the Hartesveldt experiments in Redwood Canyon established the necessity of repeated fire for both the reproduction of the giant sequoia and natural-fuel management. In response, the 1976 *Resources Management Plan* confirmed the 1968 decision that designated almost 600,000 acres of the two parks as a "natural fire zone." In such a zone, natural fires would be monitored but otherwise allowed to burn unimpeded, as long as they did not threaten facilities, recreational users, or the parks' boundaries. During the next several years, a number of natural fires burned thousands of acres of backcountry, with the largest occurring in the Sugarloaf/Roaring River country of southern Kings Canyon National Park. At the same time, a program of deliberate fires began in the more accessible sequoia groves and, especially, in the Giant Forest, where annual fires occurred starting in 1979. Park managers called these events "prescribed burns," because they were perceived as a prescribed therapy for forests that had accumulated unnatural amounts of woody fuel and because they occurred only "under prescription"; that is, only under carefully specified environmental conditions. The fires usually reduced both accumulated fuels and the density of the forest to levels similar to those hypothesized to have existed in the early nineteenth century.

During the early 1980s, as the effects of the prescribed-burn program began to spread across the landscape, the program generated both strong support and equally impassioned opposition. To most ecologists and even to many visitors, reintroduction of fire into the groves of sequoia was a logical process that added value by making the groves more natural. To these supporters of fire, the scorched bases of the giant sequoia and sometimes drastically thinned forest were nothing more than a return to the way things ought to be. Only a few ecologists questioned the return of fire, and their concerns were not about the appropriateness of the goal but the ability of fire as a natural process to restore effectively a forest so changed by humankind. Other park visitors, however, found the entire process visually and ethically objectionable. Often, these individuals perceived the groves as "natural cathedrals"—places where any human-made change was for the worse. Eventually, in 1985–1986, the level of criticism grew so intense that it required a public airing.

On June 30, 1986, a public review of the prescribed-fire program began at Lodgepole in Sequoia National Park. To sift through the comments and draw them together into recommendations for future action, the NPS created a special committee, consisting entirely of non–NPS personnel and chaired by Dr. Norm Christiansen, of Duke University. The committee visited a number of recent prescribed-burn sites and listened to both criticism and support for the program. In March 1987, the committee, dominated by ecologists, released a report suggesting only minor modifications in the parks' fire management program.[33] Ultimately, the gap between those who supported prescribed burning and those who described it as "government vandalism" could not be bridged, even through the careful efforts of a scientific panel. Anti-burn forces challenged not technical methods but rather the philosophical premises supporting the fire program. Thus, the NPS again was forced to recognize that abrupt shifts in management philosophy, such as the Leopold Report and the infusion of ecology-trained managers, could stir a backlash from those who had accepted older, traditional policies.

Under the supervision of the NPS's Division of Natural Resource Management, activity also increased significantly in the area of wildlife management. With the deer crisis in the Giant Forest resolved and almost forgotten, new problems demanded attention. Programs began to protect native fish and re-establish additional herds of the sadly reduced native bighorn sheep. But no other wildlife issue received as much attention during the period as the interaction between black bears and park visitors. In the aftermath of the Leopold Report, a new perspective slowly took hold. The new position held that bears must be managed as wild animals, not as semi-tame camp followers. From this position came a prolonged and challenging effort to separate bears from human foods. First, came "bear-proof" garbage cans, standard trash cans held in place by solid pipes set in concrete and topped with heavy lids that opened like mail boxes. These cans, within a few seasons, largely accomplished their task of taking garbage away from bears. Unfortunately, this did not cause bears to stop searching for human food. Instead, the bears simply shifted their search to focus on less well-protected food supplies. The new weak spot turned out to be automobiles. For decades, campers had been trained to protect their food from bears by placing it in their cars. This policy had worked reasonably well, as long as garbage was easily available. With access to garbage now denied, the bears instead turned to cars with a vengeance. By the early 1980s, damage to automobiles by bears approached $100,000 annually. Eventually, park managers, adopting an idea first tried in Yosemite, installed bear-proof metal food lockers in each campsite in the frontcountry of the two parks.

It was also during the late 1970s and early 1980s when a new and potentially devastating resource threat within the parks was confirmed: air pollution. During the 1960s, visibility in areas of the San Joaquin Valley west of Sequoia and Kings Canyon National Parks dropped noticeably, reflecting the rapidly increasing levels of human activity in the area. By the late 1960s, many summer days passed in Visalia without the towering wall of the Sierra being visible at all. In the following decade, reduced visibility in the parks became more commonplace, especially in the western third of Sequoia. Concern began to develop that air pollution, which consisted of a complex mix of dust, auto exhaust, farm chemicals, and industrial emissions from as far away as the San Francisco Bay area, might also have a biological effect. By 1980, this had been proven to be true, with damage from ozone similar to that already identified in the mountains of Southern California becoming clearly visible in the parks. Several years later, an elaborate state study demonstrated that the alpine zone of the two parks was potentially at risk from acid rain during the summer, when thunderstorms pulled up smog from the lowlands and mixed chemically active pollutants with rainwater. Yet another study, in the same years, suggested that sequoia seedlings suffered significant damage from ozone pollution. The identification of these problems opened a new chapter in the long history of resource protection in the two parks. For the first time in the modern era, the source of a problem that threatened the parks' resources was outside the parks' boundaries and thus outside NPS's control.

Closely tied to the growing natural-resource management program, during the 1970s and 1980s, was the smaller but equally important natural-science research program. Most of the program's early efforts focused on fire, but, by the mid-1970s, a broader approach appeared. This reflected the parks' need for information on a wide variety of issues, ranging from impacts of wilderness to stock grazing and the behavior of black bears. Additional major projects during the 1980s included support for the state's air-quality work, research focusing on the frequency of natural fires and reproduction among giant sequoias, and attempts to reconstruct the paleoecology of the Sierra. By the late 1980s, a decade of inquiry by NPS scientists and cooperating research institutions had significantly enhanced the ability of NPS managers to understand their increasingly complex resource issues. Perhaps the most ambitious and complex program undertaken by the research office, during the 1980s, was the development of a geographic information system (GIS). Taking advantage of the power of computerization, the GIS project aimed to collect and refine all the parks' many decades of resource information into one centralized computer system that stored and presented the information in a geographical framework. As a part of the same project, the parks began an ambitious and detailed full inventory of vascular plants and vertebrate animals—a step long overdue in the face of modern-management demands. Additional encouragement and support were also given to outside-supported research efforts designed to increase knowledge of the parks' resources. This was in sharp contrast to earlier years, when managers believed that most research such as tree coring or animal drugging had too severe an impact on the physical resources of the parks.

During the last two decades of their first century, the two parks, while faced with rapidly accelerating resource threats, nevertheless attempted to realize the vision contained in the Leopold

Report. Through small but professional staffs in the Division of Natural Resources Management and the research office, Sequoia and Kings Canyon aggressively pursued the elusive goal of shifting towards a more ecological and systemic version of resource preservation and management. Because the NPS tried to implement and increase resource-management and research programs without undertaking any significant reduction in visitor services, the result was often programs that reacted to problems instead of anticipating what might happen next to the increasingly isolated and fragile resources of the two parks.

COMPLETING THE FIRST CENTURY

On September 25, 1990, Sequoia National Park celebrated its centennial. A full century had passed since George Stewart and his allies had succeeded in creating a small federal reserve dedicated to the perpetuation of the giant sequoia trees of the Sierra Nevada. In the succeeding century, Stewart's small seed of a national park had grown many times over to become a globally significant biological reserve and a famous tourist destination. Sequoia had also gained an equally complex and significant twin: Kings Canyon National Park. All this called for celebration.

The first commemorative event of 1990 occurred six months before the actual centennial. On March 4, park staff marked the Golden Anniversary of the 1940 establishment of Kings Canyon National Park Act with a special day of activities at Grant Grove. Visitors and staff alike took the day to remember the contentious battle to create the park and the many challenges the reservation had weathered in the years that followed. All this was mere prelude to the much-awaited summer calendar of centennial events. In early August, Superintendent Tom Ritter hosted NPS Director James Ridenour on a trip to the backcountry that took their party over part of the route that had been ridden by Steven Mather and Horace Albright on their famous 1915 pack trip. Two weeks later, the park hosted an employee reunion that brought together more than 600 past and present employees for a picnic at Wolverton. In conjunction with these events, the first edition of this book went on sale.

Sequoia's centennial party moved into high gear with a park-wide open house on Sunday, September 23. Using a special issue of *The Sequoia Bark*, the parks' newspaper, as a guide, the NPS set out to share with the public all the things the agency did to sustain the parks. Visitors that day found crews demonstrating their work at numerous locations, from Ash Mountain to Lodgepole. Trail crews, interpreters, fire crews, mule packers, search-and-rescue rangers, and utility-system operators all told their stories. More than 7,000 visitors participated in the event.

On the actual centennial day, September 25, the park organized a media event that centered around the naming of Centennial Peak, a previously unnamed 13,288-foot-high summit on the

Kings–Kern Divide. The mountain, located on the boundary between the two parks, had been selected the previous summer.[34] A party of park rangers ascended the peak that morning, and, after establishing radio communications with a public event at Lodgepole, they formally christened the massive granite summit as media representatives listened in.

Two weeks later, the NPS convened the final and most significant event of the centennial year, the Sequoia and Kings Canyon National Parks' "Second Century Conference." Chaired by NPS Management Assistant William Tweed and educator Richard Stowell, of Ventura, and held at Beetle Rock in the Giant Forest, the conference brought together a broadly selected spectrum of perspectives to consider the future of Sequoia and Kings Canyon. The fifty attendees came not only from the NPS, but also from groups as varied as the Automobile Club of Southern California, Backcountry Horsemen of America, San Joaquin Valley Air Pollution Study Agency, Sierra Club, USFS, GSI, California Air Resources Board, and a number of colleges and universities. Dale Crain, representing the National Parks and Conservation Association, presented a keynote talk, in which he both celebrated the successes of the national park system to date and outlined a series of challenges clearly visible on the horizon. Crain identified several trends as particularly threatening. In his talk, he worried about demographic change that weakened societal support for the national parks and changes in government that were shifting money away from natural resources.[35]

The following morning, NPS Alaska Regional Director Boyd Evison, a past superintendent at Sequoia and Kings Canyon, shifted the focus towards the importance of science and education, a theme that was strongly reinforced by the next speaker, Jerry Franklin, of the University of Washington. Adding more than little irony to the emphasis was the fact that, during the conference, a budget dispute in Washington, D.C., had led to a government shutdown, and all the parks' "non-essential personnel," including interpreters and scientists, had been sent home on administrative leave.

Moving beyond the world of politics, Jerry Franklin pointed out that biological science had some very critical things to say about national parks and their underlying ideas. He reminded the group that "you don't hold anything in place on this planet," even if you want to, and that global change threatened the parks with "tremendous uncertainty." He ended on a somber note, warning that the NPS must identify its "basic assumptions" and realize that it cannot "insulate itself from the progress of science." In many ways, Franklin's words that October morning established themes that would haunt Sequoia and Kings Canyon in the years that would follow.[36]

The physical extent of the High Sierra, as captured by Richard Frear, of the National Park Service in the 1970s, gives Sequoia and Kings Canyon National Parks much of their character. A backpacker can wander for weeks on the twin parks' 700-plus miles of wilderness trails. The photograph shows the Kaweah Basin, looking southwest from above Kern Point.

CHAPTER TEN

The Challenge of a Second Century (1990–2015)

As predicted at the second-century conference, new and unprecedented challenges awaited Sequoia and Kings Canyon National Parks in the years ahead. Even as the long-projected restoration of the Giant Forest area moved toward completion, external issues deeply threatened the integrity of the parks. These new challenges included problems as varied as invasion by growers of marijuana, increasing limitations on the parks' ability to manage fire, recognition of the impacts of regional air pollution, and acceptance of the fact that global climate change seemed likely to change profoundly the parks' natural systems. At the same time, powerful demographic and cultural shifts in California's population and changing thoughts about the role of government seemed likely to prove just as significant. The second century did not begin easily for the twin parks of the southern Sierra.

ENDURING PARKS IN A CHANGING WORLD

Helping to define the era was a pattern of significant demographic change in Central California. Between 1990 and 2013, Tulare County's population grew from 368,000 to 454,000 residents; during the same period, neighboring Fresno County saw its population increase from 798,000 to 955,000.[1] Equally important was the demographic shift that saw persons of Hispanic descent increase to more than sixty percent of Tulare County's residents and fifty percent of Fresno County's. Increasingly, the view westward from the parks looked out over a world of sprawling cities and shifting cultural identity.

Significantly, this continued rapid increase in regional population, which mirrored larger trends in California as whole, was not reflected in visitation to the parks. After decades of steady increase, park use remained largely flat after 1980 (see Appendix A). Sequoia first reported more than 1,000,000 visitors in 1975, yet, between 1988 and 2015, the park surpassed that milestone only fourteen times. At Kings Canyon, after changes were made in the way the visitation was calculated, the northern park began reporting significantly lower numbers. Between 1996 and 2015, reported annual visitation at Kings Canyon only once exceeded 600,000 persons.[2] Visitation in the wilderness and backcountry mirrored the same phenomena. During the first decade of the new century, the National Park Service (NPS) calculated that wilderness users in the two parks averaged between 18,000 and 22,000 persons annually, a level approximately half that reported during the peak years of the 1970s.[3]

This continuing plateau in park-visitation levels reflected larger patterns, for visitation across the entire national park system stopped growing in the 1990s. In fact, during this period, visitation as a percentage of the national population declined. Critics drew conflicting messages from this shift. Some argued that the parks needed to "modernize" themselves and provide more enticing recreational experiences. Others saw not only an expression of more complex patterns, but also the maturation of a highly competitive recreational market that offered an almost unimaginable variety of options.

At Sequoia and Kings Canyon, even as overall visitation remained essentially flat, the nature of the parks' users shifted in important ways. Reflecting changes in regional population, traditional "Anglo" families constituted a reduced portion of visitation to the park, while use by California's Hispanic and Asian populations as well as by international travelers grew. For the first time in their history, the parks began to sound genuinely cosmopolitan on many summer afternoons, with multiple languages being spoken at places like the General Grant and General Sherman Trees. At the same time, increases in Hispanic and Asian visitation, much of it coming from first-generation immigrants, challenged the parks to master new communication skills and redesign facilities to meet the needs of extended family groups that often exceeded in size the Anglo family groups that had dominated visitation in earlier times. This led to the redesign of some of the parks' camping and picnicking sites.

With visitation levels relatively static and the character of visitors continuing to evolve, the parks' managers found themselves facing a new set of issues. The demand for campsites in the frontcountry eased, especially on summer holiday weekends, as did interest in traditional rustic housekeeping cabins. The fact that overall camping in the two parks saw little growth in a time of rapid regional population growth demonstrated the changing recreational role of the two parks.

A visitor study in 2012 documented many of these trends. Visitation remained primarily California-based, with seventy-three percent of park users coming from the Golden State. At the same time, demographic diversity showed that twenty-one percent of visitors came from outside the United States, and twenty-one percent self-identified as Hispanic and another eleven percent as Asian.[4] Perhaps the most distinctive result was that barely ten percent of all visitors reported staying overnight in either the parks' lodging or government campgrounds. Most visitors (seventy-eight percent) still visited the parks for more than a single day, but now the great majority of them (sixty-eight percent) stayed outside the parks at night. This involved the use of motels in places such as Three Rivers, Visalia, and Fresno as well as lodging and campgrounds located within the neighboring Sequoia National Forest. The extensive facilities built in recent years at Hume Lake also provided a base for many visitors. All of this reflected a major shift in park use from the days when the great majority of visitors resided in the parks, often for long periods, while they hiked, fished, and enjoyed ranger-guided walks.[5]

THE ROAD TO WUKSACHI

Within this context of change, the biggest single operational challenge of the 1990s for park managers remained the restoration of the Giant Forest. The 1980 *Giant Forest/Lodgepole Development Concept Plan* had laid out a general vision for the redevelopment of the area but left much detail undefined. As the 1990s began, questions about those details became the focus of park managers. At Clover Creek, a significant start had been made on the construction of physical infrastructure to support the new development site for concessions, but no one yet knew what would ultimately be built there or by whom. Numerous questions also haunted the parts of the project located physically within the Giant Forest. The 1980 *DCP* had called for the removal of all parking from the grove and its relocation to a 1,700-vehicle, multi-story parking garage. But the potential cost of this proposed structure and the transportation system that would be required to support it seemed highly problematic. And what about the biological restoration that would be required once the nearly 300 buildings slated for removal actually disappeared?

Responsibility for addressing these questions fell to a new team. Superintendent Tom Ritter came on board in January 1989, replacing Jack Davis. Working closely with Superintendent Ritter to manage the Giant Forest project were Scott Ruesch, the new chief of maintenance, and William Tweed, who assumed responsibility for the parks' planning and concessions management functions. During the next decade, Ruesch would oversee the design and construction program, while Tweed coordinated planning. Supporting this small group of park-based managers was the professional staff of the NPS's Denver Service Center (DSC). During the next several years, the staff at Sequoia worked closely with DSC's Western Team to assemble a complex, interdisciplinary working group that included landscape architects, engineers, planners, specialists in environmental compliance, the management of concessions, and contracts. All would be needed to move the project forward.

Helping to define this new phase in the Giant Forest restoration project was a new name for the Clover Creek site. Few at the park liked calling the site "Clover Creek," a name applied before the creation of the park by cattlemen. The actual creek, far from being adorned with clover, was incised into barren granite, and it did not even flow directly through the development area. A contest began to find a new name. The winning proposal, submitted by Chief Park Interpreter Larry Waldron, harkened back to the parks' history. Henceforth, the development area adjacent to Clover Creek would be known as "Wuksachi Village." The name came from the band of Western Mono Indians, who had long made their home in what later became the northwestern section of Sequoia National Park. The new name was distinctive, all agreed, and its origins paralleled the name of Potwisha Campground, which celebrated another Western Mono band.

In the fall of 1991, at one of the periodic "work sessions" that brought together staff from the DSC, Western Regional Office in San Francisco, and the twin parks, DSC planners presented a briefing on the overall situation at Sequoia National Park. Many problems needed attention. With existing concessioner Guest Services, Inc. (GSI) standing on the sidelines, the issue now before the NPS was to develop economically feasible plans for Wuksachi without GSI's input. This puzzle brought the NPS to a momentous decision: The government would design the new lodges itself. In the Giant Forest, meanwhile, conditions continued to deteriorate. Wastewater systems there had reached a critical state, with the leaking collection system spilling raw sewage regularly and the treatment facility failing entirely to meet state standards. Work to date had also disclosed the need for more planning for the Giant Forest's new day-use facilities. How would visitors move about within the grove? Was the parking garage proposal in the development concept plan (DCP) feasible? And what about the proposed public transportation system?[6]

By the spring of 1992, park managers were working with DSC planners and designers to address many of these issues. Key to this new round of planning was the concept of the "visitor experience." If the NPS was going to design the new lodges at Wuksachi Village without significant input from its concessioner, the agency would do so by envisioning facilities that would provide a quality national park experience. To bring this new approach into focus, the project team convened a "design charrette," an intensive team meeting, at Lodgepole in late April 1992. Desired products included a new program for the development of concessions, a phasing plan to coordinate construction, and an architectural concept package that would define the various types of accommodations. A long list of "givens" provided a starting point for the new planning effort. These included the requirement that the development be attractive to private development, that the recently completed architectural guidelines be followed, and that the utility and roadwork completed to date be incorporated to the greatest degree possible.[7]

The charrette had the desired effect of jump-starting a new design effort for Wuksachi Village. It also formally killed the "grand lodge" proposal for Wuksachi that had been on the table since it was first proposed by GSI in 1984. Fresh analysis of the concept concluded that such a building would not be economically feasible and that it conflicted with the park's new *Architectural Character*

Guidelines, which called for smaller buildings that would be subordinate to their natural settings. For similar reasons, the charrette also killed any further discussion of moving existing motel units and cabins to Wuksachi. As a result, in January 1993, the NPS purchased GSI's remaining possessory interest in the Giant Forest for an additional $1,868,493 and added the buildings to the list of structures to be razed, once they were closed.[8] GSI had now, in essence, closed out most of its investment in Sequoia National Park, a factor that further weakened the company's interest in the future of the park.[9]

The NPS again engaged the firm of Esherick, Homsey, Dodge, and Davis, this time to lead the Wuksachi design effort. Supporting the firm were subordinate companies that specialized in landscape architecture, resort management, and industrial kitchen design.[10] By September 1992, the design team had completed a first draft of a "Wuksachi Village Facilities Concept Plan" that provided four alternative visions. As the work continued, in June 1993, architect George Homsey, the NPS regional concessions chief, and park staff met with the resort-management consultants in Oregon to make choices. After this, work on the concept plan progressed quickly, and, by September, Homsey and his team had produced what they called a "preliminary program" for the proposed new complex.[11]

The 1993 plan for Wuksachi differed significantly from that developed a decade earlier, when the NPS had attempted to work with GSI. Instead of a central "High Vista Lodge" surrounded by motel units and cabins moved from the Giant Forest, Wuksachi would now consist of four separate clusters of accommodations, each connected by pedestrian walkways to a central dining and retail center. An economic analysis of the plan concluded that a development that included two of the four proposed accommodations areas and the "village center," together with support facilities, would cost $33,000,000 and produce a return on investment of 9.8 percent, which was tantalizingly close to the government's goal of ten percent.[12] Armed with a plan that it liked and that also seemed to be economically feasible, the NPS felt that it was finally ready to move forward with a concessions contract to build Wuksachi Village.

OUT WITH THE OLD—IN WITH THE NEW

Into this picture entered a new player: the California Regional Water Quality Control Board. In 1994, even as the Park Service was finalizing its plan for Wuksachi Village, the board reminded the NPS that state water engineers had allowed the seriously deficient wastewater collection and treatment systems in the Giant Forest to remain open only because the NPS had promised, in 1980, to close those facilities in the near future. More than a decade had now passed, the board noted, and the time had come to close the utility systems in the Giant Forest. Such a closure, of course, meant that all remaining visitor facilities in the grove would have to shut their doors. Caught in a difficult situation, the NPS had no choice but to negotiate. With the opening date for the new lodging at Wuksachi still highly uncertain, the NPS responded to the Water Quality Control Board by proposing a five-year-long phase-out of the old facilities in the Giant Forest. The first service to go away would be winter accommodations in the grove, and this would be followed, during the next several years, by the scheduled closure of one area after another.[13] Pinewood and Lower Kaweah would go first, to be followed by the Giant Forest Lodge area adjacent to Round Meadow. The last facilities to close would be the motel units in Upper Kaweah and the adjoining Giant Forest Village complex, which would be allowed to operate through the summer of 1998.[14] The state accepted the proposal. The NPS now knew that Wuksachi had to open no later than 1999 to provide uninterrupted service.

Concessioner GSI's long-term contract expired in December 1991, and, after that date, the company's presence in the parks relied upon year-to-year contract extensions. Based on its 1974 contract, which included a "limited preferential right of renewal," GSI believed it held a position that would allow it to retain control of the concessions business at Sequoia and Kings Canyon National Parks under any new contract. In the spring of 1995, the NPS issued business prospectuses for two new concessions contracts. The fact that there were two proposed contracts was the first surprise. Since the early 1920s, when Director Stephen Mather had pushed to consolidate contracts with concessioners in order to facilitate larger and better-financed operations, Sequoia and General Grant and, later, Sequoia and Kings Canyon had enjoyed one primary concession company. Now, in a major policy change, the NPS proposed to split the concessions operation into two separate units, one for each park. Driving this decision was the agency's conclusion, based on the 1988 plan for Grant Grove, that the NPS needed a major investment in concessions not only at Wuksachi in Sequoia, but also at General Grant in Kings Canyon National Park. All the lodging at the key location in the northern park occupied structures built before 1940, and many of these had not aged well. The solution the NPS selected was to split the concession business into two separate companies with two fully separate contracts. Each would be responsible for building a new lodge.

Since GSI still held a limited preferential right of renewal, it was clear to all interested parties that this game was really the existing concessioner's to win or lose. Thus, it came as no surprise, when the bidding period ended on August 20, 1995, that GSI submitted the only bid. What came next, however, was a surprise, especially to the company. Believing it still held substantial leverage, GSI had submitted plans in its bid packages that differed significantly from the agency's requirements. It did not take the NPS long to respond: To the shock of GSI, the agency declared the concessioner's bid "unresponsive" and informed the company that, by not responding positively to the government's proposal, it had forfeited its preferential rights. GSI's initial response was to threaten litigation, but cooler heads prevailed within the company, and the threatened lawsuit did not materialize. By October, the government was re-advertising the two concession opportunities, this time without preferential rights for any operator. The deadline for submitting bids was set for February 21, 1996.[15]

By June 1996, the NPS was ready to announce the results of the second round of bidding for the two contracts. A new company made up of Monterey-area interests submitted a responsive bid for the Kings Canyon concession opportunity and was awarded that contract. The agreement there included a commitment to build a new thirty-room lodge at Grant Grove. The news for Sequoia was not so positive. Once again, the government did not receive a responsive bid for Wuksachi and the other Sequoia operations. As Superintendent Mike Tollefson, who had replaced Tom Ritter in January 1995, put it in the news release: "We are disappointed but not discouraged. We consciously aimed high . . . looking for the best option for park visitors."[16] In truth, park management was more than a little discouraged. Finding a company willing to build Wuksachi had proven more difficult than anyone had imagined.[17]

GSI received yet another short-term extension of its contract at the beginning of 1996, this time to run through October 31 of that year.[18] As the year progressed, it became apparent that the 1996 season would be the company's last at Sequoia and Kings Canyon. The long-time concessioner had by now sold all of its possessory interest in its Giant Forest facilities to the government and had seen its preferential right of contract renewal cancelled. By early summer, there was also a new concessioner in the wings waiting to take over GSI's operations in Kings Canyon National Park. Pondering all this, GSI concluded that it had no reason to remain and began making plans to pull out altogether when its contract expired in October. This presented the NPS with yet another concessions problem. As promised earlier to the Water Quality Control Board, the commercial facilities in the Giant Forest would close for good in the fall of 1998, but, in the meantime, someone needed to operate them during the summers of 1997 and 1998. In desperation, the government approached its new Kings Canyon concessioner and asked it to assume responsibility for the two final years of operations in the Giant Forest. The company, now organized as Kings Canyon Park Services (KCPS), agreed, and, when it began operations on November 1, 1996, it became responsible not only for Kings Canyon National Park, but also for the final two seasons at the Giant Forest and associated facilities at Lodgepole and Bearpaw Meadow.

Moving forward to carry out its contractual responsibilities, KCPS began to plan new accommodations for Grant Grove. The 1988 *DCP* for Grant Grove had already designated a location for a new lodge between the existing Grant Grove Lodge and the Meadow Camp's rustic housekeeping cabin area. During the 1920s, the NPS had developed this site as its maintenance yard, but most of those functions had long since moved elsewhere. Responding to the parks' *Architectural Character Guidelines*, KCPS designed and won approval for an L-shaped, two-story lodge that had strong rustic elements. Construction began on what would become the "John Muir Lodge," and, after a much delayed building process, the lodge opened formally on April 21, 2000.

With the concessioner situation at Kings Canyon National Park moving forward, the NPS initiated yet another effort to find a concessioner to build Wuksachi. A revised bid package went out in September 1997, and, this time, to its great relief, the NPS succeeded in attracting a responsive bidder.[19] The new proposal came from Delaware North Companies (DNC), a large, privately held hospitality and food-service company based in Buffalo, New York. Several years earlier, DNC had won the concessions contract in Yosemite National Park, and now it provided a bid the NPS could accept for building and operating Wuksachi Village. The resulting contract, signed in April 1998 and good for fifteen to thirty years, depending upon the ultimate level of investment, accepted a level of development that was less than the NPS desired. The first phase of construction at Wuksachi, which was all the new company firmly committed to, called for three thirty-four-room lodges to be built in the South Terrace area together with a village center containing a dining room, registration/lobby area, and gift shop. Housing for employees would be minimal in the first phase, which was estimated to require an investment by DNC of about $15,000,000.

After that, matters moved quickly. DNC broke ground at Wuksachi in a small ceremony on July 1, 1998, and the company pushed construction forward aggressively in succeeding months. Meanwhile, in the Giant Forest, the Kings Canyon company oversaw the final summer of commercial operations within the Giant Forest, which by now had been reduced to only the eighty-three motel units in the Kaweah Area and the adjoining cafeteria and market. On Saturday, September 26, 1998, the Sequoia and Kings Canyon National Parks Foundation held a final banquet at Beetle Rock, and the last of the Giant Forest's accommodations closed a few days later. At Wuksachi, construction continued through the winter of 1998–1999, and the new lodge opened quietly on May 14, 1999. After a few weeks of test operations, DNC staged a formal dedication on June 10. The goal of removing commercial facilities from the Giant Forest had at long last been achieved.

NEW VISIONS FOR THE GIANT FOREST

Even as the effort to build Wuksachi moved forward, many questions remained unanswered regarding the future of the Giant Forest area. In early 1994, the NPS initiated an effort to develop a detailed plan for new day-use facilities within the grove. With advice in hand from Regional Director Albright in San Francisco that the 1,700-car parking garage proposed in the 1980 *DCP* was too expensive to build, NPS staff addressed the challenge of coming up with an alternate vision for making the grove work. The big questions were: What role would public transportation play, and, critically, where would visitors' automobiles and RVs (recreational vehicles) be parked?

By early summer, the planning team at the DSC had worked out several alternatives for the grove. A "no action" alternative assumed that the grove would be developed exactly as proposed in the 1980 *DCP,* the approach the NPS knew it could not afford to implement. In contrast to this now-too-expensive concept, the planners offered three additional alternatives. One preserved all of the grove's existing roads and parking areas in their existing state, a direction that did little to solve the area's many problems. To implement this plan, no visitor shuttle service would be needed. A second alternative dispersed both parking and visitors. A shuttle system would connect parking areas at the site of the old Sunset Rock Campground (270 spaces), Giant Forest Village (254), Pinewood (150), and Wolverton (300). Access to the General Sherman Tree and the Moro Rock/Crescent Meadow corridor would come via the shuttle system from these parking areas. A third new alternative, described as "transitional," maintained only eighty seasonal parking spaces at the site of Giant Forest Village and concentrated most summer visitors to one of two large parking areas at either Sunset Rock (380 parking slots) and Wolverton (300). Again, access to the General Sherman Tree and the Moro Rock/Crescent Meadow corridor would be by shuttle bus.[20]

In late August, the planning team presented the draft alternatives to Regional Director Albright, who knew the Giant Forest well, since he had served as the superintendent of Sequoia and Kings Canyon from 1975 to 1977. After listening to the presentation, Albright said that he liked the idea of using the previously disturbed areas at Sunset Rock and Pinewood as parking areas, but he was uncomfortable with the planned reliance on a mandatory shuttle system for visitors. This was not likely to be funded in the "foreseeable future," he warned. He asked the planners to consider a visitor reservation system that would allow continued use of the Moro Rock/Crescent Meadow road by private vehicles.[21]

During the winter of 1994–1995, the planning team worked to finalize a plan and environmental compliance package for the Giant Forest. Arguments continued about how many parking places were required and what role a shuttle might play, and a transportation analyst was added to the team. In May, the DSC team completed the *Draft Interim Implementation and Forest Restoration Plan/Environmental Assessment, Giant Forest, Sequoia National Park, California.*[22] The title emphasized the temporary nature of the plan and promised that the NPS still intended to implement the 1980 *DCP* in its entirety at some unspecified future date. Despite a winter of spirited debate within the team, the draft plan advanced essentially the same alternatives that had first been laid out internally the previous August. Interestingly, the document did not identify a preferred alternative, an admission the government was not yet sure where it wanted to go.

As required by the National Environmental Policy Act (NEPA), the NPS sought public comment on the draft plan. Meetings occurred in San Francisco, Visalia, Bakersfield, Three Rivers, Los Angeles, and Buena Park.[23] The park also organized an effort to generate comment directly from the park's visitors, and fourteen "Future of Giant Forest" workshops occurred at either Giant Forest Lodge or Lodgepole Visitor Center. By October, an analysis of the 260 worksheets generated by these events provided a window into what visitors and other concerned citizens thought of the proposed plan. The feedback was mixed. While the data suggested that ninety-two percent of visitors would accept a transportation system and eighty-five percent were willing to pay for the service, the reaction to the proposed major parking development at Sunset Rock was very negative. Many responses argued that the site had recovered nicely since the campground there had closed two decades earlier and that the area should not be re-disturbed. Looking over all the comments received during the summer, park management concluded that it did not yet have a workable plan.[24]

Superintendent Tollefson now pulled his staff together with the goal of developing a park-generated alternative more in tune with local conditions and visitor attitudes. A concept quickly emerged. The proposed parking at Sunset Rock disappeared, to be replaced by 240 parking spaces across the Generals Highway from the interpretive center proposed for the Giant Forest's old 1928 market building. All of these parking spaces would occupy previously disturbed lands. Moreover, the proposed parking would be within easy walking distance of the new museum. To provide access to the General Sherman Tree, the plan proposed that up to 300 parking spaces be developed a quarter mile uphill from the tree on a site just outside the giant sequoia grove that had long been used by the NPS as a borrow pit and log dump. A shuttle system would connect all the major features in the grove with Lodgepole and Wuksachi, and the Moro Rock/Crescent Meadow Road would ultimately close to public use. To meet the needs of day-use visitors, Pinewood would become a picnic area.[25] The day after the park finished its plan, Tollefson and his team sat down with the DSC planning team. Two days of hard debate followed, but, when the meetings ended, the park plan had prevailed. As the summary memo put it: "Alternatives have been explored to the point of exhaustion . . . ," and the NPS needed to heed public comment "to not develop Sunset Rock but rather use Lower Wolverton and Upper/Lower Kaweah for parking . . . "[26]

After this, events moved forward quickly. Superintendent Tollefson sent the head of the park planning team to DSC to draft the new planning documents. All the key players addressed the resulting package at meetings in Denver that began on December 5, 1995.[27] By late January, the document, now entitled *Interim Management Plan and Finding of No Significant Impact, Giant Forest, Sequoia National Park*, had been finalized.[28] In a departure from the usual outline, the plan included a special "Discussion" section that asked and then answered basic questions about the plan. Included were statements that the plan was driven by the realization that the cost of the proposed parking garage was "currently prohibitive" and that the NPS had abandoned the Sunset Rock idea because of negative public comment. Once it went out, the revised plan generated mostly positive public reaction, and, in April, the regional director approved it.[29] It had taken longer than expected, but Sequoia National Park now had a vision to guide its effort to develop visitor facilities for day-use in the Giant Forest.

During the same period, a parallel planning effort explored the question of how to initiate the biological restoration of disturbed sites where buildings and parking lots were slated for removal. Athena Demetry, a Master of Science candidate at the University of Wisconsin-Madison, assumed responsibility for this daunting question. Demetry fell into the role almost by accident when, after having spent the summer of 1991 working in the parks, she became interested in the Giant Forest project and opted to make the proposed restoration of the grove the focus of her graduate research. Pursuing this line of study, she won a National Science Foundation graduate fellowship that allowed her to delve more fully into the subject. Her work grew to become the official approach to the problem, when project managers realized that, although they had millions of dollars to spend in the Giant Forest on physical facilities, the NPS's budget rules forbid any expenditure from the project for research. So, almost by default, Demetry found herself taking the lead.[30]

Demetry's research led to a simple but powerful model for restoring disturbed areas. Working from information collected during the park's prescribed-burn program, Demetry conceptualized that the best way to advance the recovery of a giant sequoia grove would be to envision the removal of human development as a process closely related to the disturbance created in sequoia groves by wildfires. Building on this perspective, she spent the summer of 1994 quantifying the natural distribution of vegetation in fire-produced gaps in the forest canopy. In her 1995 master's thesis, she analyzed this data and produced restoration models that could be applied to disturbed areas as they were cleansed of past human development. At the heart of the restoration process was the assumption that many of the areas within the grove that had been the sites of visitor developments were so significantly impacted that natural regrowth would occur only very slowly. The models put forth an alternative vision that "jump started" the recovery process by either the purposeful planting of native species or the importation of enough woody fuel to allow the areas in question to burn. (Over time, it would become obvious that fire produced better results than planting.) Yet other areas received no treatments at all and thus served as control plots during the monitoring process. No treatments were applied outside the areas where buildings or other developments were removed; in those undeveloped areas natural processes, including fires, were allowed to proceed.[31]

The last commercial facilities designed to service visitors in the Giant Forest area closed in the autumn of 1998. During the next several years, the old buildings were removed, thus finally bringing to an end the many decades of controversy that had shadowed Sequoia National Park during much of the twentieth century. Photographs by Athena Demetry, (top) 1999 and (bottom) 2011.

The actual physical shutdown of the old commercial facilities in the Giant Forest began in the fall of 1994, and, during the next several years, the commercial operations in the Giant Forest continued to shrink. As these areas closed, demolition work began. Representing the times in which they were constructed, the old buildings contained a wide variety a toxic materials, including asbestos, lead paint, and PCB-laden electrical components. Just getting to many of the structures with modern machinery presented another challenge. Steep hillsides and sometimes dense stands of trees made access difficult. The work proceeded slowly. Contractors first erected protective fencing around specimen sequoias and other key trees and then proceeded to salvage fixtures such as iron bathtubs and porcelain toilets. Next, safety-suited hazardous-waste workers removed toxic materials. Only after all this had been accomplished could physical razing of the nearly 300 buildings proceed. Utilizing everything from chainsaws to front-end loaders, crews broke apart the old wooden buildings and fed the resulting debris through giant shredders. The remains of the once-proud structures were reduced to truckloads of wood chips that could be fed into an electrical co-generation plant in the San Joaquin Valley. Proceeding area by area, the entire process took several years to complete. By September 1999, demolition crews were knocking down the Giant Forest's cafeteria, the last of the 282 buildings slated for removal in what had once been Giant Forest Village, Camp Kaweah, Giant Forest Lodge, and Pinewood Shelter Camp.

By the time demolition ended, only a handful of original structures remained. Most visible was the Giant Forest's historic market, which now began its metamorphosis into an interpretive center. Also retained were a nearby comfort station and a ranger house, the latter intended to ensure that someone was in the area at night. Across the street, in the Upper Kaweah Area, only a single building survived, the Beetle Rock Recreation Hall. The *Interim Management Plan* called for this building to become an education center for the park's visitors, but since the federal plan for the Giant Forest did not include funding for the conversion, responsibility for it fell to the Sequoia and Kings Canyon National Parks Foundation, which eventually raised $250,000 to support the rehabilitation of the building.

As work progressed at the site of the old village, the area took on a distinctly new appearance. Where visitor cars had once parked, a pedestrian plaza took shape with interpretive exhibits. A roofed pavilion, designated as the "Trail Center," was erected to serve as a portal to the area's extensive trail system, including the new "Big Trees Trail," a fully accessible, self-guided nature trail that took visitors on a one-mile-long loop to the many large specimen sequoias at Round Meadow. All of this landscape work, as called for in the *Architectural Character Guidelines*, featured rustic design.

The conversion of the old market into an interpretive facility took several years. First, the building, designed by Gilbert Stanley Underwood, of Ahwahnee Hotel fame, had to be rehabilitated. This involved stripping the seventy-year-old edifice of decades of accretions and then repairing or replacing worn elements, including its roof and flooring. Installation of modern utility systems, appliances, and insulation followed. Finally, the exhibits arrived, telling the story of the Giant Forest and its sequoias. Attempting to reinforce the traditional national park character of the site, the new facility was christened the "Giant Forest Museum." It opened to the public on December 13, 2001.

Half a mile to the north along the Generals Highway, another construction project took place just outside the giant sequoia zone. Here, workers constructed a new picnic area on the ridge where the rustic cabins of the Pinewood Shelter Camp had once stood. Farther north along the same highway, a larger project moved forward at the General Sherman Tree. Automobile congestion had plagued that area for decades. The existing parking layout, developed in the 1930s, provided fewer than 100 parking spaces, and summer demand far exceeded that number. Lack of parking prevented many visitors from seeing the world's largest tree. Under the *Interim Management Plan*, the area received a major remodeling. Taking advantage of the grade of an abandoned roadway, the General Sherman Tree received an entirely new pedestrian approach. Able-bodied visitors would henceforth visit the tree via a trail leading down into the grove from parking installed on the site of an abandoned gravel pit just outside the sequoia zone. Vehicle access to this new parking area came from the Wolverton Road, and the new parking area contained more than 250 spaces, making it nearly three times as large as the parking area it replaced. Once the new trail opened, crews removed the old parking area to the south of the tree and also rebuilt the small all-year parking area along the Generals Highway to serve as a shuttle bus drop-off point and handicapped parking area. Contracting disputes, litigation, and a change in construction companies delayed the work, and the complex finally opened to the public late in the summer of 2005.

As work on the ground wound up in the Giant Forest, a series of events and awards confirmed the magnitude of what had been accomplished. First to arrive was President George W. Bush, whose staff scheduled a media event for him at the still-unfinished Giant Forest Museum on May 30, 2001. Interior Secretary Gale Norton introduced the president as not only a "compassionate conservative" (his 2000 campaign slogan), but also a "compassionate conservationist." President Bush spoke to the news media and a small audience of invited guests about the importance of America's natural heritage.

A year later, on May 30, 2002, with the Giant Forest Museum now open, the NPS organized a formal event to celebrate the completion of the museum and all of its supporting infrastructure, including the Big Trees Trail and the Beetle Rock Education Center. The following summer, another event rededicated the Booker T. Washington Tree, which had been designated by U.S. Army officer Charles Young while serving as the acting superintendent of the park in 1903 and promptly forgotten by his successors.[32] In 2004, responding to a groundswell of interest about Young, the NPS formally named a tree for the early black park manager, giving him an honor

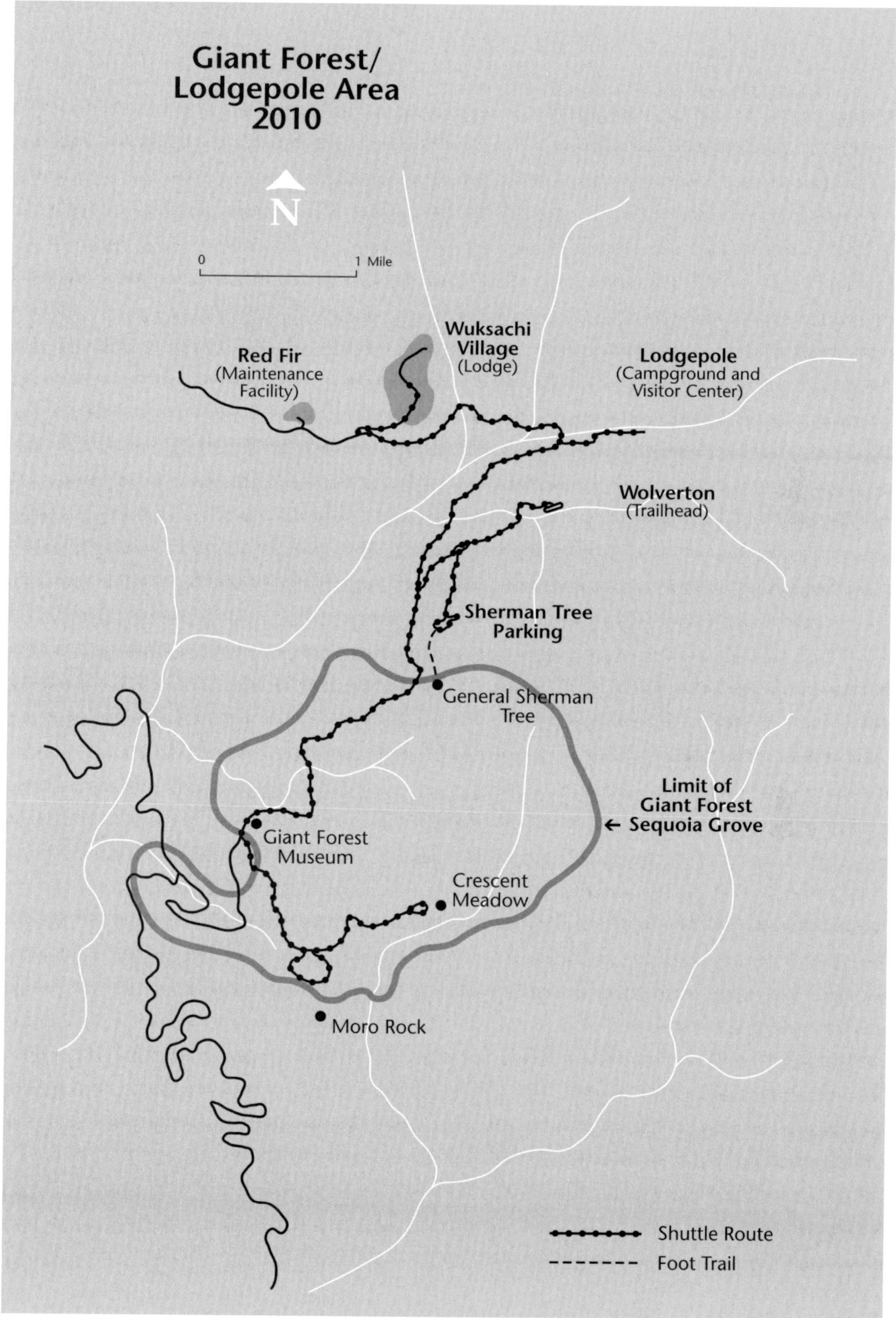

Giant Forest/
Lodgepole Area
2010
N
0
1 Mile
Red Fir
(Maintenance
Facility)
Wuksachi
Village
(Lodge)
Lodgepole
(Campground and
Visitor Center)
Wolverton
(Trailhead)
Sherman Tree
Parking
General Sherman
Tree
Limit of
Giant Forest
Sequoia Grove
Giant Forest
Museum
Crescent
Meadow
Moro Rock
Shuttle Route
Foot Trail

few had received since the wide-scale naming of trees ended during the late 1930s. Finally, in October 2007, at its national convention in San Francisco, the American Society of Landscape Architects recognized the entire Giant Forest project, awarding it a General Design Honor Award and lauding it as an "unprecedented restoration effort" that demonstrated "true leadership [and] sustained vision . . . "[33]

Even as the awards trickled in, the effort continued to implement one last key element of the Giant Forest plan: a shuttle for visitors. Serious planning for the shuttle began at a transportation charrette in November 2000. The challenge was how to test and implement the transportation vision embedded in the 1996 *Interim Management Plan*. For the next several years, a series of teams studied and restudied the proposal, analyzing both its potential benefits and likely costs. Planning efforts peaked during 2004, but it was not until the summer of 2007 that the service finally began. Authorized initially as a three-year-long experiment and funded by the designation of $10.00 of the park's entrance fee as a "transportation fee," the free, summer-only service centered at the Giant Forest Museum and ran to Moro Rock and Crescent Meadow to the south and the General Sherman Tree, Lodgepole, and Wuksachi to the north. This within-park system soon proved its worth to visitors. Use grew quickly from 136,000 riders in the summer of 2007 to more than 437,000 in 2013. The NPS also began providing shuttle service in the area during busy winter holiday periods. Using non-park funds, the City of Visalia also initiated a new summer-only bus line linking the Giant Forest Museum with the city. Working as an official cooperator, the city government of Visalia ran both the within-park and Visalia-connection bus systems.

A NEW LOOK AT THE TWO PARKS AS A WHOLE

The impending completion of the Giant Forest restoration project drew the attention of the Park Service to the need for broad-scale planning to pull the rest of the two parks into the twenty-first century. No general park-wide planning had been undertaken at Sequoia and Kings Canyon since the completion of the 1971 *Master Plan*, an effort that predated the decision to move commercial facilities out of the Giant Forest. In the years since the completion of that document, the NPS had restyled its park-wide plans and re-named them "general management plans" (GMP). During the mid-1990s, with the *Master Plan* for Sequoia and Kings Canyon now more than two decades old, park managers at the twin parks set out to obtain funding to undertake a multiple-year-long project to develop a GMP. By 1997, they succeeded, and that summer a newly constituted "GMP Team" issued its first newsletter and scheduled scoping meetings with park visitors to begin the effort to identify key issues.

Building on public feedback received from the initial scoping exercise, the planning team, led by DSC planner Susan Spain and park-based NPS Senior Scientist David Graber, published a planning workbook, in the spring of 1999, that generated 745 responses. Out of this feedback came both a much clearer view of what the participating public cared about and a basis for developing a series of planning alternatives. The public responses also documented a phenomenon that would shadow the entire decade-long GMP effort. Even as the NPS sought to define long-term philosophical goals for managing the two parks, public comment focused primarily on a small number of controversial issues.

To the NPS, the GMP was first and foremost about providing a management philosophy for the parks in a changing world. Were the guiding principles of the parks' first century still applicable in its second century? How could the parks relate more successfully to California's changing demographic structure? What facilities would the parks need to meet the needs of twenty-first-century visitors? The GMP would also need to address significant legal requirements.[34] One of these resulted from the passage, in 1987, of legislation that designated both the South Fork of the Kern River in Sequoia National Park and the Middle and South Forks of the Kings River in Kings Canyon National Park as units of the National Wild and Scenic River System. This designation required that the NPS develop plans for the protection and management of the three river corridors, a goal the GMP would need to address.

In addition, other questions had arisen, including whether the *Interim Management Plan* decisions for the Giant Forest area would be made permanent and whether a parks-wide public transportation system was needed. Another set of questions arose from the designation of additional cultural resources within the parks, a process that had barely begun in 1971. By the late 1990s, the two parks contained several dozen sites listed on or eligible for nomination to the National Register of Historic Places (National Register). These represented everything from pioneer cattle ranches to buildings associated with the New Deal–era programs of the 1930s. In the Mineral King area, questions had arisen as to whether the special-use-permit cabins constituted a cultural resource and what such a designation might mean for the cabins and families that occupied them. Local Congressman George Radanovich had taken a particular interest in the fate of the Mineral King permit-cabin community, and the NPS promised the congressman that the GMP would address questions related to that issue. This promise undoubtedly strengthened the parks' bid for planning money for the project.

Unfortunately for the agency, it was also this last question that became the most visible and debated GMP issue, eclipsing several broader issues that had larger implications for the parks as a whole. The legislation in 1978 that ended Walt Disney's dream of a ski development at Mineral King and added the area to Sequoia National Park required that the NPS phase out private cabin privileges in the area. Permits issued by the U.S. Forest Service (USFS) prior to 1978 authorized approximately sixty specifically "temporary" cabins on public land in the Mineral King area. The legislation allowed the continued use of these summer residences but specified that, after November 1978, permits could be renewed only to the "permittees of record" and that permits could not be transferred, even to heirs. The permittees had grudgingly gone along with these provisions in 1978 in order to bring an end to the proposed ski development, but, as time passed and a generation of permittees began to pass from the scene, the permit-cabin community increasingly chafed against a legal requirement that threatened its continued existence. As the GMP project moved forward, the NPS would hear a great deal about Mineral King and its cabin community.

A second issue surfaced repeatedly during public meetings associated with the GMP, and, although it did not attract as much public comment as the Mineral King cabin question, it also generated considerable passion. These comments revived issues that had led to considerable debate during the mid-1980s, as the parks' *Stock Use and Meadow Management Plan* and *Backcountry Management Plan* were being developed. The parks' 1971 *Master Plan* had called for the long-term phasing out of pack stock in the backcountry of the two parks.[35] Instead, in the years that followed 1971, the NPS had backed away from that decision. The two plans, finalized in 1986, confirmed that shift as well as the continued traditional role of stock in the parks. The new plans even allowed stock to continue to graze in high-altitude meadow areas, a provision that had been phased out on most other national parks. For a segment of high-country users, this shift in policy came as a step backwards and further evidence that the NPS could not be trusted to manage pack stock within the wilderness areas of Sequoia and Kings Canyon.

Out of this controversy arose two lobbying groups which would each play a significant role in the early years of the twin parks' second century. Pack-stock users organized first, affiliating themselves in 1981 as the High Sierra Stock Users. This group played a major role in determining the character of the 1986 plans for the backcountry, and, during that debate, it affiliated with similar groups in Montana, Idaho, and Washington to create a national organization known as the Back Country Horsemen of America. In 1990, reacting to the perceived political effectiveness of the stock users, another group, one that included several individuals who had served as seasonal backcountry rangers at Sequoia and Kings Canyon, created an opposing organization, the High Sierra Hikers Association (HSHA).

The event that brought the hikers' lobby together was a management effort, initiated in 1989, to develop consistent party-size limits for stock and hiking parties in all of the wildernesses of the central and southern Sierra Nevada, including those managed by both the NPS and the USFS. At first, the initiative progressed rapidly. An interagency working group developed a proposal for new, consistent party-size limits of fifteen persons and twenty-five stock animals. Few objected to the proposed limits on party size for humans, but the section dealing with horse and mules was more problematic. The interagency proposal had the effect of reducing stock use significantly on a number of wilderness areas in the national forest, while at the same time increasing the stock limit in Sequoia and Kings Canyon from the previous limit of twenty animals. Some areas administered by the USFS then possessed no limits whatsoever. An interagency letter went out with this proposal to 1,200 wilderness users, and the government received more than 200 responses. Comments ranged widely. There was clear support, according to a USFS analysis, for the fifteen-person limit, but seventy-six percent of the respondents wanted stock to be limited to no more than twenty per party. After reviewing this data, and noting that twenty stock would inadequately support the proposed new party size of fifteen persons, the USFS and NPS moved forward to implement their original recommendation of a twenty-five-animal limit. In April 1991, a notice in *The Federal Register* announced the new limits, and a second notice, in October, formally promulgated the new rules and shared that they would be phased in during the 1992 and 1993 seasons.[36]

Missing from the process, however, was any environmental compliance as required by the National Environment Protection Act (NEPA). As the USFS explained later in an internal briefing book: "We did not feel that it was necessary to go through the NEPA process on this as we felt that it was primarily a social issue, and each of the Forest Supervisors and Superintendents have the authority to promulgate regulations."[37]

The HSHA had opposed this proposal from the beginning. A letter to the NPS, in December 1990, advised that there was no justification to increase group-size limits for stock within the twin parks. During the next year, as the new policies moved toward implementation, the HSHA became increasingly vocal. By November 1991, the association was asking why the NPS was proposing to promulgate these new rules without any environmental compliance, and, in the fall of 1992, the group warned Superintendent Ritter that it was prepared "to take whatever action is necessary" to stop the implementation of the new rules without environmental compliance.[38]

At this point, sensing it was on thinner ice than it preferred to admit, the NPS retreated, suspended the new rules, and initiated the preparation of an environmental assessment for the proposed rules within Sequoia and Kings Canyon. The short document, a mere nine pages, came out in the spring of 1993, and the NPS's Western Regional Office promptly approved a "Finding of No Significant Impact" statement to accompany it.[39]

The HSHA responded by filing suit. *High Sierra Hikers Association v. Roger Kennedy* alleged that, in promulgating the new party-size limits, the NPS had violated both the Wilderness Act of 1964 and NEPA, and the suit sought a permanent injunction voiding the new rules. Judge Claudia Wilken accepted evidence, and, in June 1995, ruled in favor of the hikers' group, declaring that the environmental assessment had been "inadequate" and ordering the NPS to reinstate the previous limit of twenty pack and riding animals per party.[40] Both sides appealed, but the judge's ruling convinced the NPS that it did not have a strong position. A settlement was reached before the appeals could be resolved, and, in the resulting stipulations, negotiated in early 1996, the NPS gave in on nearly all points. It agreed not to change the twenty-animal limit without preparing a full environmental impact statement and also to pay the plaintiffs $50,000 in legal fees.

The outcome in *High Sierra Hikers Association v. Roger Kennedy* confirmed what the NPS already knew: Neither the *Stock Use and Meadow Management Plan* nor the *Backcountry Management Plan* provided adequate guidance for the management of the Sequoia-Kings Canyon Wilderness. As formally designated wilderness, these lands needed to be managed under the tenets of the Wilderness Act. Included in that act were standards such as the "minimum requirement" clause, which specified that management should do only those things in wilderness required to maintain the wilderness in its "untrammeled state," and the "minimum tools" clause, which instructed managers to carry out their actions in as non-mechanized a manner as possible.

The NPS had, in fact, already started work on a "Wilderness Management Plan" for the Sequoia and Kings Canyon National Parks in the winter of 1990–1991. The effort had progressed slowly, but new energy went into the plan as a result of the HSHA's lawsuit. During the summer of 1996, park staff conducted public-scoping workshops in seven cities.[41] More than 200 people attended the meetings, and the NPS received approximately 150 letters of comment. On April 30, 1997, *The Federal Register* published a formal notice that Sequoia and Kings Canyon intended to prepare a plan for wilderness management that would be supported by an environmental impact statement. Still moving forward, the parks issued a *Wilderness Planning Workbook* in the spring of 1998, inviting public comment on nine topics closely tied to management of the parks' wilderness.[42] Shortly after that, however, the effort stalled. The process to draft a management plan for the Sequoia-Kings Canyon Wilderness had collided with the newly initiated *General Management Plan* effort. Under agency policy, the GMP would need to take precedence and set direction for all other plans. Preparation of the wilderness plan would have to wait.

THE GMP MOVES FORWARD

So, in 1999, the Park Service witnessed not the drafting of a wilderness management plan, as had been promised two years earlier, but rather public meetings for a parks-wide GMP. By January 2000, the GMP Team turned the information received at these events into four alternatives.[43] Driving the development of these alternatives was the overarching question: How should the parks respond to issues generated by social change? All four alternatives assumed that the parks would carry out their legally mandated mission of preserving the parks' significant resources "unimpaired for future generations." All four alternatives also assumed that the numerical demand for visitor experiences would continue to grow, as had been the case throughout most of the twentieth century. Beyond that, however, the alternatives differed significantly.

Building around the NEPA-required "no-action" alternative, which would see the parks continue along their current and largely reactive path, the GMP Team developed three new philosophical alternatives. The first of these, which emphasized the protection of natural ecosystems and biodiversity, proposed to reduce visitor use and development, in effect making the parks more of a nature preserve and less of a recreational center. A second alternative, responding to the visitors' comments about wanting the national park experience to remain as unchanged as possible, called for managing the parks to emphasize their traditional character. This alternative would continue to emphasize the experiences and supporting infrastructure that had dominated the parks during a theoretical "golden era" in the years before World War II. A third alternative took yet another path, guiding growth in a manner that would both "preserve basic character and adapt to changing user groups."

As always, these alternatives were released for public comment. Once the comments came in, the team addressed the challenging task of distilling the resulting responses. Out of this analysis rose the draft of a new "preferred" alternative. This approach to parks management came with the awkward title: "Accommodate Sustainable Growth and Visitor Enjoyment, Protect Ecosystem Diversity, and Preserve Basic Character While Adapting to Changing User Groups." Work also began on a draft *Environmental Impact Statement* that would identify and analyze the impacts of the proposed actions upon the human and natural environment.

Further complicating the situation, several additional issues had by now surfaced. These included the designation, in April 2000, of the Giant Sequoia National Monument on USFS lands adjoining the two national parks and the addition, in December 2001, of the Dillonwood grove of giant sequoias to Sequoia National Park. Also affecting the process was the arrival of a new park superintendent, Dick Martin, who replaced Mike Tollefson in January 2001. The biggest change the planners faced, however, was the creation of the Mineral King Road Cultural Landscape District and its listing on the National Register.

The permit-cabin community at Mineral King had long asserted that both the cabins they occupied during the summer months and their human community itself deserved recognition as cultural resources.[44] This point of view had been loudly and clearly voiced during the GMP's scoping process and had been endorsed by local Congressman George Radanovich. The National Historic Preservation Act of 1960 offered little in the way of protection for the human community, but designation of the physical structures seemed more plausible. The NPS did not respond

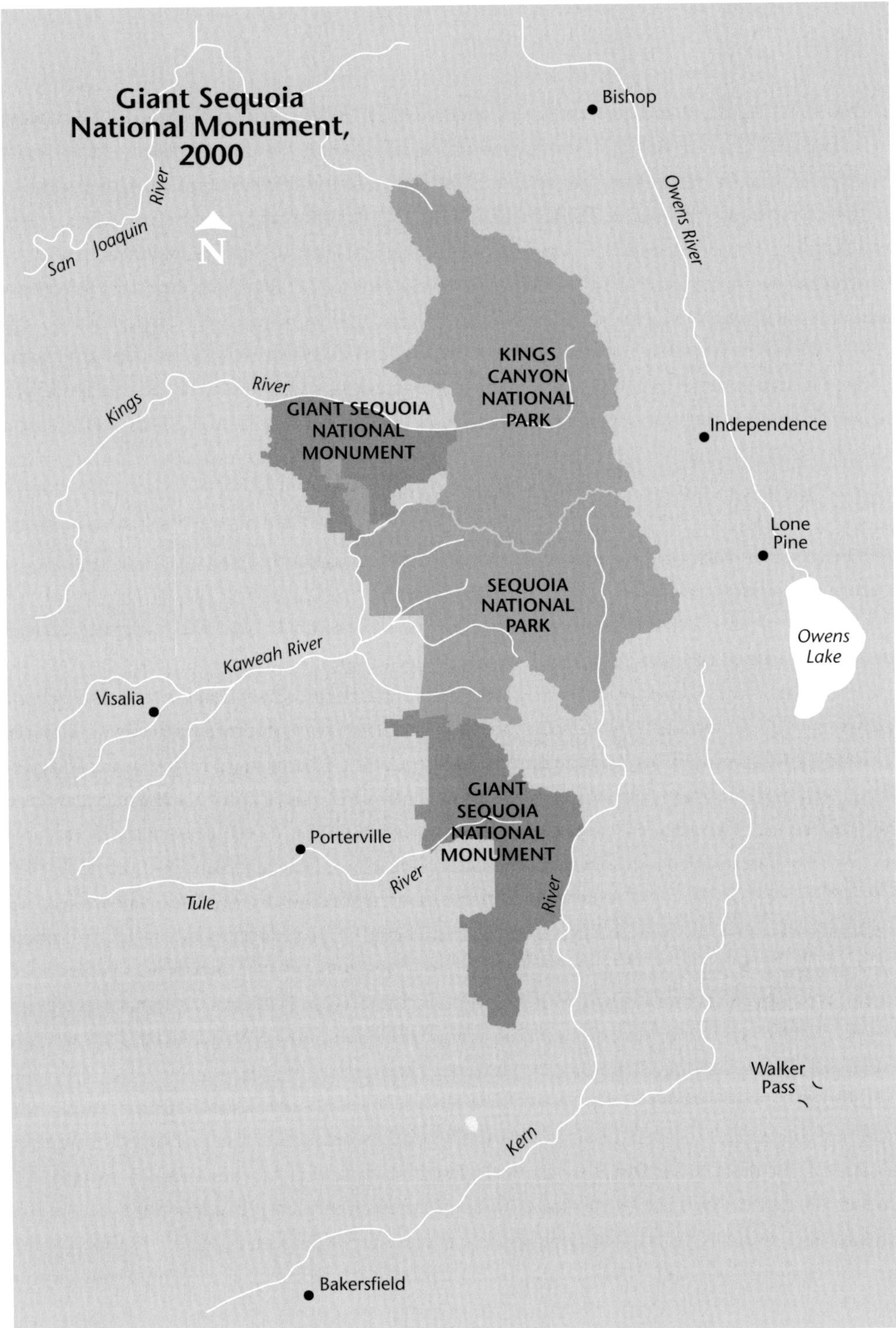
Giant Sequoia
National Monument,
2000
N
San Joaquin River
Bishop
Owens River
KINGS
CANYON
NATIONAL
PARK
Kings River
GIANT SEQUOIA
NATIONAL
MONUMENT
Independence
Lone
Pine
SEQUOIA
NATIONAL
PARK
Owens
Lake
Kaweah River
Visalia
GIANT
SEQUOIA
NATIONAL
MONUMENT
Porterville
Tule River
River
Walker
Pass
Kern
Bakersfield

with enthusiasm to this pressure, but the argument that the buildings deserved study was too powerful to reject, and, ultimately, the agency commissioned a study. In 1999, Ethan Carr, an historian of landscape architecture in the NPS who was based at the agency's DSC, produced a "determination of eligibility" report that recommended the creation of a cultural landscape district that included the entire Mineral King Road corridor within Sequoia National Park.[45] (The concept of a cultural landscape was relatively new at this point to the National Register and centered on the relationship between human activities and landscapes.) Included within the new proposed landscape district were not only the roadway itself, but also sixty-three structures along the way, including a majority of the permit cabins at Cabin Cove and in Mineral King Valley. With some reluctance, the NPS accepted the recommendation and proceeded to prepare a formal nomination of the district to the National Register. The nomination was accepted, and the district achieved formal listing on October 24, 2003.[46]

The determination that a major part of the permit-cabin community at Mineral King needed to be seen as a cultural resource significantly changed the planning game for that portion of the park. The challenge for the NPS was now to find a way to bring together the existing law that ordered the eventual termination of the cabin permits and a cultural-resources program that now saw the structures, if not the people, as historic park features.

By May 2004, when the draft GMP went out to the public for formal comment, it had grown to fill two phone-book-sized paperback volumes. Forming the heart of the effort was a complex matrix in the first volume that explored 395 specific issues, each one addressed five times to specify how it would play out under each of the five alternatives.[47] As the complex title of the preferred alternative suggested, that approach sought middle ground on most significant issues. Highlights included sustaining the parks' natural and culture resources, seeking to make the parks more relevant to the increasingly diverse population of California, and preserving a modified version of the parks' traditional character. Specific details included retaining a role for pack stock in the parks, making the 1997 *Interim Management Plan* for Giant Forest permanent, and committing to removing some of the parks' administrative facilities from within the parks.

The draft plan's approach to questions about the future of the Mineral King permit-cabin community drew immediate public attention. Still attempting to carry out the intent of the 1978 law, the NPS sought to be creative. In its preferred alternative, the agency proposed to acquire and retain the now-historic cabins and partner with either a commercial or nonprofit organization to make the cabins available for public use.[48] Unsurprisingly, the permit-cabin community did not respond favorably to this proposal, and, working through the Mineral King Preservation Society, the permittees negotiated behind the scenes with new local Congressman Devin Nunes.[49] This strategy worked, and the NPS's proposals for the future of the cabins were made moot on

December 8, 2004, when President Bush signed a $388,000,000,000 omnibus federal spending bill that included a clause repealing the 1978 requirement that Mineral King's special-use permits be phased out.

Congress did not intervene in the backcountry's stock issue, but neither did the NPS attempt a full resolution of the issue through the GMP. The draft preferred alternative did cancel the provision in the 1971 *Master Plan* that called for the eventual phase-out of all stock use in the backcountry but then deferred all the resulting questions to a stewardship plan for the wilderness that it promised would be prepared after the GMP was approved.

In response to the draft *General Management Plan* and accompanying *Environmental Impact Statement*, the NPS received another 400 comments, but, as the agency would state when it issued the final *Record of Decision* for the planning package: "Based on careful consideration of all responses received . . . [t]here were no substantive changes as a result of public commentary."[50] Nonetheless, two more years passed before the agency issued its "final" planning documents in November 2006, and yet another year would slide by before the GMP received formal approval from Regional Director Jonathan Jarvis in September 2007.

IMPLEMENTING THE GMP

In many ways, the vision embodied within the 2007 *General Management Plan* confirmed the historically conservative nature of Sequoia and Kings Canyon National Parks. After a decade of work, the plan reiterated that the integrity of the parks' resources remained paramount; that the parks would attempt to connect with diverse user groups but not abandon their traditional character; that overnight facilities would remain largely unchanged; that pack stock had an appropriate role in the backcountry; and that educational programming would be encouraged.[51] Questions about how to manage the permit-cabin community at Mineral King were largely deferred with a promise that the NPS would work with the California State Historic Preservation Officer and the Mineral King Preservation Society to develop a management plan for the cultural landscape district.[52]

Also unresolved by the GMP were many policy and operational issues related to management of the Sequoia-Kings Canyon Wilderness, and the situation there had, if anything, become even more complicated, while the GMP crept toward finalization. During the years that Sequoia and Kings Canyon had been drafting the GMP, the HSHA had been broadening its campaign to reduce the impacts of pack stock in the wilderness areas of the Sierra Nevada. The association's campaign moved along two parallel tracks. On one hand, it involved itself deeply in the twin parks' GMP process by drafting a series of detailed letters about wilderness management and stock use in the parks. In a letter dated October 5, 2004, for example, the association detailed what it argued were deep flaws in the alternatives and analysis that the parks had released earlier that same year. The letter, which ran to twenty-six pages, argued that the NPS had improperly framed its alternatives, failed to consider pertinent information, and ineffectively analyzed the impacts of its proposed actions.[53] A detailed bibliography accompanied the correspondence. A similar document in March 2006, as the NPS moved to finalize the GMP for the two parks, added yet more material.[54] These letters, together with other correspondence, face-to-face meetings, and Freedom of Information Act document requests, all established not only that the HSHA did not agree with the decisions the NPS was making, but also that the HSHA was laying the administrative-record groundwork for a potential lawsuit. In December 2006, in a final "shot across the bow" of the NPS, the association formally requested that NPS Regional Director Jarvis withdraw the essentially complete but not yet approved GMP for Sequoia and Kings Canyon National Parks, an action that did not occur.[55]

At the same time, the HSHA, in cooperation with Wilderness Watch and the Forest Service Employees for Environmental Ethics, initiated a lawsuit against the USFS regarding its management of the Ansel Adams and John Muir Wilderness areas of the Sierra and Inyo National Forests. The lawsuit, known as *High Sierra Hikers Association v. Blackwell*, challenged the joint management plan the forests had finalized, in April 2001, for the two wilderness areas. In its suit, the HSHA argued that the USFS had not only failed in its environmental compliance for the plan, but also, and more significantly, failed to meet the requirements of the Wilderness Act. The argument on this latter point was based on a section of the 1964 law that specified that commercial activities—in this case, commercial packing—be provided in wilderness areas only "to the extent necessary."[56] Although aimed at the USFS, it was clear that the case had broad implications for wilderness areas in national parks as well. A preliminary decision in November 2001 reduced limits for pack station use in the two forest wilderness areas until the USFS could prepare an environmental impact statement.

The case moved forward slowly, and it was not until August 25, 2004, that the court announced the next round of decisions. Magistrate Judge Elizabeth Laporte, presiding over this phase of the suit for the Ninth Circuit Court of Appeals, resolved a number of issues in favor of the HSHA. Not only did she find that the USFS had violated NEPA by failing to consider adequately the impact of commercial stock use authorized by its 2001 wilderness plan, but also that the agency had violated the Wilderness Act by not determining the *extent* to which stock use was necessary to meet the goals of the wilderness management in the John Muir and Ansel Adams Wilderness areas. This latter point, all agreed, was a new interpretation of wilderness law and one with consequences for other areas, including Sequoia and Kings Canyon National Parks.

The HSHA and the USFS continued to battle over the management of the John Muir and Ansel Adams Wilderness areas after 2004, and, by the time the court issued a final judgment, in May 2008, regarding all the issues that had been litigated during the past seven years, it was clear that Judge Laporte had rejected and rewritten key sections of the USFS's plan for the two wildernesses areas. On issue after issue, the USFS's arguments and tentative decisions had failed to hold sway. These successes emboldened the HSHA to prepare for another legal fight. This time it would challenge wilderness management at Sequoia and Kings Canyon.

On September 30, 2009, two years after the approval by the NPS of the *General Management Plan* for Sequoia and Kings Canyon National Parks, the HSHA filed suit against the Department of the Interior to overturn the plan. In its initial filing of *High Sierra Hikers Association v. United States Department of the Interior*, the association asserted that the NPS had violated the Wilderness Act of 1964, the National Park Organic Act of 1916, and the National Environmental Policy Act of 1969. Many of the allegations were the same ones that had prevailed in *High Sierra Hikers Association v. Blackwell*. Citing the extensive administrative record that it had built as a part of the GMP process, the HSHA alleged that the NPS had failed to consider a full range of alternatives in the environmental impact report that supported the GMP. Specifically, although the NPS did propose (and reject) an alternative that would have ended all use of pack stock in the parks, it did not consider alternatives that would have ended grazing in the parks or prohibited stock only in fragile, high-altitude areas. Early in the scoping process, the HSHA had suggested both of these alternatives. After observing closely the six-year-long court battle between the HSHA and the USFS, the NPS sought a different path. Four months after the suit was filed, in January 2010, both the NPS and the association endorsed a court order moving the case into formal mediation.[57] That effort failed, however, and the battle over stock use in the high country, one that had, in theory, been resolved forty years earlier in the parks' 1971 *Master Plan*, entered yet another phase.

In a decision issued by U.S. District Judge Richard Seeborg in January 2012, the court held that, although the NPS had met all NEPA requirements in the preparation of the GMP, it had failed to meet the requirements of the Wilderness Act, as defined in the *Blackwell* ruling. In response, the NPS announced it would suspend the issuing of commercial-use authorizations for wilderness areas in Sequoia and Kings Canyon. Public reaction to this decision in local news media soon took on a highly negative tone, and local Congressman Devin Nunes quickly announced a position in defense of continued use of commercial stock in the parks' wilderness areas. Seeking to moot the ongoing court case, Nunes introduced H.R. 4849, a bill that *required* the NPS to continue to issue permits to its long-time commercial stock users. Support for the bill came not only from Nunes's Republican colleagues, but also from California's two Democratic U.S. senators,

Diane Feinstein and Barbara Boxer. Organizations usually as far apart as the Wilderness Society and the Backcountry Horsemen of America joined the effort. No one, it seemed, except initially the HSHA, was ready to fight for full implementation of Judge Seeborg's ruling. In late May, the bill passed, and the NPS thus received not only permission to continue issuing permits, but also a requirement that the agency complete a wilderness-management plan for the Sequoia-Kings Canyon Wilderness within two years. A new *Wilderness Stewardship Plan* for the two parks was completed in May 2015. The plan, which largely preserved existing management policies, was subsequently challenged unsuccessfully by HSHA in the courts.

Meanwhile, still working to implement the GMP, the NPS also began work on a plan to resolve the remaining management issues associated with the Mineral King area. Following the now-familiar NEPA planning path, the parks initiated a public scoping process. As promised in the GMP, park planners met with staff representing the California State Historic Preservation Officer and representatives from the Mineral King Preservation Society. Public meetings in Three Rivers, Visalia, and Bakersfield, in May 2010, were followed, in June, by a similar event in Mineral King Valley. Written comments were sought, and the park ultimately received thirty-five pieces of correspondence. Comments came in from cabin permittees, the Mineral King Preservation Society, and the HSHA. An analysis of the comments reflected a familiar set of issues. Generally, nearly everyone agreed that Mineral King was a special place and that its character needed to be protected and sustained. Beyond that, significant issues broke the letters into familiar groups. Whether the area needed a pack station generated nearly as many comments as did the question of who should pay to bring the utility systems that supported the cabins into compliance with contemporary health and safety codes.[58] As the planning effort progressed, Mineral King, like the parks' wilderness areas, showed every indication of continuing its long-established capacity to generate controversy.

SEQUOIAS, BOUNDARIES, NEIGHBORS, AND PARTNERS

During the decade that the NPS labored to create the *General Management Plan*, other parties labored to make changes in neighboring parts of the southern Sierra Nevada. Ultimately, these efforts succeeded in making significant modifications to the regional setting of the two parks.

Reflecting on the compromises struck between the NPS and the USFS, in 1926 and 1940, many giant sequoias remained under USFS's management. Most of the Big Trees grew within two geographical zones, both located on the Sequoia National Forest: One set of groves occupied terrain adjoining the old General Grant National Park, while the other groves were south of Sequoia National Park, mostly in the Tule River drainage. Taken together, these two regions contained nearly as many giant sequoias as did the national parks themselves. But, as early as the 1970s, controversies had arisen over the USFS's management of these areas. Working under its multiple-use management policies, the USFS not only logged forest areas that adjoined its sequoia groves but also began to log within the groves, removing pine and fir. USFS staff argued that thinning out the forest by logging achieved many of the same results that fire provided for groves of giant sequoia within the national parks, while at the same time producing lumber. Environmental groups reacted with anger and frustration and initiated a campaign to halt logging within and around the groves.

The full story of this campaign falls outside the scope of this book, but, suffice it to say, by the last year of the Clinton administration, the environmentalists who wanted to force change upon the USFS had gained important political allies. After much internal politicking, the Clinton White House acted, in April 2000, issuing an Antiquities Act proclamation creating a Giant Sequoia National Monument to be managed by the USFS.[59] Comprised entirely of lands that were a part of the Sequoia National Forest, the 327,000-acre monument included most of the USFS's Hume Lake Ranger District in and around the Grant Grove Section of Kings Canyon National Park as well as extensive additional lands to the south of Sequoia National Park. As for ending logging, the proclamation was clear in its intent:

> No portion of the monument shall be considered to be suited for timber production, and no part of the monument shall be used in a calculation or provision of a sustained yield of timber from the Sequoia National Forest. Removal of trees, except for personal use fuel wood, from within the monument area may take place only if clearly needed for ecological restoration and maintenance or public safety.[60]

Both the USFS and the political power structure of Tulare County strongly opposed the creation of the Giant Sequoia National Monument. The county's Board of Supervisors sued to overturn President Clinton's proclamation on the grounds that it failed to comply with the provisions of the Antiquities Act of 1906, which gives the President the authority to designate national monuments. President Clinton's proclamation, they argued, took in too much land that did not contain sequoia trees. The suit reached the U.S. Supreme Court, where the justices rejected it. For its part, the USFS prepared a management plan for the monument that deemed that continued logging within the reserve to be necessary for ecological purposes. Environmental groups challenged the document, and, in 2006, a federal court cancelled the plan and instructed the USFS to try again. This second attempt went better, and the USFS, in September 2012, finally approved a management plan for the monument. This plan guaranteed that on-the-ground management of the controversial reservation would be carried out within the context of twenty-three advisory recommendations made by an independent scientific advisory board.

During these controversies, the NPS maintained a low profile. Park managers at Sequoia and Kings Canyon knew they had little to gain by angering either local environmental groups or the USFS and its friends. What the NPS did know, however, was that, for Sequoia and Kings Canyon, the creation of the national monument was a positive event. No longer did multiple-use management lands, with their timber-production activities, immediately adjoin the two parks. Through President Clinton's proclamation, Sequoia and Kings Canyon National Parks had gained a beneficial ecological buffer.

Another significant change in the management of giant sequoias in the southern Sierra occurred only a few months after President Clinton created the Giant Sequoia National Monument. The tract in question, known as the Dillonwood Grove, stood on the southern flank of Dennison Mountain along the boundary of Sequoia National Park and had been in private hands since the nineteenth century. Because access to Dillonwood best occurred from Springville in the Tule River watershed, most descriptions of the grove described it separately from the Garfield Grove within Sequoia National Park. Yet a close reading of the map disclosed that the Dillonwood and Garfield groves were simply two halves of the same giant sequoia forest that spread down both sides of Dennison Mountain. The various private owners of Dillonwood had logged in the area over the years, but, after the Reed family gained control in 1960, it managed the grove with considerable care. Many large sequoias remained on the 1,540-acre tract. Although privately owned, Dillonwood fell within the administrative boundaries of the Sequoia National Forest. When placed in a Sierra Nevada-wide context, Dillonwood represented nearly seventy percent of the giant sequoia forest remaining in private hands.

As early as the mid-1990s, David Reed and his sister, Susan Matthews, had concluded that the time had come to sell the grove, but they did not want to see its resources subjected to intense logging by new private owners. Sensitive to the controversies that were continuing over the USFS's management of its sequoia groves, the Reeds also concluded that they did not wish to see the grove become part of the Sequoia National Forest. Instead, they set out to add their sequoia grove to Sequoia National Park. To accomplish this goal, the Reeds sought and received the support and assistance of the Save the Redwoods League, a San Francisco-based conservation organization committed to acquiring for preservation both California redwood and giant sequoia forests.[61] Working with U.S. Senator Barbara Boxer and Congressman George Radanovich, a Republican from Fresno, the league lobbied successfully to have Congress modify the boundaries of Sequoia National Park to include the Dillonwood Grove.[62] At the same time, the league began a fundraising effort intended to buy out the Reed Family's interest in the grove. Ultimately, the purchase price of approximately $10,000,000 came from both federal and private funds. California Senator Diane Feinstein worked to obtain a federal appropriation of $5,000,000, while the league raised a similar sum with assistance from the Goldman Foundation, Packard Foundation, Oracle Foundation, San Francisco Foundation, and California Wildlife Conservation Board.[63] Dillonwood became a part of Sequoia National Park on December 6, 2001.

EXTENDING WILDERNESS

Among the issues that the General Management Plan left in the hands of Congress was the designation of additional lands within the parks as wilderness. The GMP noted that the two parks contained a number of areas that were suitable for such designation, including the Hockett Plateau, the North Fork Kaweah and Chimney Rock areas, and Redwood Canyon. Also potentially eligible was a portion of the 1978 Mineral King addition. The GMP committed the park to managing these areas in a manner compatible with wilderness designation but noted that only Congress could formally place these lands under permanent wilderness protection.

U.S. Senator Barbara Boxer and Congressman Jim Costa, a Democrat from Fresno, began work on wilderness status for these lands in the years following the Dillonwood addition, but it took time to generate the required support among California's congressional delegation. Finally, in July 2007, Representative Costa introduced a bill that proved successful. Costa had done his homework, and the bill moved forward, this time with the support of Congressman Devin Nunes, a conservative from Tulare who was generally skeptical of environmental legislation. The support of Nunes was all the more surprising, because Costa's bill proposed that the Hockett Plateau country become the "John Krebs Wilderness," in honor of the Democratic Congressman who had led the fight to add Mineral King to Sequoia National Park in 1978 and lost his congressional seat in 1980 as a result.

In October 2007, the NPS testified in favor of Costa's bill, H.R. 3022. The agency supported both the designation of the proposed lands as wilderness and the "John Krebs Wilderness" title, and the bill passed the House on a voice vote the following June. Over subsequent months, Costa's bill was swept up along with 160 other pieces of public-lands legislation to form the 1,200-page Omnibus Public Land Management Act of 2009. As the bill worked its way towards approval, concerns arose related not to the designation of wilderness per se but to its relationship to the two issues that had proved so troublesome during the parks' GMP effort. Cabin permittees in Mineral King Valley and private-property owners in Silver City insisted on language that would insure that their rights and privileges would remain uncompromised. Recreational pack-stock users also succeeded in inserting language into the bill that specified their desires: "Nothing in this subtitle

Boundary Changes and Wilderness Additions 2001–2009
N
KINGS CANYON NATIONAL PARK
Tehipite Valley
SEQUOIA-KINGS CANYON WILDERNESS (1984)
Cedar Grove
Grant Grove
Kings Canyon National Park
Addition to SEQUOIA-KINGS CANYON WILDERNESS, 2009
Lodgepole
Giant Forest
SEQUOIA NATIONAL PARK
Ash Mountain
Mineral King
Three Rivers
JOHN KREBS WILDERNESS, 2009
DILLONWOOD addition to SEQUOIA NATIONAL PARK, 2001
0
10 Miles

precludes horseback riding in, or the entry of recreation or commercial saddle or pack stock into, an area designated as wilderness by this subtitle." But even this provided insufficient assurance for advocates of pack stock and, as a final requirement for their support, they insisted that the southern part of the Hockett Plateau be dropped from bill. As finally signed into law, on March 30, 2009, the John Krebs Wilderness consisted not of 69,500 acres, as initially proposed, but a much smaller 39,740 acres, a loss of forty-three percent of Costa's original proposal.

Those who knew the history of the Hockett Plateau could not ignore the irony of the reduction. The area had been omitted from the 1984 wilderness bill not because it lacked wilderness character but because Congressman Charles Pashayan, Jr., a Republican from Fresno, needed to show his local constituents that he could oppose and negatively affect environmental legislation. Twenty-five years later, when an attempt was made to correct this oversight, political concerns that had little to do with the actual nature of the land in question again intervened to limit the designation of wilderness in the Hockett country. Surprisingly, while all this controversy swirled around the Mineral King and Hockett areas, the part of the bill that added the 45,000-acre North Fork Kaweah and Redwood Canyon areas to the already existing Sequoia-Kings Canyon Wilderness breezed through, without amendment or opposition.[64]

AN ERA OF LIMITS

Operational challenges also remained a part of the parks' world as the twenty-first century began. In the years after 1990, the twin parks' federally appropriated operating budget continued to increase numerically, but the increases often failed to meet growing operational demands. In ways that were more similar than many realized at the time, both the Clinton and George W. Bush administrations sought to keep the overall budget of the discretionary portion of the government, including that of the NPS, as small as possible. This trend showed up in several ways. Perhaps the most subtle was the congressional tactic of providing cost-of-living raises to federal employees without providing funds to cover those increases. The result, largely invisible to the public, was to reduce the purchasing power of the parks' federal budget by two to three percent each year. Seasonal staffing, in particular, suffered, since reducing summer jobs was one of the most expedient ways to control overall salary obligations.

One of the most striking losses was the severe reduction of the parks' traditional interpretive programs. By 2010, the ranger-guided nature walks that had once defined the parks had almost disappeared. Wrestling with funding limitations and changing public expectations, the parks' interpretive program moved in new directions. Interpretive rangers found themselves involved more and more in social media and outreach activities. Day-to-day staffing of the park's visitor centers shifted significantly to the nonprofit Sequoia Natural History Association. The parks' nonprofit fundraising organization, the Sequoia and Kings Canyon National Parks Foundation, came up with funding for an outreach program called "Rangers in the Classroom," which took the parks' message to schools in the San Joaquin Valley.

Yet not all was doom and gloom. Between FY 1991 and FY 2010, the parks' basic operating budget increased from $8,234,000 to $17,306,000. Even when corrected for inflation, the parks' budget actually increased during these years by approximately sixty percent. The competition within the parks for this new money was often intense. Each operating program had unmet needs, which varied from things as basic as meeting increasingly professional standards for water and waste-water treatment to responding to the invasion of the parks by growers of marijuana, to identifying and addressing changes in the parks' natural resources resulting from climate change. Most fundamentally, the parks' increase in fiscal capacity expressed itself in additional permanent staffing. In the fifteen years leading up to 2010, the parks' staff grew by the equivalent of eighty-five new full-time positions, most of which were concentrated in maintenance, law enforcement associated with the control of marijuana, and natural-resource management.[65]

Beginning with FY 2011, this trend of steadily increasing support faltered. Fiscal austerity became the goal in Washington, D.C., and the national parks were not immune to the change. Funding for basic park operations dropped slightly in FY 2011 and then again in FY 2012. Fiscal year 2013 saw the parks lose a full million dollars to an across-the-board cut in federal spending known as the Sequester Program. During these three years, a full ten percent of the federal operating budget for the two parks disappeared, the first significant and prolonged reduction in park funding since World War II. These reductions showed up in many ways. Campgrounds opened later and closed earlier each year. Winter snowplowing of the Generals Highway north of Lodgepole was discontinued, and, for the first time in seventy years, no camping was available for winter visitors in the Giant Forest/Lodgepole area. The overall size of the parks' staff, as measured by hours worked, dropped by more than twenty percent.[66]

Haunting the budget challenges of the entire two-decade-long period was the problem of sustaining the parks' complex and still-growing physical infrastructure. The challenge of deciding which facilities would receive investment (and which would not) became more and more difficult. As the parks' infrastructure aged, keeping track of everything became a project in itself. Responding to new agency-wide requirements, Sequoia and Kings Canyon implemented a computer-based facility management software system. By 2010, according to the database, the NPS found itself attempting to sustain at Sequoia and Kings Canyon National Parks a total of 136 miles of paved highway, thirteen miles of unpaved roadway, 842 miles of trails, fourteen campgrounds containing 1,264 campsites, 468 buildings, twenty-two water systems, five wastewater-treatment plants, and a good deal more. The total estimated replacement value of these facilities, which had accumulated over more than a century, exceeded $1,100,000,000. Equally significant was the parks' calculation that it had a backlog of deferred maintenance that exceeded $190,000,000. Of this, more than half represented deferred road maintenance. [67]

Adding a bit of good news to this situation was the implementation of the system-wide Recreation Fee Demonstration Program in 1996. For decades, all visitor fees collected in the parks had gone to the U.S. Department of the Treasury. Beginning in 1996, eighty percent of these revenues, which came from park-entrance and campground fees, were allowed to remain in the parks for local use. By 2014, this program delivered about $2,500,000 annually for the two parks in support of park maintenance and the enhancement of visitor experiences. Unlike most other sources of project funding, the prioritization and use of these funds remained at the park level. This program allowed on-the-ground managers to argue for everything from wayside exhibit rehabilitation to campground and trail repairs.[68]

Aside from the Giant Forest project, by far the largest infrastructure investment in the parks during the 1990–2010 period focused on the Generals Highway. Originally constructed to varying standards between 1921 and 1934, the roadway had deteriorated over the years, especially the oldest section between Ash Mountain and the Giant Forest. In 1992, using federal gas-tax funds from the Federal Lands Highway Program, the parks began the phased reconstruction of the highway—a project everyone knew would involve many years of work.

Before physical work could begin, decisions needed to be made about the role and nature of the highway itself. These decisions involved not only the NPS but also the Federal Highway Administration, the agency responsible for the design and construction of highways on federal lands. It came as no surprise that an initial analysis by the Highway Administration found the Generals Highway to be obsolete and deficient in many ways and suggested radical changes. These recommendations aimed particularly at the section of the highway that provided access to the Giant Forest from the south, the same segment that had so bothered directors Mather and Albright during the 1920s. Pointing out that the existing roadway placed severe constraints on both traffic volume and vehicle size, the Highway Administration proposed a program to widen and straighten the road, so it could safely support tours buses and other large vehicles. On some of the sharpest switchback corners, this would have required very extensive road widening, so as to allow large vehicles to pass through hairpin turns without crossing over the centerline.[69]

Park managers wrestled with these proposals and ultimately rejected them, preferring a more conservative approach. Driving the parks' decision were the realizations that the existing roadway was already capable of bringing more vehicles into the upland portions of Sequoia National Park than existing or proposed parking facilities could accommodate and the corollary that an improved highway would intensify overcrowding and degrade the visitor experience. Also recognized was the role the southern half of the Generals Highway played in defining the character of Sequoia National Park. By providing an entry experience that slowed visitors down and gave the park a sense of separation from the outside world, the highway made Sequoia a distinctive and special place. Following up on this new appreciation of the highway's character, the NPS sought a "determination of eligibility" on the National Register for the roadway, and, in 1991, the entire route was determined to have sufficient significance to warrant listing. Henceforth, the Generals Highway project proceeded under the assumption that the character of the highway was a resource worthy of protection.[70]

With decisions in place that the reconstructed road would maintain its character as a slow and winding "parkway," work could now proceed. The first phase began, in October 1993, between the Ash Mountain entrance and the Ash Mountain headquarters complex.[71] Succeeding contracts advanced the project to Potwisha, Hospital Rock, Big Fern Spring, and Amphitheater Point. By the summer of 2013, contractors had completed the difficult task of rebuilding the roadway between Amphitheater Point and Deer Ridge; the reconstruction of the highway between Eleven Range Point and Wolverton Junction, a stretch that took the road through the Giant Forest, occurred during the summer of 2014. Each phase included replacing deteriorated retaining walls and culverts and laying down a new road surface. Subtle widening occurred locally with the goal of making the highway's width more consistent. The result was a "new" Generals Highway that had the character of the original highway but also now had modern guard walls, culverts, and pavement. Visitors remarked that they appreciated the distinctive use of stone on the many retaining and guard walls.

Several less complex highway projects also took place along the northern half of the highway between Lodgepole and Grant Grove. In those areas where the highway had originally been built to a higher standard, less work was required. North of the Giant Forest, highway rehabilitation consisted primarily of culvert replacement, re-grading to smooth out seventy years of settling, and repaving. Another project on the highway's northern reaches saw the correction of highway-caused stream diversions at Halstead Meadow that had done grievous harm to that wetland.

MANAGING RESOURCES IN A COMPLEX WORLD

During the opening decades of the twin parks' second century, Sequoia and Kings Canyon faced many challenges, but none carried as much significance for the future as those relating to the management of the parks' natural and cultural resources. As Jerry Franklin had warned at the 1990 centennial conference, the parks had entered a period of "tremendous uncertainty" when it came to the ability of managers to preserve these treasures in an unimpaired state.[72] Particularly after the beginning of the new millennium, a profound sense of change swept over natural resource managers. Outside influences—including air pollution, invasions by alien plants and pathogens, and changes in the state of adjoining lands—all emphasized that the parks could no longer be managed as biological islands separate from the surrounding world. The specter of global climate change, with its huge implications for natural systems, confirmed the somber mood.

The character of these threats to the integrity of the parks varied considerably. Some stemmed from advances in science that led to new understandings of the fragility of ongoing ecological processes. Others reflected new versions of more traditional problems. Of the latter, the invasion of marijuana growers in the parks' foothills-wildlands came to be, by far, the most publicized and the easiest for the NPS to discuss with the public. Since the expulsion by the cavalry of illegally grazing herds of sheep during the 1890s, the two parks had been largely free of direct trespass activities that damaged the parks' resources. Admittedly, poaching of wildlife continued over the decades but generally at a level that could be controlled by ranger patrols. This status changed, however, early in the twenty-first century with the arrival of large-scale but clandestine trespass by growers of marijuana. By 2002, the problem had reached a crisis point. During a one-month period late that summer, park staff located and removed nineteen illegal plantations, containing more than 34,000 plants.[73] During the next several years, despite hard work by park rangers, the problem grew. During the 2004 growing season, rangers uprooted 44,000 plants, and, by the close of the summer of 2005, the total number of plants removed from the two parks had grown to more than 100,000.[74]

Several factors, all of them outside the control of the NPS, came together to lead to the illegal development of extensive marijuana plantations within Sequoia and Kings Canyon National Parks. The continuing national "war on drugs" kept street prices high for marijuana, and increased efforts to tighten the national border with Mexico provided incentives for domestic production. Adding further encouragement were laws that confiscated private property when it was employed in the production of illegal substances. Together, these policies had a major unintended consequence: It suddenly made sense for international drug cartels to grow marijuana on public lands in the U.S., and, once this conclusion became obvious, scouts for those cartels rapidly discovered that Sequoia and Kings Canyon contained regions that were potentially suitable and only lightly policed.

The requirements of marijuana cultivation attracted growers to the twin parks' foothill region. These areas, mostly in Sequoia National Park below 6,000 feet, had originally been given park status to provide a geographic buffer between the giant sequoia groves and private ranchlands to the west. Often covered with thick vegetation in the form of oak and brushy chaparral, this terrain had remained some of the wildest and least visited anywhere in the two parks. By the beginning of the parks' second century, the foothill lands along the several forks of the Kaweah River had become, perhaps, the parks' truest wilderness, with many locations receiving no human footprints in decades. This attribute of wildness, combined with the presence of thick, obscuring vegetation, water from streams, and reasonable foot access from park roads, made the foothills a particularly good place to grow marijuana. Growers imported hand crews, who cleared out understory vegetation, deployed camouflage netting, planted marijuana, and built drip-irrigation systems to sustain the plants. Armed guards protected the valuable crop. Finding plantations, even from the air, proved difficult. At the same time, ground patrols put ranger staff at unprecedented risk. For many rangers, seeking armed growers in thick chaparral felt like tropical guerilla warfare. When sites were successfully identified, rangers found much evidence of resource damage, including extensive use of herbicides and pesticides as well as animal remains associated with poaching.

Even in hindsight, it is not easy to determine the overall scale of this activity during the early years of the twenty-first century. For obvious reasons, marijuana growers worked hard to obscure both the location and scale of their activities. Statistics collected by rangers reflected the problem; they document only how much marijuana was discovered and eradicated, not how much the parks actually supported. The severity of the marijuana problem attracted the attention of many support groups, including the National Parks Conservation Association, and a campaign for more funding for the suppression of marijuana bore fruit in FY 2006, when the parks received a base increase of $448,000 specifically to increase law enforcement of marijuana. The parks continued to wrestle with the problem and, in FY 2009, they received another base increase for marijuana's suppression, this time for $493,000.[75] Despite these increases in funding, which emphasized law enforcement and largely left unfunded the costs associated with restoration, the law-enforcement staff at Sequoia and Kings Canyon still found itself forced to work extensively with the State of California, the Sheriff's Office of Tulare County, and National Guard.

And then, almost as suddenly as it began, the marijuana problem faded away. Outside issues had driven the growers onto federal land, and, as those conditions evolved, the need to use the parks' lands ebbed. Foremost among these changes was the legalization of the cultivation and use of medical marijuana in California, a change that made it easier to grow the drug-producing plants in places more amenable to agricultural activity. As growers shifted to fields in the San Joaquin Valley (both legal and illegal), cultivation in the parks dropped off quickly. Statistics document the shift. As late as 2010, park rangers located and removed more than 40,000 plants from illegal gardens within the parks. The following year, that number plummeted to barely 1,300 plants. In the two seasons after that, no plants at all were found within the parks.[76]

The abrupt rise and fall of the marijuana gardens within the parks demonstrated just how closely the parks were now tied to the surrounding culture and economy. During a period of ten years, park rangers located and eradicated more than 240,000 plants that had a theoretical street value of more than $500,000,000. In yet another way, the NPS had come to understand that it could no longer manage Sequoia and Kings Canyon as an insular unit.

THE EVOLVING ROLE OF FIRE

Managing wildland fire in the twenty-first century presented the parks with another issue that demonstrated the increasing connection between activities in the parks and the outside world. Traditionally, the NPS had maintained clear control over both its fire-management policy and fire operations. Mutual-aid agreements provided assistance from other agencies when needed, but the parks remained largely autonomous when it came to fire. This remained true even during the 1970s, as the parks shifted to a policy that saw fire not as a threat but as a critical natural process. In the following decade, Sequoia and Kings Canyon applied this new policy with minimal regulatory oversight. The parks' fire-management program possessed the freedom to burn when and where managers thought appropriate.

Over time, however, this freedom faded, as additional constraints developed. First came complaints from the parks' neighbors about smoke. NPS burns, particularly those in late summer and fall, often resulted in substantial amounts of smoke filling the canyons to the west of the two parks. The community of Three Rivers proved particularly susceptible to smoke, when fire activity occurred in the Kaweah watershed, but smoke could also concentrate in the communities below Grant Grove, at Hume Lake, and, even occasionally, on the eastern side of the Sierra Nevada in the Owens Valley. Although most of the parks' visitors accepted the necessity of burning, these neighboring communities, especially when residents faced smoke for prolonged periods, found the situation harder to accept. The resulting angry comments, often made to the news media and to elected officials, became more significant, as new regulatory structures for air quality began to emerge in Central California.

The amendments in 1990 to the Clean Air Act of 1963 placed substantial pressure on the newly created San Joaquin Valley Air Pollution Control District (APCD). Of particular concern were very high levels of ozone and particulate pollution in both the San Joaquin Valley and the adjacent Sierra Nevada. Under the provisions of the 1990 amendments, the U.S. Environmental Protection Agency (EPA) declared the entire region to be in "non-attainment status," and correction of this situation became a major goal for the regional pollution-control agency. When local concerns about smoke merged with regional pollution concerns and new federal goals, the APCD concluded that it needed to develop a program to regulate fire in the Sierra Nevada.

As it drafted these policies, the regional agency concluded that, although little could be done to regulate emissions from genuine wildfires, opportunities did exist to work with the NPS and the other land-management agencies to manage smoke emissions from both management-ignited prescribed fires and naturally ignited fires that were allowed to burn to achieve resource goals. In 1999, the APCD finalized regulations that asserted control over when and where the national parks of the southern Sierra could use fire as a resource-management tool. Another regulation charged the NPS a per-acre fee for management burns. Such regulations were made possible by the fact that the federal Clean Air Act transferred enforcement of its provisions to the states and thus to state-authorized agencies. This delegation of authority had the effect of removing air-quality issues from the parks' exclusive jurisdiction list and placing the NPS's activities under state control.

In practice, this new level of oversight led initially to considerable friction between the fire-management program in the twin national parks and the air district. The goals of the two agencies did not mesh well. While the NPS sought to manage fires to enhance forest health, the regional air agency had as its primary goal the limitation of smoke moving westward into the San Joaquin Valley. The two organizations also perceived fire very differently. Professional staff at the APCD assumed that fire could be closely managed and that smoke occurred when the government allowed it to. The NPS's fire managers came to the table with a very different view. Their experience told them that fires were necessary to sustain the forest's health and that, once a fire started, extinguishing even a prescribed burn could, in many cases, be difficult, dangerous, or sometimes impossible.

Not surprisingly, these divergent views led to repeated conflicts about the location, timing, and seasonality of the parks' fire projects. These frustrations came to head in June 2004, when the NPS's fire-management staff, acting under instructions from Superintendent Dick Martin, ignited a fire in Sequoia National Park that had not been authorized by the APCD. In response, the district issued a violation notice and, after a review, proposed to fine the NPS $75,000 for its unpermitted fire-management actions. The NPS's regional office in San Francisco negotiated the fine down to $25,000, but the public fining of the parks for an air-quality violation generated considerable negative public comment.[77] Eventually, tempers cooled and, as the APCD had no doubt hoped, the fining of the parks led ultimately to serious discussions and a better working relationship. Out of this period came an agreement, the *Unified Guidelines and Procedures for Smoke Management*, which was endorsed not only by the NPS and the APCD, but also by the USFS and other land-management agencies. [78] With this tool in hand, the ability of the NPS and the APCD to work together improved. For the first time, the NPS's fire staff began to feel that the air district understood the challenges they faced.

Changes in smoke-management policy and strategy came about as a part of larger patterns of the change in the fire-management program at Sequoia and Kings Canyon. The finalization of a new *Fire and Fuels Management Plan*, in 2003, documented just how far the fire program had come since park managers had begun to perceive fire as a forest-management tool during the late 1960s. In the new plan's mission statement, the NPS set forth an overall goal of seeking "to benefit park resources and society by restoring and maintaining the natural fire regime in a manner consistent with firefighter and public safety."[79] To achieve this mission, the plan established procedures for everything from its planning process for individual fires to how to work with fire in the presence of identified "sensitive values," including both giant sequoia groves and designated wilderness. Supporting these procedures were new computer programs that forecast the spread and behavior of fire and documented divergence from historic fire regimes on a very detailed scale. In short, the *Fire and Fuels Management Plan* demonstrated a level of sophistication and complexity in management almost unimaginable a generation earlier.[80]

Illustrative of this complexity was the parks' experience with the Washington Tree, a monarch giant sequoia located within the Giant Forest. Late in the summer of 2003, lightening ignited a fire within the grove. Applying the procedures defined by the *Fire and Fuels Management Plan*, fire-management staff analyzed the situation and concluded that the fire, if allowed to spread, would benefit the central part of Sequoia National Park's most visited sequoia grove. The fire did spread, ultimately burning some 275 acres of sequoia forest, but along the way flying embers ignited the Washington Tree, a massive old monarch tree, with extensive damage from past natural fires. After sparks from the burn kindled a fire within the tree's hollow upper trunk, and despite efforts to suppress the fire, the upper half of the tree eventually collapsed.[81] Because the tree had long been listed as one of the largest giant sequoias, this event attracted critical attention. The resulting controversy saw the parks' fire-management program both damned for allowing the "destruction" of a magnificent old tree and praised for returning the natural process of fire to the same feature.[82]

Masked by such controversies was a more significant trend. Despite its idealistic intentions, the fire-management program at Sequoia and Kings Canyon continued to find it beyond its means to burn enough acreage annually to move the parks any closer to what had been defined as the desired natural state. Work by ecologists over the years had led to the estimate that a "natural fire regime" within the two parks would see 15,000–20,000 acres burn in an average year, but the NPS never came close to achieving that goal. In the twenty-two years following 1991, only three fire seasons witnessed more than 10,000 acres treated by some sort of fire, and sixteen saw fewer than 5,000 acres touched by fire.[83] No single cause determined this outcome. Limiting factors included air-quality concerns related to smoke, weather that limited the season for good prescribed burning, diversions of crews to other fires outside the parks, and limitations in funding. Fire staff, however, came to believe that the most limiting factor they faced, more than any other single pressure, had become the complexity of the entire process. The parks' fire-management program, which had entered a new era during the 1970s relatively unfettered by either tradition or procedure, had now become a complex, data-rich program with numerous checks and balances. Management plans for even small fires often ran to 100 or more pages. And each year, according to its own data, the fire-management effort fell further behind, as management pursued its goal of restoring wildland fire to its full natural role in Sequoia and Kings Canyon National Parks.

PROTECTING THE PARKS' WILDLIFE

Throughout their first century, Sequoia and Kings Canyon took pride in their role as places where wildlife prospered. Aside from the obvious loss of the grizzly bear, which disappeared from the southern Sierra during the 1920s, park managers liked to believe that they had preserved all the parks' other native vertebrates. Moreover, during the second half of the twentieth century, the parks had managed to resolve most of the wildlife issues that had plagued the parks in earlier years. With populations of mountain lions restored, for example, earlier problems related to overpopulation of deer faded away. Management of black bears in developed areas, where bears continued to seek human food, remained a nuisance that required much management time, but the installation of food-storage lockers in all the parks' campgrounds and a strong educational effort had reduced the problem to one that could be endured. Certainly, no one worried that black bears were in danger of disappearing.

After 1990, however, even as these earlier issues faded away, new problems appeared. Perhaps no animal better captured the challenges facing wildlife managers in this new era than the Sierra Nevada bighorn sheep. This subspecies of *Ovis canadensis* had been declining in the Sierra since intense grazing of domestic sheep overran the high country during the last third of the nineteenth century. A century later, the species had reached a very fragile state, and only two small herds of wild sheep remained in the range. These two groups, one located around Mt. Baxter and the other near Mt. Williamson, both summered on the Sierra Crest along the eastern boundary of Sequoia and Kings Canyon and wintered primarily on Inyo National Forest's terrain immediately to the east.

In 1980, efforts began to enhance populations of bighorn sheep in the Sierra. Pursuing the goal of increasing the number of bighorn in the Sierra, wild sheep were translocated from the two surviving herds to several other locations along the Sierra Crest, including the Mount Langley area of Sequoia National Park. Initially, these efforts produced encouraging results, but then trends again turned downward. By 1997, the continued existence of the Sierra Nevada bighorn sheep in the wild had become a critical concern. The known population of breeding females within the Mt. Williamson herd, for example, had declined to a mere five ewes. In that same year, Sierra Nevada bighorn sheep achieved "endangered" status under the federal Endangered Species Act, and a new effort began to stabilize and grow the small surviving population of wild sheep. An interagency team produced a draft recovery plan for the sheep by July 2003, and a final plan followed in February 2008.[84] Careful husbanding by the interagency team, including the removal of selected predatory mountain lions and the vacating of domestic sheep grazing allotments on the Inyo National Forest, allowed the total Sierra Nevada population to increase by the end of the decade to about 200 breeding females. Of the five major wild sheep herds in the Sierra Nevada, three, including those based at Mt. Langley, Mt. Williamson, and Mt. Baxter, spent part of their time within Sequoia and Kings Canyon. Encouragingly, a new small herd, apparently a spinoff of the Mt. Baxter group, appeared in the lower Bubbs Creek Canyon of Kings Canyon National Park. But after nearly three decades of intense management, the Sierra Nevada bighorn sheep remained an endangered species whose long-term future appeared precarious.

The plight of the mountain yellow-legged frog documented another story of the degradation of habitat and collapse in population. During the late-nineteenth and early-twentieth centuries, three species of yellow-legged frogs occupied the southern Sierra Nevada. The foothill yellow-legged frog lived at lower altitudes, while two closely related species of mountain yellow-legged frogs lived in the sub-alpine and alpine zones. All three creatures were common. By the late 1970s, however, the foothill species had disappeared completely, an event that took place essentially without notice, and, in the following years, the two mountain species also entered a pattern of severe decline.

Unlike the foothill yellow-legged frog, the mountain species lived in habitats that traditionally made the three-inch-long amphibians easy to see. For decades, users of the high country had been accustomed to finding large populations of frogs in and around the parks' many high-altitude lakes and ponds. By the end of the 1990s, however, estimates suggested that the High Sierra's population of mountain yellow-legged frogs had declined by approximately ninety percent.[85] Intensifying the mystery was the fact that, at least superficially, the mountain lakes and streams that formed the home for these frogs did not appear to be damaged significantly in any of the regular ways. The collapsing populations were in remote wilderness areas within national parks, places with the highest level of protection given to any lands within the United States. What was going on?

A decade of research eventually discerned at least three interrelated factors, each of which placed significant negative pressure on the ability of the mountain yellow-legged frogs to survive in the southern Sierra Nevada. Early work disclosed a strong relationship between the presence of introduced trout and the absence of frogs. Before fish-planting, which began in the late-nineteenth century and continued into the 1970s, the high country of Sequoia and Kings Canyon had been almost completely devoid of fish. By the late twentieth century, most of the parks' major lakes and streams harbored introduced trout. In 2001, in order to explore whether a reversal of this condition might benefit frogs, the natural-resource staff at the parks issued an environmental assessment that proposed to remove fish from a small set of lakes and related streams located at the head of Le Conte Canyon in Kings Canyon National Park.[86] During the next several years, using gill nets and devices that temporarily stunned fish with electricity, park staff succeeded in removing fish from these lakes and then monitored the results: By 2009, in nine of the eleven lakes treated, frog populations had blossomed; the density of tadpoles increased thirteen-fold in the nine lakes, while the presence of mature frogs increased fifteen-fold; and populations of mountain garter snakes also increased by a factor of seven.[87]

Unfortunately, even while this fish-removal experiment produced encouraging results, it became apparent that other factors were also causing declines of mountain yellow-legged frog populations. Attention shifted to air pollution, and studies identified the fact that significant amounts of chemical pollution could be detected in the lakes of the High Sierra. A joint study conducted by the NPS and the EPA announced, in early 2008, that several years of monitoring at Emerald and Pear Lakes east of Lodgepole in Sequoia National Park disclosed that fish there contained within their bodies "significant levels" of mercury, DDT, PCB, hexachlorobenzene, chlordanes, and dieldrin. Upslope summer winds apparently transported these toxic materials into the parks from the agricultural and urban lands of the San Joaquin Valley. The study went on to state that three of the twenty fish taken at the study site contained enough toxic material to make them unfit for human consumption.[88]

Then, yet another factor surfaced, and it turned out to be difficult to separate the effects of toxic chemicals from the ravages wrought on frog populations by the arrival of amphibian chytrid fungus (*Batrachochytrium dendrobatidis*), an easily transported disease extirpating frog populations worldwide. By 2009, of the 512 sites where frogs had been detected in the Sierra in 1997, fewer than 300 still had frogs present. In response, the NPS authorized an experiment that allowed the experimental inoculation of individual frogs against the fungal disease.[89]

The plight of the mountain yellow-legged frog demonstrated how fundamentally external factors had come to threaten the biological resources of Sequoia and Kings Canyon. Even if the introduction of alien predatory trout could be reversed, the presence within the parks of wind-blown toxic pollution and the infection of the parks' aquatic ecosystems by chytrid fungus cast a dark shadow over not just the future of these frog species, but also the ability of the NPS to protect the many other native species under its management. As 2014 began, the agency was analyzing public comments on an environmental impact report to allow the chemical removal of frog-eating trout from up to about five percent of the parks' 3,500 high-altitude lakes and ponds. Half a century earlier, who could have imagined a world in which the NPS would consider poisoning trout in high-country lakes and allowing frogs to be inoculated against diseases?

AND IF THE WHOLE WORLD CHANGES, THEN WHAT?

Even as the parks' staff wrestled with natural-resource problems related to fire, bighorn sheep, decline of amphibians, and pollution, it became increasingly apparent that one global issue—climate change—might ultimately take precedence over all the parks' other natural-resource issues in the twenty-first century. As scientific research on and awareness of the implications of climate change exponentially grew, the twin parks began to wrestle with how to respond. No one could deny the potential of climate change to affect them. A rise in temperature of only six degrees Fahrenheit, a shift viewed as conservative by many climate-forecast models, would have the likely effect of shifting climate zones sufficiently upward to disrupt or displace nearly all of the parks' plant communities and dependent wildlife. At risk was the very assumption around which the park had been created in 1890: the belief that a "fence of law," when properly applied to a tract of wild land, could sustain that land in an "unimpaired" state essentially forever.[90]

As the first decade of the new century progressed, it became apparent that, although national parks might be unable to do much internally to prevent climate change, they could provide particularly good sites for studying its effects. At Sequoia and Kings Canyon, two areas of study stood out: forest demography and glacial melting.

The forest-demography work undertaken by Phil van Mantgem and Nate Stephenson, of the U.S. Geological Survey (USGS), involved the review of long-term data on tree mortality collected between 1983 and 2004 at twenty-one permanent plots, and the two research ecologists concluded that mortality over the period had been increasing at a rate of about three percent per year. After reviewing a broad spectrum of possible causes for this phenomenon, the two ecologists concluded that the most likely cause was "a temperature-driven increase in the estimated climatic water deficit . . . "; in other words, drought driven by climate change.[91] In their concluding discussion, the two scientists voiced a perspective that said a great deal about the importance of national parks such as Sequoia and Kings Canyon to science:

> We have provided the first demonstration of long-term, chronic changes in demographic rates in otherwise undisturbed old-growth temperate forests, and have linked those to a

> possible climatic driver. Our work contributes to a growing body of evidence indicating that ongoing environmental changes may be driving both chronic and acute changes in forests worldwide.[92]

Meanwhile, Hassan Basagic, a graduate student at Portland (OR) State University, set out to document the decline of glaciers in the Sierra Nevada, including those in and near Sequoia and Kings Canyon. Using historic photographs as a baseline, Basagic revisited most of the Sierra's remaining glacial features and documented the changes he found. In his 2007 master's thesis, Basagic concluded that the glaciers he studied had all shrunk during the twentieth century and that, using the year 1900 as a baseline, the average loss in ice surface area had been fifty-five percent.[93]

As the first decade of the twenty-first century closed, compelling evidence of climate change in the Sierra Nevada continued to accumulate. Various studies documented earlier peak snowmelt in the Sierra's rivers, warming high-altitude lakes, rising alpine tree lines, and longer and more intense fire seasons. All of these trends challenged the century-old mission of Sequoia and Kings Canyon National Parks in ways that could not have been imagined a generation earlier.

BUILDING A PROFESSIONAL RESPONSE TO A CHANGING WORLD

In many ways, the biological issues facing Sequoia and Kings Canyon since their centennial anniversary in 1990 paralleled those facing most national parks, especially in the American West. In response to this pattern of broad deterioration of natural resources, the Department of the Interior and the NPS instituted several programs that had as their goals the development of enhanced professional capacity to deal with increasingly complex biological issues.

One of the first major efforts in this initiative did not turn out well. The election of President Bill (William Jefferson) Clinton, in November 1992, brought new leaders into many critical jobs at the highest levels of the federal government. Among them was Bruce Babbitt, who came into the new administration as Secretary of the Interior, a position that gave Babbitt broad influence over the land-management agencies within the Department of the Interior, including the NPS. Secretary Babbitt, who had served as the governor of Arizona prior to coming to Washington, D.C., brought an interesting mix of perspectives to his new role as overseer of the nation's public lands. Babbitt's family had deep roots in the ranching industry, but, as he moved through a variety of elected positions in Arizona, Babbitt also developed an appreciation for the importance of conservation and held a deep belief in the efficacy of science as a way of resolving resource-management controversies. In the spring of 1993, full of enthusiasm as he began his new job,

Babbitt proposed a major reorganization of science within the Department of the Interior. In late April, he announced the creation, by secretarial order, of a new agency within his department. The National Biological Survey (NBS), to begin operations on October 1, 1993, would bring together some 1,600 existing federal scientists and support personnel to form a consolidated science bureau dedicated to public-lands issues.[94] About eighty percent of the personnel in the new agency would come from the Fish and Wildlife Service, but, altogether, staff came from seven different agencies within the Interior Department, including the NPS.

This announcement had significant implications for the science program at Sequoia and Kings Canyon. The NPS had begun building a professional staff dedicated to park science in 1968, when it appointed Bruce Kilgore as the twin parks' first resident scientist. By the early 1990s, this function had become one of the parks' treasured assets. Two Ph.D.-level ecologists formed the core of a staff that provided scientific advice to the parks' management. Research activities focused on questions directly related to the parks, including wildlife, fire, air pollution, and wilderness use. The two lead scientists, David Parsons and David Graber, participated in management-team meetings, served on the parks' committees, and were involved in most decisions about the parks. Suddenly, however, on October 1, 1993, they were no longer NPS employees. What had been the parks' science program now became a field office for the NBS.

Both park managers and what had been the parks' science team struggled to adjust to these new circumstances. Initially, the scientists continued to advise the parks' management, but research priorities in their new agency began to shift to include a broader suite of concerns. Meanwhile, in Congress, another major change in public-land science began to take form. The federal elections of 1994 witnessed a major shift in national politics, and, for the first time in a generation, the Republican Party controlled both the Senate and House of Representatives in Congress. The incoming majority's platform, the "Contract with America," included an explicit repudiation of many of the positions taken by Interior Secretary Babbitt, including his work to modify old mining and grazing policies on public lands in the western part of the nation. Also indicted was Babbitt's vision of the NBS as a federal tool for monitoring the condition of the nation's natural resources.

A campaign within Congress to abolish the new research agency accelerated during the FY 1996 budget hearings.[95] Since the agency had been created by secretarial order, it had no founding legislation to protect it. As a result, the agency could be attacked through the budget process. The FY 1996 federal budget dissolved the National Biological Survey, so the field staff of the short-lived bureau, including those at Sequoia and Kings Canyon, became employees of the USGS. At the same time, the parks' research station became the Sequoia and Kings Canyon Field Station of the Western Ecological Research Center.

This new structure ultimately brought both organizational stability and new research priorities to what had been the parks' science office. The USGS's field station, still physically located at the parks' headquarters in Ash Mountain, henceforth would pursue a wider program of cooperative research that aimed to provide value not only to Sequoia and Kings Canyon, but also to other land managers and organizations. The role of serving as advisors to the parks' management, which had begun to atrophy during the short-lived NBS period, continued to shrink. Ultimately, noting how important that advisory role had been to the parks, the NPS created a new type of position known as a "science advisor," and Sequoia and Kings Canyon became one of the first park units in the nation to have one of these positions. David Graber returned to the NPS to fill the new role. The work of science advisors differed from that of research scientists in that the new positions did not conduct actual research, a function that remained with the Geological Survey's field station staff. Sequoia and Kings Canyon sustained the position of science advisor for a decade, and the position played a major role in many of the parks' issues, including the development of the GMP. Ultimately, the position disappeared when Graber, still working out of his office at Ash Mountain, became Chief Scientist for the Pacific West Region, formerly the Western Regional Office, of the NPS.

In a more positive trend, during these same years, the parks' natural-resource management program grew in responsibility and capacity. Again, as with the NPS's research program, much of what happened to the natural-resources function at Sequoia and Kings Canyon took place within a national park system-wide context. The catalyst for much of this change was a book. In 1997, Yale University Press published *Preserving Nature in the National Parks: A History* by Richard West Sellars.[96] In this highly detailed and powerful work, Sellars made the case that the fundamental mission of the national parks—the preservation of nature in an "unimpaired" state—had been compromised badly by the continuing refusal of the NPS to consider ecological principles in the management of its natural resources. And the agency had not only tended to ignore its biologists, Sellars argued, but also underfunded their work to an almost criminal degree.

Sellars's premise found support both within the NPS and in the broader world outside the parks. Increasing natural-resource problems in many parks reinforced the message that a new approach must be pursued. Out of this ferment came a system-wide initiative, the Natural Resources Challenge. NPS Director Robert Stanton announced the new program during a visit, in August 1999, to Mt. Rainier, in Washington. As envisioned, the Resources Challenge would seek permanent funding from Congress for professionalization of natural resources staff as well as for a broad suite of new natural resources programs. Reflecting the Clinton administration's support for the initiative, the President's budget proposal for FY 2000 included a permanent increase of

$20,000,000 for natural-resources work in the national parks.[97] Congress endorsed the request for new funding, and those increases continued in each of the next seven fiscal years. Significantly, two-thirds of this new money went into programs that could be broadly categorized as "inventory and monitoring." These programs were designed to gain knowledge about the parks' natural resources and the trends affecting them.[98]

In FY 2001, following closely upon the first Resources Challenge funding, Sequoia and Kings Canyon received a base increase of $367,000 to enhance the parks' natural-resources management program. This funding supported the equivalent of more than six new professional positions in natural resource management. Included were a full-time aquatic biologist and a supporting seasonal field crew, a new position for monitoring air quality, another new position for restoring disturbed lands together with a supporting field crew, and yet another new position to support management of caves.[99] Additional, albeit smaller, increases occurred in following years, and the twin parks of the southern Sierra ultimately received, between 2001 and 2009, almost half a million dollars annually of additional money for long-term staffing in resources management.[100] Supporting all these functions and greatly increasing their effectiveness was a growing geographical information system (GIS) program that organized data both digitally and spatially, as it flowed in from the enhanced programs.

Another part of this new focus on the parks' resources was the development of inventory and monitoring networks. Ultimately, the NPS created thirty-two such networks nationwide, each of them providing services to a cluster of parks with similar resources. Sequoia and Kings Canyon found themselves part of the Sierra Nevada Network, which the two parks shared with Yosemite and Devils Postpile National Monument in California. Funding for this effort began in 2004, and, by 2009, the network was receiving more than $700,000 annually to support inventory and monitoring activity in the four park units. More than ninety percent of this funding went into a program called "Vital Signs Monitoring," which was an effort to identify and track those organisms and processes most likely to be indicative of environmental health.

By 2015, Sequoia and Kings Canyon National Parks, along with the rest of the units of the national park system, had come an enormous distance from the state of affairs Richard Sellars had documented in his book. In response to the clear and present danger to parks resources presented by intensifying external pressures, the NPS had responded with an aggressive and professional monitoring program that sought to document the parks' condition and identify and track its vital signs. In the twin parks of the southern Sierra, more attention had been paid to documenting the parks' natural resources during the first decade of the twenty-first century than in the rest of the parks' history combined. As in so many other areas, management of natural resources at Sequoia and Kings Canyon had moved into new territory.

TWO DECADES INTO A SECOND CENTURY

As Sequoia and Kings Canyon approached their 125th anniversary in 2015, Jerry Franklin's somber warning in 1990 that the parks would face a challenging future had been proven to be inescapably true. The completion of the Giant Forest project had been a huge, positive accomplishment, but on many other fronts the situation in the parks had deteriorated. Overall funding for the parks' operations had increased significantly but mostly in response to targeted problems. Other traditional services such as interpretation programs had dwindled alarmingly. The development of a more sophisticated management program for natural resources had led to much new knowledge, but the overall condition of the parks' resources had continued to deteriorate, largely as the result of large-scale environmental problems such as air pollution and invasive organisms that were beyond the control of the parks. The capacity of the parks' staff to manage fire had been augmented by new scientific tools, but, forty years after park managers committed to restoring fire to its full natural role, fuels continued to accumulate in the parks' forests faster than fires could remove them. Other problems had arisen seemingly out of nowhere. Among these, the invasion of the parks by growers of marijuana stood out as a symptom of the increasing difficulty of protecting the parks from physical assault. Most ominously of all, global climate change had shifted from something that might impact the parks eventually to an attack on the parks' resources that had already begun.

Demographic and social trends had proven equally problematic since 1990. Located in a region growing more rapidly than many Third World countries, the two parks had seen little increase in use. Visitation had remained little better than stagnant, and broad societal trends seemed to be doing little to increase interest in either nature or national parks. Increasingly, visitors came to the parks for only a few hours, ignoring the range of experiences the parks had long been so good at providing. Jerry Franklin had been right. Sequoia and Kings Canyon National Parks had entered a new period of "tremendous uncertainty."

Although known primarily for the giant sequoias, the twin national parks of the southern Sierra Nevada preserve countless other life-forms. Among the most spectacular are the foxtail pines (*Pinus balfouriana*) that cling to the high, rocky ridges of the southernmost end of the High Sierra. Growing resolutely upward in a region where most other woody plants hug the ground, foxtails often endure for a thousand years or more before they succumb to the elements. Even in death, they add beauty to the landscape. Photograph (original in color) by William C. Tweed, 1997.

Epilogue

ULTIMATELY, the success of a national park can be evaluated in three ways. First, to what extent has the park achieved the goals of its creators? Second, to what extent has the park been useful to the society that created it? By yet a third criterion, to what extent has the park been able to sustain the myriad natural and cultural resources and systems it features?

By the first two measures, Sequoia and Kings Canyon National Parks have succeeded impressively, seemingly achieving the goals expressed in the legislation of 1890, 1926, and 1940. The parks' sequoia forests remain untouched by loggers, and the High Sierra remains wild. There can be no doubt but that the extent and character of the two parks today far exceed the dreams of George Stewart, who worked so hard to establish the twin parks during the late-nineteenth century. Colonel John R. White, who spent a quarter-century wrestling with the parks' development, and Secretary of the Interior Harold Ickes, who politicked so diligently to create Kings Canyon National Park, would recognize their creations and be pleased that, since 2003, more than 1,500,000 visitors annually use the two parks for nature-based recreation. And those visitors like what they see and find. The National Park Service (NPS) annually surveys satisfaction by visitors, and the results for Sequoia and Kings Canyon National Parks document that more than ninety percent of those who respond each year rate their experiences in the parks as "good" or "excellent."

When the third standard is applied—integrity of resources—the situation becomes more complex. After 125 years of management by various government organizations, including the U.S. Army, Department of Interior, NPS, and U.S. Forest Service, the lands and natural resources now contained within Sequoia and Kings Canon are less modified from their natural condition than those in any other portion of the Sierra Nevada. Yet they are also more threatened than ever before. Many measures have been developed to protect the parks, including strict limits on facilities, a management philosophy increasingly focused on preserving all of the parks' natural elements (including natural processes such as fire), and sophisticated resource-management and research programs. At the same time, threats to the parks continue to intensify. In years past, these challenges centered on issues within the parks such as insufficient funding, ever-heavier visitation, and the resistance of certain groups to curtail their traditional uses. Now, local problems such as these are being submerged into a larger matrix of issues that function on a much grander—sometimes even global—scale. There is a general recognition that the parks have become fragile biological islands, and there is a growing suspicion that the founding idea at the heart of the parks—that a fence of law can be drawn around a place and change prevented—may not be fully possible.

In the twenty-first century, Sequoia and Kings Canyon are more connected to the outside world than ever before. Air pollution and pesticide drift, invasions by alien species, and other environmental issues ignore the parks' boundaries. Management of fire within the parks requires careful coordination with regional regulatory authorities. And, most powerfully of all, climate change carries with it the potential for huge disruptions, to the extent that nearly every geographically fixed organism and ecosystem within the two parks could ultimately be in the wrong place due to rising temperatures and other climatic adjustments.

Even as these issues may darken the integrity of the preserved landscape, the developing science of "island biology" casts additional shadows. Much has been learned about how large a tract of land is required to preserve biological resources, if those resources have disappeared from surrounding lands. From these studies come new answers to questions: Why did Sequoia and Kings Canyon lose their grizzly bears during the early twentieth century? Why did animals such as bighorn sheep become so rare? And how might global climate change extirpate numerous additional organisms? For many species, it now appears, the parks are simply not big enough to sustain their ecological welfare.

As Sequoia and Kings Canyon National Parks move forward beyond their first 125 years, it is apparent that this new century will be fraught with insidious and complex threats. The original purposes of the twin parks, as defined in both their founding acts of legislation and the Organic Act of 1916, have been overwhelmed by events far too large for the parks to resist. Even national parks as large as Sequoia and Kings Canyon will not survive as untouched places forever, "unimpaired for the enjoyment of future generations." Whether we like it or not, factors such as global climate change and the fragmentation of habitat will modify the parks' ecosystems in profound ways far beyond our current ability to anticipate or prevent. It is likely that the parks' future may include biological shifts in the Sierra Nevada that equal in magnitude those that occurred at the end of the great Pleistocene Ice Age.

In opposition to this somber background of accelerating environmental threats stand significant beams of hope. The social value of these parks remains obvious. Here grow not only the world's largest trees, but also a stunning myriad of other life-forms, all of them occupying what has come to be the heart of the least-disturbed region of California's beloved Sierra Nevada. Just as valuable are the human experiences the parks offer: stunning scenery, wonderful opportunities to wander quietly in natural settings, and the challenge of travel in wilderness areas. Beyond doubt, Sequoia and Kings Canyon offer what literally can be found nowhere else on Earth.

The power of these national park experiences at Sequoia and Kings Canyon to affect human beings has surprised again and again. From their beginning in 1890, the regions now within the twin parks have motivated amazing human behavior. This book has documented many such stories. There have been capable and powerful visionaries such as John Muir, leaders such as George Stewart and Harold Ickes, those who sought knowledge like Lowell Sumner and Richard Hartesveldt, and those such as Bud Gearhart and John Krebs who risked political careers to support the parks' values. Finally, there have been those whose lives were devoted to managing the parks, among them Walter Fry, Colonel John White, and Boyd Evison. Without their collective contributions, the two parks could never have come to mean so much to so many millions of visitors who come to this special place from all over the world.

At the same time and with equal importance, countless citizens have acted to protect the parks. During the 1880s, such people took a course contrary to the public land policy of the United States at that time, a direction that promoted the sale of all public lands and private use. Against all reasonable odds, they triumphed and created Sequoia and General Grant National Parks. During the 1920s and 1930s, committed citizens again diverged from the mainstream of their time to resist popular attempts to "improve" the great canyons of the Kings and Kern Rivers with reservoirs and power plants. Amazingly, they won again, even at a time when dams and diversion structures emasculated nearly every other major river system in the Sierra Nevada. After 1965, when "progress" sought to enter the mountains in the form of a ski development in Mineral King, those who cared deeply about the region fought anew, and once again popular wisdom said their efforts could only be futile. In 1978, these people who cared for nature won yet another victory for the integrity of the mountains, canyons, and Big Trees when Mineral King became a part of the parks. In the last third of the twentieth century, concerned individuals arose yet again to support the long-delayed idea of removing all commercial development from the heart of the Giant Forest. And again, because of their commitment and determination, their efforts succeeded.

To conclude, no landscape is immune to human impact; no natural place is too remote to be threatened. For more than 125 years, committed individuals have fought repeatedly to preserve the priceless heritage contained within Sequoia and Kings Canyon National Parks. As the twenty-first century continues, even more commitment will be necessary to sustain the twin parks. It will fall to those who know and love these magical places to rise to this challenge of the Big Trees.

Managers at Sequoia and Kings Canyon National Parks have done their best to document levels of visitation since the very earliest days of the parks. Since the late nineteenth century, levels of visitor use have risen from a few hundred persons per year to more than a million. No other location in the two parks draws as many visitors as does the General Sherman Tree in the Giant Forest of Sequoia National Park. Photograph (original in color) by William C. Tweed, 1985.

APPENDIX A: Visitation to the Twin Parks, 1890–2015

YEAR	GENERAL GRANT*	SEQUOIA
1890–1905	7,000 (total)	6,000 (total)
1906	900	700
1907	1,100	900
1908	1,773	1,251
1909	798	854
1910	1,178	2,407
1911	2,160	3,114
1912	2,240	2,923
1913	2,756	3,823
1914	3,735	4,667
1915	10,523	7,647
1916	15,360	10,780
1917	17,390	18,510
1918	15,496	15,001
1919	21,574	30,443
1920	19,661	31,508
1921	30,312	28,263
1922	50,456	27,514
1923	46,230	30,158
1924	35,032	34,468
1925	40,517	46,677
1926	50,597	89,404
1927	47,996	100,684
1928	51,988	98,035
1929	44,783	111,385
1930	43,547	129,221
1931	51,995	143,573
1932	40,806	131,398
1933	50,081	126,464
1934	56,024	147,533
1935	116,729	205,783
1936	148,565	230,714
1937	157,810	234,661
1938	145,750	260,139
1939	161,080	272,329

* *General Grant* becomes *Kings Canyon* after 1939.

YEAR	KINGS CANYON	SEQUOIA
1940	201,454	282,198
1941	172,271	300,012
1942	113,949	166,964
1943	63,100	70,240
1944	36,771	54,066
1945	62,710	126,221
1946	219,855	312,556
1947	230,468	370,197
1948	274,437	392,472
1949	295,093	376,375
1950	330,913	379,699
1951	446,795	447,888
1952	444,644	468,371
1953	435,548	501,259
1954	551,541	484,653
1955	556,139	517,995
1956	669,801	538,080
1957	638,543	535,846
1958	683,910	512,183
1959	701,384	528,074
1960	740,260	592,359
1961	731,544	592,801
1962	809,609	676,369
1963	745,199	625,570
1964	802,000	648,570
1965	848,890	877,270
1966	923,360	797,840
1967	909,950	746,810
1968	1,064,000	874,300
1969	945,990	919,310
1970	1,018,990	875,670
1971	896,670	881,980
1972	1,058,040	869,600
1973	906,780	846,280
1974	887,410	686,940
1975	1,124,655	1,067,411
1976	1,127,902	1,040,575
1977	1,046,614	978,573
1978	869,877	973,448

YEAR	KINGS CANYON	SEQUOIA
1979	809,292	799,950
1980	823,795	862,762
1981	782,472	1,095,064
1982	831,044	1,020,500
1983	765,755	854,233
1984	938,262	979,632
1985	874,456	939,468
1986	1,028,785	1,056,527
1987	1,081,172	1,139,389
1988	1,007,695	1,031,129
1989	1,056,020	1,037,349
1990	1,062,867	1,063,552
1991	1,071,022	1,120,278
1992	637,446*	961,095
1993	636,515	1,066,552
1994	725,930	1,034,133
1995	832,794	844,582
1996	502,749	838,060
1997	484,718	1,008,931
1998	540,212	861,303
1999	559,534	873,229
2000	528,987	838,974
2001	541,787	870,327
2002	545,420	920,292
2003	555,987	979,297
2004	525,035	1,000,177
2005	594,893	1,004,843
2006	552,766	954,507
2007	580,129	979,537
2008	574,870	930,011
2009	609,296	965,170
2010	598,205	1,002,979
2011	566,810	1,006,583
2012	591,033	1,006,584
2013	567,544	909,274
2014	529,596	1,024,703
2015	468,106	1,097,464

*Reflects a modification in the formula used to calculate visitation; there was no significant change in visitation between 1991 and 1992.

Civilian superintendents under the supervision of the Secretary of the Interior have overseen Sequoia, General Grant, and Kings Canyon National Parks since 1914. Prior to that time, officers from the U.S. Army managed the parks. In this photograph, Superintendent Thomas J. Ritter takes a break after riding to the summit of Franklin Pass east of Mineral King in Sequoia National Park. Photograph (original in color) by William C. Tweed, 1990.

APPENDIX B

Superintendents of Sequoia, General Grant, and Kings Canyon National Parks

During the summer seasons of 1891 through 1913, Sequoia and General Grant National Parks were supervised by military officers assigned by the Department of War. Each officer received the title of "Acting Superintendent of Sequoia and General Grant National Parks" from the Secretary of the Interior. Generally, these appointments began in May and expired in October. Beginning in 1900, civilian rangers served as "Park Ranger in Charge" during the remainder of the year. After 1912, the civilian officer in charge of the parks during the winter also took the title "Acting Superintendent." The first formally designated "Superintendent" took charge of the parks in 1914, after the War Department discontinued its park-protection program at Sequoia and General Grant. In 1933, the Superintendency of General Grant National Park was separated from that of Sequoia National Park. In 1940, when Kings Canyon National Park came into being, it also functioned initially as a separate park with a separate superintendent. In 1943, as a wartime economic measure, the two superintendencies were again merged. Since that date, the two parks have been administered jointly.

Acting Superintendents under the Department of War

Captain Joseph H. Dorst, 1891 and 1892
Captain James Parker, 1893
Lieutenant Alexander Tracy Dean, 1894
Captain James Lockett, 1895
Captain George Henry Goodwin, 1896 and 1897
George Langenberg (Civilian appointee in lieu of military personnel during the Spanish–American War), 1898
Captain Bennent X. Smith, 1898 (Replaced Langenberg late in the season)
Lieutenant James Alfred Moss, 1899
Second Lieutenant Henry Benjamin Clark, 1899
Captain Frank West, 1900
Ernest Britten (Winter) Ranger in Charge, 1900–1904

Captain Lincoln Clarke Andrews, 1901
Captain Frank Arthur Barton, 1902
Lieutenant George Blanchard Comply, 1902
Captain Charles Young, 1903
Captain Lester Warren Cornish, 1903
Captain George French Hamilton, 1904
Captain John O'Shea, 1905
Walter Fry (Winter) Ranger in Charge, 1905–1912
Captain Kirby Walker, 1906 and 1907
Captain Cornelius Cole Smith, 1908 and 1909
Captain Edmund Sehon Wright, 1910
Captain James Bryan Hughes, 1911
Captain Walter Monteith Whitman, 1912
Captain Douglas McCaskey, 1913
Lieutenant Hugh S. Johnson, 1913

Superintendents and Acting Superintendents of Sequoia National Park under the Department of the Interior prior to October 1, 1943

Walter Fry (Acting) March 1912 to July 1914
Walter Fry, July 1914 to July 1920
John R. White, July 1920 to January 1939
Eivind T. Scoyen, January 1939 to July 1941
John R. White, July 1941 to October 1943

Superintendents and Acting Superintendents of General Grant National Park prior to March 4, 1940

John R. White (Acting), July 1920 to March 1933
Guy Hopping (Acting), March 1933 to October 1936
Guy Hopping, October 1936 to March 1940

Superintendents of Kings Canyon National Park prior to October 1, 1943

Eivind T. Scoyen (Acting), March 1940 to July 1941
Eivind T. Scoyen, July 1941 to October 1943

Superintendents of Sequoia and Kings Canyon National Parks

John R. White, October 1943 to October 1947
Eivind T. Scoyen, November 1947 to January 1956
Thomas J. Allen, May 1956 to November 1959
John M. Davis, November 1959 to February 1966
Frank Kowski, March 1966 to September 1967
John S. McLughlin, October 1967 to November 1972
Henry G. Schmidt, November 1972 to July 1975
Stanley T. Albright, October 1975 to September 1977
David D. Thompson, Jr., October 1977 to March 1980
Quincy Boyd Evison, August 1980 to August 1985
John H. Davis, August 1985 to January 1989
J. Thomas Ritter, January 1989 to May 1994
Michael J. Tollefson, January 1995 to September 2000
Richard H. Martin, January 2001 to June 2005
Craig Axtell, January 2006 to October 2009
Karen Taylor-Goodrich, December 2009 to January 2013
Woody Smeck, August 2013 to the time of this book's publication (September 2016)

LIST OF ACRONYMS

Note: These acronyms appear in the text and/or the notes.

APCD	San Joaquin Valley Air Pollution Control District
BCE	Before the Common Era (also known as B.C.)
BLM	Bureau of Land Management (formerly the GLO before 1946)
CCC	Civilian Conservation Corps
CE	Current Era (also known as A.D.)
DCP	Development Concept Plan
DNC	Delaware North Companies
DSC	Denver Service Center (of the National Park Service)
EIS	Environmental Impact Statement
EPA	U.S. Environmental Protection Agency
GIS	Geographical Information System
GLO	General Land Office (later the BLM beginning in 1946)
GMP	General Management Plan
GSI	Guest Services, Inc. (formerly Government Services, Incorporated)
HSHA	High Sierra Hikers Association
KCPS	Kings Canyon Park Services
NA	National Archives
NBS	National Biological Survey
n.d.	No date (or date unknown)
NEPA	National Environmental Protection Act
NPS	National Park Service
USDA	U.S. Department of Agriculture
USDI	U.S. Depart of the Interior
S&GG	Sequoia and General Grant National Parks
SEKI	Sequoia and Kings Canyon National Parks
SPRR	Southern Pacific Railroad Company
USFS	U.S. Forest Service
USGS	U.S. Geological Survey

NOTES

General Notes: Whenever possible, the authors refer to specific Indian tribes; otherwise, they comply with the National Park Service's guidelines in the general use of "Native Americans" for unknown and unspecified "native peoples." Likewise, the authors use terminology of the National Park Service such as "pillow limit," "management philosophy," "visitor use," and "visitor experience," even as they refrain from using nouns as adjectives throughout the text. Also, refer to the *List of Acronyms* (on page 350) for abbreviations used in the notes.

INTRODUCTION

1. The 1990 edition of this book was published by the Sequoia Natural History Association with the title *Challenge of the Big Trees: A Resource History of Sequoia and Kings Canyon National Parks.*
2. Despite the highly cooperative nature of this book, the authors ultimately each took lead responsibility for drafting separate sections. William C. Tweed is the primary author of Chapters 1–4, 9–10, and the Epilogue; Lary M. Dilsaver wrote Chapters 5–8. Both authors, however, read and reviewed the other's text and responded collectively to revisions suggested by the publisher.

CHAPTER ONE

1. Useful descriptions of the Sierra Nevada and its natural history can be found in Verna R. Johnson, *Sierra Nevada* (Boston, MA: Houghton Mifflin and Company, 1970); and Stephen Whitney, *A Sierra Club Naturalist's Guide to the Sierra Nevada* (San Francisco, CA: Sierra Club Books, 1979).
2. Nowhere can the effects of glaciers on the southern Sierra be better studied than in the illustrations contained within Francois Matthes, *Sequoia National Park: A Geological Album*, Fritiof Fryxell, ed. (Berkeley: University of California Press, 1956). For a more contemporary account, see Bill Guyton, *The Glaciers of California* (Berkeley: University of California Press, 1998).
3. William L. Preston, *Vanishing Landscapes: Land and Life in the Tulare Lake Basin* (Berkeley: University of California Press, 1981).

CHAPTER TWO

1. C. Kristina Roper Wickstrom, "Issues Concerning Native American Use of Fire: A Literature Review," *Yosemite Research Center Publications in Anthropology*, No. 6 (1987): 15.

2. Lorin E. Berryman and Albert B. Elsasser, *Terminus Reservoir: Geology, Paleontology, Flora and Fauna, Archeology, History* (Sacramento, CA: U.S. Army Corps of Engineers, 1966), 14–27; and Albert B. Elsasser, *Indians of Sequoia and Kings Canyon National Parks* (Three Rivers, CA: Sequoia Natural History Association, 1962; revised edition, 1988), 14–23.
3. A. L. Kroeber, *Handbook of the Indians of California* (Washington, DC: Bureau of American Ethnology of the Smithsonian Institution, 1925), 581–92.
4. Elsasser, 28.
5. Kroeber, 585–86.
6. Elsasser, 31–41.
7. A fascinating description of the Monache camp at Hospital Rock, based on interviews from the first Euro-American to visit it, can be found in Walter Fry, "Hospital Rock in the Sequoia National Park," *Sequoia Nature Guide Service Bulletin*, No. 5 (February 17, 1925).
8. Kroeber, 587.
9. The best book on this complex and still controversial subject is Kat Anderton, *Tending the Wild: Native American Knowledge and the Management of California's Natural Resources* (Berkeley: University of California Press, 2005).
10. Fry, 2.
11. Wickstrom, *op. cit. passim.*
12. A more complete exploration of this perspective can be found in William C. Tweed, *Uncertain Path: A Search for the Future of National Parks* (Berkeley: University of California Press, 2010).

CHAPTER THREE

1. Francis P. Farquhar, *History of the Sierra Nevada* (Berkeley: University of California Press, 1966), 15–21.
2. Ibid., 23–29.
3. Ibid., 31–39.
4. Ibid., 59–60.
5. Wallace Smith, *Garden in the Sun*, 4th Edition (Fresno, CA: California History Books, 1960), 74.
6. Walter Fry, "The Discovery of Sequoia National Park, "*Sequoia Nature Guide Service Bulletin*, No. 1 (November 22, 1924).
7. Ibid.
8. Walter Fry, "Hospital Rock in Sequoia National Park," *Sequoia Nature Guide Service Bulletin*, No. 5 (February 17, 1925).
9. Fry, "The Discovery of Sequoia National Park."
10. Herbert Junep, "A Chronological History of Sequoia National Park," an unpublished manuscript (1937), 4; and Fry, "The Discovery of Sequoia Park."
11. Francis Farquhar, "Early History of the Kings River Sierra," *Sierra Club Bulletin*, Vol. 26, No. 1 (February 1941): 31.
12. Fry, "Hospital Rock in Sequoia National Park," 3.
13. Floyd Otter, *The Men of Mammoth Forest* (Ann Arbor, MI: Edwards Brothers, 1963), 37.
14. Ibid., 39.
15. Ibid., 29–30.

16. Ibid., 31–35.

17. Farquhar, 129.

18. As quoted in William Alsup, ed., *Such a Landscape: A Narrative of the 1864 California Geological Survey Exploration of Yosemite, Sequoia, and Kings Canyon from the Diary, Fieldnotes, Letters & Reports of William Henry Brewer* (Yosemite and Three Rivers, CA: Yosemite Association and Sequoia Natural History Association, 1987), 46.

19. Ibid., *passim.*; and Farquhar, 129–53.

20. Two wonderful volumes by geologist James G. Moore detail the story of Clarence King and the California Geological Survey: *Exploring the Highest Sierra* (Stanford, CA: Stanford University Press, 2000) and *King of the 40th Parallel: Discovery in the American West* (Stanford, CA: Stanford General Books, 2006).

21. Farquhar, "Early History of Kings Canyon," 38.

22. Samuel Thomas Porter, *The Silver Rush at Mineral King, California, 1873–1882* (self-published, 1966), 4.

23. Ibid., 10.

24. Ibid., 45.

25. Tulare County Historical Society, "Early Sawmills in Northern Tulare County," *Los Tulares*, No. 6 (October 1950).

26. William C. Tweed, "John Muir in the Southern Sierra," *Valley Trails* (Stockton, CA: Stockton Corral of Westerners, 1976), 4–6.

27. John Muir, *Our National Parks* (New York, NY: Houghton Mifflin and Company, 1901), 268–330.

28. John Muir, "On the Post Glacial History of the Sequoia Gigantea," *American Association for the Advancement of Science Proceedings,* Vol. 25 (August 1876): 242–53.

29. Tweed, "John Muir in the Southern Sierra," 12–14.

30. Farquhar, 179–80 and 194–95.

31. Hubert Dyer, "The Mt. Whitney Trail," *Sierra Club Bulletin*, Vol. 1, No. 1 (January 1893): 7–8.

32. Farquhar, 180–81 and 194–95.

33. Hank Johnston, *They Felled the Redwoods* (Los Angeles, CA: Trans-Anglo Books, 1966), 23–25; Douglas H. Strong, *Trees—or Timber? The Story of Sequoia and Kings Canyon National Parks* (Three Rivers, CA: Sequoia Natural History Association, 1968), 20–21 and 38; and Otter, 70.

34. William C. Tweed, *Kaweah Remembered, The Story of the Kaweah Colony and the Founding of Sequoia National Park* (Three Rivers, CA: Sequoia Natural History Association, 1986), 1–6; see, also, Jay O'Connell, *Co-Operative Dreams: A History of the Kaweah Colony* (Van Nuys, CA: Raven River Press, 1999), 3–36.

CHAPTER FOUR

1. William R. Dudley, "Forest Reservations: With a Report on the Sierra Reservation, California," *Sierra Club Bulletin,* Vol. 1, No. 7 (January 1896): 264–65.

2. Francis P. Farquhar, "Colonel George W Stewart, Founder of Sequoia National Park," *Sierra Club Bulletin*, Vol. 17, No. 1 (February 1932): 49.

3. Douglas Hillman Strong, "A History of Sequoia National Park," an unpublished dissertation (Syracuse, NY: Syracuse University, 1964), 65.

4. Ibid., 68–69.

5. Ibid., 82.

6. Ibid., 84–86.
7. *The Visalia Delta* (June 12, 1890), as quoted in Strong, 92.
8. Strong, 93.
9. Ibid., 100.
10. Ibid., 108.
11. *An Act to set apart a certain tract of land in the State of California as a public park, approved September 25, 1890* (26 Stat. 478).
12. Holway R. Jones, "Mysterious Origins of the Yosemite Park Bill," *Sierra Club Bulletin*, Vol. 48, No. 9 (December 1963): 69–79.
13. Strong, 119.
14. Oscar Berland, "Giant Forest's Reservation: The Legend and the Mystery," *Sierra Club Bulletin*, Vol. 47, No. 9 (December 1962): 74–79.
15. Jones, 77.
16. Berland, 77 and 79–80.
17. "Rules and Regulations Prescribed for the Sequoia National Park . . . , Department of the Interior, October 21, 1890," National Archives, Record Group 79, Entry 1, Sequoia and General Grant (S&GG). (Hereinafter, all National Archives record groups, entry numbers, and file sections will be abbreviated, for example, NA 79:1, S&GG.)
18. Letter, Secretary of the Interior to the Secretary of War (October 21, 1890), NA 79:1, S&GG.
19. Strong, 127, 130; Letter, Andrew Cauldwell to Thomas J. Newsham (November 29, 1890), NA 79:1, S&GG.
20. Letter, William Stone, Assistant Commissioner, General Land Office (GLO), to Secretary of the Interior (November 20, 1890), NA 79:1, S&GG; letter, Cauldwell to Newsham (November 29, 1890), NA 79:1, S&GG; and letter, Cauldwell to Vandever (December 5, 1890), NA 79:1, S&GG.
21. Letter, Secretary Noble to Commissioner, GLO (April 6, 1891), NA 79:1, S&GG; and letter, Commissioner, GLO, to Secretary of the Interior (May 25, 1891), NA 79:1, S&GG.
22. Strong, 133–34.
23. Letter, Cauldwell to Commissioner, GLO (June 1, 1891), NA 79:1, S&GG.
24. "Special Report to the Secretary of the Interior Relative to Cutting Timber at Atwell's Mill" (hereinafter referred to as "Special Report"), September 8, 1891, NA 79:1, S&GG, 4–5; and letter, Commissioner, GLO, to Secretary of the Interior (June 18, 1891), NA 79:1, S&GG.
25. Letter, Lt. Nolan to Captain Dorst (June 28, 1891), NA 79:1, S&GG; and "Special Report," 5.
26. "Special Report," 4–6. The paragraphs that follow draw from this same source.
27. Letter, Lt. Nolan to Captain Dorst (August 9, 1891), NA 79:1, S&GG.
28. Letters, Sgt. P. Daugherty to Dorst (August 19, 1891) (August 31, 1891), NA 79:1, S&GG.
29. Special Report," 13; letter, Cauldwell to Commissioner, GLO (August 12, 1891), NA 79:1, S&GG.
30. U.S. Department of the Interior (USDI), "Report of the Acting Superintendent of the Sequoia National Park, 1891," 9–10. (Hereinafter, the annual reports of the superintendents of Sequoia and General Grant National Parks will be cited as *Annual Report* followed by the *year.*)
31. Letter, W. W. Bowers to Secretary of the Interior (September 17, 1891), NA 79:1, S&GG.
32. Letter, Cauldwell to John Noble (September 17, 1891), NA 79:1, S&GG.
33. Strong, 139–40.
34. Ibid., 140–42.

35. Tweed, "John Muir in the Southern Sierra," *Valley Trails* (Stockton, CA: Stockton Corral of Westerners, 1976), 14–16.
36. Strong, 141–44.
37. Report of Special Agent Allen (February, 1893), as quoted in Strong, 144.
38. *Annual Report 1899*, 3–4.
39. Ibid., 4–5 and 10–11.
40. Strong, 160–61.
41. *Annual Report 1900*, 4–5 and 9–10.
42. Letter, J. W. Dobson to Charles S. Newhall, Supt. of Forests, California (June 1, 1899), NA 79:1, S&GG.
43. Letters, Ernest Britten to Secretary of the Interior (December 22, 1899, and January 22, 1900), NA 79:1, S&GG.
44. Letter, Acting Supt. West to Secretary of the Interior (September 18, 1900), NA 79:1 S&GG.
45. *Annual Report 1901*, 10.
46. William C. Tweed, "Sequoia National Park Concessions: 1898–1926," *Pacific Historian*, Vol. 16, No. 1 (Spring 1972): 37–39.
47. Letter, Britten to Secretary of the Interior (May 9, 1901), NA 79:1, S&GG.
48. *Annual Report 1903*, *passim*.
49. *Annual Report 1907*, 10.
50. Michael P. Cohen, *The History of the Sierra Club, 1892–1970* (San Francisco, CA: The Sierra Club, 1988): 9.
51. For a full account of this trip, see Joseph N. Le Conte, *A Summer of Travel in the High Sierra* (Ashland, OR: Lewis Osborne, 1972): 11.
52. Shirley Sargent, *Solomons of the Sierra: The Pioneer of the John Muir Trail* (Yosemite, CA: Flying Spur Press, 1989).
53. Sierra Club, "Report of the Outing Committee," *Sierra Club Bulletin*, Vol. 4, No. 3 (February 1903): 236.
54. Letter, William Hammond to Secretary of the Interior (January 29, 1902), NA 79:1, S&GG.
55. Rudolph Van Norden, "System of the Mt. Whitney Power and Electric Company," *Journal of Electricity, Power and Gas*, Vol. 21, No. 26 (December 27, 1913): 8–10.
56. Louise Jackson, *Beulah: A Biography of the Mineral King Valley of California* (Tucson, AZ: Westernlore Press, 1988), 111–12.
57. William R. Dudley, "Forestry Notes," *Sierra Club Bulletin,* Vol. 5, No. 2 (June 1904): 146–48.
58. William R. Dudley, "Forestry Notes," *Sierra Club Bulletin,* Vol. 5, No. 4 (June 1905): 326–27.
59. As quoted in Otter, *The Men of Mammoth Forest* (Ann Arbor, MI: Edwards Brothers, 1963), 113–14.
60. *Annual Report 1913*, 3–4.
61. By 1914, in addition to Yellowstone and the three California national parks, Congress had created Mount Rainier (1899), Crater Lake (1902), Mesa Verde (1906), and Glacier (1910) National Parks. Presidents Theodore Roosevelt, William Howard Taft, and Woodrow Wilson, using the authority granted to them by the Antiquities Act of 1906, had also designated fourteen national monuments by 1914, including the first at Devils Tower on September 24, 1906.
62. For a first-person account of this trip and its significance, see Horace Marden Albright and Marian Albright Schenck, *The Mather Mountain Party of 1915: A Full Account of the Adventures of Stephen T. Mather and His Friends in the High Sierra of California* (Three Rivers, CA: Sequoia Natural History Association, 1990).
63. *An Act to establish a National Park Service and for other purposes*, approved August 25, 1916. (39 Stat. 535).
64. Richard C. McLaren and Henry J. LaSala, "Historical Grazing Records," manuscript in the Sequoia and Kings Canyon National Parks Library (1966), *passim*.

CHAPTER FIVE

1. For discussion of the early days of the National Park Service (NPS), see, especially, Horace Albright and Robert Cahn, *The Birth of the National Park Service: 1913–33* (Salt Lake City, UT: Howe Brothers, 1985); Ronald Foresta, *America's National Parks and Their Keepers* (Washington, DC: Resources for the Future, Inc., 1984), especially Chapter 2; John Ise, *Our National Park Policy: A Critical History* (Baltimore, MD: The Johns Hopkins University Press, 1961); and Robert Shankland, *Steve Mather of the National Parks*, 3rd Edition (New York, NY: Alfred A. Knopf, 1970). The best existing summaries of the administration of Sequoia National Park during these formative years are Herbert Junep, "A Complete and Chronological History of Sequoia National Park," an unpublished manuscript (1937), and Douglas Hillman Strong, "A History of Sequoia National Park," an unpublished dissertation (Syracuse, NY: Syracuse University, 1964). Junep's Civilian Conservation Corps (CCC)-era manuscript is largely a compilation of superintendents' annual reports, while Strong devotes most of his attention to the policies of the park's creation and expansion, but both contain some reference to administrative policies and goals.
2. Letter, Secretary of Interior Franklin Lane to Stephen Mather (May 13, 1918). The entire text of the letter can be found in NPS, *Administrative Policies for Natural Areas of the National Park System* (Washington, DC: USDI, 1968), Appendix A, 68–71, or in Albright and Cahn, 69–73.
3. Albright and Cahn, 69–73.
4. Information on Walter Fry can be found in William C. Tweed, "The Early Naturalist Program in Sequoia National Park," an unpublished document (1978); Colonel White is the subject of Rick Hydrick's, "The Genesis of National Park Management: John Roberts White and Sequoia National Park, 1920–1947," *Journal of Forest History*, Vol. 28, No. 2 (April 1984): 68–81.
5. Hydrick, ibid.; see, also, Sequoia and Kings Canyon *Annual Reports 1920–1931*, for an eloquent personal expression of Colonel White's ideas and actions.
6. An excellent treatment of this subject is provided in Strong, 165–92.
7. Daniel J. Tobin, "A Brief History of Sequoia National Park," an unpublished manuscript (n.d.); for an exhaustive account of the campaign to enlarge Sequoia National Park, see Strong, 193–292.
8. See, especially, Albright and Cahn, 81–93; Shankland, 42–55 and 114–28; and letter, Secretary Lane to Mather (May 13, 1918).
9. National Park Service, *The Sequoia and General Grant National Parks: Season of 1916* (Washington, DC: Government Printing Office, 1916); and "Our Big Trees Saved," *National Geographic Magazine*, Vol. 31, No. 1 (January 1917); see, also, *Annual Reports 1920–1926*.
10. For a detailed description of the evolution of the interpretive program, particularly as it affected Sequoia National Park, see William C. Tweed, "The Early Naturalist Program in Sequoia National Park," an unpublished manuscript (1981).
11. Ibid.
12. Ibid.
13. Jim Corson, "A Brief History of the Generals Highway," an unpublished chronology (June 4, 1963), filed under D30.
14. Ibid.
15. Ibid.

16. *Annual Reports 1920–1926, 1935*; Corson; letter, John White to H. E. Petterson of Fresno, CA (July 16, 1921); and letter, Arno Cammerer to W. B. Greeley, of the U.S. Forest Service (USFS) (July 20, 1922).
17. *Annual Report 1926.*
18. "Notes on the Construction of the Wolverton Creek, Lodgepole, Silliman Creek, Clover Creek, and Suwanee Creek Bridges on the Generals Highway," excerpts from *Monthly Superintendent's Reports* (March 22, 1977).
19. For a good indication of the rising control of landscape architects, see, especially, the *Annual Reports 1920–1932.*
20. SEKI (Sequoia and Kings Canyon National Parks), "Press Bulletin on Completion of Generals Highway" (June 19, 1935).
21. Letter, George Goodwin to John White (October 19, 1920); and memorandum, Arno Cammerer to George Goodwin (May 4, 1921).
22. Letter, Arno Cammerer to Ben Maddox (June 24, 1921); memorandum, George Goodwin to John White (March 31, 1922); and memorandum, W. M. Austin to John R. White (March 22, 1927).
23. Memorandum, John White to Horace Albright (May 3, 1929).
24. Foresta, 26–27.
25. Letter, John White to Howard Hays (December 1, 1933).
26. See the voluminous correspondence on Colonel White's "attitude" toward the concessioners and their presence in the Giant Forest, filed under "Giant Forest Development."
27. Memorandum, Frank Kittredge to Horace Albright (August 3, 1933), filed under "Middle Fork Road."
28. Letter, John White to Francis Farquhar (August 29, 1934), filed under "Middle Fork Road."
29. Letter, John White to Horace Albright (March 4, 1938).
30. Tobin, 10–11.
31. Letter, John White to Thomas Vint (January 10, 1928); memorandum, Frank Kittredge to Horace Albright (March 12, 1930); and letter, John White to Chief N.P.S. Engineer (April 4, 1930), all filed under "Roads and Trails."
32. See the early years of *The Sierra Club Bulletin* (especially 1893–1915), for frequent references to the pressing need for new and more trails in the high Sierra. See, also, the extensive correspondence between Colonel White and William Colby and Francis Farquhar of the Sierra Club, filed under "Roads and Trails" and "Sierra Club."
33. Memorandum, Guy Hopping to John White (February 9, 1938), filed under "Roads and Trails."
34. USFS, "John Muir Trail, History," a segment of a larger and apparently lost the Forest Service's report (March 8, 1933); see, also, Edward Hyatt, "History of John Muir Trail" (January 14, 1929), given to Colonel White and filed under the trail name.
35. There is a thick file of correspondence and reports in the SEKI Archives labeled "High Sierra Trail," but, for a synopsis, see William C. Tweed, *The High Sierra Trail* (Three Rivers, CA: Sequoia Natural History Association, 1982).
36. John White, "Some Notes on the Development of Sequoia National Park" (December 14, 1933): 1–2.
37. Ibid.
38. Ibid.; Tobin, 10–11; and *Annual Reports, 1920–1931.*
39. Letter, John White to Stephen Mather (September 20, 1923); letter, Stephen Mather to holders of semi-permanent camps (October 9, 1924); and "Private Camping Sites Definitely Banned in Park," *The Exeter Sun* (July 27, 1933).
40. Letters, John White to H. B. Hommon (February 14, 1923); H. B. Hommon to John White (April 26, 1923).
41. White, "Some Notes"; and *Annual Reports 1920–1932.*

42. White, ibid.
43. Tweed, "Sequoia National Park Concessions," 36–60.
44. Ibid., 49–49.
45. Ibid., 53–54.
46. Ibid., 55–57.
47. Ibid.; "Fred Harvey Co. Buys Parks Firm," *The Fresno Bee* (April 1, 1966).
48. Letter, Howard Hays to John White (August 26, 1927).
49. Ibid.
50. Letter, George Mauger to John White (January 25, 1930).
51. Letter, Howard Hays to John White reporting concession profits (January 1930). The old letter is torn, and no other copy exists. Although the month and year are clear, the specific date is unreadable.
52. SEKI, *Fire Management Plan: An Amendment to the Natural Resources Management Plan* (April 1984 Revision): 14–16.
53. Emilio Meinecke, "Memorandum on the Effects of Tourist Traffic on Plant Life, Particularly Big Trees, Sequoia National Park, California," an unpublished report (May 1926).
54. *Annual Reports 1930–1931.*
55. Letter, John White to Mrs. Edward Breck (April 2, 1930); memorandum, Horace Albright to John White (April 16, 1930); memorandum, John White to Horace Albright reporting on destruction of predators (August 26, 1931); and Horace Albright's response to the above by John White (November 10, 1931).
56. SEKI, *Wildlife Management Plan* (March 1987): 11–15.
57. Ibid., 15–23; and *Annual Reports 1921–1931.*
58. SEKI, *Wildlife Management Plan* (March 1987): 11–15.
59. Marcella M. Sherfy, "The National Park Service and the First World War," *Journal of Forest History*, Vol. 22, No. 4 (October 1978): 203–05.
60. Memorandum, Walter Fry to Stephen Mather (June 17, 1918); memorandum, John White to Stephen Mather (April 22, 1924); letter, Horace Albright to Earl Schlaman (April 15, 1931); and Tobin, 5.
61. Walter Fry, "A Twenty-Five Year Survey of the Animals of Sequoia National Park," described and heavily quoted in George Wright, Joseph Dixon and Ben Thompson, *Fauna of the National Parks of the United States* (Washington, DC: U.S. Department of Interior Fauna Series), Vol. 1, No. 1 (May 1932): 129–31.
62. Referred to in the *Wildlife Management Plan* (1987), 16.
63. Meinecke; John White, "Retrospect," a five-page memorandum to the files on development in Sequoia National Park (1932); and White, "Some Notes."
64. Meinecke, ibid.
65. Letter, Stephen Mather to John White (June 17, 1927); and White, "Some Notes."
66. Letter, Mather to White (June 17, 1927).
67. White, "Some Notes."
68. *Annual Report 1930.*
69. Ibid.
70. Letter, Howard Hays to John White (March 14, 1931).
71. Memorandum, John White to Director (November 23, 1944), summarizing events and conditions for planning, especially in the Giant Forest.

72. See, especially, memoranda, John White to Horace Albright (February 14, 1930) (March 28, 1932); see, also, Albright to White (March 15, 1932).
73. Memorandum, Horace Albright for Washington office files (July 10, 1931), copy filed under "Giant Forest Development."
74. Memorandum, White to Director (November 23, 1944).

CHAPTER SIX

1. John White, "Atmosphere in the National Parks," address to Special Superintendent's Meeting, Washington, D.C. (February 10, 1936), in Lary Dilsaver, ed., *America's National Park System: The Critical Documents*, Revised Edition (Lanham, MD: Rowman & Littlefield, 2016), 123–30.
2. For an excellent summary of CCC operations in the national parks, see John C. Paige, *The Civilian Conservation Corps and the National Park Service, 1933–1942: An Administrative History* (Washington, DC: National Park Service, 1985).
3. Ibid., 66–70 and 131–32.
4. See, especially, *Annual Reports 1933–1938*, and White, "Atmosphere in National Parks."
5. Paige, 70–73; and "Seasonal Narrative Reports of ECW [Emergency Conservation Work] Projects, 1933–1941."
6. Paige, 66–93.
7. Filmore Criss, interview conducted by Dana Abell (August 1974), a two-page interview summary filed under "CCC."
8. Ray DeVoe, interview conducted by Peter Pellegrin (September 23, 1982), a two-page interview summary filed under "CCC."
9. SEKI, "Statement of Conditions in Sequoia National Park Before CCC (1933) and Now (1941)," a list and description of changes and accomplishments (1942).
10. *Annual Reports 1918*, *1940*, and *1941*.
11. Paige, 51–52.
12. White, 123–25.
13. Ibid.
14. *Annual Reports 1931* and *1941*.
15. Rick Hydrick, "The Genesis of National Park Management: John Roberts White and Sequoia National Park, 1920–1947," *Journal of Forest History*, Vol. 28, No. 2 (April 1984): 75.
16. Ibid.; White, "Atmosphere in National Parks"; Letters, Howard Hays to John White (December 6, 1937); Arno Cammerer to John White (September 6, 1931); John White to Horace Albright (May 31, 1930); and John White to Regional Director (March 18, 1946).
17. See *Annual Reports 1936–1938* under "Winter Use."
18. Letter, Lawrence Cook to John White (September 15, 1933).
19. Letter, Daniel Tobin to Yosemite Superintendent C. C. Thompson (September 26, 1934).
20. Ernest Davidson, "A Study Plan and Schedule for Completion of Development Removal Program Giant Forest Area, Sequoia National Park," an in-house report by the Regional Landscape Architect (December 1943).
21. Ibid.
22. Hydrick; and letter, John White to William Colby (May 14, 1938).
23. Letter, Horace Albright to John White (March 15, 1932).
24. Letter, John White to Horace Albright (March 28, 1932).

25. Davidson; *Annual Reports 1935–1938.*
26. Letter, John White to Landscape Architect Thomas Carpenter (May 9, 1933).
27. Letter, John White to George Mauger (October 3, 1933).
28. Letter, George Mauger to John White (August 24, 1936).
29. Letter, John White to George Mauger (September 7, 1936).
30. Letters, John White to Harold Bryant (September 17, 1937); Ernest Davidson to Regional Director (September 15, 1938); and John White to George Mauger (March 4, 1938); and *Annual Report 1940.*
31. Letters, John White to Eivind Scoyen (February 25, 1941) and Eivind Scoyen to John White (March 3, 1941).
32. Memorandum, John White to Regional Director (September 13, 1941).
33. Charles C. Adams, *An Ecological Survey in Northern Michigan: A Report from the University Museum* (Ann Arbor: University of Michigan, Michigan Board of Geological Survey Report, 1905); *An Ecological Survey of Isle Royale, Lake Superior* (East Lansing: Michigan State Biological Survey, 1908); and "Ecological Conditions in National Forests and National Parks," *The Scientific Monthly*, Vol. 20, No. 6 (June 1925): 561–93.
34. Lowell Sumner, "Biological Research and Management in the National Park Service: A History," *The George Wright Forum* (August 1983): 3–27.
35. Ibid.
36. George M. Wright, Joseph Dixon, and Ben Thompson, *Fauna of the National Parks of the United States*, Fauna Series No. 1, USDI, National Park Service (1933).
37. Sumner, 5–13.
38. SEKI, *Wildlife Management Plan* (March 1987): 24–26.
39. Ibid., 17–24.
40. Sumner, 22–25.
41. SEKI, *Development Zone Vegetation Management Plan* (September 1987): 4–26.
42. Emilio Meinecke, "Relocation of Public and Operator Developments in Sequoia National Park," a confidential memorandum to the NPS (November 1944).
43. Newton Drury, "Park Meadows and Tree Encroachment," excerpt from the minutes of the Regional Director's Conference of the NPS, Chicago, Illinois (January 6–15, 1944).
44. John Armstrong, "A Study of Grazing Conditions in the Roaring River District, Kings Canyon National Park, with Recommendations," a report submitted to the Superintendent, Sequoia National Park (April 21, 1942).
45. Letter, John R. White to Mrs. W. K. Webber (January 17, 1927); "Seven Counties Concerned in Greatest Summit-Parks Highway; Plan Organization," *The Visalia Daily Times* (January 17, 1927); and "Proposed New Routing for Parks Highway," *The Fresno Morning Republican* (July 15, 1929).
46. See the minutes of the meetings of the Sierra National Parks Highway Association, filed under "Sierra Way."
47. Ward P. Webber, "Report on the Reconnaissance of a North and South Road Sequoia National Park and Approaches," Office of Chief Engineer, Branch of Engineering, National Park Service (September 1931), filed under "Sierra Way."
48. Letters, John White to Arno Cammerer (December 28, 1935 and January 4, 1936).
49. Letter, Frank Kittredge to Arno Cammerer (January 8, 1936).
50. Letter, Arthur Demaray to Frank Kittredge (March 18, 1935).
51. Letter, Acting Director Demaray to Secretary Harold Ickes (November 30, 1935); and "Minutes of the San Joaquin Valley Council of the California Chamber of Commerce" (December 12, 1935).

52. H. A. Alderton, Jr., and E. E. Erhart, "Route Study of the Proposed Western Divide Highway Between Greenhorn Summit and South Boundary of Sequoia National Park," USDA (U.S. Department of Agriculture), Bureau of Public Roads (September 1935).
53. The Commonwealth Club of California, "Should We Stop Building New Roads into California's High Mountains?" *The Commonwealth*, Vol. 12, No. 22 (June 2, 1936): 327–86.
54. Memorandum, Frank Kittredge to Arno Cammerer (March 19, 1936).
55. "Sierra Way Revived to Handle 'Stub' Freeway Traffic," *The Sierra Club Bulletin*, Vo.. 46 (January 1961).
56. Letters, Arno Cammerer to Allen Hughes (December 15, 1936); and Frank Kittredge to Arno Cammerer (January 8, 1936); and memorandum, John White to Newton Drury (April 18, 1944).
57. Memorandum, John White to Frank Kittredge (July 15, 1944).
58. *Annual Reports 1941–1945.*
59. Letter, Daniel Tobin to Lt. Colonel Joe Myer (April 10, 1944).
60. Memorandum, Herbert Maier to Western Region Superintendents (December 9, 1942); letter, John White to B. M. Hobbick (October 22, 1943); memorandum, Daniel Tobin to Newton Drury (February 7, 1945); and *Annual Reports 1943–1945.*
61. Newton Drury, "The National Parks in Wartime," *American Forests*, Vol. 49, No. 8 (August 1943): 375–78 and 411; Duncan McDuffie, "Grazing in Recreational Areas," *The Sierra Club Bulletin*, Vol. 27, No. 4 (August 1942): 115–16; and John R. White, "Grazing Article for National Parks Magazine," a draft of a position statement (May 7, 1943).
62. Reference to this memorandum is contained in a memorandum from Regional Director Owen Tomlinson to John White (June 10, 1942).
63. Davidson.
64. Letter, Howard Hays to Newton Drury (June 1, 1945).
65. Memoranda, Lawrence Cook to Newton Drury (January 19, 1944), Thomas Vint to Drury (September 4, 1944), and John White to Drury, containing a recapitulation of Olmsted's conclusions (November 3, 1944), Meinecke; Davidson; and John White, "Arguments for and Against Removal of Giant Forest Lodge and Village to New Site," memorandum to the Director (September 16, 1944).
66. Memorandum, John White to Owen Tomlinson (June 4, 1945).
67. See the files under "Giant Forest Development" for the years 1945 and 1946.
68. Memoranda, John White to Newton Drury (September 22, 1945); and Eivind Scoyen to Lawrence Merriam (January 8, 1951).
69. Memorandum, John White to Owen Tomlinson (June 4, 1945).
70. Memorandum, Eivind Scoyen to Lawrence Merriam (January 8, 1951).
71. *Annual Reports 1920* and *1947.*

CHAPTER SEVEN

1. John Muir, "A Rival of the Yosemite—The Canyon of the South Fork of the Kings River," *The Century Magazine,* Vol. 42, No. 1 (November 1891): 77–82.
2. Francis Farquhar, "Kings Canyon National Park," an unpublished manuscript in the Bancroft Archives, University of California, Berkeley (ca. 1938).

3. Alfred Runte, *National Parks: The American Experience* (Lincoln: University of Nebraska Press, 1979).
4. Joseph B. Lippincott, *Storage of Water on the Kings River, California* (Washington, DC: United States Geological Survey (USGS), 1902).
5. Ralph Randell, *Storage Resources of the South and Middle Forks of the Kings River, California* (Washington, DC: Federal Power Commission, 1930).
6. Letters, Chester Warlow to John White, Frank Kittredge, and William Colby (1927–1933), filed under "Kings Canyon."
7. Douglas Hillman Strong, "A History of Sequoia National Park," an unpublished dissertation (Syracuse, NY: Syracuse University, 1964), 219–92; see, also, the extensive correspondence between William Colby and Francis Farquhar of the Sierra Club, Stephen Mather and John White of the NPS, Chester Warlow of Fresno, Congressman Barbour, and representatives of Southern California Edison (1921–1939).
8. Letter, Chester Warlow to John White (ca. 1931), filed under "Kings Canyon."
9. Strong, ibid.
10. Sierra Club, "Kings River Power Development," a confidential memorandum in the Francis Farquhar papers, Bancroft Archives, University of California, Berkeley (1948).
11. Randell; Letter, Chester Warlow to Regional Forester S. B. Show (March 30, 1931), attached to the Randell Report.
12. Randell, ibid.
13. George Gibbs, "Preliminary Plan for Development of Kings River Canyon for Recreation," USFS (1933); George Gibbs, "Reappraisal of the Development Plan for the Kings River Canyon," USFS (1934); and letter, F. L. Olmsted, Jr., to George Gibbs (February 23, 1934), attached to the 1933 Gibbs report.
14. Joseph Elliott, "Description of the Master Plan for the Kings River District," Sequoia National Forest, by the Forest Supervisor (1935).
15. Memorandum, Frank Kittredge to NPS Director Arno Cammerer (January 8, 1936); and San Joaquin Council, California Chamber of Commerce, "Minutes of the Meeting on Sierra Way" (March 13, 1936).
16. See, especially, Barry Mackintosh, "Harold Ickes and the National Park Service," *Journal of Forest History*, Vol. 29, No. 2 (April 1985): 78–84.
17. For a full treatment of Ickes, see T. H. Watkins, *Righteous Pilgrim: The Life and Times of Harold L. Ickes, 1874–1952* (New York, NY: Henry Holt and Company, 1990).
18. Mackintosh; see, also, S. B. Show, "Background and Events of Kings Canyon Controversy," Part 4 of an unpublished interview by Amelia R. Fry, Bancroft Archives, University of California, Berkeley (1963): 175–211.
19. William Colby, an unpublished interview by Corrinne Gibb, Bancroft Archives, University of California, Berkeley (1951): 51–56.
20. As quoted in Mackintosh, 82.
21. Ibid., 78–84.
22. Memorandum, Harold Ickes to Arno Cammerer (September 20, 1935), Francis Farquhar Papers, Bancroft Archives, University of California, Berkeley.
23. Frank Kittredge, "Kings Canyon National Park," an unpublished memoir of the former Regional Director of the NPS (1950), 20; and B. F. Manbey, seventeen unpublished memoranda to the Regional Director of the NPS reporting on meetings with San Joaquin Valley citizens and associations (1938).
24. Kittredge, ibid.

25. Manbey.
26. Ibid.
27. Corson, J. W., "A Brief Talk on the Future of Cedar Grove and Tehipite Valley," a transcript of a presentation made February 17, 1964; memorandum, B. E Manbey to the NPS Regional Director (July 27, 1949); and NPS, "Résumé of Correspondence and Actions regarding the exclusion of Cedar Grove and Tehipite areas from Kings Canyon National Park" (February 14, 1952).
28. NPS, "A List of Organizations Opposed to the Creation of Kings Canyon National Park" (March 1939).
29. Kittredge; and Show.
30. Kittredge; and letter, Chester Warlow to Frank Kittredge (date unclear; ca. 1939).
31. Irving Brant, *Adventures in Conservation with Franklin D. Roosevelt* (Flagstaff, AZ: Northland Publishing Company 1989). See, especially, Chapter 10 on Kings Canyon.
32. Show.
33. Mrs. Charles Edge, "Statement on H.R. 3794 to House Committee on Public Lands," in *Establishing the John Muir–Kings Canyon National Park, California, hearings before the Committee on the Public Lands of the 76th Congress* (March 1939): 428–34; James A. Foote, "Statement on H.R. 3794 to House Committee on Public Lands," ibid., 290–99; and Brant, 204.
34. The entire account of Elliott's misdeeds, Gearhart's response, and the reaction of House members is available in *The Congressional Record*, House, Vol. 84, 76th Congress, 1st Session (May 2, 1939), 5033–45; See, also, Brant, 204–05.
35. Brant, 147–217.
36. Ibid.
37. *The Congressional Record,* House, Vol. 84, Appendix to the 76th Congress, 1st Session (August 4, 1939).
38. John Ise, *Our National Park Policy* (New York, NY: Arno Press, 1979); and Kittredge.
39. *Annual Report 1940*.
40. Memorandum, Acting Director Arthur Demaray to Secretary Ickes (May 14, 1940).
41. Memorandum, C. M. Granger to Regional Forester Show (July 11, 1940).
42. Memorandum, M. E. Griffith, U.S. Commissioner, Sequoia National Park, to Eivind Scoyen (July 14, 1949).
43. Memorandum, Eivind Scoyen to the Regional Director (May 20, 1949).
44. Letters, Chester Warlow to Arthur Demaray (December 30, 1938, and May 24, 1940) and to George Mauger (September 14, 1954).
45. See, especially, letters, William Colby to Newton Drury (September 5, 1946) and John White to Arno Cammerer (November 11, 1940).
46. Letter, John White to Guy Hopping (October 23, 1940).
47. Frederick Law Olmsted, Jr., "A Report on Kings Canyon Development Plans," *The Sierra Club Bulletin*, Vol. 32 (1947): 112–24; and letter, John White to Guy Hopping (November 1, 1940).
48. Letter, Warlow to Demaray (December 30, 1938).
49. Ibid.
50. Letter, Demaray to Warlow (January 20, 1939).
51. Letter, Warlow to Demaray (May 24, 1940): 2.
52. Letter, Warlow to Arthur (June 10, 1940); and letter, Warlow to Eivind Scoyen (March 5, 1952).

53. Olmsted, 112–24.
54. Letter, Thomas Carpenter, NPS Landscape Architect, to Regional Director O. A. Tomlinson (July 27, 1948); *Sierra Club Bulletin*, Vol. 34 (1949): 13.
55. Letter, Carpenter to Tomlinson (July 27, 1948).
56. Olmsted.
57. Ibid.; and memorandum, Superintendent Eivind Scoyen to Director Newton Drury (February 3, 1950).
58. Olmsted.
59. David Brower, "Kings Canyon National Park; Landscape Planning in the South Fork Canyon," an introduction to the report by Frederick Law Olmsted, Jr., 112.
60. Olmsted; and memorandum, Regional Director O. A. Tomlinson to Director Newton Drury (January 27, 1950).
61. National Park Service, "Kings Canyon Development Plan," a three-page summary of the proposed development on the canyon of the South Fork, prepared for the Sierra Club (ca. Spring 1947).
62. Letter, Regional Director O. A. Tomlinson to Warlow (August 1947).

CHAPTER EIGHT

1. *Annual Reports* 1943–1945.
2. Conrad Wirth, *Parks, Politics and the People* (Norman: University of Oklahoma Press, 1980), 61.
3. As quoted in W. A. Carnes, "A Look Back to Look Ahead," a paper delivered at the "Mission 66 Frontiers Conference" (April 24, 1961): 4; see, also, Edward K. Muller, ed., *DeVoto's West: History, Conservation, and the Public Good* (Athens: Swallow Press/Ohio University Press, in association with the Center for American Places, 2005), in particular Part Four: "Protection of the National Parks," 179–218.
4. *Annual Reports 1940, 1947,* and *1955*.
5. "Road Will Open New Scenic Area in Kings Canyon," *The Fresno Bee* (March 25, 1947); and *Annual Reports 1948, 1952,* and *1954–1958*.
6. *Annual Reports 1947* and *1952–1955*.
7. Wirth, 237–45.
8. Ibid., 237–38.
9. Ibid., 237–63.
10. Ibid.
11. Ibid.
12. SEKI, "Mission 66 for Sequoia and Kings Canyon National Parks," a narrative report on plans released in Washington D.C., 1956; "Summary of Mission 66 Objectives and Program for Sequoia and Kings Canyon National Parks" (Detailed Bulletin, May 7, 1956); and "Statistical Report for Mission 66: Sequoia and Kings Canyon National Parks" (November 9, 1955).
13. "Statistical Report."
14. *Annual Report 1959*.
15. "Mission 66 Accomplishments, July 1, 1956–June 30, 1966."
16. Letter, Howard Hays to Conrad Wirth (August 15, 1955).

17. Letters, Newton Drury to George Mauger (February 4, 1941) and Secretary of Interior J. Krug to Representative J. H. Peterson (July 7, 1949).
18. Letter, George Mauger to John White (January 5, 1945); and memorandum, John White to Newton Drury (January 8, 1945).
19. "Master Plan Development Outline, Kings Canyon Area, South Fork Region" (May 1957) 10–12; and "Master Plan for the Preservation and Use of Sequoia and Kings Canyon National Parks, California" (October 1961): Chapter 5, 4–7. For information on the concession contract, see memorandum, Chief of Concessions Management Donald Lee to Regional Director Merriam (November 12, 1953).
20. See, especially, memorandum, NPS Administrative Officer to Assistant Superintendent of SEKI (February 24, 1972), and also the large volume of correspondence between the NPS in both Washington, D.C., and the regional office, George Mauger, B. F. Quinn, and Walter Lindborg of the concession company, and representatives of the Pacific Gas and Electric Company, filed under Cedar Grove Development (1957–1972).
21. See two memoranda, Eivind Scoyen to Regional Director Tomlinson (June 4, 1948, and August 31, 1949).
22. Memorandum, Acting Superintendent Carlson to Regional Director Merriam (March 3, 1952); and memorandum, Los Angeles Department of Water and Power to the California State Board of Water and Power Commissioners (April 1952).
23. Charles Kaupke, "Summary of Development of the Pine Flat Project," Kings River Water District (December 1952); memorandum, Acting Director Wirth to W. A. Hoyt, Commissioner of Reclamation (September 12, 1949); and Michael Straus and Richard Boke, North Fork Kings River Development, Central Valley Basin Plan, California, Bureau of Reclamation Project Planning Report No. 2–4, 23–3 (August 1949).
24. Corson, "A Brief Talk on the Future of Cedar Grove and Tehipite Valley" (February 17, 1964).
25. Ibid.
26. Letter from Attorney Northcutt Ely to Howard Hays (August 4, 1954).
27. See the voluminous correspondence between George Mauger and NPS officials from SEKI, the regional office, and the Washington, D.C., office during the period 1960–1963, filed under "Cedar Grove Development."
28. *Annual Reports 1965–1972.*
29. SEKI, "Master Plan Development Outline, Sequoia and Kings Canyon: Kings Canyon Area, South Fork Region" (May 1957).
30. SEKI, "Draft of Proposed Replacement of National Park Service and Concessioner Facilities, Cedar Grove, Kings Canyon National Park" (July 15, 1972).
31. See, especially, correspondence under files for "Development" in the two parks to note the preponderance of attention given to reports accepted from landscape architects from 1925 to the 1950s. See, also, reports of the park scientist and *Annual Reports* for the same period. It is worth nothing that landscape architecture began to embrace more fully the principles and practices of ecological design and planning, especially during the 1950s and 1960s, when the modern environmental movement in the U.S. emerged. The key book in this development remains Ian L. McHarg, *Design with Nature* (Garden City, NY: Natural History Press, 1969), which was a finalist for the National Book Award; see, also, George F. Thompson and Frederick R. Steiner, eds., *Ecological Design and Planning* (New York, NY: John Wiley and Sons, 1996), which also became a landmark book.
32. Memoranda, Director Demaray to Regional Director Merriam (June 22, 1951); Superintendent Scoyen to Regional Director Tomlinson (August 18, 1948); and Merriam to Director Wirth (February 8, 1954); and *Annual Reports 1948–1952.*

33. See the correspondence between George Mauger and Howard Hays on one side and SEKI and Western Region officials on the other from 1947 through 1952, filed under "Development—Giant Forest" and "Concession Relations."
34. Memoranda, Demaray to Merriam (June 22, 1951); Merriam to Wirth (February 8, 1954); and Scoyen to Tomlinson (April 28, 1948). White predicted what the concessioner would do in a memorandum to Regional Director Tomlinson (June 4, 1945).
35. See, especially, memoranda, Demaray to Merriam (June 22, 1951) and Thomas Carpenter to Merriam (March 3, 1955); and SEKI, "Master Plan Development Outline," section on concessions (1952).
36. Letter, George Mauger to Assistant Superintendent Oscar Carlson (June 6, 1947), which gives an inventory of concession structures.
37. Memorandum, Landscape Architect William Rosenberg to Chief, Western Office, Division of Design and Construction (February 21, 1957).
38. Ibid.; and *Annual Report 1950–1953*.
39. See, especially, letters, John Davis to George Mauger (February 5, 1964) and George Mauger to John Davis (January 23, 1965); and correspondence listed under "Roads and Trails" and "Development—Giant Forest" between Mauger and park officials.
40. Letters, George Mauger to Thomas Allen (July 7, 1956, August 13, 1956, and January 17, 1957) and Thomas Allen to George Mauger (May 3, 1957).
41. Memoranda, Eivind Scoyen to Regional Director Tomlinson (September 15 and September 25, 1950); letter, Howard Hays to Secretary Oscar Chapman (October 25, 1950); and memorandum, Regional Forester Burnett Sanford to Superintendent Scoyen (October 9, 1950).
42. See, especially, George Mauger, "Felling the Leaning Sequoia Tree," an unpublished essay (November 1950); see, also, memorandum, Newton Drury to Regional Director Tomlinson (October 30, 1950).
43. See the general correspondence in file "Hazard Trees" for the period September through November 1950.
44. Memoranda, Eivind Scoyen to Owen Tomlinson (September 25, 1950); Scoyen to Lawrence Merriam (June 23, 1953); and Mauger, "Felling the Leaning Sequoia Tree."
45. SEKI, "Mission 66 for Sequoia and Kings Canyon National Parks."
46. Ibid.
47. Yosemite National Park, "Report on the Effects of Human Impact Upon the Giant Sequoias of the Mariposa and Tuolumne Groves—Yosemite National Park," Committee Report to Superintendent Preston (1954).
48. Emilio Meinecke, "Relocation of Public and Operator Developments in Sequoia National Park," a report to Superintendent White (November 1944).
49. Richard Hartesveldt, "The Effects of Human Impact upon Sequoia Gigantea and Its Environment in the Mariposa Grove," a preliminary report to the NPS (1959). Hartesveldt completed his extensive dissertation with the same title for the University of Michigan in 1962.
50. Memorandum, John Davis to Regional Director Merriam (June 20, 1960)
51. "Recommendations from the Giant Forest Development Meeting" (June 1960).
52. Memorandum, Conrad Wirth to Lawrence Merriam (August 16, 1960).
53. Bureau of Public Roads, "Reconnaissance Report of Generals Highway Route from Ash Mountain Park Headquarters to Vicinity of Red Fir, Sequoia, and Kings Canyon National Parks, Tulare County, California." U.S.

Department of Commerce (1961); Bureau of Public Roads, "Supplementary Report of Generals Highway Route 1 . . . " (1962). Much of the data in these reports can be found on the enclosed maps.

54. D. Jackson Faustman, "Traffic Analysis, Master Plan Studies Sequoia and Kings Canyon National Parks, California, Report to the National Park Service" (October 1969).

55. Letter, Regional Director Chapman to Senator John Tunney (October 15, 1974).

56. Memorandum, Superintendent John McLaughlin to Regional Director William Bowen (September 2, 1969)

57. *Master Plan.*

58. Without any explanation, all correspondence and planning documents from 1965 on discuss a pillow limit of 1,200 or 1,240, while those of 1963 specifically maintain the original 1,000. There is no documentation extant concerning this important change.

59. Memorandum, Park Forester Chris Cameron to Chief Ranger R. Stenmark (January 3, 1967).

60. "Draft of Construction and Development Program Proposed for Inclusion in Written Supplemental Agreement with Government Services, Incorporated for Sequoia and Kings Canyon National Parks" (November 6, 1972).

61. *Master Plan.*

62. For a more complete view of this important trend, see Richard West Sellars, *Preserving Nature in the National Parks: A History* (New Haven, CT: Yale University Press, 1997).

63. As quoted in Lowell Sumner, "Biological Research and Management in the National Park Service: A History," *The George Wright Forum* (August 1983): 18.

64. Ibid.

65. A. Starker Leopold, Stanley Cain, Ira Gabrielson, Clarence Cottam, and Thomas Kimball, "A Vignette of Primitive America," *Sierra Club Bulletin*, Vol. 48, No. 3 (March 1963): 2–11. Also published as "Advisory Board on Wildlife Management Appointed by Secretary of the Interior Udall," in Lary Dilsaver, ed., *America's National Park System: The Critical Documents*, Revised Edition (Lanham, MD: Rowman & Littlefield, 2016), 210–24.

66. Ibid.

67. *American Men of Science*, 11th Edition (New York, NY: R. R. Bowker Company, 1966). Of note, a children's book on the Leopold family was recently declared "the best children's book for the State of Wisconsin" by the Library of Congress. See Nancy Nye Hunt, *Aldo Leopold's Shack: Nina's Story* (Chicago, IL: Center for American Places at Columbia College Chicago, 2011).

68. Cain, et al., 4.

69. Ibid., 5.

70. Ibid., 8.

71. Lowell Sumner, "Biological Research and Management in the National Park Service: A History," *The George Wright Forum* (August 1983): 18–23; memoranda, Assistant Director to All Field Offices (October 14, 1965), Director Hartzog to All Field Offices (September 22, 1967); and letter, Secretary Udall to Leopold Committee Members, printed with the report in *Sierra Club Bulletin*, *op. cit.*, 3.

72. Sumner, ibid.; and *Annual Report 1963.*

73. See the correspondence and memoranda from both the Research Biologist and Chief Ranger for the period 1965–1972, filed under "Wildlife"; see, also, *Master Plan.*

74. Cain, et al., 6.
75. *Wildlife Management Plan*, 24–25.
76. Ibid.; and memorandum, Park Biologist Sumner to Superintendent Scoyen (August 12, 1955) on the deer-reduction program of 1955 and summarizing actions up to that time.
77. See the annual reports from the Park Biologist to the Superintendent on the deer-reduction program, filed under "Wildlife."
78. "1964–65 Deer and Range Management Plan for Sequoia and Kings Canyon National Parks" (1964).
79. *Wildlife Management Plan*.
80. See SEKI, *Bighorn Sheep Management Plan* (August 1986): 15; see, also, letter, Forest Supervisor Rodel, USFS, to Superintendent McLaughlin (January 5, 1971).
81. See, especially, *SEKI, Bear Management Plan* (December 1987 and subsequent revisions).
82. *Wildlife Management Plan*, 10–11.
83. Hartesveldt, " The Effects of Human Impact upon Sequoia Gigantea and Its Environment in the Mariposa Grove."
84. Cain, et al., 211; and SEKI, *Fire Management Plan* (April 1984 Revision): 21–31.
85. SEKI *Fire Management Plan*.
86. Ibid.
87. John Armstrong, *A Study of Grazing Conditions in the Roaring River District, Kings Canyon National Park, with Recommendations* (1942); Lowell Sumner, *Special Report on a Wildlife Study of the High Sierra in Sequoia and Yosemite National Parks and Adjacent Territory* (1936); Lowell Sumner, *Special Report on Range Management and Wildlife Protection in Kings Canyon National Park* (1940); and Lowell Sumner, *Erosion in the Roaring River District, Kings Canyon National Park—A Checkup after Six Years* (1947).
88. Lowell Sumner, *Tourist Damage to Mountain Meadows in Sequoia and Kings Canyon National Parks, 1935–1948* (1948).
89. Bruce Black, *Erosion in the Roaring River District, Kings Canyon National Park: A Pictorial Review after Ten Years* (1952).
90. Memorandum, Stanley Bechtel to Chief Ranger (May 2, 1952).
91. John A. Rutter and Bruce Black, *Back Country Use Report* (February 1953).
92. Ibid., 32.
93. Memorandum, Lowell Sumner to NPS Regional Naturalist, April 1, 1953 (also included at the back of the *Back Country Use Report*).
94. Letters, Superintendent Scoyen to B. F. Bole (October 18, 1951, April 25, 1952, and June 1, 1953); Superintendent to Richard Leonard, Sierra Club (October 1, 1951); and Mrs. Virginia Romaine to Superintendent Scoyen (October 5, 1951).
95. Henry M. Brown, "Lewis Camp," *Los Tulares*, No. 80 (March 1969); and memorandum, Ranger John Nealis to Chief Ranger (November 11, 1952).
96. Memorandum, Howard Stagner to Superintendent Scoyen (January 3, 1952).
97. See the enormous amount of correspondence between these two associations and the parks between 1945 and the present, filed under "Stock Use" and "Backcountry Management."
98. Memorandum, Assistant Director Thomas Allen to Superintendent Scoyen (November 7, 1953).
99. Letter, Chief Ranger Irwin Kerr to Superintendent, Lassen Volcanic National Park (March 10, 1955).
100. See the correspondence between Hugh Traweek and his many supporters and the NPS, filed under "Traweek" (dating from January 1, 1958, to September 14, 1961).
101. *Annual Report 1958*.

102. Carl W. Sharsmith, *A Report on the Status, Changes and Ecology of Back Country Meadows in Sequoia and Kings Canyon National Parks* (1959).
103. Ibid.
104. See, especially, William J. Briggle, *A Report on the Restrictions Imposed on Public Camping and Grazing at Kearsarge Lakes and Bullfrog Lake in Sequoia and Kings Canyon National Parks,* Report to the Superintendent (January 19, 1960).
105. "Backcountry Report" (1960), Annual Report to the Chief Ranger and Superintendent.
106. Maurice Thede, Lowell Summer, and William Briggle, *Backcountry Management Plan for Sequoia and Kings Canyon National Parks* (Washington, DC: USDI, NPS, 1963).
107. See *Annual Backcountry Reports* filed for the years 1960–1969 as well as correspondence filed under "Stock Use" for the same dates.
108. *Annual Backcountry Reports 1959* and *1972*.
109. *Annual Backcountry Report 1971*, 9–10.
110. H. T. Harvey, R. J. Hartesveldt, and J. T. Stanley, *Wilderness Impact Study Report, Interim Report to the Sierra Club Outing Committee* (September 1972).
111. Rendel Alldredge, *Some Capacity Theory for Parks and Recreation Areas, Report from the NPS to the Secretary of the Interior* (June 1972); and memorandum, Howard Chapman to superintendents, Western Region, November 27, 1972.
112. Memoranda, Bruce Kilgore to Chief Scientist, Washington, D.C., office of the NPS (February 1, 1972; Gordon Boyd to Superintendent Henry Schmidt (January 23, 1973); and *A Use Limit Plan for Portions of the John Muir Wilderness and Kings Canyon National Park*, Interagency Plan by the USFS and NPS (March 16, 1973).
113. *The Wilderness Act,* Public Law 88–577, 88th Congress (September 3, 1964).
114. Ibid.
115. SEKI, "Wilderness Proposal for Sequoia and Kings Canyon" (November 1975). This proposal includes a two-page synopsis of the events and actions that occurred in the planning and public-hearing procedures from the time of the original proposal of November 1966.
116. Ibid.
117. Ibid.
118. Although strongly biased against the USFS and Walt Disney Productions, the most complete account of the Mineral King controversy remains John L. Harper, *Mineral King, Public Concern with Government Policy* (Arcata, CA: Pacifica Publishing Company, 1982). Harper worked as an activist for the Sierra Club during the controversy.

CHAPTER NINE

1. USDI, *Master Plan, Sequoia and Kings Canyon National Parks* (1971): 10–18.
2. Ibid.
3. Sasaki, Walker Associates, *Development Concept Plan, Giant Forest and Lodgepole, Sequoia and Kings Canyon National Parks, California* (1974): 7.
4. Ibid., 28.
5. NPS News Release, "Sequoia Park Development Plan Being Revised" (November 20, 1974).
6. NPS, *Development Concept Planning Alternatives* (May 1975); see, also, the attached "Planning Alternatives Response Booklet."
7. NPS News Release, "Sequoia and Kings Canyon National Parks to Hold Public Meetings" (December 21, 1977).

8. NPS, *Draft Development Concept Plan, Giant Forest/Lodgepole Area of Sequoia and Kings Canyon National Park* (September 1977), inside cover, 21–51.
9. NPS, *Draft Environmental Statement, Proposed Development Concept Plan, Giant Forest/Lodgepole Area, Sequoia and Kings Canyon National Parks (November 1977)*: 266/39–266/41.
10. NPS, *Final Environmental Statement, Proposed Development Concept Plan* (June 1979): 266/39–266/41.
11. "Briefing Statement—Concessions Issues, Sequoia and Kings Canyon National Parks" (December 7, 1988), filed under "Park Development, GSI Move and Contract Negotiation."
12. Ibid.
13. Memorandum, Superintendent, Sequoia and Kings Canyon to Regional Director, Western Region, "Clover Creek Comprehensive Design Plan Comments" (March 1, 1985).
14. "Briefing Statement—Concessions Issues, Sequoia and Kings Canyon National Parks" (December 7, 1988), filed under "Park Development, GSI [Guest Services, Inc.] Move and Contract Negotiation."
15. "Minutes of Meeting" (December 6, 1989), filed under "Park Development, GSI Move and Contract Negotiation."
16. Laura Soulliere Harrison, *Architectural Character Guidelines Study, Sequoia and Kings Canyon National Parks: Inventory of Significant Structures,* NPS, Denver Service Center (DSC) (1989); and NPS, *Architectural Character Guidelines: Sequoia & Kings Canyon National Parks*, DSC (1989).
17. NPS, *Planning Alternatives Draft, Cedar Grove, Kings Canyon National Park* (1975): 6–21.
18. NPS, *Environmental Review, Development Concept Plan, Cedar Grove, Kings Canyon National Park* (May 1976); and NPS, *Development Concept Plan, Cedar Grove, Kings Canyon National Park* (May 1976).
19. *The Visalia Times-Delta*, "High Court Rejects Sierra Club Suit" (April 19, 1972).
20. *The San Francisco Chronicle* (May 5, 1972).
21. USFS, *Draft Environmental Statement, Mineral King Recreation Development* (1974).
22. USFS, *Summary, Final Environmental Statement, Mineral King Recreation Development, Sequoia National Forest* (1976).
23. NPS, "Department of the Interior, Feasibility Report, Mineral King, California," 46.
24. Letter, John Krebs to John Maguire, Chief, USFS (February 17, 1977).
25. *The San Francisco Chronicle*, "Mineral King Plan Appears Doomed" (January 26, 1978).
26. NPS, *Comprehensive Management Plan, Mineral King, Sequoia and Kings Canyon National Parks* (November 1980): 3.
27. NPS, *Environmental Assessment for the Development Concept Plan, Grant Grove and Redwood Mountain, Sequoia–Kings Canyon National Parks* (1983): 21–32.
28. NPS, *Final Environmental Impact Statement, Development Concept Plan, Grant Grove/Redwood Mountain* (1987): 4–5.
29. NPS, *Plan for the Management of Backcountry Use* (May 22, 1973).
30. Letter, Superintendent Evison to Interested Citizens (February 27, 1984).
31. NPS News Release, "Comment Period Extended" (March 28, 1984).
32. NPS, *Natural Resources Management Plan and Environmental Assessment* (December 1976).
33. NPS, News Release, "Park Service to Modify Way of Managing Fire in Sequoia Groves in Response to Report of Committee of Independent Experts" (March 2, 1987).
34. William C. Tweed, co-author of this book, had the pleasant assignment of finding the right mountain.
35. William C. Tweed, ed., *Proceedings of the Sequoia and Kings Canyon National Parks Second Century Conference: Held at Giant Forest, Sequoia National Park, California, October 5–7, 1990* (Three Rivers, CA: Sequoia Natural History Association, 1991).
36. Ibid.

CHAPTER TEN

1. United States Census Bureau data are available at www.quickfacts.census.gov/qfd/states/06/06019.
2. Data from the NPS Statistical Webpage: www.nature.nps.gov/stats.
3. Data provided by the SEKI Wilderness Office (2014).
4. Executive Summary, Sequoia and Kings Canyon National Parks—VSP Visitor Study 258 (August 2012).
5. Philip S. Cook, *Impacts of Visitor Spending on the Local Economy: Sequoia and Kings Canyon National Parks*, Natural Resource Report NPS/NRSS/EAD/NRR—20134/713, NPS Park Studies Unit, University of Idaho.
6. Report on October 1991 Work Session, "The Future of Giant Forest and Wuksachi: Package 200."
7. Briefing Statements, *"Management Objectives" for Wuksachi Village* and *Concessions Charrette for Wuksachi Village, Sequoia National Park*, by William C. Tweed (March 23, 1992).
8. NPS News Release, "Park Service Completes Purchase of Concessioner Facilities in Sequoia's Giant Forest" (January 20, 1993).
9. Another casualty of this era was the downhill skiing facility at Wolverton. Operated by GSI, the facility had been a money loser for years, and the NPS allowed the concessioner to close the facility after the 1992 season.
10. "Sequoia National Park, Wuksachi Village, Village Center and South Terrace Lodging, Preliminary Program" (draft version) (August 1993).
11. Ibid.
12. Memorandum, Steve Spickard, Economic Research Associates, to Wuksachi Village Planning Team, "Title I 50% Preliminary Design, Revised Economic Forecast" (June 8, 1994).
13. Because the effluent from the Giant Forest's wastewater-treatment plant in the Lower Kaweah River was sent to a spray field after being processed, the system was particularly unsatisfactory when snow covered the ground. In essence, the NPS disposed of partially treated winter effluent in the Giant Forest by spraying it onto the snow and allowing it to disperse when the snowpack melted in the spring.
14. NPS News Release, "Sequoia's Giant Forest Village Closes for Season" (October 29, 1994).
15. NPS News Release, "Park Business Opportunities Re-advertised" (October 24, 1995).
16. NPS News Release, "Mixed Results on Two Park Concessions Contracts" (June 5, 1995).
17. William C. Tweed, co-author of this book, was a part of the parks' management team at this point, and he took part in numerous discussions about the difficulty of attracting a new concessioner.
18. NPS News Release, "Sequoia Concessioner Receives Contract Extension" (January 10, 1996).
19. NPS News Release, "Sequoia Park Business Opportunity Re-advertised" (October 24, 1995).
20. Draft maps of proposed alternatives, Giant Forest, Sequoia National Park, dated June 13, 1994, filed under "Project SEKI 200JA."
21. Memorandum, Kevin Percival (DSC) to William C. Tweed, et al., "SEKI/WRO Videoconference (August 24, 1994)," filed under "Project SEKI 200JA."
22. *Draft Interim Implementation and Forest Restoration Plan/Environmental Assessment, Giant Forest, Sequoia National Park, California* (May 1995), filed under "Project SEKI 200JA."
23. NPS News Release, "Public Invited to Workshops on Future of Giant Forest in Sequoia National Park" (August 11, 1995).
24. *Alternatives for Interim Management and Environmental Assessment, Giant Forest, Sequoia National Park, California, Analysis of Public Comment Worksheets*, prepared by Mark Lellouch, a graduate student at Stanford University

(October 1995), filed under "Project SEKI 200JA ."

25. "Park Alternative for the Interim Management of Giant Forest, Sequoia National Park" (October 11, 1995), filed under "Project SEKI 200JA."

26. Memorandum, Kevin Percival and Suzy Stutzman, landscape architects at the DSC, to Marvin Wall, Project Manager, DSC, "Selection of Alternative Meeting at Park October 12–13 1995; reference Package 200JA, Giant Forest Interim Management Plan" (October 16, 1995), filed under "Project SEKI 200JA."

27. All of this took place in the midst of a major political showdown between the Republican majority in Congress and Democratic President Bill Clinton. The entire federal government shut down for several days, due to the lack of a budget on November 14, 1995, and then again on December 18. During this second impasse, which went on for three full weeks, Sequoia and Kings Canyon National Parks were closed to the public, and most staff members were idled.

28. NPS, *Interim Management Plan and Finding of No Significant Impact, Giant Forest, Sequoia National Park, California* (January 1996).

29. NPS News Release, "New Plan for Giant Forest Approved" (April 16, 1996).

30. Personal correspondence, Athena Demetry to William C. Tweed (October 5, 2010).

31. Athena Demetry, *Regeneration within canopy gaps in a giant sequoia–mixed conifer forest: Implications for forest restoration*, Master of Science thesis (Flagstaff: University of Northern Arizona, 1995). (Midway through her graduate work, Demetry moved from the University of Wisconsin-Madison to Northern Arizona University.)

32. The rediscovery of the Booker T. Washington Tree required considerable sleuthing by park employees. A historic photo showed the tree marked with a sign nailed to its trunk. Using the photo, park curator Ward Eldredge studied the many sequoias along Moro Rock Road, which had been constructed the same year the tree was named. His lucky guess paid off when he found the tree. The nail that had held the original sign still protruded from the trunk.

33. *ASLA 2007 Professional Awards*, www.asla.org/awards/2007.

34. NPS, *Draft General Management Plan and Comprehensive River Management Plan/Environmental Impact Statement*, DSC (2004), Volume 1, iii.

35. NPS, *Master Plan,* 24.

36. NPS News Release, "Sierra Wilderness Managers Standardize Use Limits" (March 26, 1992).

37. Contained within the "Briefing Notebook on Wilderness Group Size Changes at Sequoia and Kings Canyon National Parks" (April 6, 1993). The notebook is in the files of the SEKI Wilderness Office.

38. Certified letter, Peter Browning to Ritter (September 17, 1992). A copy is in the files of the SEKI Wilderness Office.

39. NPS, *Environmental Assessment, Revise Wilderness Group Size Limits for Persons and Stock, Sequoia and Kings Canyon National Parks* (May 5, 1993).

40. Judge Wilken did absolve the NPS of acting in "bad faith."

41. NPS News Release, "Public Input Needed for Park Wilderness Plan" (June 3, 1996).

42. NPS, *Sequoia & Kings Canyon National Parks Wilderness Planning Workbook* (May 1998): 2–3. The nine "topics" identified by the NPS for discussion in the Wilderness Management Plan were (1) campfires, (2) bears and food storage, (3) party size, (4) camping/campsites, (5) toilets/sanitation, (6) trail, (7) the "Minimum Requirement," (8) stock use and meadow management, and (9) commercial use and wilderness permits.

43. NPS, *General Management Plan News Letter 5* (January 2000).

44. Indicative of earlier work in this area by the cabin community is John Elliott, *Mineral King Historic District: Contextual History and Description* (Exeter, CA: Mineral King Preservation Society, 1994).

45. Ethan Carr and Steve McNeil, *The Cultural Landscape of Mineral King, Sequoia & Kings Canyon National Parks: Determination of Eligibility for the National Register of Historic Places* (Denver, CO: NPS, DSC, 1999).
46. NPS, *Mineral King Road Cultural Landscape District: Sequoia and Kings Canyon National Parks* (2008), un-numbered introductory section.
47. NPS, *Draft General Management Plan and Comprehensive River Management Plan/Environmental Impact Statement*, DSC (2004), Volume 1, 77–159.
48. NPS, *Sequoia and Kings Canyon National Parks: Draft General Management Plan and Comprehensive River Management Plan/Environmental Impact Statement*, Volume 1, 148.
49. In a redistricting that resulted from the 2000 U.S. Census, Congressional boundaries were redrawn in Central California, and the two parks became a part of the 21st District. In November 2002, in the first election after the new boundaries were established, Devin Nunes was elected to the seat.
50. NPS, *Final General Management Plan and Comprehensive River Management Plan/Environmental Impact Statement, Sequoia and Kings Canyon National Parks, Tulare and Fresno Counties California, Record of Decision*, approved September 14, 2007, Volume 1, 11.
51. Ibid., 2–4.
52. Ibid., 158, 164.
53. Letter, Peter Browning, Coordinator, High Sierra Hikers Association, to Richard Martin, Superintendent, Sequoia and Kings Canyon National Parks (October 5, 2004); available on the HSHA's Website: http://www.highsierrahikers.org/.
54. Letter, Peter Browning, President, High Sierra Hikers Association, to David Graber, General Management Plan Coordinator, Sequoia and Kings Canyon National Parks (March 28, 2006).
55. Letter, Peter Browning, President, High Sierra Hikers Association, to Jon Jarvis, Regional Director, Pacific West Region, NPS (December 14, 2006).
56. Public Law 88–577, *The Wilderness Act of 1964*, Section 4 (d)(6). This subsection reads in full as follows: "Commercial services may be performed within the wilderness areas designated by this act to the extent necessary for activities which are proper for realizing the recreational or other wilderness purposes of the areas."
57. *High Sierra Hikers Association v. United States Department of the Interior et al.*, Stipulation and Order Referring Case to Mediation, United States District Court, Northern District of California (January 25, 2010).
58. NPS, *Public Scoping Summary Report: Mineral King Management Plan and Environmental Assessment* (October 2010), *passim*.
59. President Clinton's decision to assign management of the Giant Sequoia National Monument to the USFS rather than to the NPS reflected an initiative undertaken by Bruce Babbitt, President Clinton's Secretary of the Interior. Seeking to broaden environmental stewardship within all the federal land-management agencies, Babbitt successfully lobbied within the Clinton administration for the creation of new national monuments that would continue to be managed by their previous agencies. Under this policy, both the USFS and the BLM found themselves managing Clinton-era national monuments.
60. Presidential Proclamation 7295, *Establishment of the Giant Sequoia National Monument* (April 15, 2000).
61. This was not the first time the Save the Redwoods League was involved in the acquisition of lands for Sequoia National Park. In 1986, the League purchased 422 acres of giant sequoia forest within the East Fork Grove near Silver City on Mineral King Road and arranged for the ultimate transfer of that land to federal ownership.

62. Public Law 106–574, approved December 28, 2000, accomplished this goal.
63. Save the Redwoods League Press Release, "Save-the-Redwoods (*sic*) League makes 1,540-acre gift to National Park Service" (December 6, 2001).
64. Public Law 111–11, Subtitle M, Sections 1901–3.
65. Data from the SEKI Budget Office, personal communication with William C. Tweed (January 28, 2011).
66. Data from the NPS, February 2014.
67. Ibid.
68. Figures from the NPS, January 2014.
69. NPS, DSC, *Environmental Assessment, Road Improvements, Generals Highway, Sequoia and Kings Canyon National Parks, California*, a draft for public review (September 1988), and *Finding of No Significant Impact* (approved April 10, 1989).
70. Ibid.
71. NPS News Release, "Highway Rehab Project to Start in Sequoia National Park" (n.d.).
72. William C. Tweed, ed., *Proceedings of the Sequoia and Kings Canyon Second Century Conference.*
73. NPS News Release, "Marijuana Plantations Invading Sequoia National Park" (September 24, 2002).
74. NPS News Release, "Park Rangers Remove Marijuana Plants in Sequoia National Park" (September 21, 2005).
75. Data from the SEKI Budget Office (December 15, 2010).
76. Data from the SEKI Budget Office (January 2014).
77. "NPS Pays Fine for No-Burn Violation," *Kaweah Commonwealth* (February 25, 2005).
78. NPS, Sequoia and Kings Canyon National Parks, *Fire and Fuels Management Plan: 2009 Annual Update*, Appendix J—Smoke Management Plan.
79. Ibid., 2 ff.
80. Ibid.
81. NPS News Release, "Washington Tree Damaged in Giant Fire: Parks Take Steps to Protect 'Trees of Special Interest'" (October 23, 2003).
82. For a sense of the passion and defensiveness involved, see "Washington Tree Burned," in *The Kaweah Commonwealth* (October 31, 2003).
83. Data from the SEKI Fire Information Office, personal correspondence with William C. Tweed (December 15, 2010).
84. U.S. Fish and Wildlife Service, *Draft Recovery Plan for the Sierra Nevada Bighorn Sheep*, FR Vol. 68, No. 146, 44808, and *Recovery Plan for the Sierra Nevada Bighorn Sheep*, FR Vol. 74, No. 30, 8345–8346.
85. News release from the Center for Biological Diversity, "Mountain yellow-legged frog endangered in Sierra Nevada" (February 8, 2000).
86. NPS, *Preliminary Restoration of Mountain Yellow-Legged Frogs: Environmental Assessment* (February 20, 2001): 2–8.
87. NPS, Sequoia and Kings Canyon National Parks, *Restoration of Native Species in High Elevation Aquatic Ecosystems: Planning Participant Workbook* (March 2010).
88. NPS, Sequoia and Kings Canyon National Parks, "Frequently Asked Questions on WACAP [Western Airborne Contaminants Assessment Project] Study," a briefing statement issued in 2008.
89. Erica Rex, "Toiling to Save a Threatened Frog," *The New York Times* (October 4, 2010).
90. See William C. Tweed, *Uncertain Path: A Search for the Future of National Parks* (Berkeley: University of California Press, 2010), for a more complete exploration of this concern.

91. Phillip J. Van Mantgem and Nathan L. Stephenson, "Apparent climatically induced increase of tree mortality rates in a temperature forest," *Ecology Letters*, Vol. 10, No. 10 (November 2007): 914.

92. Ibid., 914–15.

93. Hassan Basagic, IV, *Quantifying Twentieth Century Glacial Change in the Sierra Nevada, California*, an unpublished Master of Science thesis (Portland, OR: Portland State University, 2007): 74.

94. USDI News Release, "Scientific Research to be Reorganized Under National Biological Survey at Interior Department" (April 26, 1993).

95. "New Congress Moves on Science Budgets," *Science News Magazine* (April 22, 1995): 245.

96. Richard Sellars West, *Preserving Nature in the National Parks: A History* (New Haven, CT: Yale University Press, 1997).

97. NPS, *Natural Resource Challenge: The National Park Service's Action Plan for Preserving Natural Resources* (August 1999): 18–20.

98. NPS, *Rising to the Challenge: Natural Resource Stewardship and Science Program Highlights, Fiscal Year, 2009.*

99. Data provided by SEKI's budget officer, personal correspondence with William C. Tweed (December 15, 2010).

100. NPS, *Funding the Natural Resources Challenge: FY 2009 Report to Congress* (2010): 81.

PUBLISHED SOURCES

PUBLISHED WORKS dealing directly with the history of Sequoia and Kings Canyon National Parks are surprisingly few, a situation that inspired this book. Nevertheless, a number of useful volumes shed light on portions of the history of the region. We recommend the following volumes.

As a general history, Francis P. Farquhar's *History of the Sierra Nevada* (Berkeley: University of California Press, 1966) still stands alone. This wonderful book brings together, in a way never attempted elsewhere, the broad history of California's great mountain range. Students of the southern Sierra's national parks should pay special attention to the chapters on the California Geological Survey, Kings Canyon, and Mt. Whitney. Farquhar's history drew heavily on more than forty years of research, much of which was published during many decades in *The Sierra Club Bulletin*.

The only popular history of Sequoia and Kings Canyon National Parks to appear in recent decades is the slim volume by Douglas Hillman Strong, *From Pioneers to Preservationists: A Brief History of Sequoia and Kings Canyon National Parks* (Three Rivers, CA: Sequoia Natural History Association, 1996). It summarizes Strong's much more detailed Ph.D. dissertation (Syracuse, NY: Syracuse University, 1964), in which he focuses on the founding and early enlargement of Sequoia National Park. In these areas, Strong is likely to remain the ultimate source.

Tulare County and the Tulare Lake country have inspired many books, most of which are outside our focus. Standing alone in significance, however, is William L. Preston, *Vanishing Landscapes, Land and Life in the Tulare Lake Basin* (Berkeley: University of California Press, 1981). In *Vanishing Landscapes*, Preston did for the southern San Joaquin Valley what this book hopes to accomplish for the southern Sierra.

The California Geological Survey is unique among the early western scientific endeavors in the amount and quality of the literature it generated. Two books authored by participants in the survey remain in print, and together they still present a concise and extremely readable summary of the survey's efforts and adventures. The two classics are William H. Brewer, *Up and Down California in 1860–1864: The Journal of William H. Brewer,* Francis P. Farquar, ed. (New Haven, CT: Yale University Press, 1930), and Clarence King's *Mountaineering in the Sierra Nevada* (Boston, MA: James R. Osgood and Company, 1872). Happily, both remain in print.

The logging of the Big Trees also generated a number of books, two of which stand out. Hank Johnston, in *They Felled the Redwoods* (Los Angeles, CA: Trans-Anglo Books, 1966), tells the story of the destruction of the sequoia forests surrounding General Grant Grove, while Floyd Otter, in *The Men of Mammoth Forest* (Ann Arbor, MI: Edwards Brothers, 1963), does equal justice to the Tule River country immediately south of the twin parks. We recommend both. Three other views of late-nineteenth-century logging in the Sierra Nevada deserve attention: Jay O'Connell, *Co-Operative Dreams: A History of the Kaweah Colony* (Van Nuys, CA: Raven River Press, 1999); Jackie McDougall Weiner, *Timely Exposures: The Life and Times of C.C. Curtis, Pioneer California Photographer* (self-published, 1999); and William C. Tweed, *Kaweah Remembered: The Story of Kaweah Colony and the Founding of Sequoia National Park* (Three Rivers, CA: Sequoia Natural History Association, 1986).

The story of Mineral King Valley, including its mining rush and later battles over its development, has been explored in a number of publications. The best summary of the mining rush remains Samuel Thomas Porter's *The Silver Rush at Mineral King, California, 1873–1882* (self-published, ca. December 1964). Long out of print, it is now available in a facsimile hardcover edition from the Mineral King Preservation Society. A work that adds considerably to Porter and to the story of the area's middle years is Louise Jackson, *Beulah: A Biography of the Mineral King Valley of California* (Tucson, AZ: Westernlore Press, 1988). The most complete attempt to date to summarize the ski-development controversy at Mineral King can be found in John L. Harper, *Mineral King: Public Concern with Government Policy* (Arcata, CA: Pacifica Publishing Company, 1982). Harper was a protagonist in the controversy, and his account, though quite useful, is thus tilted in favor of preservation.

A number of good books about the history of the High Sierra have appeared in recent years. For more details about the history of the Kings River region, try Gene Rose, *Kings Canyon: America's Premiere Wilderness National Park, A History* (Three Rivers, CA: Sequoia Naturalist History Association, 2011). Those seeking to learn more about the origins of the John Muir Trail should consult Shirley Sargent, *Solomons of the Sierra: The Pioneer of the John Muir Trail* (Yosemite National Park, CA: Flying Spur Press, 1989). An older book that provides a good overall history of the trail is Hal Roth, *Pathway in the Sky: The Story of the John Muir Trail* (Berkeley, CA: Howell-North Books, 1965). Two recent books about mountaineering in the southern Sierra stand out. We recommend Daniel Arnold's *Early Days in the Range of Light: Encounters with Legendary Mountaineers* (Berkeley, CA: Counterpoint, 2009), and Robert Pavlik, *Norman Clyde: Legendary Mountaineer of California's Sierra Nevada* (Berkeley, CA: Heyday Books, 2008). George F. Thompson, our publisher, helped develop the latter.

John Muir has received more historical attention than any other comparable figure in American environmental history. Many biographies exist, including *A Passion for Nature: The Life of John Muir* by Donald Worcester (New York, NY: Oxford University Press, 2008). Another way to approach Muir is through his own writings, many of which remain quite readable. Students of Sequoia and Kings Canyon National Parks should seek out Muir's still-popular *Our National Parks* (Boston, MA: Houghton, Mifflin and Company, 1901), for an interesting account of his first visit to the Giant Forest, and Frederic Grunsky, ed., *South of Yosemite: Selected Writings by John Muir* (Garden City, NY: Natural History Press, 1968). Grunsky contains a good sampling of Muir's otherwise scattered writings on the Sequoia-Kings Canyon region.

Yet another way to approach Muir is through the organization he founded: the Sierra Club. A good start is Michael P. Cohen, *The History of the Sierra Club, 1892–1970* (San Francisco, CA: Sierra Club Books, 1988). The early recreational explorations of the Sierra Club are still best read in the early editions of *The Sierra Club Bulletin*. Few other organizational journals hold interest as effectively as these wonderfully written and illustrated volumes. Look, especially, for articles prior to 1915 by Bolton Coit Brown, Joseph N. LeConte, and Marion Randall Parsons. Also by LeConte is his very pleasant volume, *A Summer of Travel in the High Sierra* (Ashland, OR: Lewis Osborne, 1972), which recounts LeConte's 1890 visit to Kings Canyon and Mount Whitney and features a preface by Ansel Adams, the renowned photographer.

Only a very few items address directly National Park Service activities in the two parks. In this department, Robert Shankland's *Steve Mather of the National Parks* (New York, NY: Alfred A. Knopf, 1954) still reads well. The important story of Colonel John R. White and Sequoia National Park is available through the efforts of Rick Hydrick, "The Genesis of National Park Management: John Roberts White and Sequoia National Park, 1920–1947," in the April 1984 issue (Vol. 28, No. 2) of *The Journal of Forest History*. Another article that still stands alone as the only exploration of its field is William C. Tweed, "Sequoia National Park Concessions: 1898–1926," in the Spring 1972 issue (Vol. 16, No. 1) of *The Pacific Historian*. See, also, William C. Tweed, *Guide and History to the High Sierra Trail* (Three Rivers, CA: Sequoia Natural History Association, 1982).

Finally, simply because they do not fit anywhere else in this bibliographic essay, we must mention two efforts which address two of the region's most colorful and eccentric figures: William C. Tweed's *Shorty Lovelace, Kings Canyon Fur Trapper* (Three Rivers, CA: Sequoia Natural History Association, 1980), and Gene Rose's *High Odyssey* (Fresno, CA: Panorama West Publishing, 1987), which tells the story of Orland Bartholomew and the first ski trip from Mt. Whitney to Yosemite in 1928–1929.

ARCHIVAL RESOURCES

Working with the archives in Sequoia and Kings Canyon National Parks is a daunting task, but rich information can be found by one who is willing to search. Three sources of material are available in government holdings. First, early records (up to 1936 and, especially, before 1915) are found in Washington, D.C., at the National Archives and Records Center. All correspondence between park superintendents and national officials prior to 1908 has been microfilmed from this source and is now available in the parks' archives in the library at the Ash Mountain Headquarters in Sequoia National Park.

In 1937, the National Park Service (NPS) was reorganized when the superintendents of Sequoia and General Grant National Parks thereafter reported to a regional director in San Francisco instead of the NPS director in Washington, D.C. The regional branch of the National Records Center at San Bruno, California, received the records and correspondence generated by the regional office and the parks since this change. Betty Knight, the former archivist at Sequoia, and the authors recalled some thirty-one boxes of the most pertinent material, and this material has now also been added to the parks' archives at the Ash Mountain Headquarters.

The third and most important holdings are those that have never left the Ash Mountain Headquarters. The greatest repository is the museum-archives collection that contains, in addition to the recalled San Bruno Center boxes, all the superintendent's annual and monthly reports, and the equivalent of some twenty file-drawers of other historical correspondence. Many old maps, reports, subject files, and nearly 12,000 historic photos loom like a lost treasure in this important archival collection. Note: When the first edition of this book was under preparation in the late 1980s, many other park offices held historic files. Today, nearly all of this material has been added to the parks' main archives.

Despite the vastness and relative richness of these collections, a researcher should check other non-government data. Principal among these are the Francis Farquhar Collection and the Sierra Club Archives, both housed at the Bancroft Library, University of California, Berkeley. The Sierra Club collection, in particular, is huge (thirty-six boxes on Sequoia and Kings Canyon alone), but it is only partially described. Colonel John R. White's papers are currently housed at the University of Oregon Library in Eugene. Each of the sources above is a worthwhile addition to the hundreds of thousands of pages of documents located at the Ash Mountain Headquarters in Sequoia National Park.

INDEX

Note: All maps and photographs appear in *italics*.

ACKNOWLEDGMENTS

THE CENTENNIAL EDITION (1990)

THE AUTHORS WISH to acknowledge, with gratitude, the assistance and support we received from many sources. From Sequoia and Kings Canyon National Parks came an enormous amount of support, including unlimited access to records, free use of copying facilities, housing for Lary Dilsaver during several long periods of archival research, and, most important, genuine interest in the project. Particular thanks go to then-Superintendent John H. Davis, to Sylvia Nichols, Anne Shepherd, Larry Bancroft, Tom Nichols, David Parsons, and especially archivist Betty Knight, for her constant and unwavering support and encouragement. Special thanks also go to Gordon Chappell, National Park Service Western Regional Historian, who brought together the two authors.

Financial assistance for the research came from the National Endowment for the Humanities and the University of South Alabama. The university also supplied research release time, clerical assistance, and technical help, without which this book might never have been completed. At the university, special thanks go to Vice-President Jeral Williams, Dean S. Gene Crossley, Geology and Geography Department Chairman Glenn Sebastian, and Debbie Hopkins. Assistance also came from Joyce Quinn at California State University, Fresno, and Stephen Jett at the University of California, Davis.

Extremely critical was the support of John J. Palmer, first as Chief Park Interpreter for Sequoia and Kings Canyon National Parks and, after May 1987, as Executive Director of the Sequoia Natural History Association. His vision brought the book to fruition.

Special thanks also go to Sylvia Haultain, who provided excellent editorial advice and endured all the frustrations inherent in a project of this sort.

To these individuals and institutions and to many, many others too numerous to list, the authors give their thanks.

THE REVISED EDITION (2016)

In addition to the many people who provided important assistance during the preparation of the first "centennial" edition of this book (1990), we now wish to acknowledge, also with our gratitude, a new and rich list of persons who helped bring this second "revised" edition (2016) to fruition. As might be expected in a work of this sort, most of those involved are associated in one way or another with Sequoia and Kings Canyon National Parks. At the top of any such list must be park superintendents Craig Axtell and Woody Smeck, under whom, respectively, work on this this revised and expanded edition was initiated and later completed. Both shared useful criticism as well as genuine encouragement. Past superintendents Tom Ritter and Mike Tollefson also provided material assistance.

Many other National Park Service employees took time out from their busy jobs to make this story as complete and accurate as possible. Special thanks go to John Austin, Athena Demetry, Dana Dierkes, Ward Eldredge, Gregg Fauth, David Graber, Paul Schwarz, Tracy Thetford, and Harold Werner. Nathan Stephenson, of the U.S. Geological Survey, also earned our sincere appreciation, for his critical analysis of our efforts.

This book relies upon its many maps, and their consistent high quality reflects the capable cartographic work done at Eureka Cartography in Berkeley, California. Thank you, also, to the Sequoia Natural History Association, for underwriting the digital updating of the maps from the first edition so they could be carried over into this new version of the book.

Special thanks, also, to the Sequoia Parks Foundation, for making the generous contribution and book order that made publication of this revised edition possible.

Finally, we owe a large debt to George F. Thompson and the team at GFT Publishing. It is their hard work, quite literally, that produced the book you now hold in your hands.

ABOUT THE AUTHORS

William C. Tweed has studied, researched, and explored Sequoia and Kings Canyon National Parks for nearly forty years as a writer, park ranger, and Chief Park Naturalist. Since 1997, he has written more than 400 essays about nature in Central California in a column for *The Visalia Times-Delta* newspaper. He is also the author of *King Sequoia: The Tree that Inspired a Nation, Created Our National Park System, and Changed the Way We Think About Nature* (Heyday, 2016), *Uncertain Path: A Search for the Future of National Parks* (University of California Press, 2010), *Death Valley and the Northern Mojave: A Visitor's Guide*, with Lauren Davis (Cachuma Press, 2003), *Exploring Mountain Highways: A Road Guide to Sequoia and Kings Canyons National Parks* (Sequoia Natural History Association, 1984), and *Sequoia and Kings Canyon: The Story behind the Scenery* (KC Publications, 1980; VistaBooks, 1997).

Lary M. Dilsaver, a native Californian, is Professor Emeritus of Historical Geography at the University of South Alabama and a thirty-year volunteer researcher for the National Park Service. He has written more than forty articles and book chapters on national parks and historic landscapes, and he has authored or edited six books, including *Preserving the Desert: A History of Joshua Tree National Park* (George F. Thompson Publishing, 2016), *America's National Park System: The Critical Documents* (Rowman and Littlefield, 1994; revised edition, 2016), and *Cumberland Island National Seashore: A History of Conservation Conflict* (University of Virginia Press, in association with the Center for American Places, 2004).

ABOUT THE BOOK

Challenge of the Big Trees: The History of Sequoia and Kings Canyon National Parks, A Revised Edition was brought to publication in a first edition of 1,300 softcover copies with gatefold flaps. The text was set in Adobe Garamond Pro and ITC Garamond book condensed, the paper is Huron Matte, 70# gsm weight, and the book was professionally printed and bound by Thompson-Shore in Michigan.

Publisher and Project Director: George F. Thompson
Editorial and Research Assistant: Mikki Soroczak
Manuscript Editors: Sherri Byrand and Purna Makaram
Book Design and Production: Ann Lowe and David Skolkin

Special Acknowledgments: The publisher extends grateful thanks to the Sequoia Parks Foundation and, especially, Mark Tilchen, Executive Director, for their institutional and personal support of this project in every way.

Published 2016. First softcover edition.
Printed in the U.S.A. on acid-free paper.

George F. Thompson Publishing, L.L.C.
217 Oak Ridge Circle
Staunton, VA 24401-3511, U.S.A.
www.gftbooks.com

24 23 22 21 20 19 18 17 16 1 2 3 4 5

The Library of Congress Preassigned Control Number is 2016950023.

ISBN: 978–1–938086–47–2